D1268127

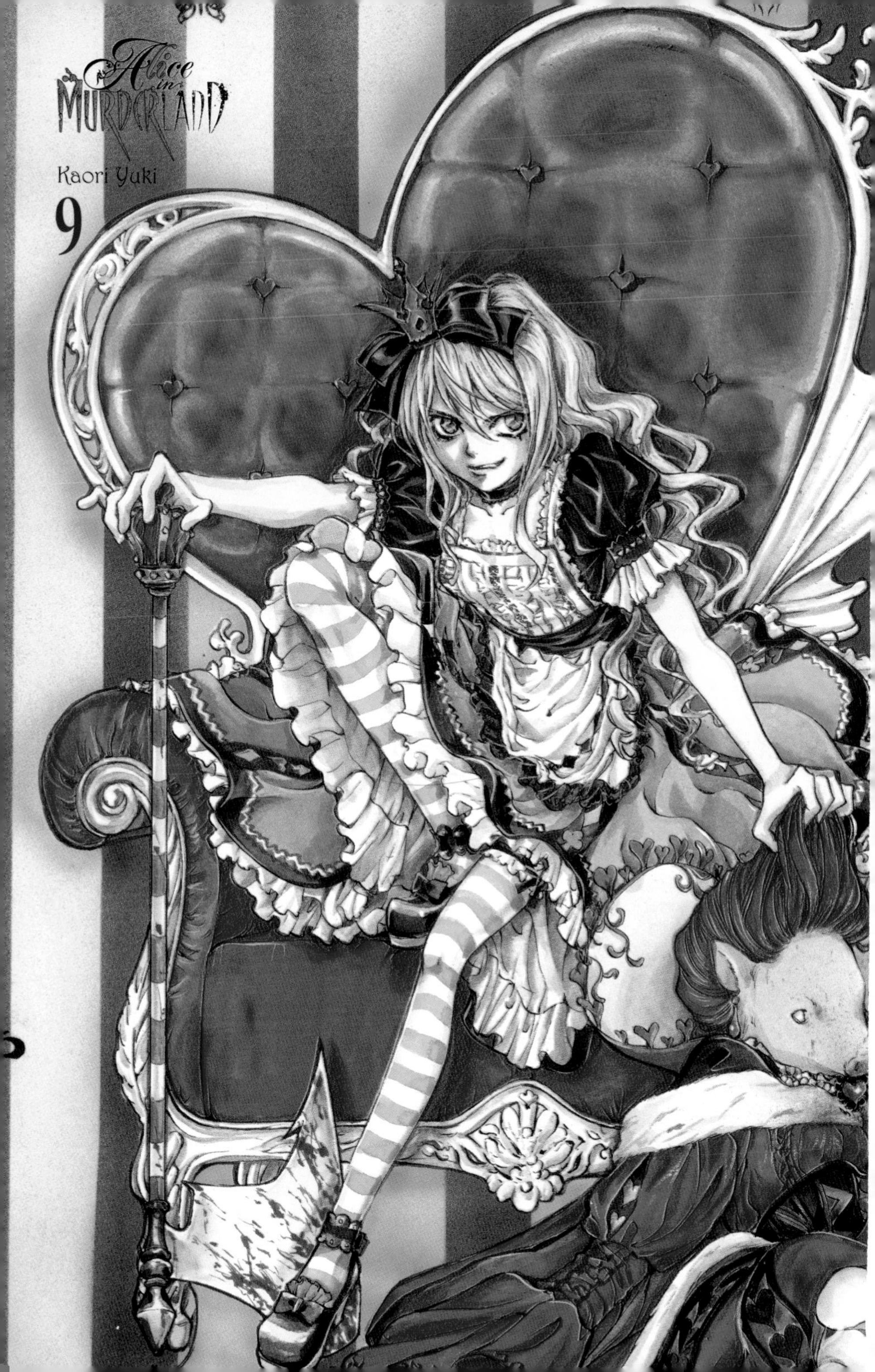
Alice in Murderland
Kaori Yuki
9

contents

Alice in Murderland

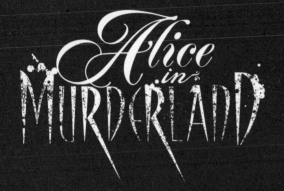

9

Kaori Yuki

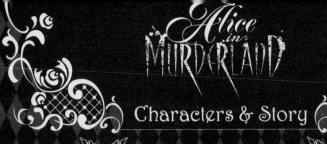

Alice in Murderland

Characters & Story

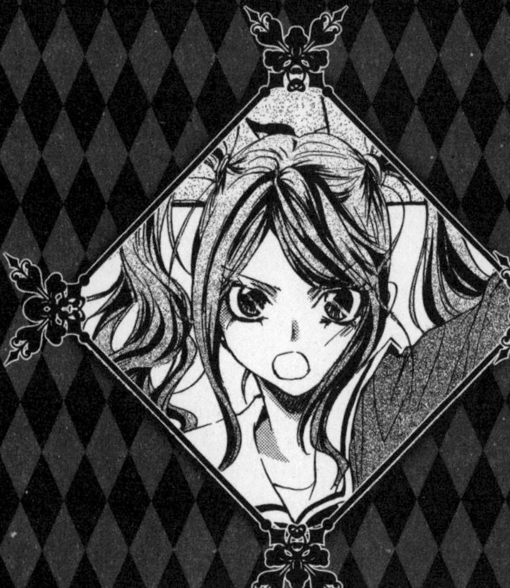

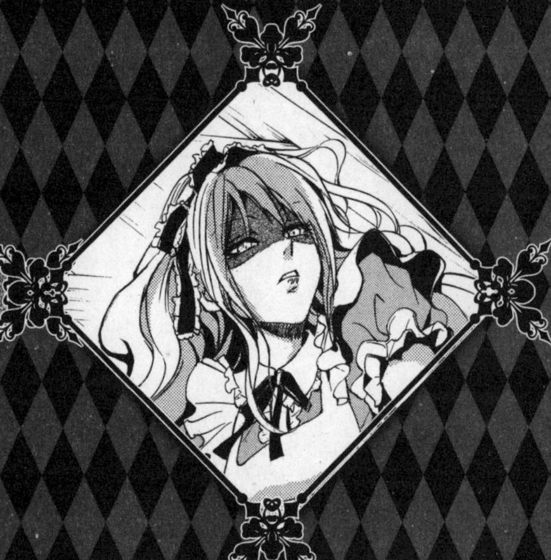

Stella Kuonji

Fourth daughter of the Kuonji family. Was taken in by the Kuonjis, along with eldest brother, Zeno. Loves Zeno.

Bloody Alice

Another personality residing within Stella that appears when she loses all reason.

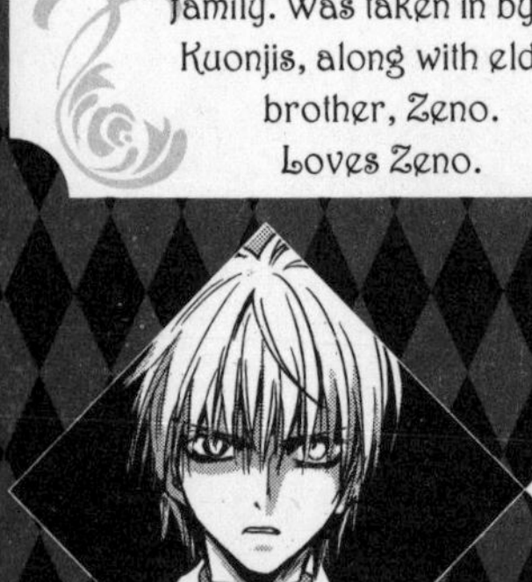

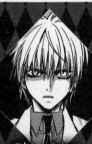

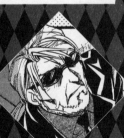

Tsukito

Grandson of Kokonoe, the chief of the Black Rabbit bodyguards. The true Zeno was a personality inside of Tsukito.

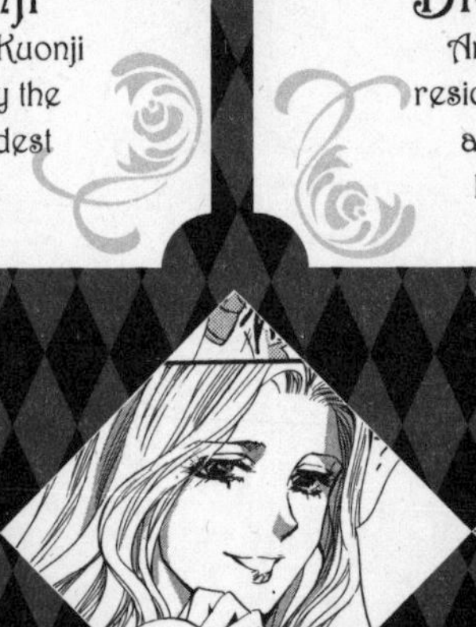

Olga

Head of the Kuonji Group and matriarch of the family.

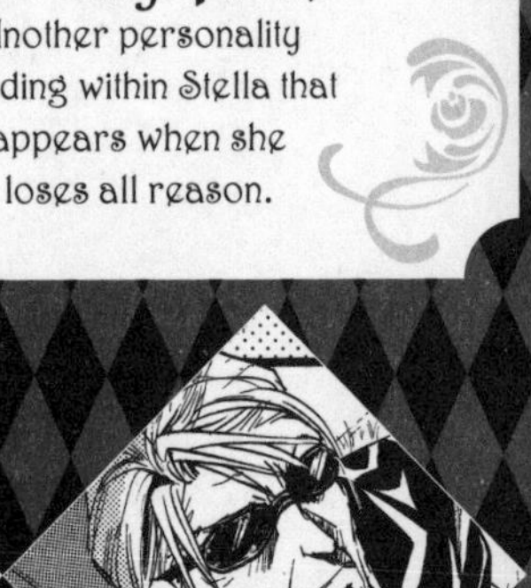

Kokonoe

Chief of the Black Rabbit bodyguards tasked with protecting the nine siblings.

The Kuonji Siblings

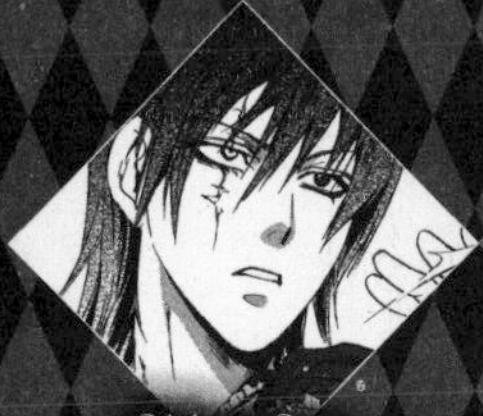

Eldest Son
Zeno
Previously thought to be Stella's beloved big brother, but actually an impostor who replaced him five years ago.

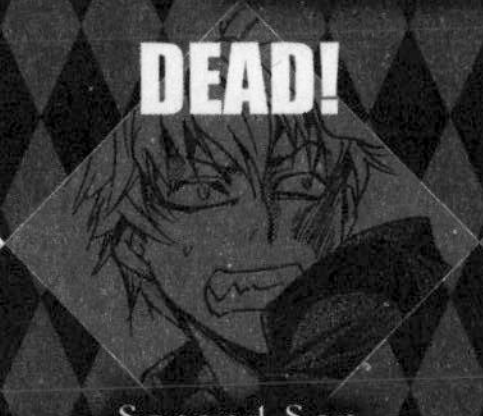
DEAD!

Second Son
Sid
The culprit behind a wave of local murders. Killed by Stella after her transformation into "Bloody Alice."

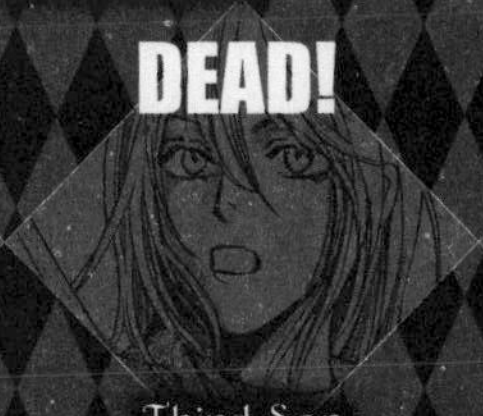
DEAD!

Third Son
Sol
Maré's older twin. Fought Stella to avenge his younger brother Maré and lost. In the end, he chose to die.

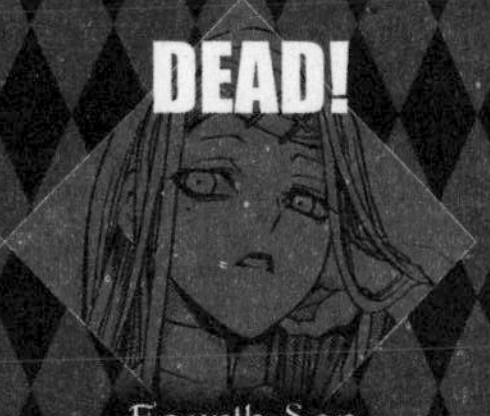
DEAD!

Fourth Son
Maré
Sol's younger twin. He and Stella had an antagonistic relationship, and he died at the end of their showdown.

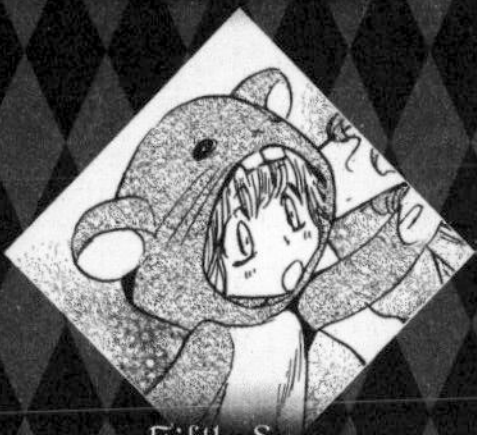

Fifth Son
Melm
The youngest of all the Kuonji siblings. Had been in Claire's care due to his youth.

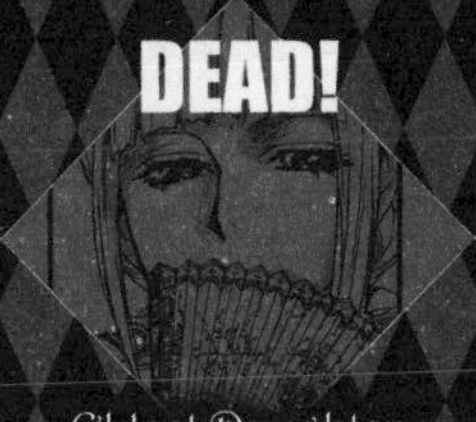
DEAD!

Eldest Daughter
Ibara
The best fighter among the siblings. She challenged Stella to a one-on-one fight, and Alice crushed her heart, killing her.

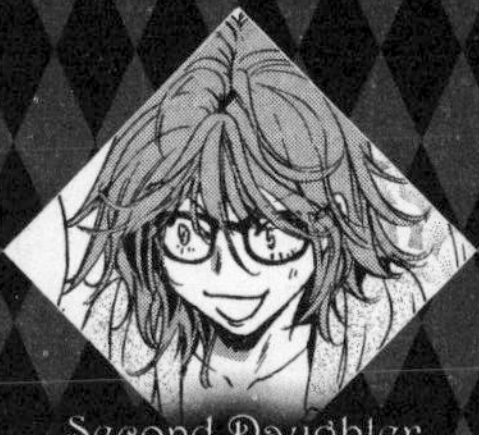

Second Daughter
Miser
Reptile *otaku*. Tricked by Maré into a showdown with Stella, but ultimately brought to her senses by the love of ex-boyfriend Io.

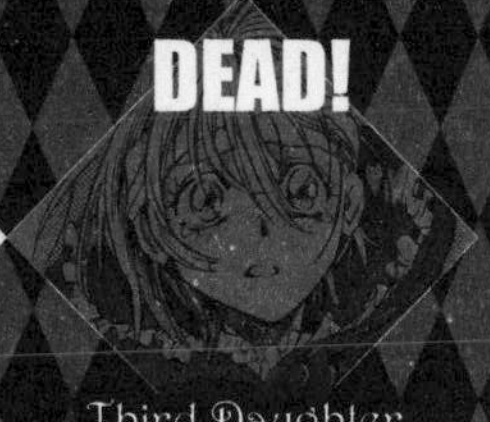
DEAD!

Third Daughter
Claire
Closest to Stella of all the siblings. Was finished off by eldest son, Zeno, after her showdown with Stella.

Story

Stella, fourth daughter of the Kuonji family, world leaders of industry, finds that she must engage in a battle royale with her siblings for the sake of her eldest brother, Zeno. As a succession of challenges comes from her siblings and numerous clashes of life or death unfold, Stella fights alongside "Bloody Alice," her second battle-awakened personality. When third son, Sol, attacks Stella with Maré's repurposed larva, he takes Tsukito hostage in the process, tying Stella's hands. But thanks to Tsukito's quick thinking, Stella manages to hold out and win, leaving just three siblings alive: second daughter, Miser, youngest child, Melm, and Stella herself. Then confirmation arrives of fake Zeno's true identity as a disciple of the anti-Kuonji Washimiya sect! What will bewildered Stella do in the face of the truth about the brother she respects and adores...!?

Key Words

Secret of Elysium • A mysterious ability passed down through the Kuonji line that grants the wielder power over life and death, as well as immortality.

Bandersnatch • The true form of the members of the Kuonji family. Attempts to grow the number of people infected with its blood and steals the souls of others for family sustenance.

Murderland Rules • The nine brothers and sisters must kill one another until only one is left standing. The game must be completed within one year, by Zeno's twentieth birthday. The lone survivor will become head of the family, inheriting the Kuonji Group and all its assets.

Black Rabbits • Bodyguards who may be used by the siblings as pawns. There are special methods by which this manipulation can be accomplished.

Alice in MURDERLAND

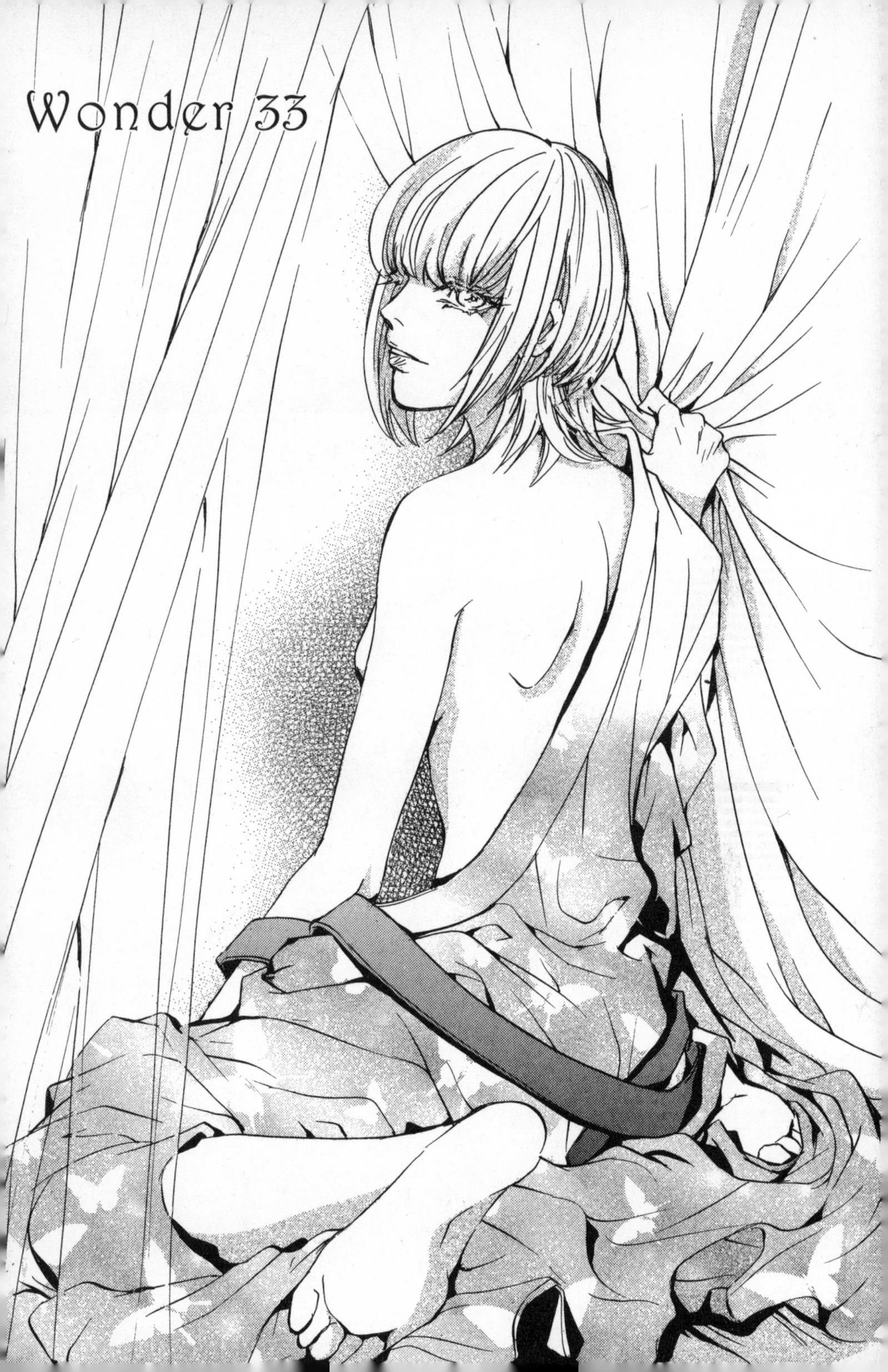
Wonder 33

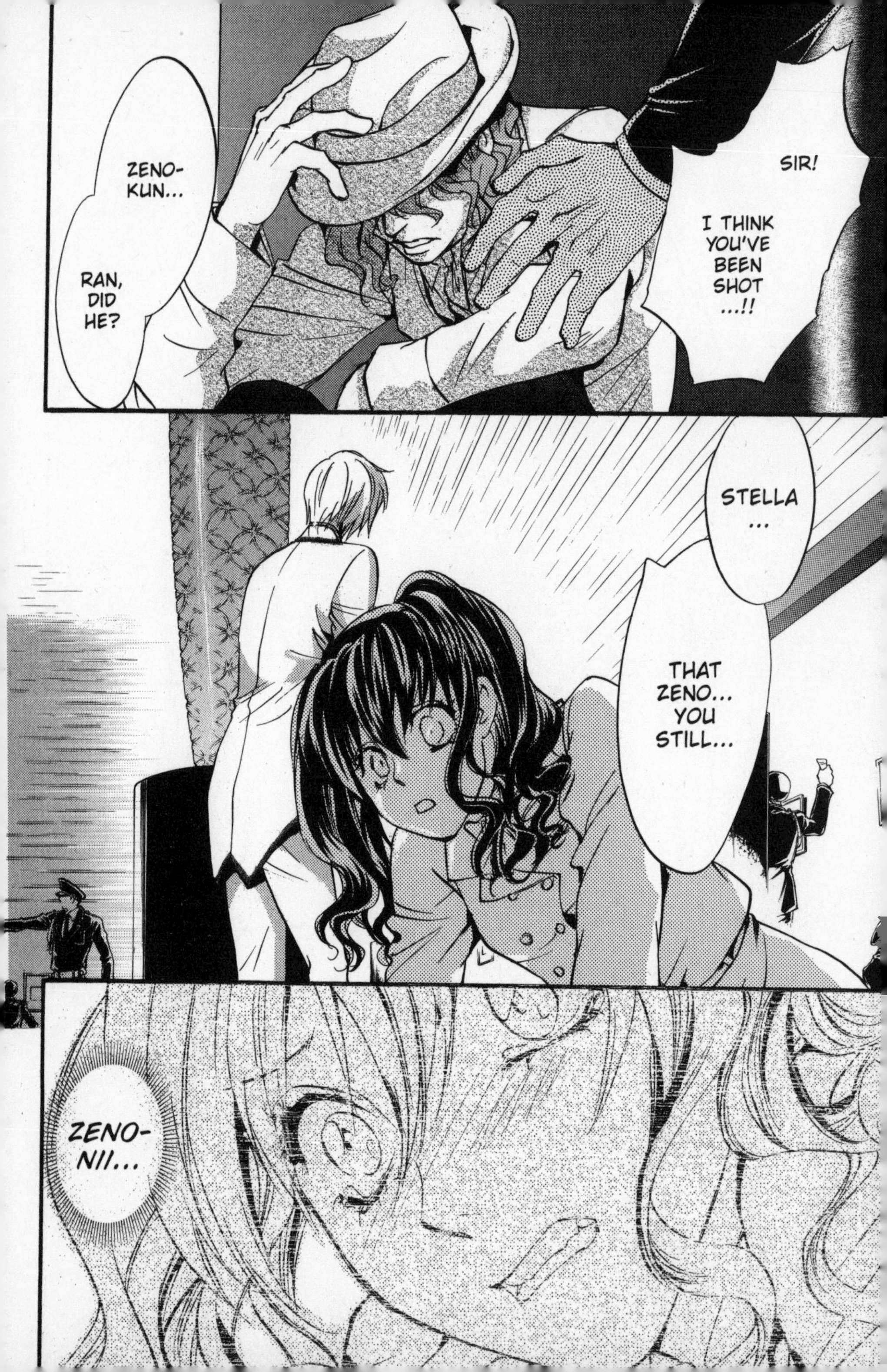
SIR!
I THINK YOU'VE BEEN SHOT ...!!
ZENO-KUN...
RAN, DID HE?
STELLA ...
THAT ZENO... YOU STILL...
ZENO-NII...

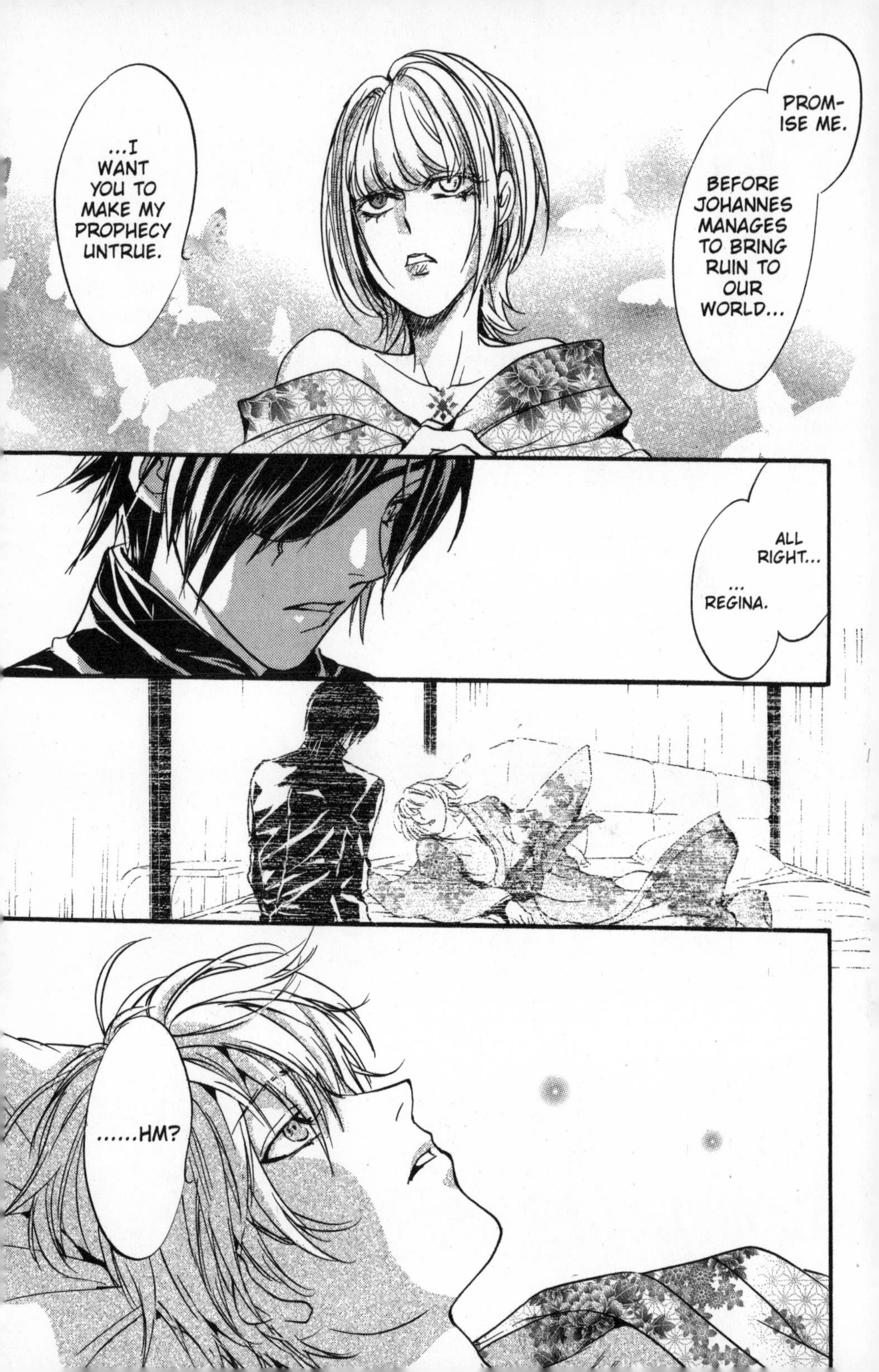
PROM-ISE ME.
BEFORE JOHANNES MANAGES TO BRING RUIN TO OUR WORLD...
...I WANT YOU TO MAKE MY PROPHECY UNTRUE.
ALL RIGHT... ...REGINA.
......HM?

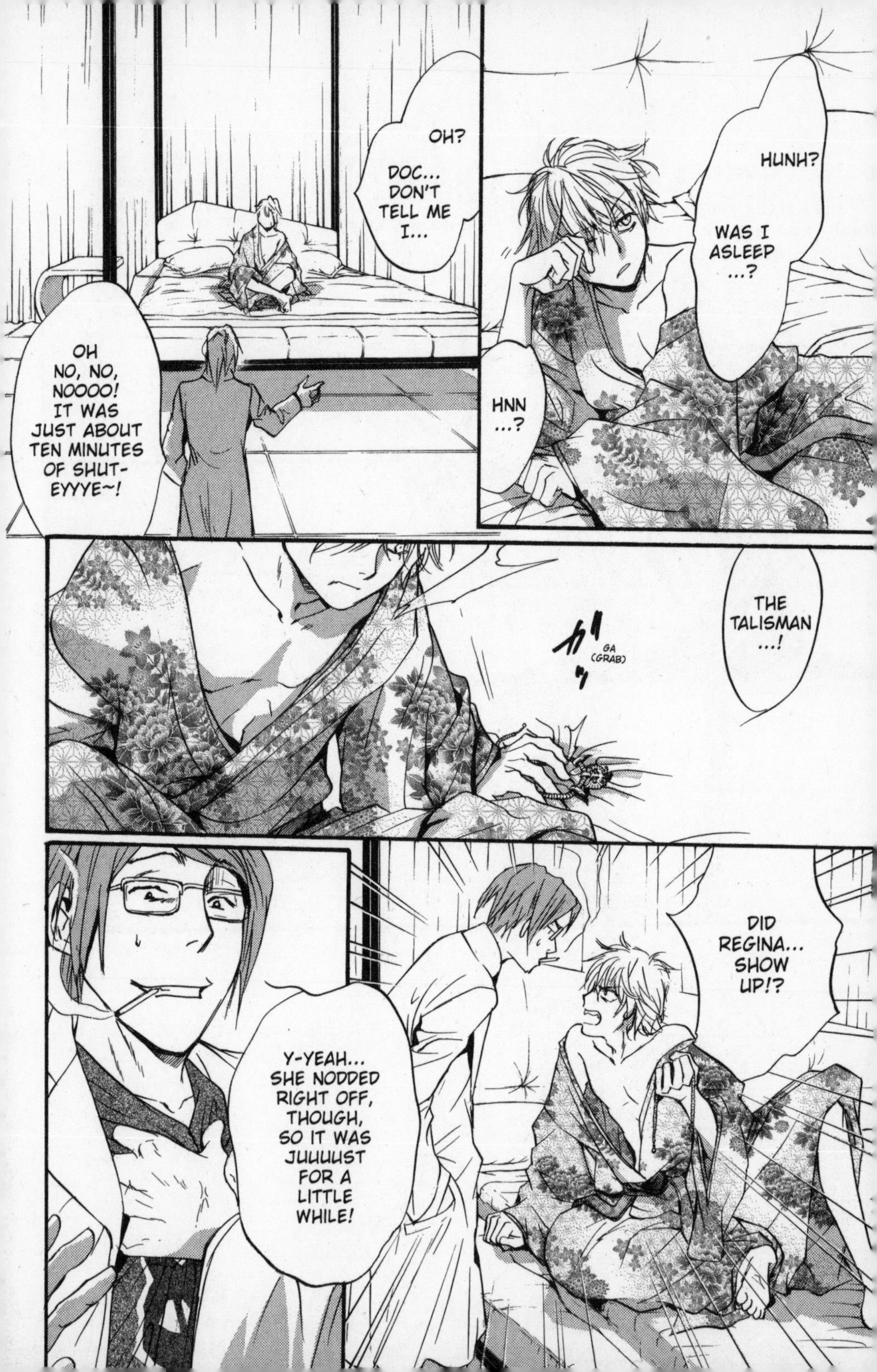
HUNH?
WAS I ASLEEP ...?
HNN ...?
OH?
DOC... DON'T TELL ME I...
OH NO, NO, NOOOO! IT WAS JUST ABOUT TEN MINUTES OF SHUT-EYYYE~!
THE TALISMAN ...!
ガッ
GA (GRAB)
DID REGINA... SHOW UP!?
Y-YEAH... SHE NODDED RIGHT OFF, THOUGH, SO IT WAS JUUUUST FOR A LITTLE WHILE!

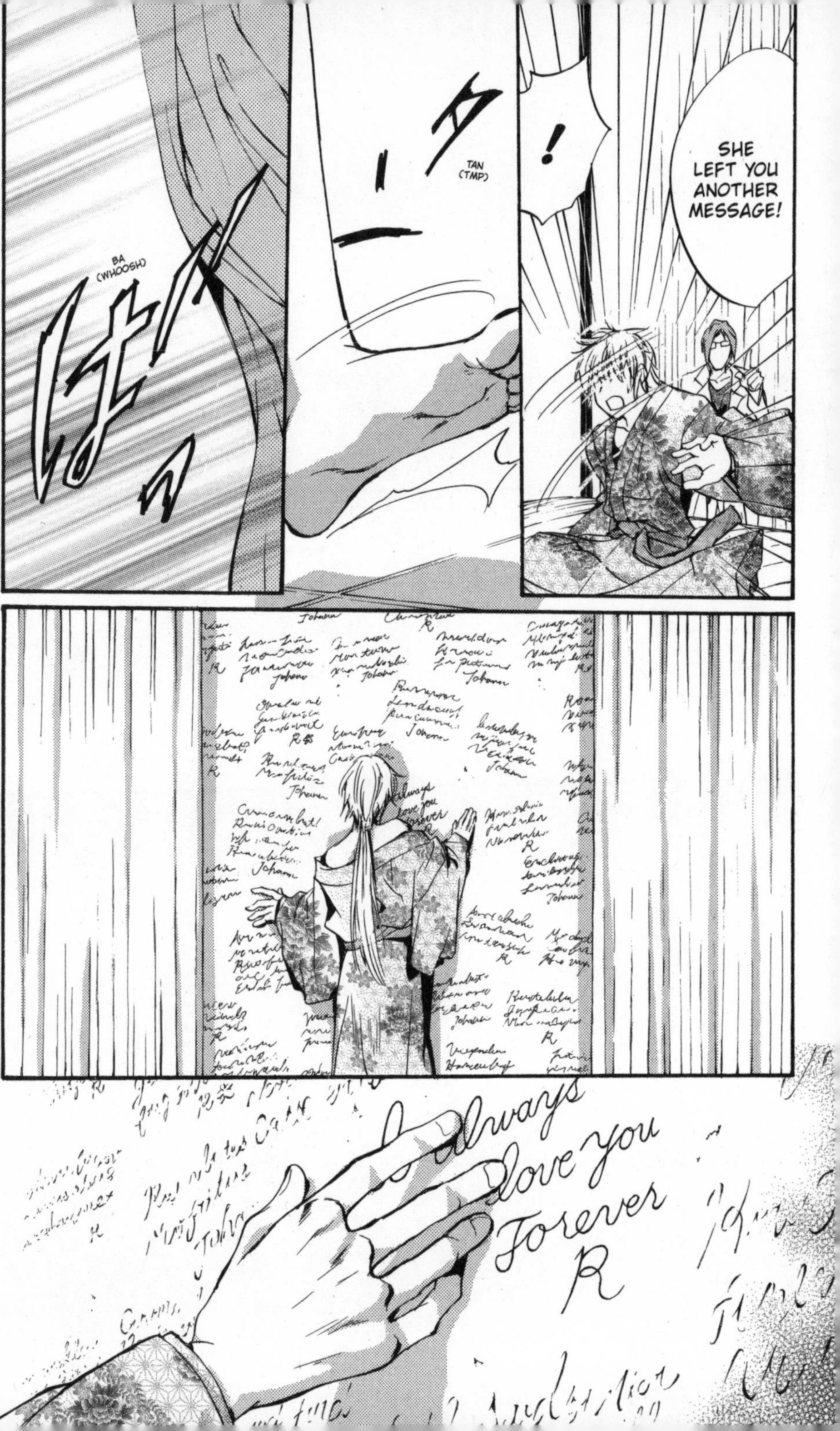
SHE LEFT YOU ANOTHER MESSAGE!
TAN (TMP)
BA (WHOOSH)
always
love you
Forever
R

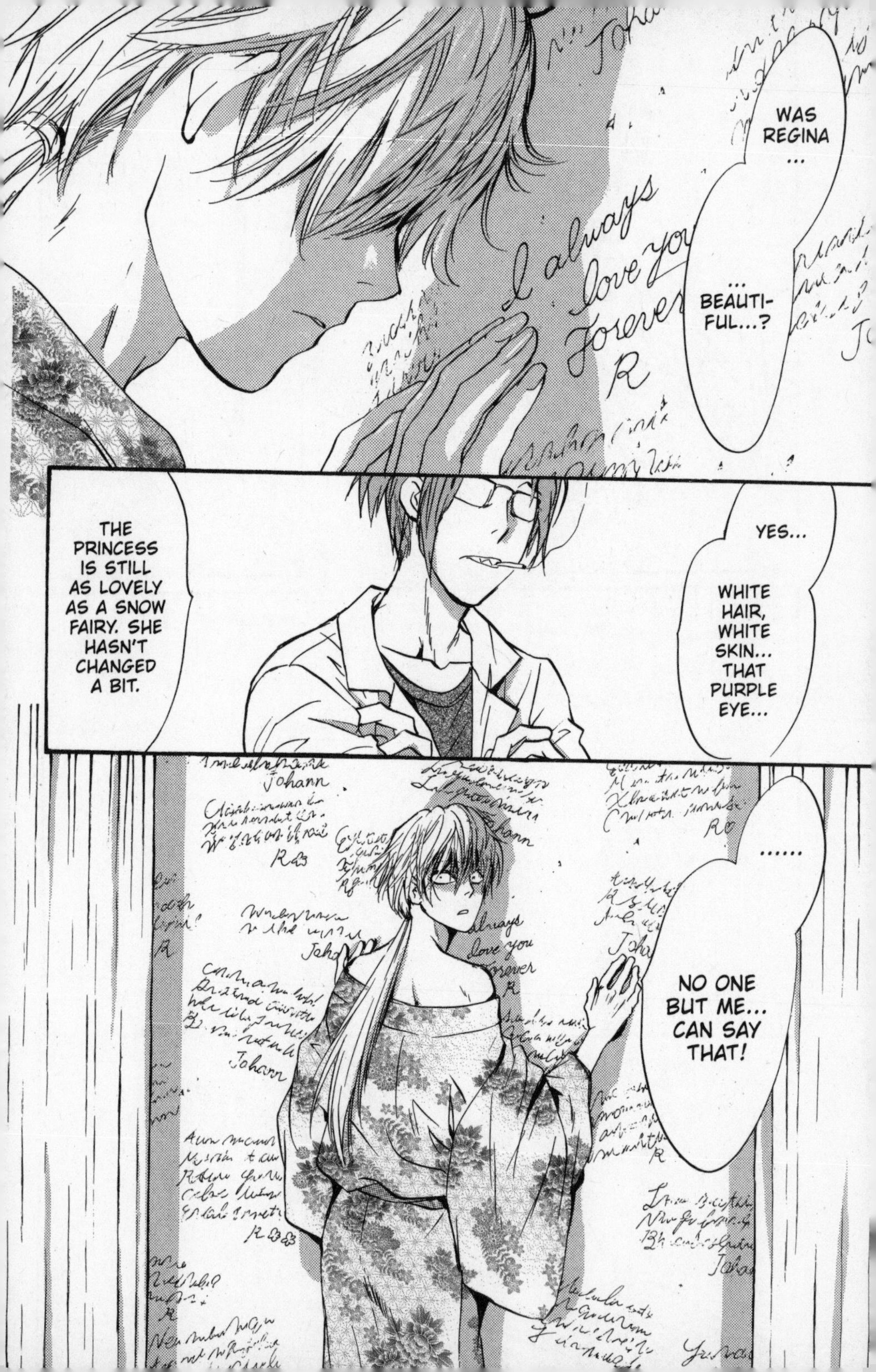
I always love you Forever R
WAS REGINA ...
... BEAUTIFUL...?
YES...
WHITE HAIR, WHITE SKIN... THAT PURPLE EYE...
THE PRINCESS IS STILL AS LOVELY AS A SNOW FAIRY. SHE HASN'T CHANGED A BIT.
......
NO ONE BUT ME... CAN SAY THAT!

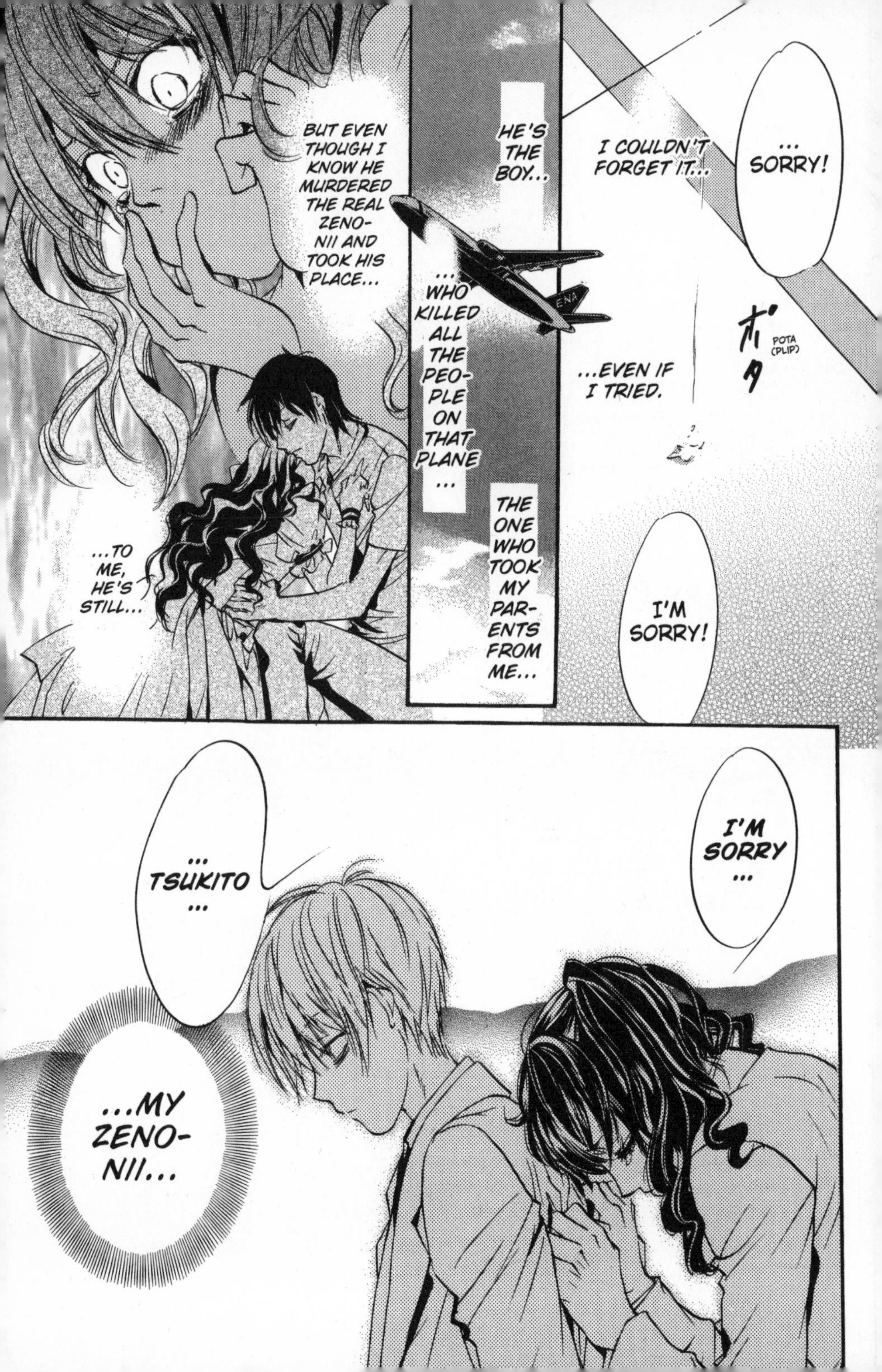
...SORRY!
I COULDN'T FORGET IT...
ポタ
POTA (PLIP)
...EVEN IF I TRIED.
I'M SORRY!
HE'S THE BOY...
...WHO KILLED ALL THE PEOPLE ON THAT PLANE...
THE ONE WHO TOOK MY PARENTS FROM ME...
BUT EVEN THOUGH I KNOW HE MURDERED THE REAL ZENO-NII AND TOOK HIS PLACE...
...TO ME, HE'S STILL...
I'M SORRY...
...TSUKITO...
...MY ZENO-NII...

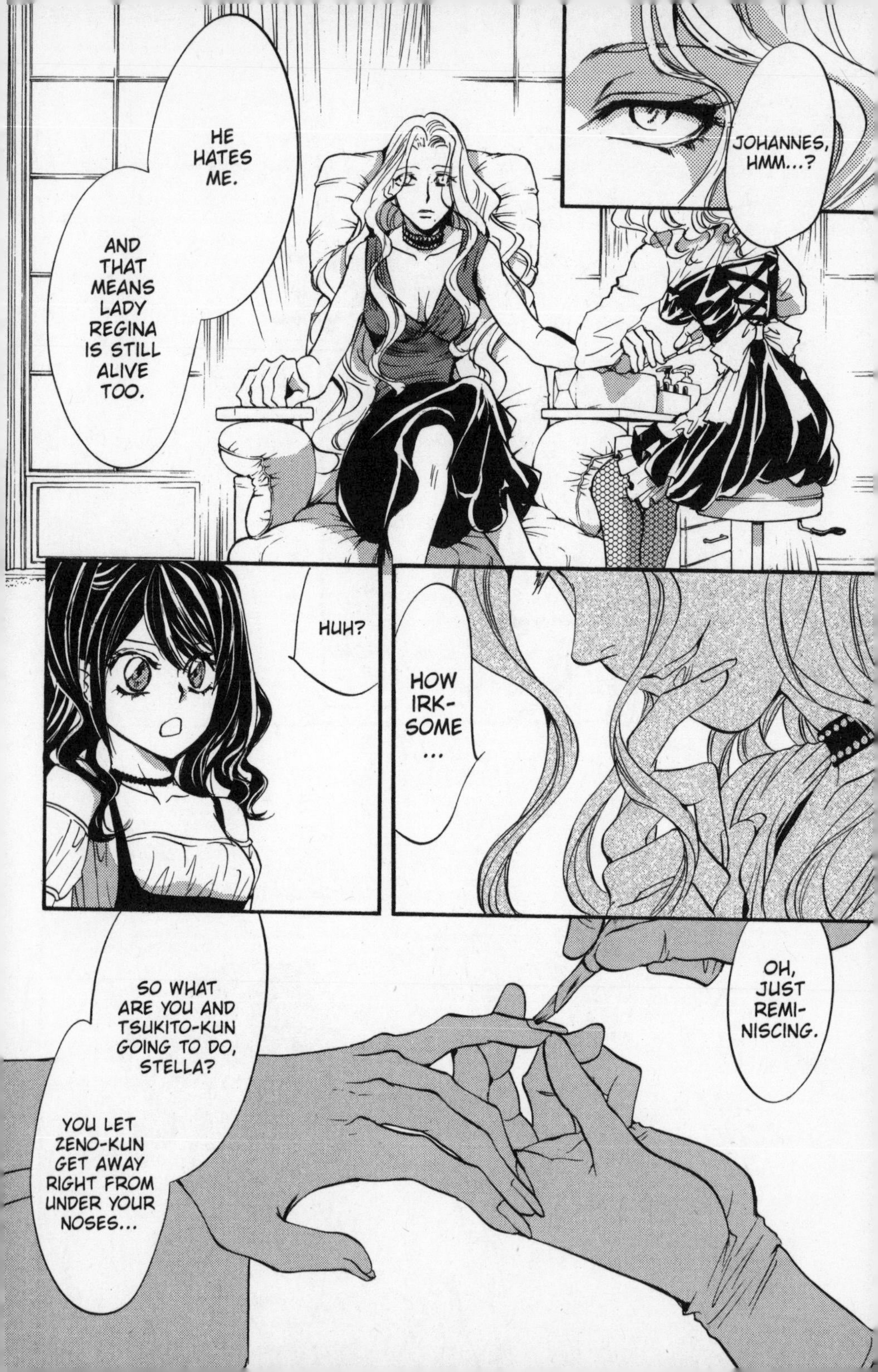
JOHANNES, HMM...?
HE HATES ME.
AND THAT MEANS LADY REGINA IS STILL ALIVE TOO.
HOW IRK-SOME...
HUH?
OH, JUST REMI-NISCING.
SO WHAT ARE YOU AND TSUKITO-KUN GOING TO DO, STELLA?
YOU LET ZENO-KUN GET AWAY RIGHT FROM UNDER YOUR NOSES...

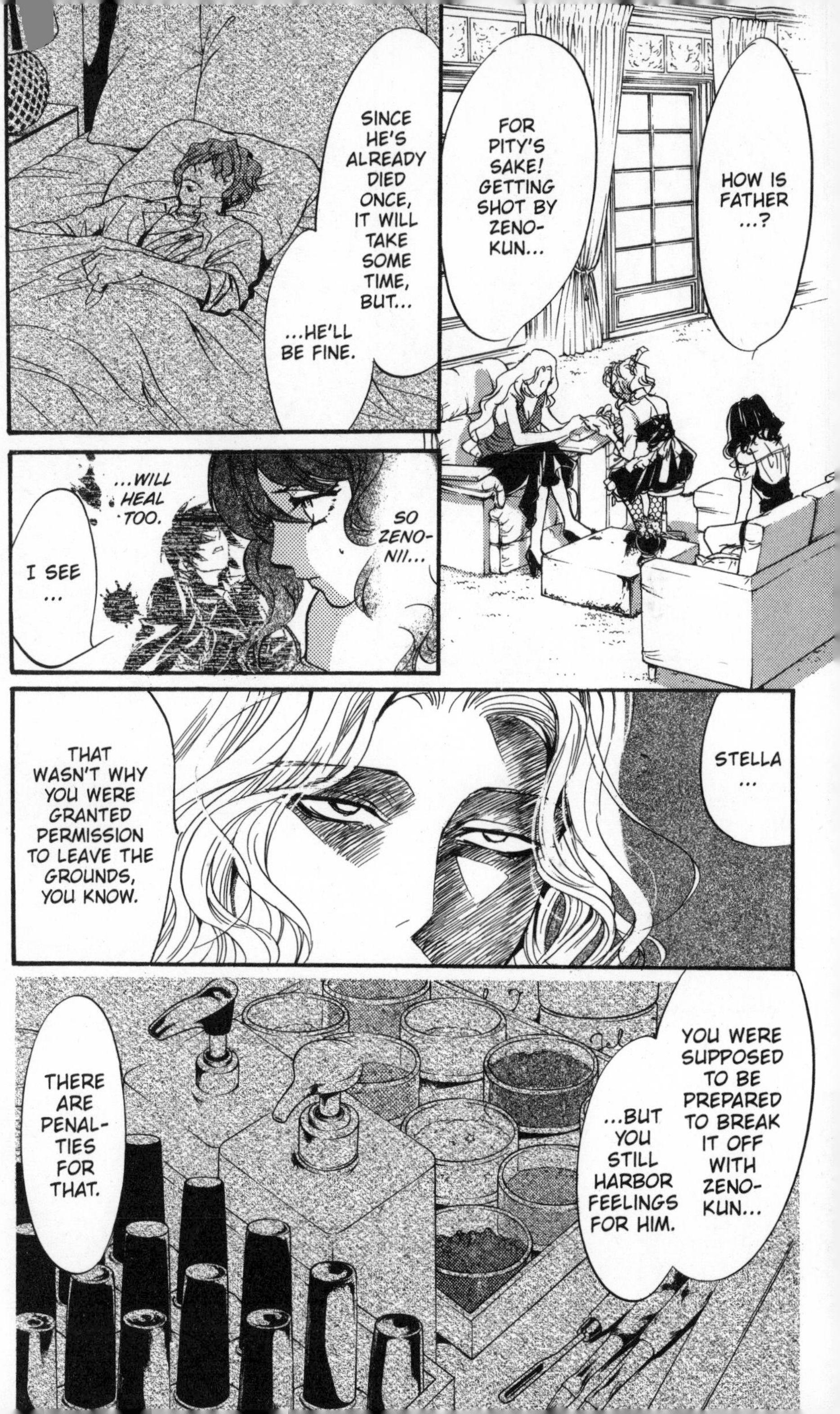
HOW IS FATHER ...?
FOR PITY'S SAKE! GETTING SHOT BY ZENO-KUN...
SINCE HE'S ALREADY DIED ONCE, IT WILL TAKE SOME TIME, BUT...
...HE'LL BE FINE.
SO ZENO-NII...
...WILL HEAL TOO.
I SEE ...
STELLA ...
THAT WASN'T WHY YOU WERE GRANTED PERMISSION TO LEAVE THE GROUNDS, YOU KNOW.
YOU WERE SUPPOSED TO BE PREPARED TO BREAK IT OFF WITH ZENO-KUN...
...BUT YOU STILL HARBOR FEELINGS FOR HIM.
THERE ARE PENALTIES FOR THAT.

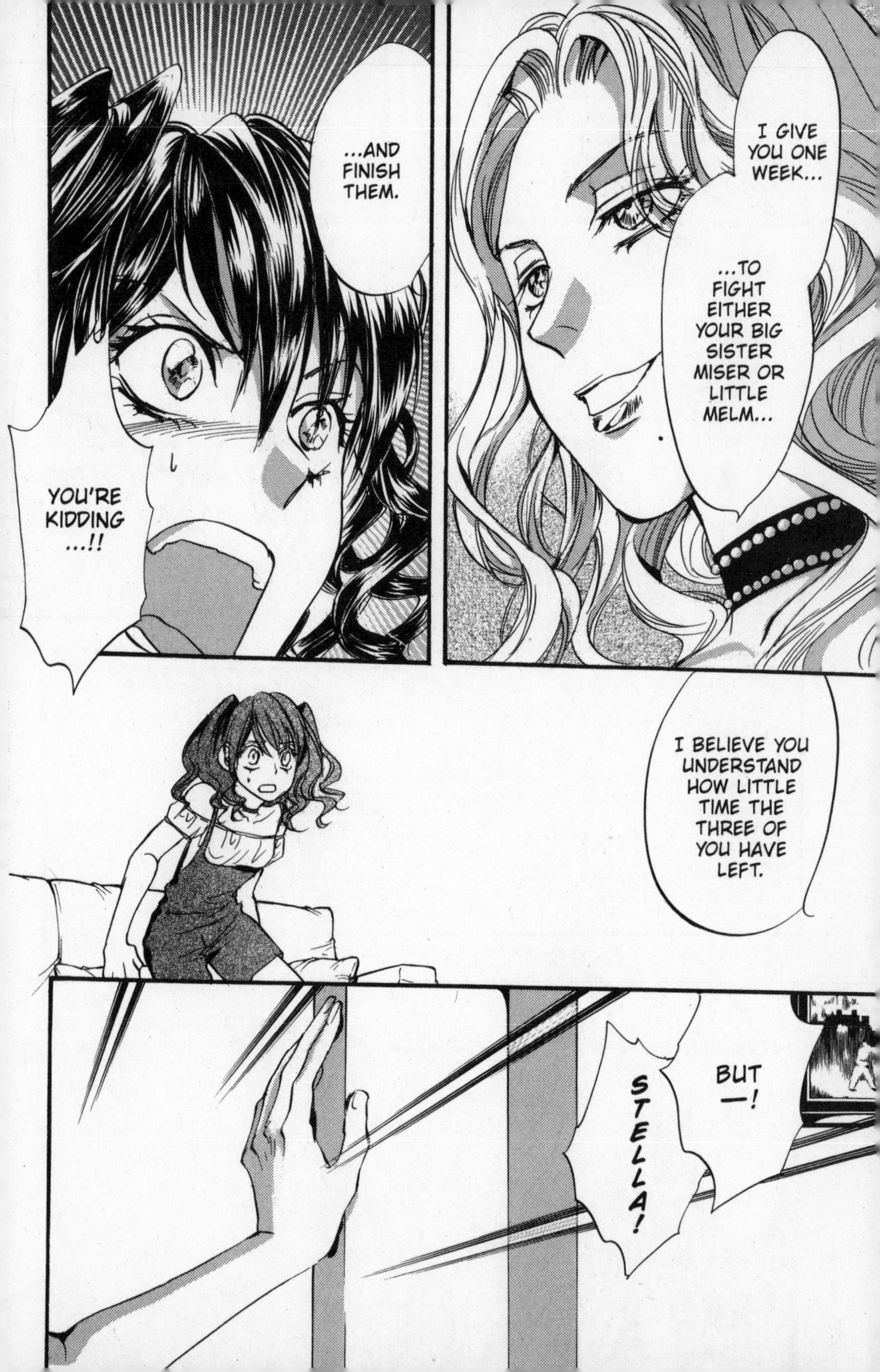
I GIVE YOU ONE WEEK...
...TO FIGHT EITHER YOUR BIG SISTER MISER OR LITTLE MELM...
...AND FINISH THEM.
YOU'RE KIDDING ...!!
I BELIEVE YOU UNDERSTAND HOW LITTLE TIME THE THREE OF YOU HAVE LEFT.
BUT —!
STELLA!

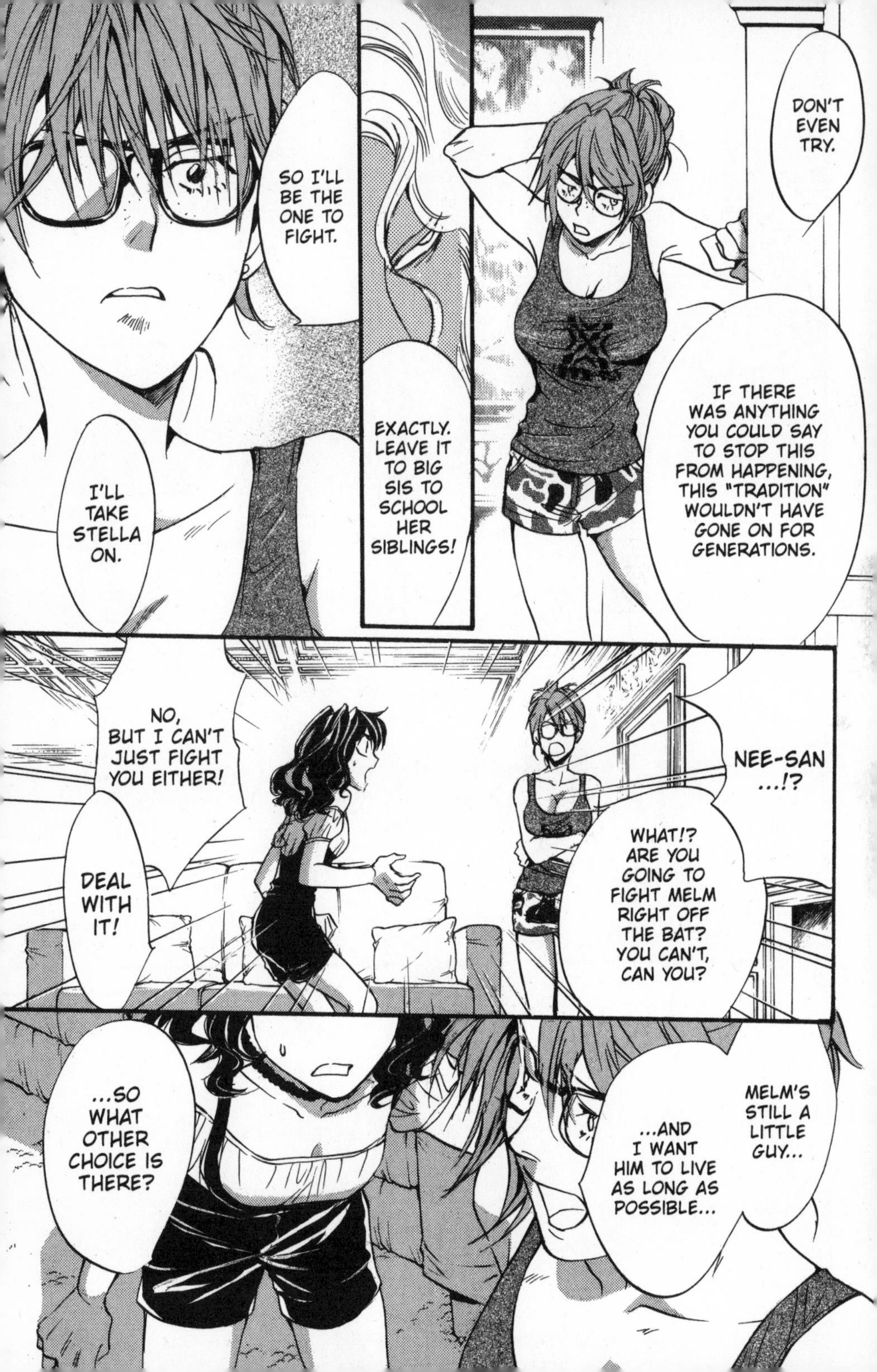
DON'T EVEN TRY.
IF THERE WAS ANYTHING YOU COULD SAY TO STOP THIS FROM HAPPENING, THIS "TRADITION" WOULDN'T HAVE GONE ON FOR GENERATIONS.
EXACTLY. LEAVE IT TO BIG SIS TO SCHOOL HER SIBLINGS!
SO I'LL BE THE ONE TO FIGHT.
I'LL TAKE STELLA ON.
NEE-SAN ...!?
WHAT!? ARE YOU GOING TO FIGHT MELM RIGHT OFF THE BAT? YOU CAN'T, CAN YOU?
NO, BUT I CAN'T JUST FIGHT YOU EITHER!
DEAL WITH IT!
MELM'S STILL A LITTLE GUY...
...AND I WANT HIM TO LIVE AS LONG AS POSSIBLE...
...SO WHAT OTHER CHOICE IS THERE?

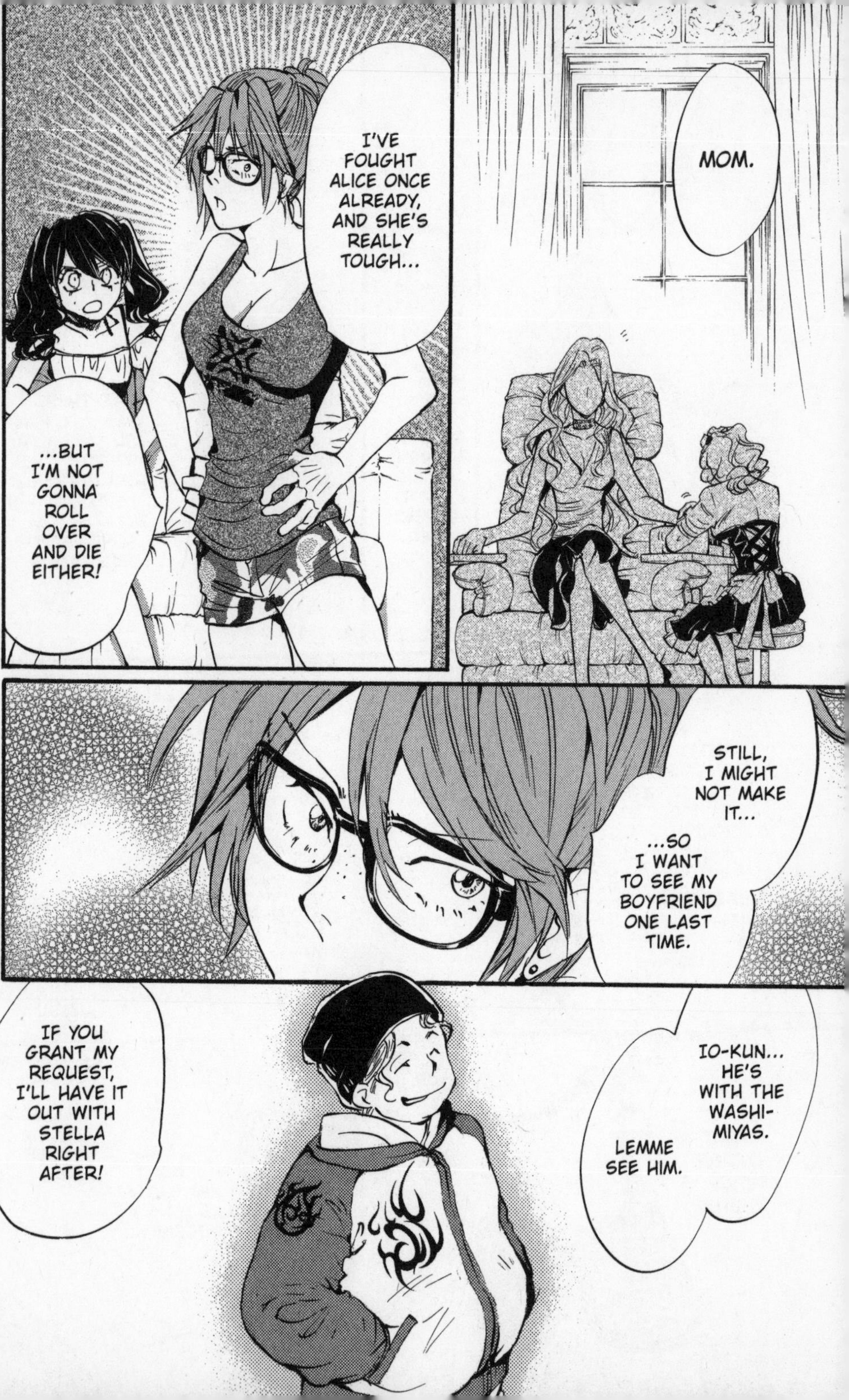

MOM.
I'VE FOUGHT ALICE ONCE ALREADY, AND SHE'S REALLY TOUGH...
...BUT I'M NOT GONNA ROLL OVER AND DIE EITHER!
STILL, I MIGHT NOT MAKE IT...
...SO I WANT TO SEE MY BOYFRIEND ONE LAST TIME.
IO-KUN... HE'S WITH THE WASHI-MIYAS.
LEMME SEE HIM.
IF YOU GRANT MY REQUEST, I'LL HAVE IT OUT WITH STELLA RIGHT AFTER!

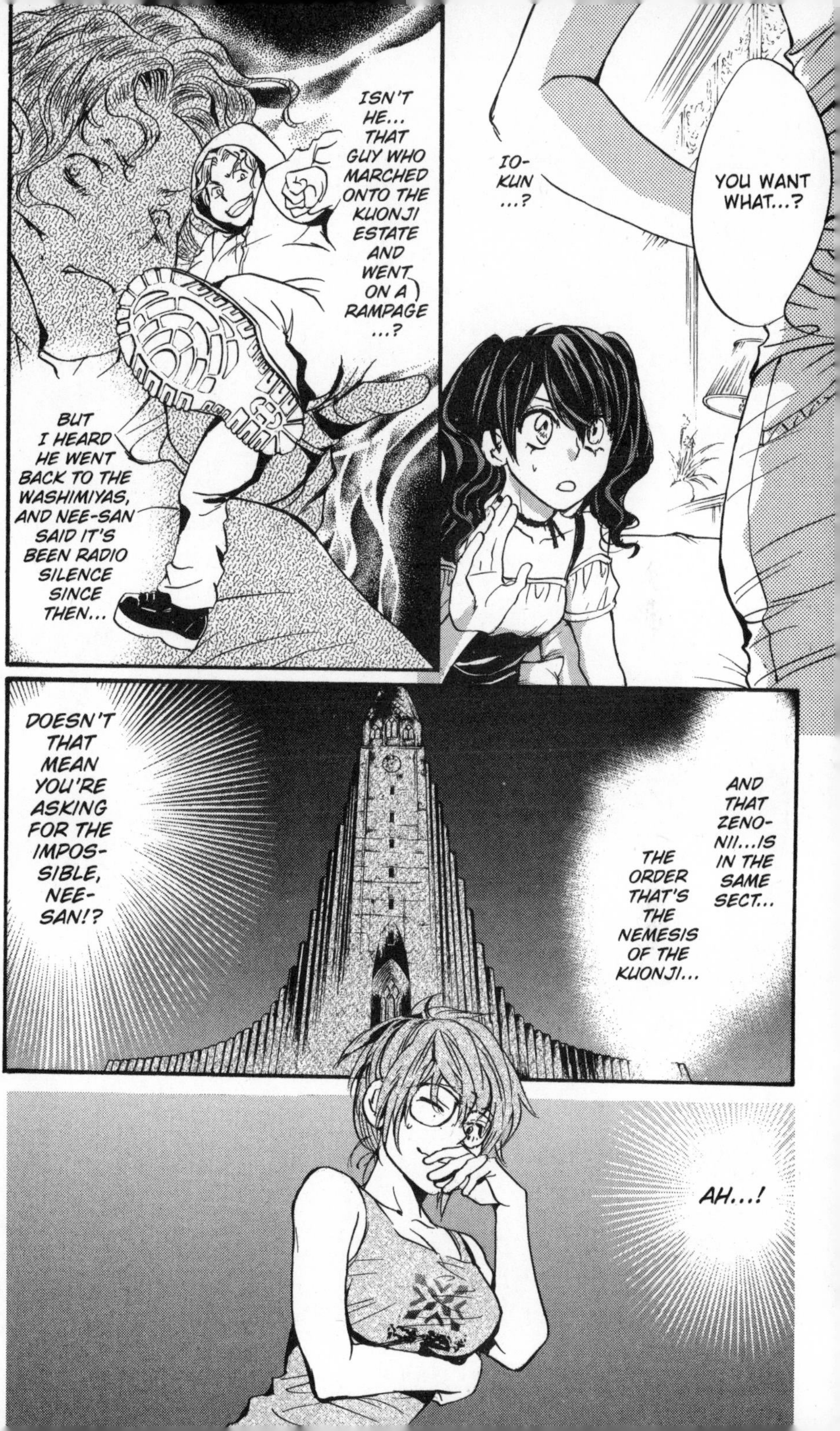
YOU WANT WHAT...?
IO-KUN...?
ISN'T HE... THAT GUY WHO MARCHED ONTO THE KUONJI ESTATE AND WENT ON A RAMPAGE...?
BUT I HEARD HE WENT BACK TO THE WASHIMIYAS, AND NEE-SAN SAID IT'S BEEN RADIO SILENCE SINCE THEN...
AND THAT ZENO-NII...IS IN THE SAME SECT...
THE ORDER THAT'S THE NEMESIS OF THE KUONJI...
DOESN'T THAT MEAN YOU'RE ASKING FOR THE IMPOS-SIBLE, NEE-SAN!?
AH...!

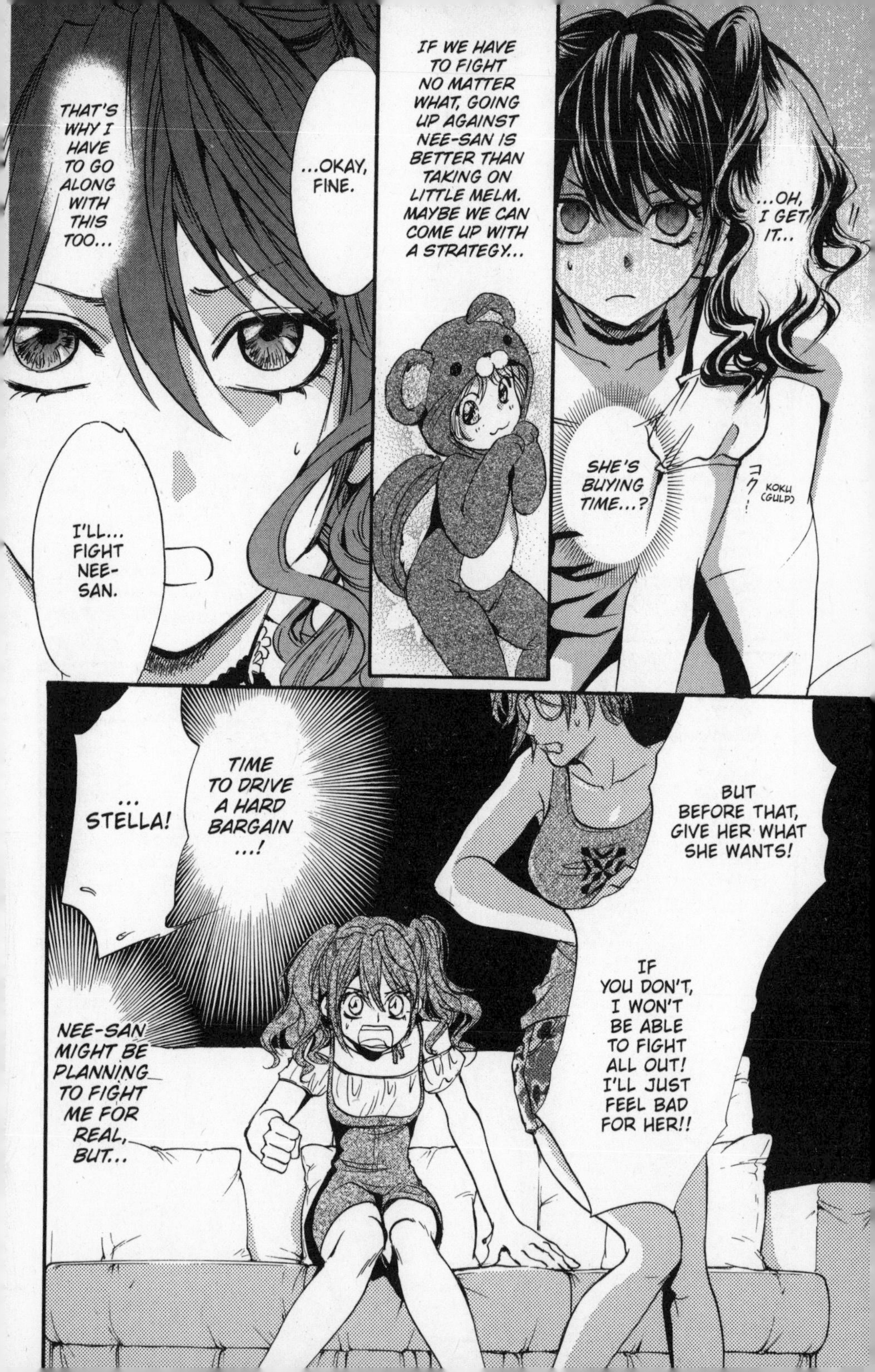
...OH, I GET IT...
SHE'S BUYING TIME...?
KOKU (GULP)
IF WE HAVE TO FIGHT NO MATTER WHAT, GOING UP AGAINST NEE-SAN IS BETTER THAN TAKING ON LITTLE MELM. MAYBE WE CAN COME UP WITH A STRATEGY...
...OKAY, FINE.
THAT'S WHY I HAVE TO GO ALONG WITH THIS TOO...
I'LL... FIGHT NEE-SAN.
BUT BEFORE THAT, GIVE HER WHAT SHE WANTS!
TIME TO DRIVE A HARD BARGAIN...!
... STELLA!
IF YOU DON'T, I WON'T BE ABLE TO FIGHT ALL OUT! I'LL JUST FEEL BAD FOR HER!!
NEE-SAN MIGHT BE PLANNING TO FIGHT ME FOR REAL, BUT...

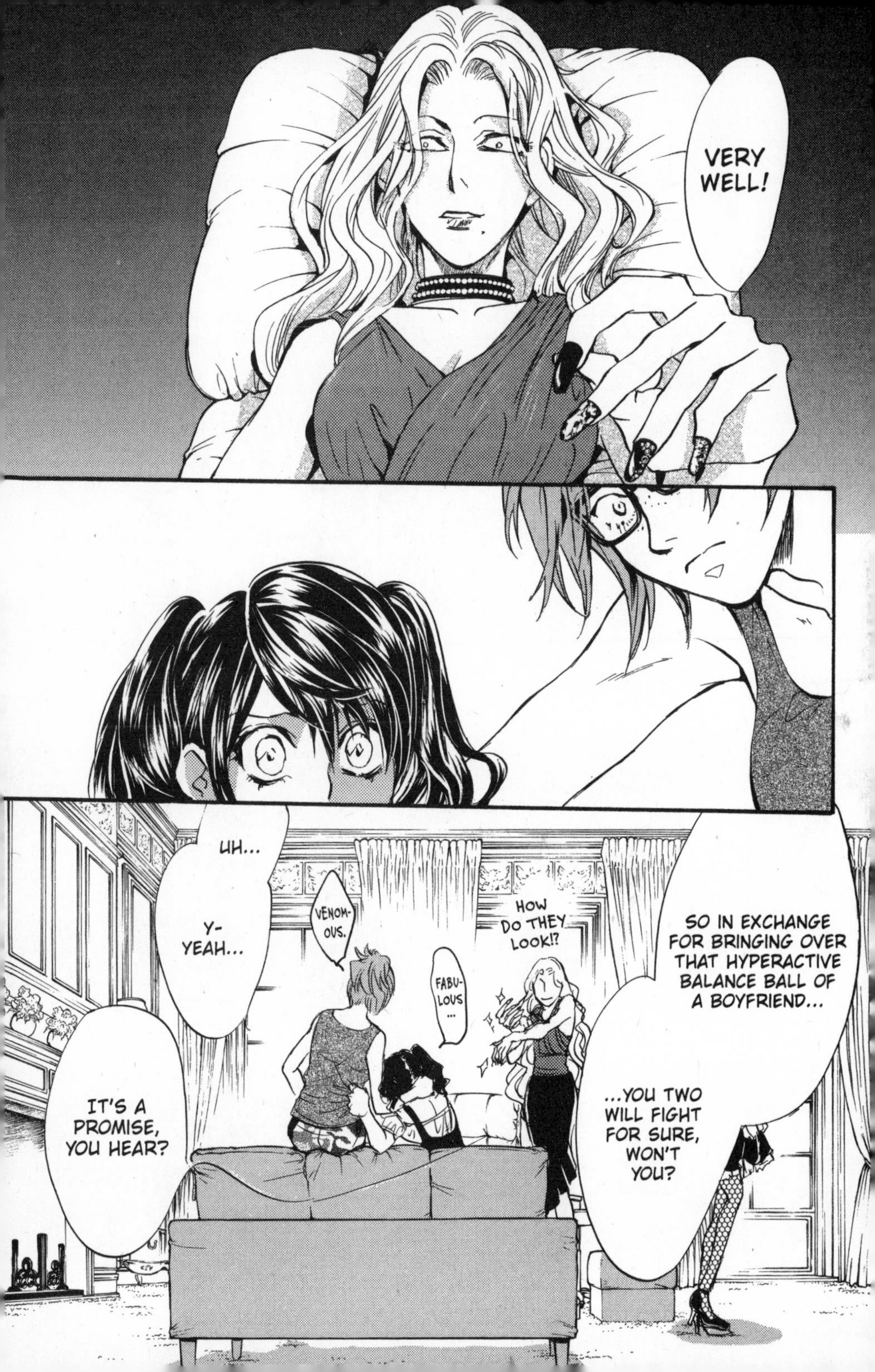
VERY WELL!
SO IN EXCHANGE FOR BRINGING OVER THAT HYPERACTIVE BALANCE BALL OF A BOYFRIEND...
...YOU TWO WILL FIGHT FOR SURE, WON'T YOU?
HOW DO THEY LOOK!?
FABULOUS...
VENOMOUS.
UH...
Y-YEAH...
IT'S A PROMISE, YOU HEAR?

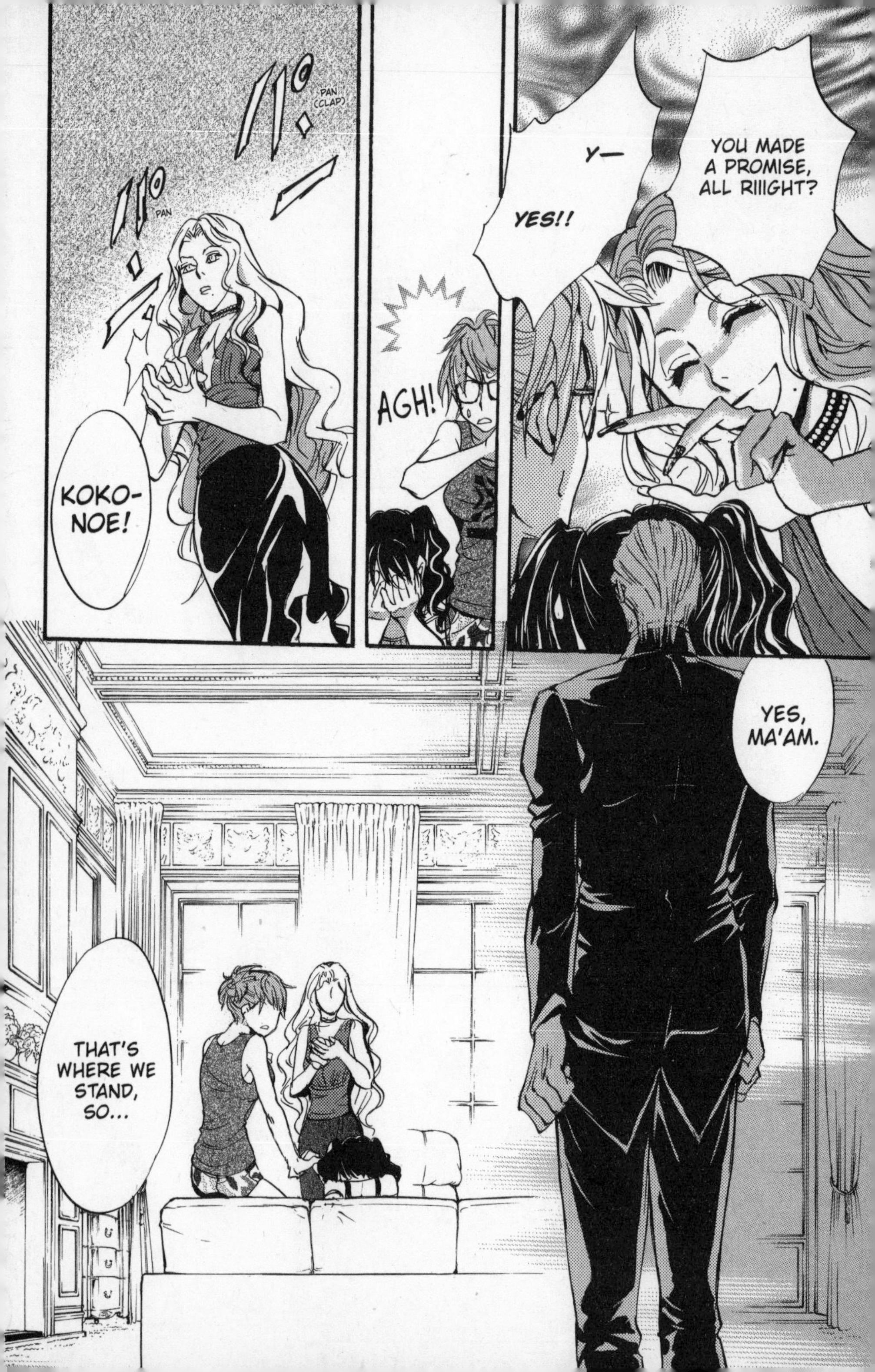
YOU MADE A PROMISE, ALL RIIIGHT?
Y—
YES!!
AGH!
PAN (CLAP)
PAN
KOKO-NOE!
YES, MA'AM.
THAT'S WHERE WE STAND, SO...

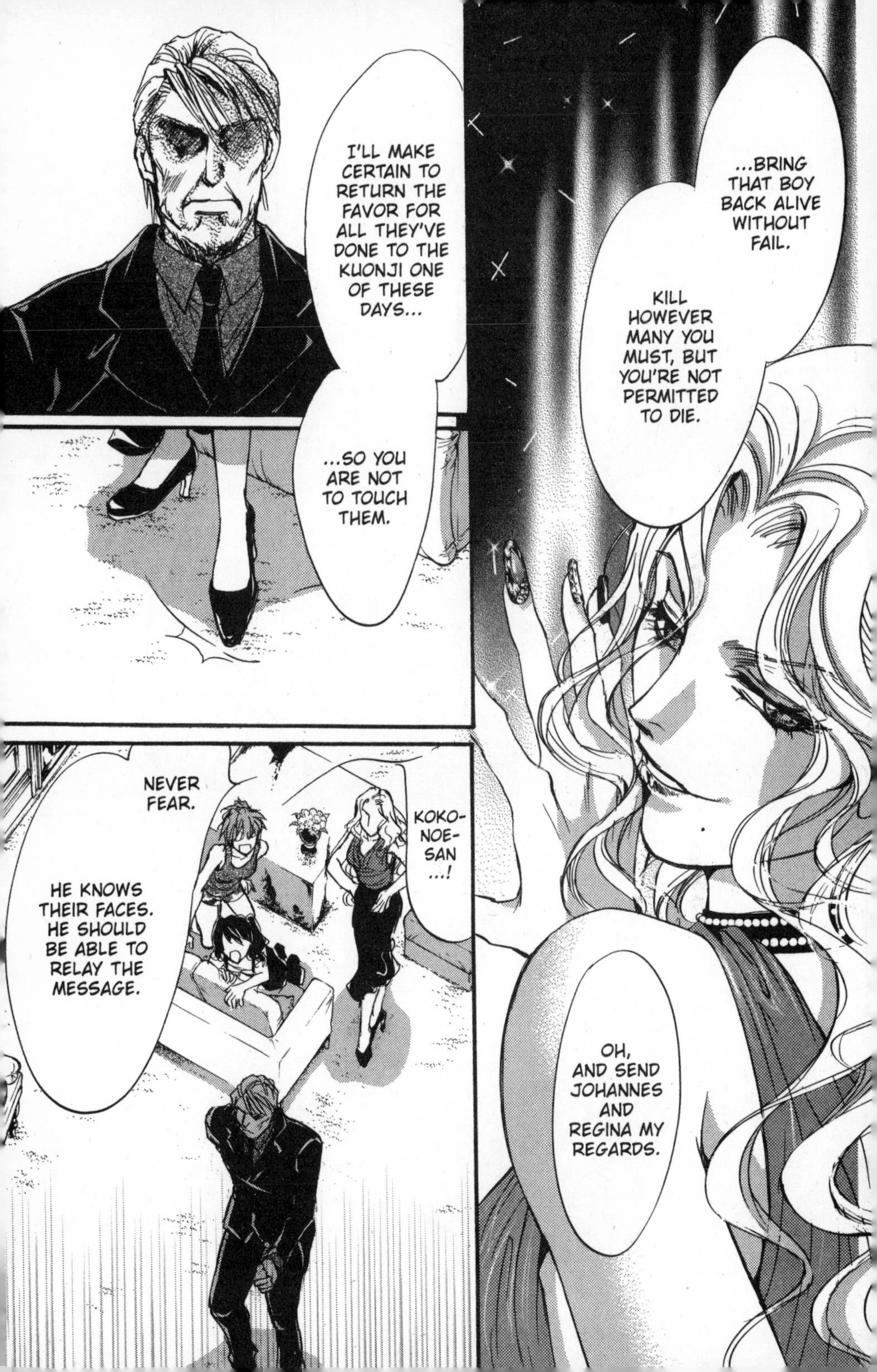
...BRING THAT BOY BACK ALIVE WITHOUT FAIL.
KILL HOWEVER MANY YOU MUST, BUT YOU'RE NOT PERMITTED TO DIE.
OH, AND SEND JOHANNES AND REGINA MY REGARDS.
I'LL MAKE CERTAIN TO RETURN THE FAVOR FOR ALL THEY'VE DONE TO THE KUONJI ONE OF THESE DAYS...
...SO YOU ARE NOT TO TOUCH THEM.
KOKO-NOE-SAN ...!
NEVER FEAR.
HE KNOWS THEIR FACES. HE SHOULD BE ABLE TO RELAY THE MESSAGE.

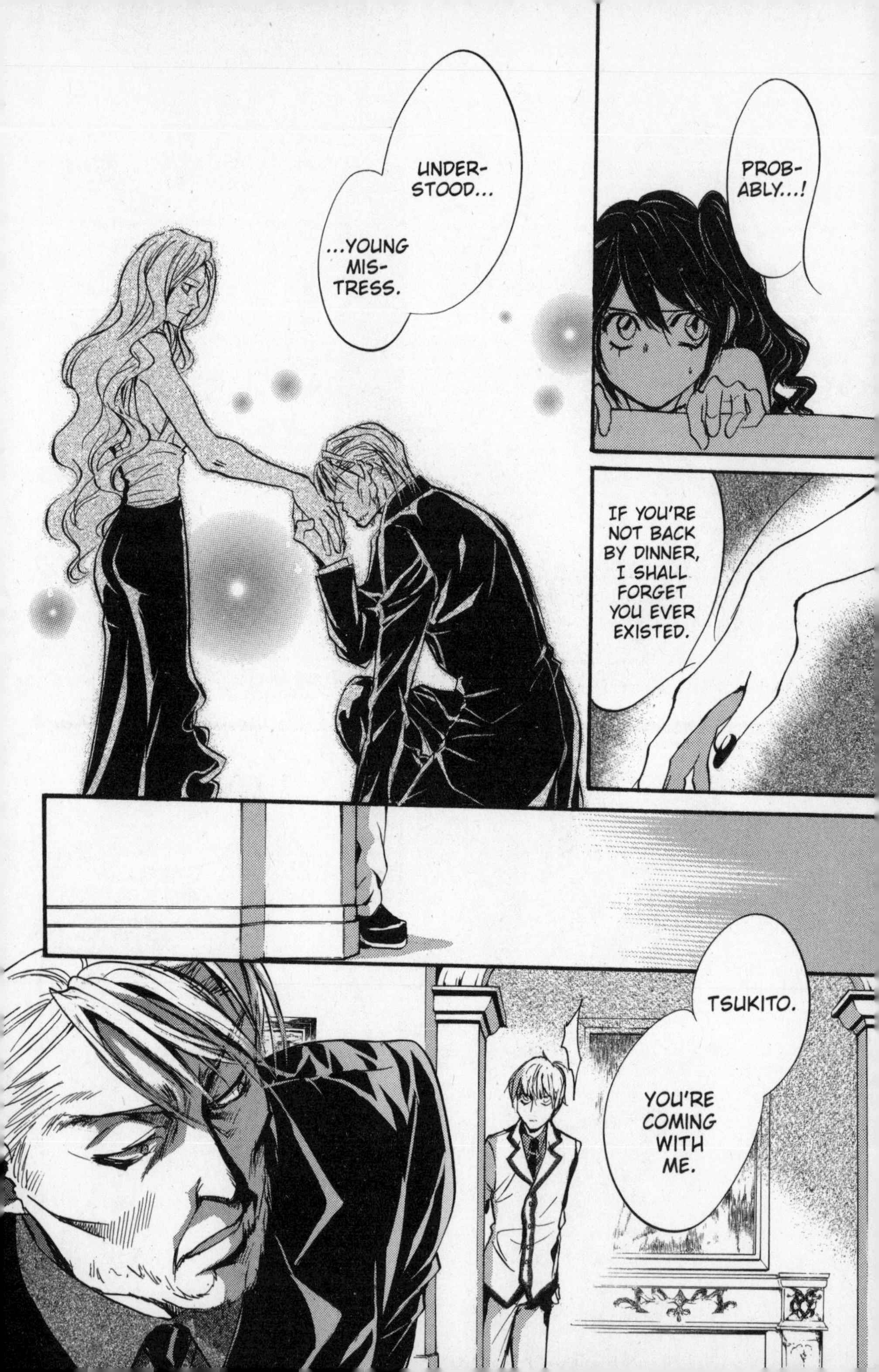
PROB-ABLY...!
IF YOU'RE NOT BACK BY DINNER, I SHALL FORGET YOU EVER EXISTED.
UNDER-STOOD...
...YOUNG MIS-TRESS.
TSUKITO.
YOU'RE COMING WITH ME.

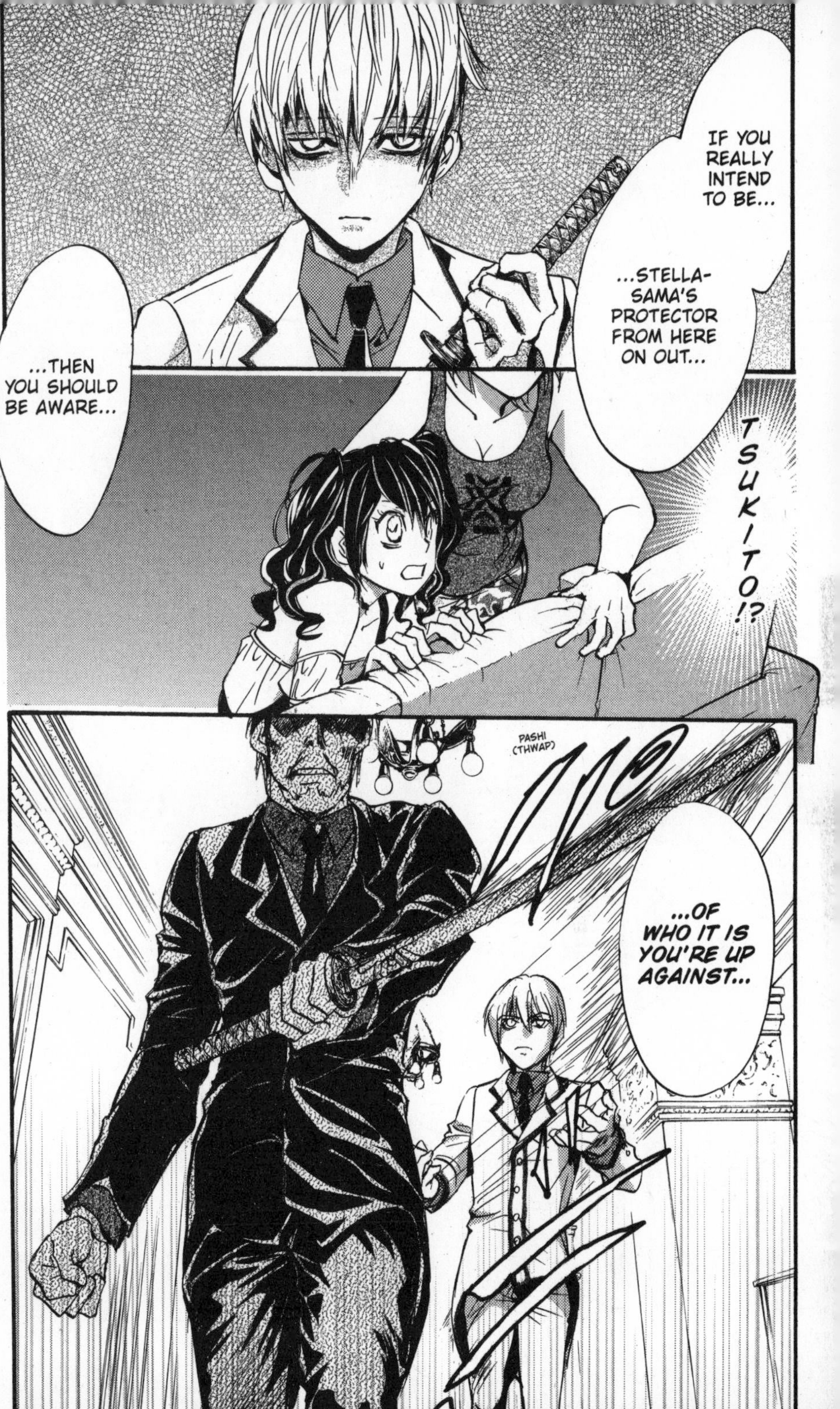
IF YOU REALLY INTEND TO BE...
...STELLA-SAMA'S PROTECTOR FROM HERE ON OUT...
...THEN YOU SHOULD BE AWARE...
TSUKITO!?
PASHI (THWAP)
...OF WHO IT IS YOU'RE UP AGAINST...

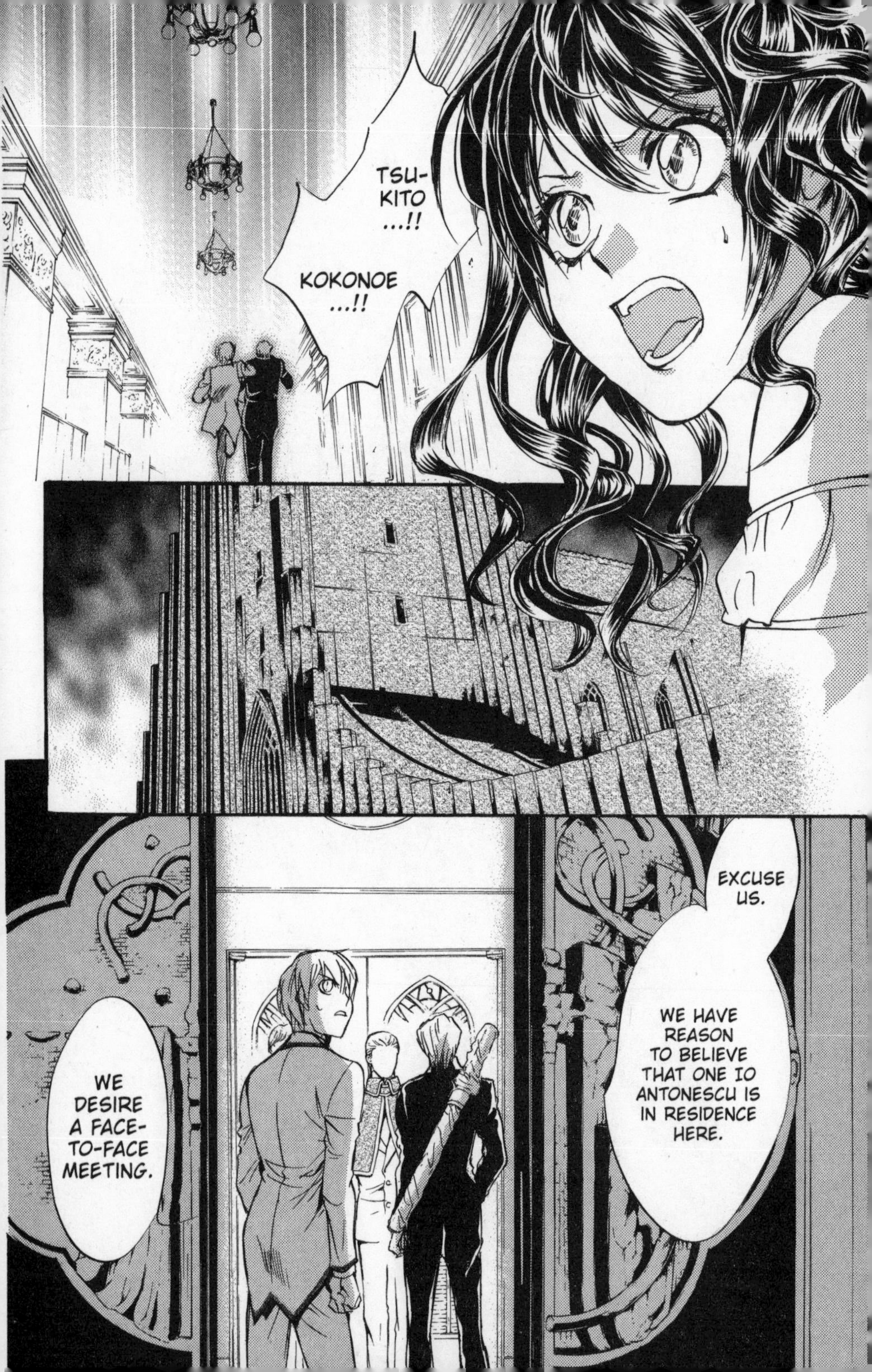
TSU-KITO ...!!
KOKONOE ...!!
EXCUSE US.
WE HAVE REASON TO BELIEVE THAT ONE IO ANTONESCU IS IN RESIDENCE HERE.
WE DESIRE A FACE-TO-FACE MEETING.

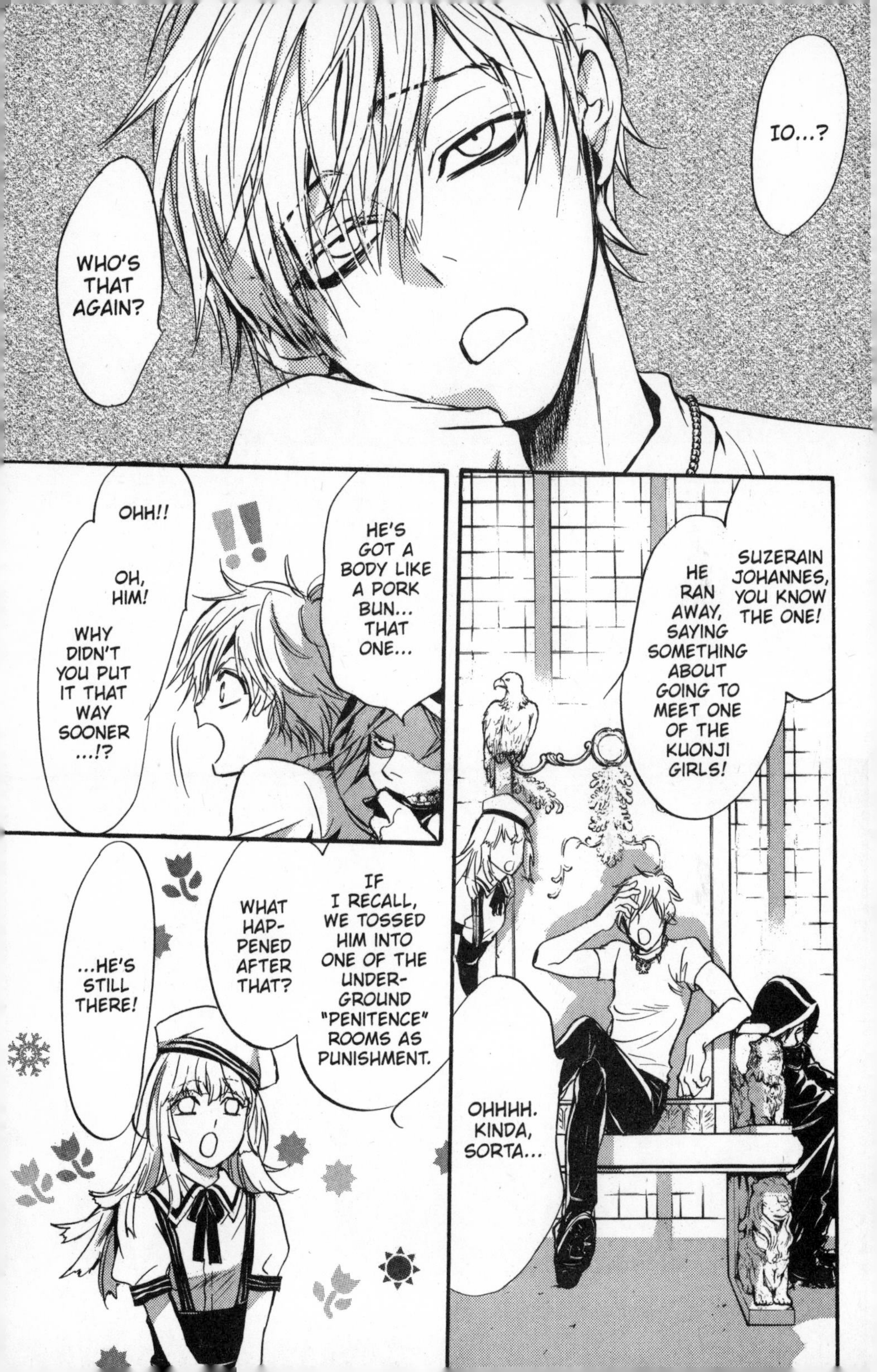
IO...?
WHO'S THAT AGAIN?
SUZERAIN JOHANNES, YOU KNOW THE ONE!
HE RAN AWAY, SAYING SOMETHING ABOUT GOING TO MEET ONE OF THE KUONJI GIRLS!
OHHHH. KINDA, SORTA...
HE'S GOT A BODY LIKE A PORK BUN... THAT ONE...
!!
OHH!!
OH, HIM!
WHY DIDN'T YOU PUT IT THAT WAY SOONER ...!?
IF I RECALL, WE TOSSED HIM INTO ONE OF THE UNDER-GROUND "PENITENCE" ROOMS AS PUNISHMENT.
WHAT HAP-PENED AFTER THAT?
...HE'S STILL THERE!

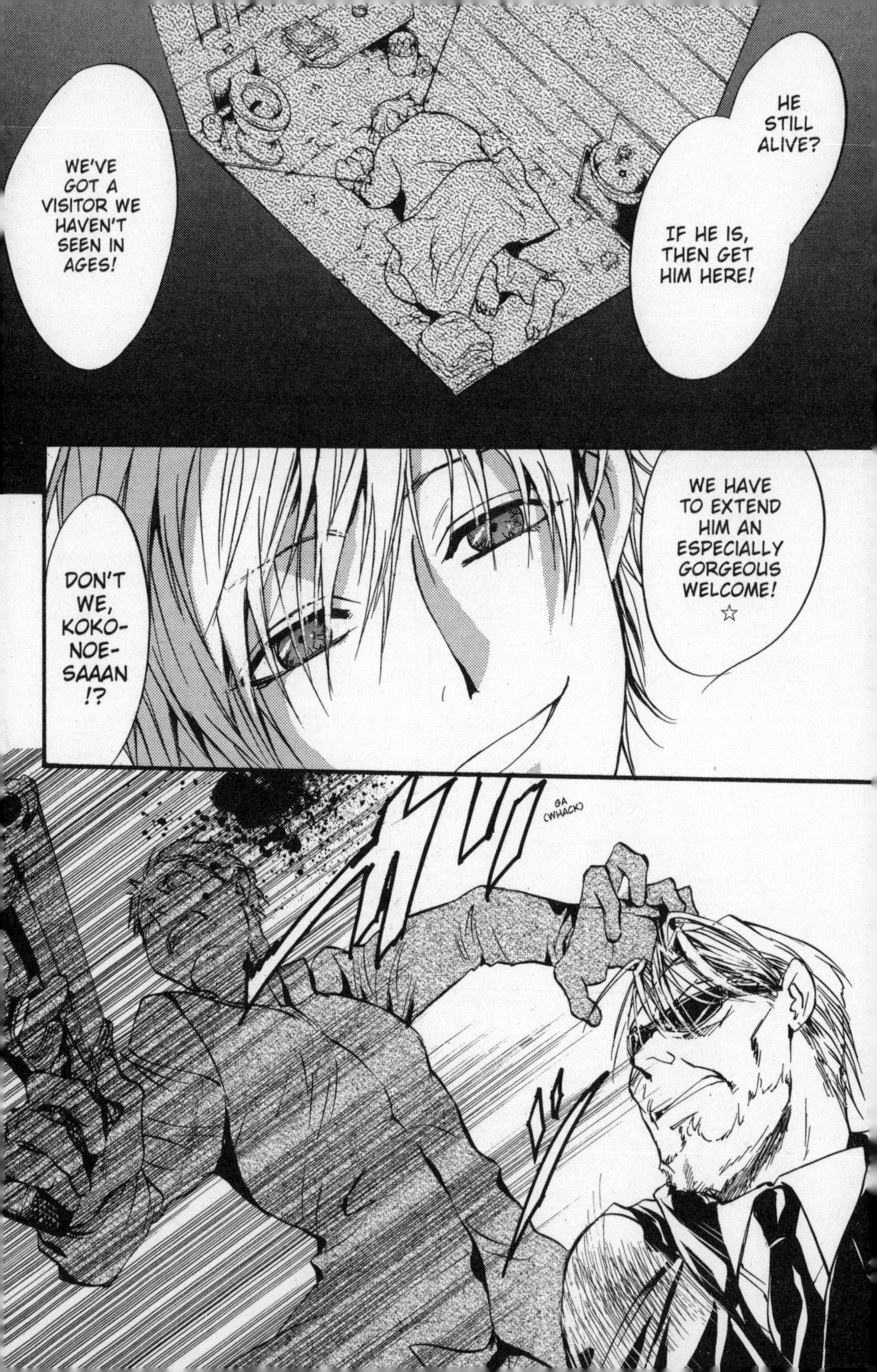
HE STILL ALIVE?
IF HE IS, THEN GET HIM HERE!
WE'VE GOT A VISITOR WE HAVEN'T SEEN IN AGES!
WE HAVE TO EXTEND HIM AN ESPECIALLY GORGEOUS WELCOME! ☆
DON'T WE, KOKO-NOE-SAAAN!?
GA (WHACK)

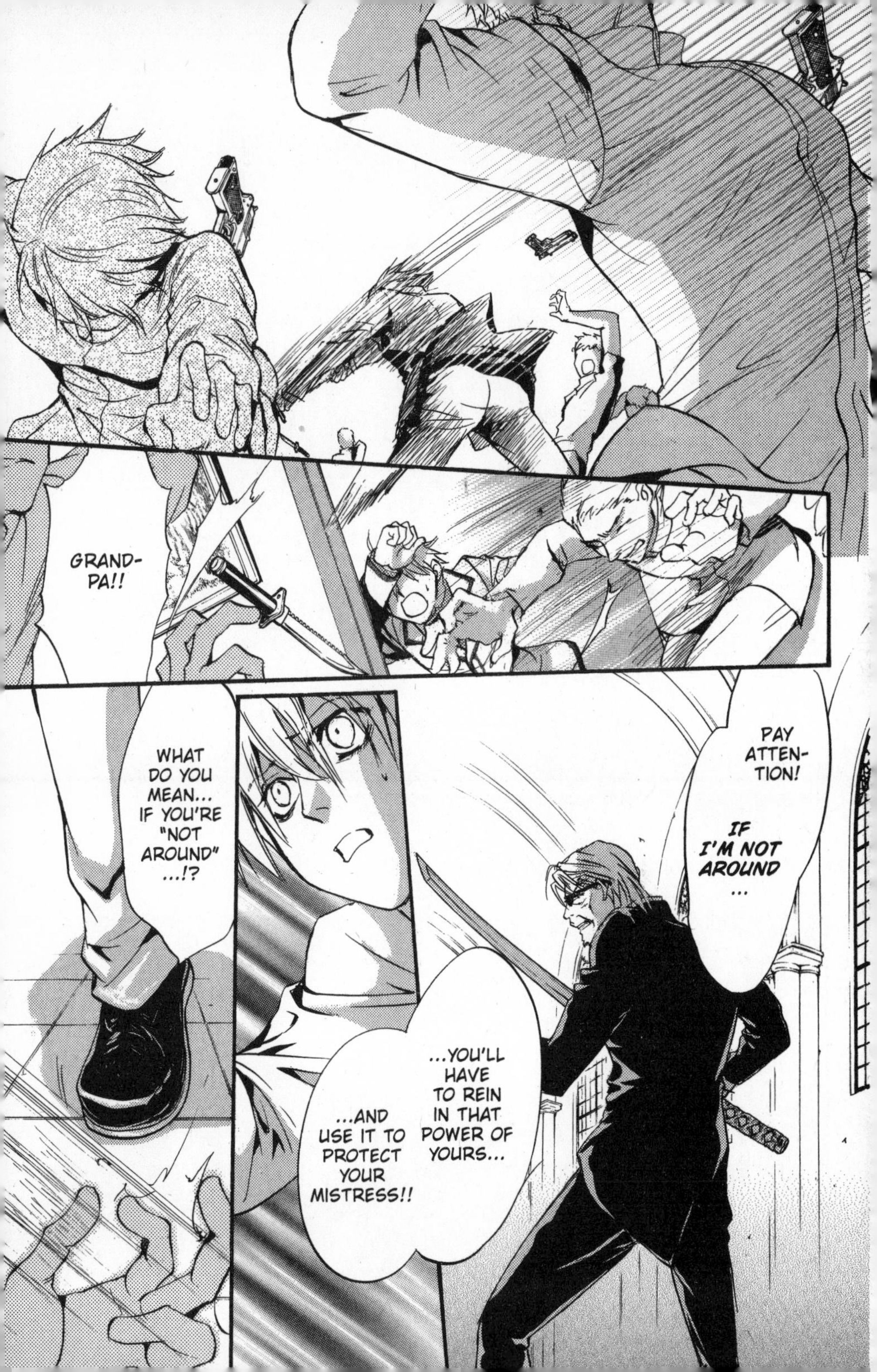
GRAND-PA!!
PAY ATTEN-TION!
IF I'M NOT AROUND...
...YOU'LL HAVE TO REIN IN THAT POWER OF YOURS...
...AND USE IT TO PROTECT YOUR MISTRESS!!
WHAT DO YOU MEAN... IF YOU'RE "NOT AROUND"...!?

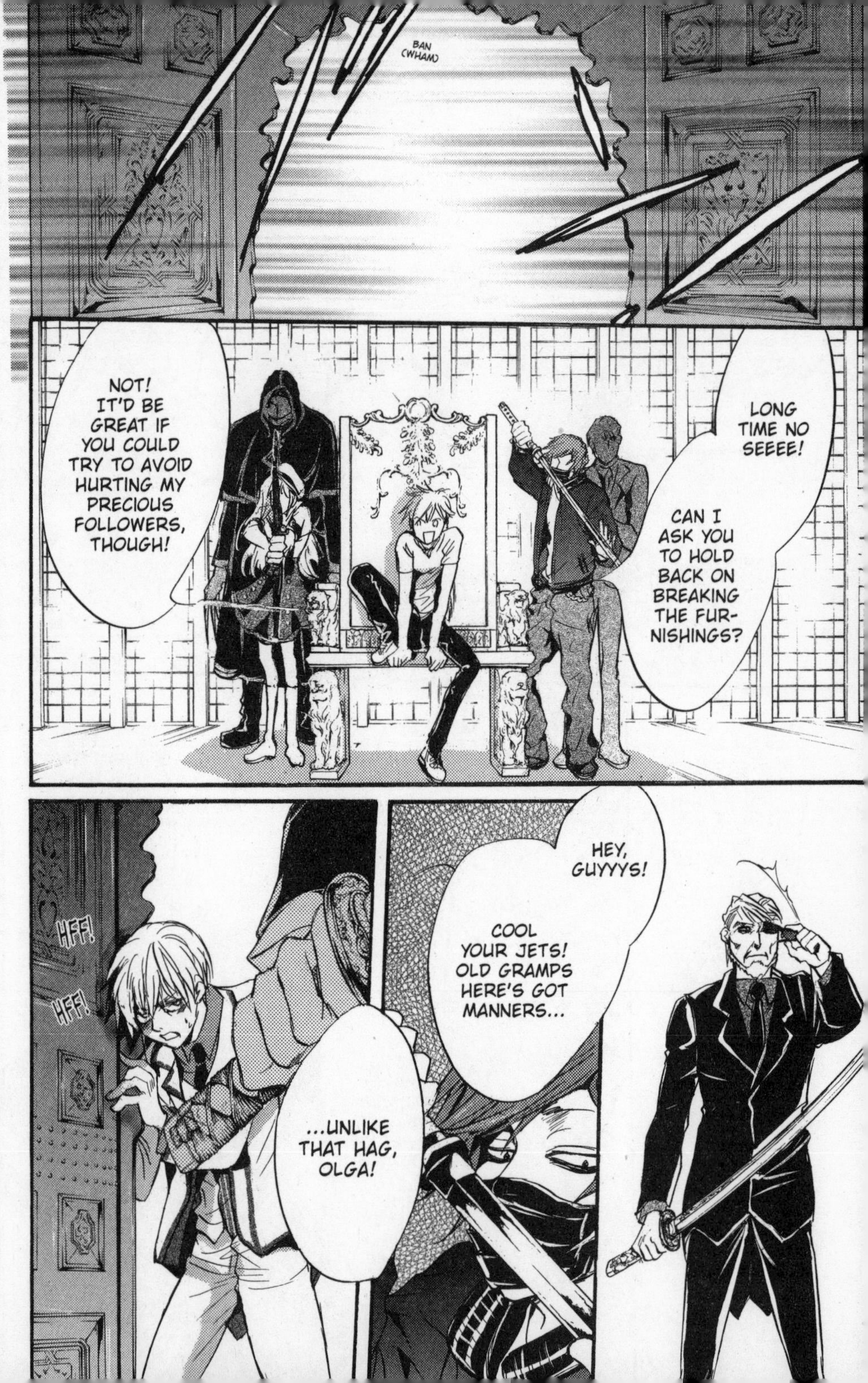
BAN
(WHAM)
LONG TIME NO SEEEE!
CAN I ASK YOU TO HOLD BACK ON BREAKING THE FUR-NISHINGS?
NOT! IT'D BE GREAT IF YOU COULD TRY TO AVOID HURTING MY PRECIOUS FOLLOWERS, THOUGH!
HEY, GUYYYS!
COOL YOUR JETS! OLD GRAMPS HERE'S GOT MANNERS...
...UNLIKE THAT HAG, OLGA!
HFF!
HFF!

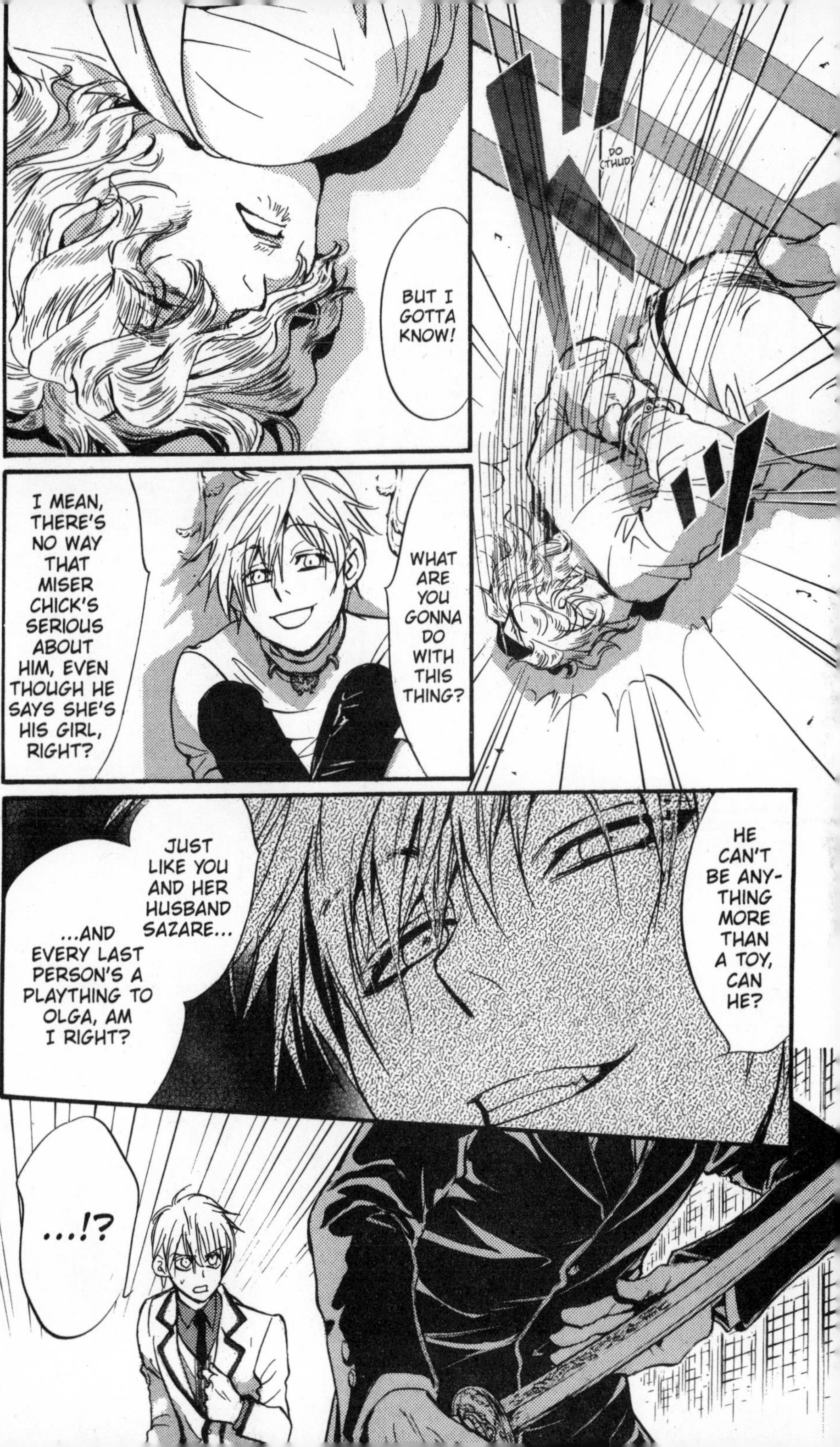
DO (THUD)
BUT I GOTTA KNOW!
WHAT ARE YOU GONNA DO WITH THIS THING?
I MEAN, THERE'S NO WAY THAT MISER CHICK'S SERIOUS ABOUT HIM, EVEN THOUGH HE SAYS SHE'S HIS GIRL, RIGHT?
HE CAN'T BE ANYTHING MORE THAN A TOY, CAN HE?
JUST LIKE YOU AND HER HUSBAND SAZARE...
...AND EVERY LAST PERSON'S A PLAYTHING TO OLGA, AM I RIGHT?
...!?

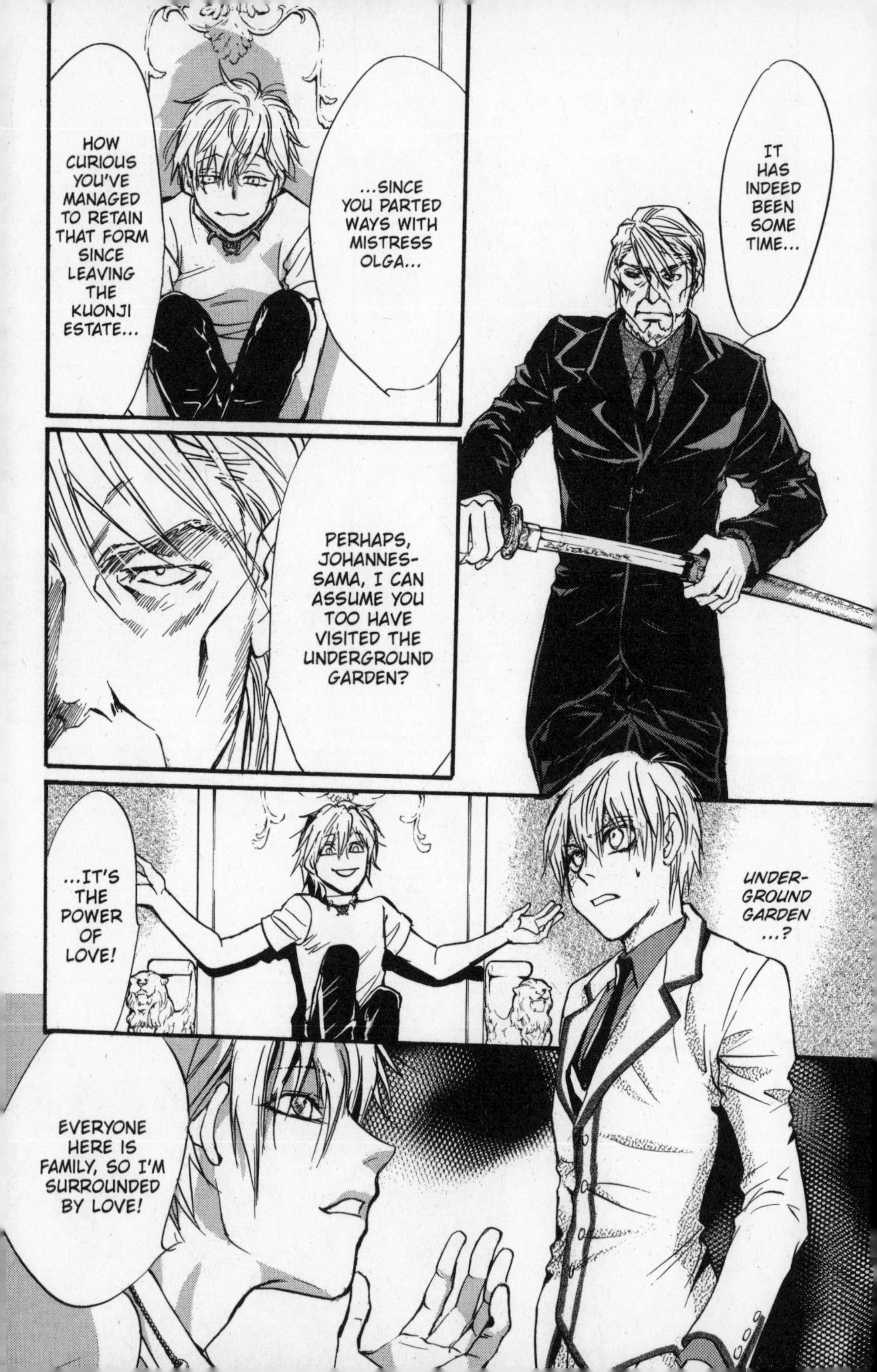
IT HAS INDEED BEEN SOME TIME...
...SINCE YOU PARTED WAYS WITH MISTRESS OLGA...
HOW CURIOUS YOU'VE MANAGED TO RETAIN THAT FORM SINCE LEAVING THE KUONJI ESTATE...
PERHAPS, JOHANNES-SAMA, I CAN ASSUME YOU TOO HAVE VISITED THE UNDERGROUND GARDEN?
UNDER-GROUND GARDEN ...?
...IT'S THE POWER OF LOVE!
EVERYONE HERE IS FAMILY, SO I'M SURROUNDED BY LOVE!

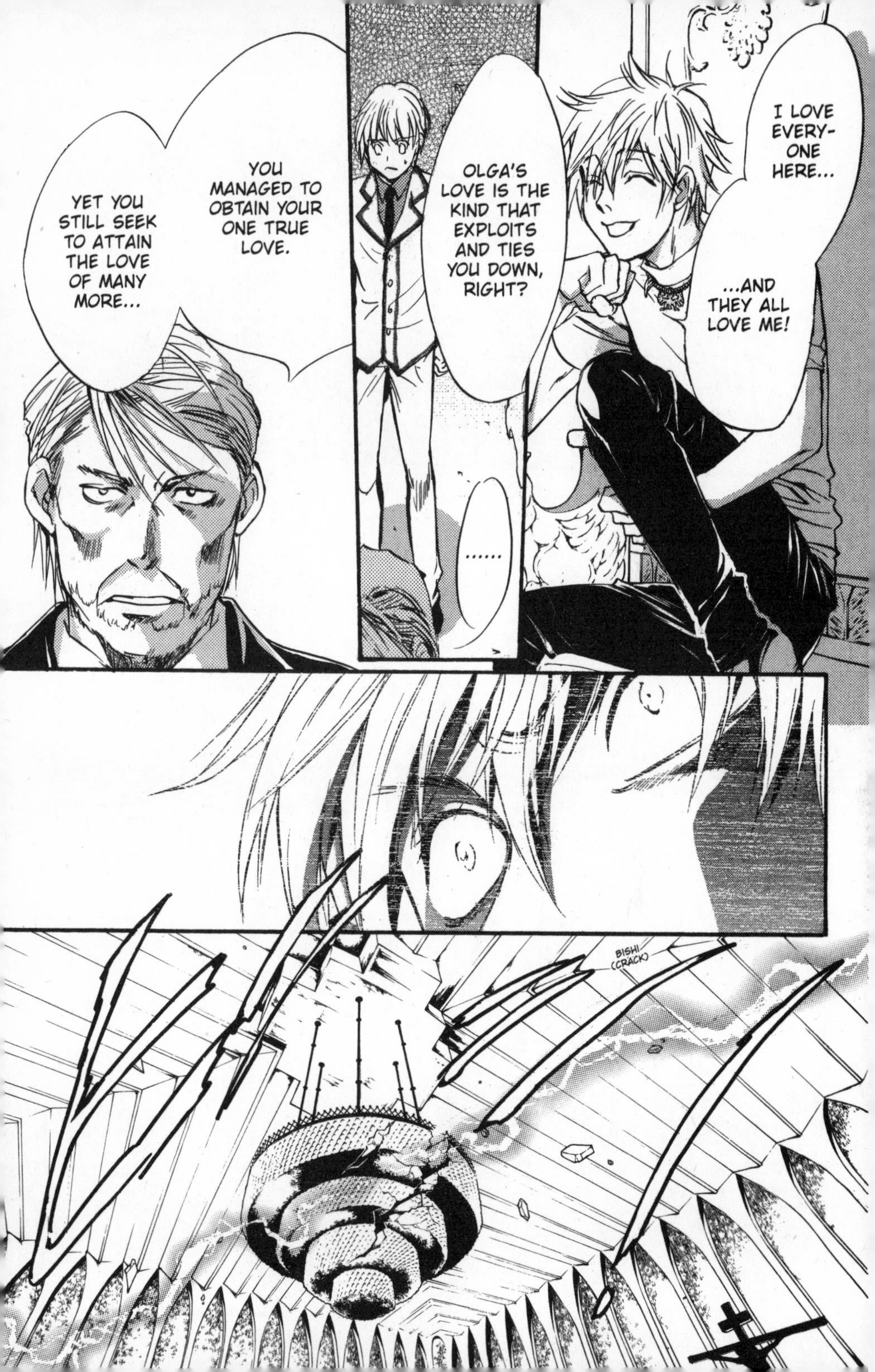
I LOVE EVERY-ONE HERE...
...AND THEY ALL LOVE ME!
OLGA'S LOVE IS THE KIND THAT EXPLOITS AND TIES YOU DOWN, RIGHT?
......
YOU MANAGED TO OBTAIN YOUR ONE TRUE LOVE.
YET YOU STILL SEEK TO ATTAIN THE LOVE OF MANY MORE...
BISHI (CRACK)

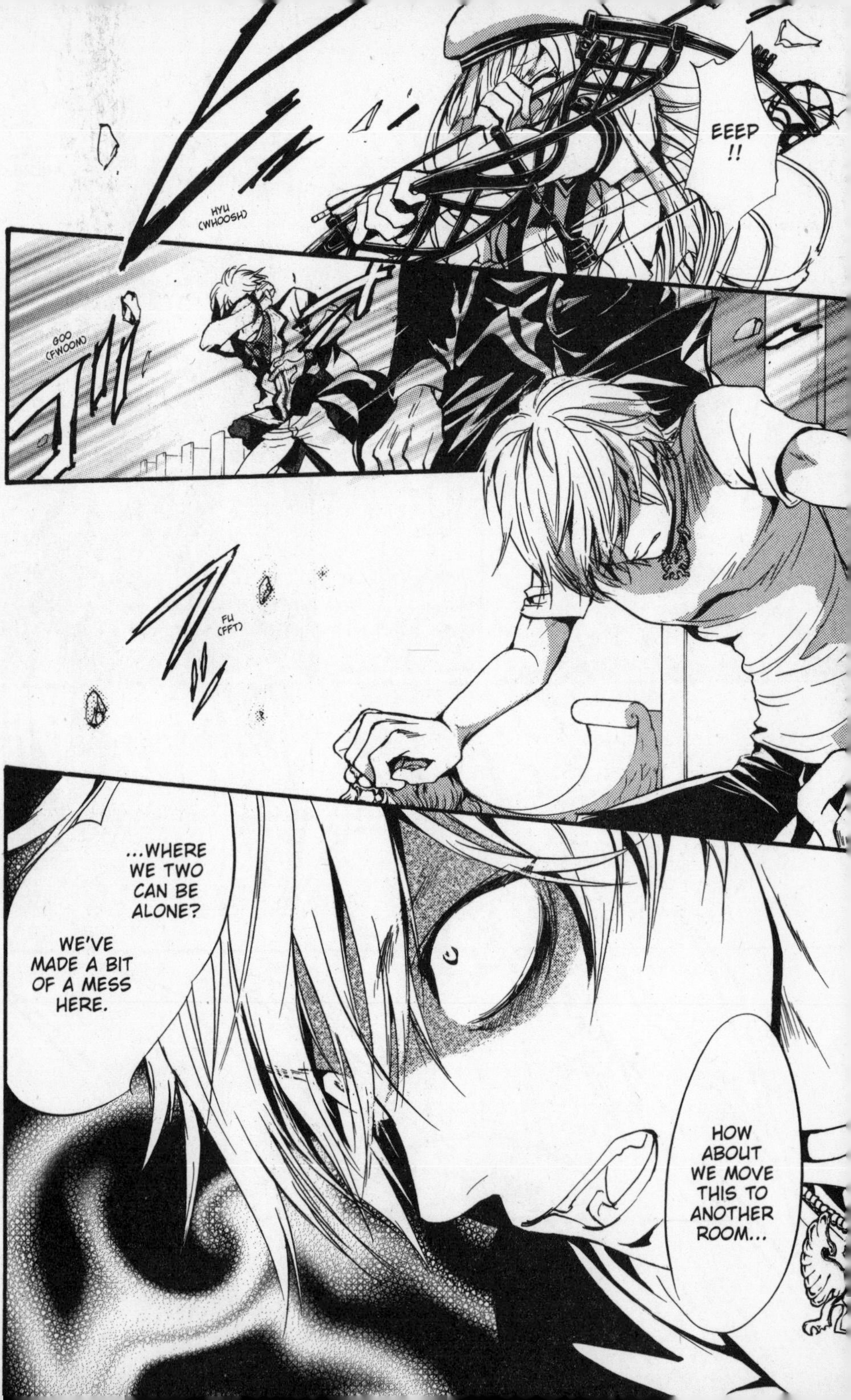
EEEP !!
HYU (WHOOSH)
GOO (FWOOM)
FU (FFT)
HOW ABOUT WE MOVE THIS TO ANOTHER ROOM...
...WHERE WE TWO CAN BE ALONE?
WE'VE MADE A BIT OF A MESS HERE.

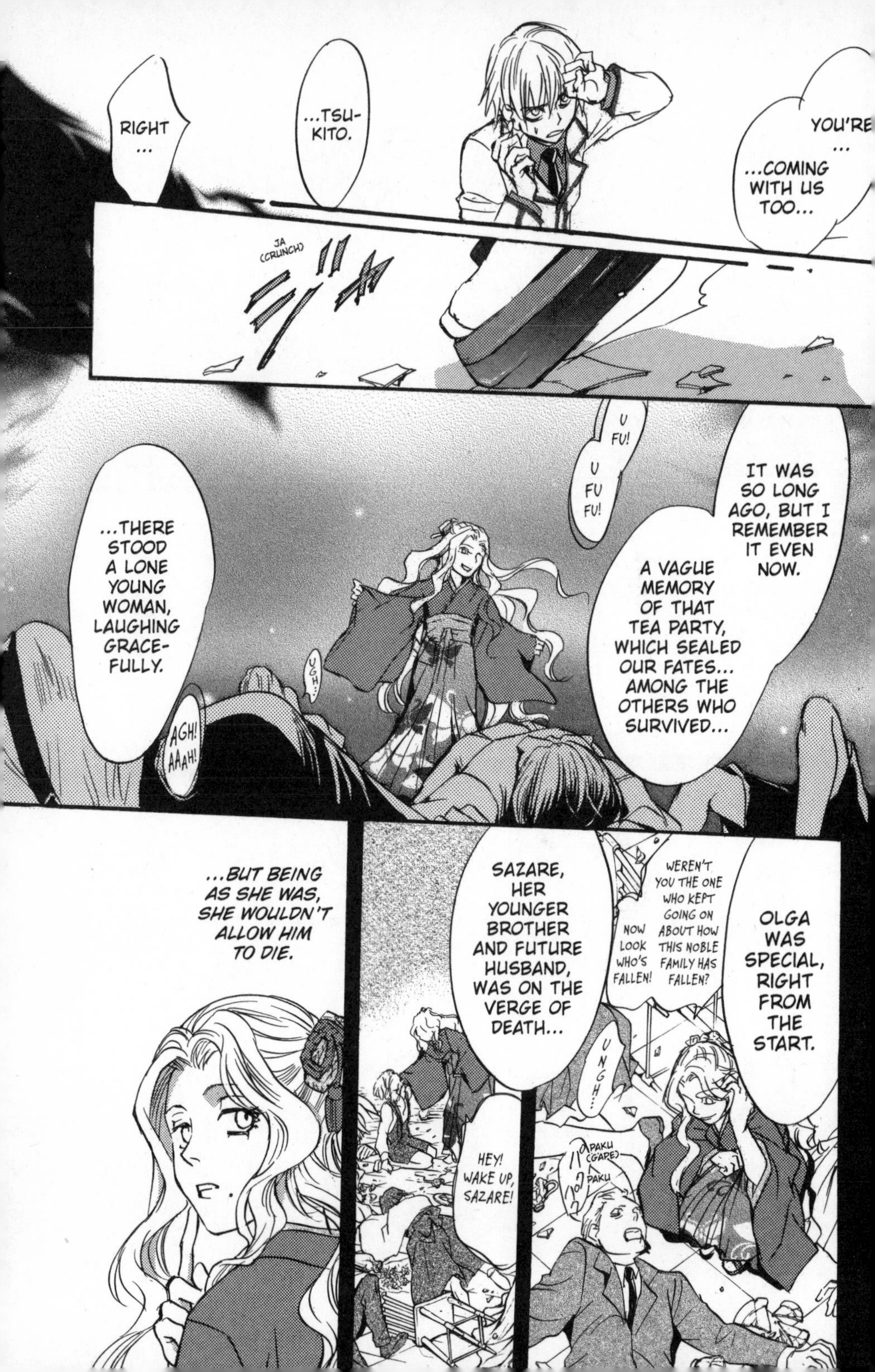
YOU'RE ... ...COMING WITH US TOO...
...TSU-KITO.
RIGHT ...
JA (CRUNCH)
IT WAS SO LONG AGO, BUT I REMEMBER IT EVEN NOW.
U FU! U FU FU!
A VAGUE MEMORY OF THAT TEA PARTY, WHICH SEALED OUR FATES... AMONG THE OTHERS WHO SURVIVED...
...THERE STOOD A LONE YOUNG WOMAN, LAUGHING GRACE-FULLY.
UGH...
AGH! AAAH!
OLGA WAS SPECIAL, RIGHT FROM THE START.
WEREN'T YOU THE ONE WHO KEPT GOING ON ABOUT HOW THIS NOBLE FAMILY HAS FALLEN?
NOW LOOK WHO'S FALLEN!
SAZARE, HER YOUNGER BROTHER AND FUTURE HUSBAND, WAS ON THE VERGE OF DEATH...
UNGH...
PAKU (GAPE) PAKU
HEY! WAKE UP, SAZARE!
...BUT BEING AS SHE WAS, SHE WOULDN'T ALLOW HIM TO DIE.

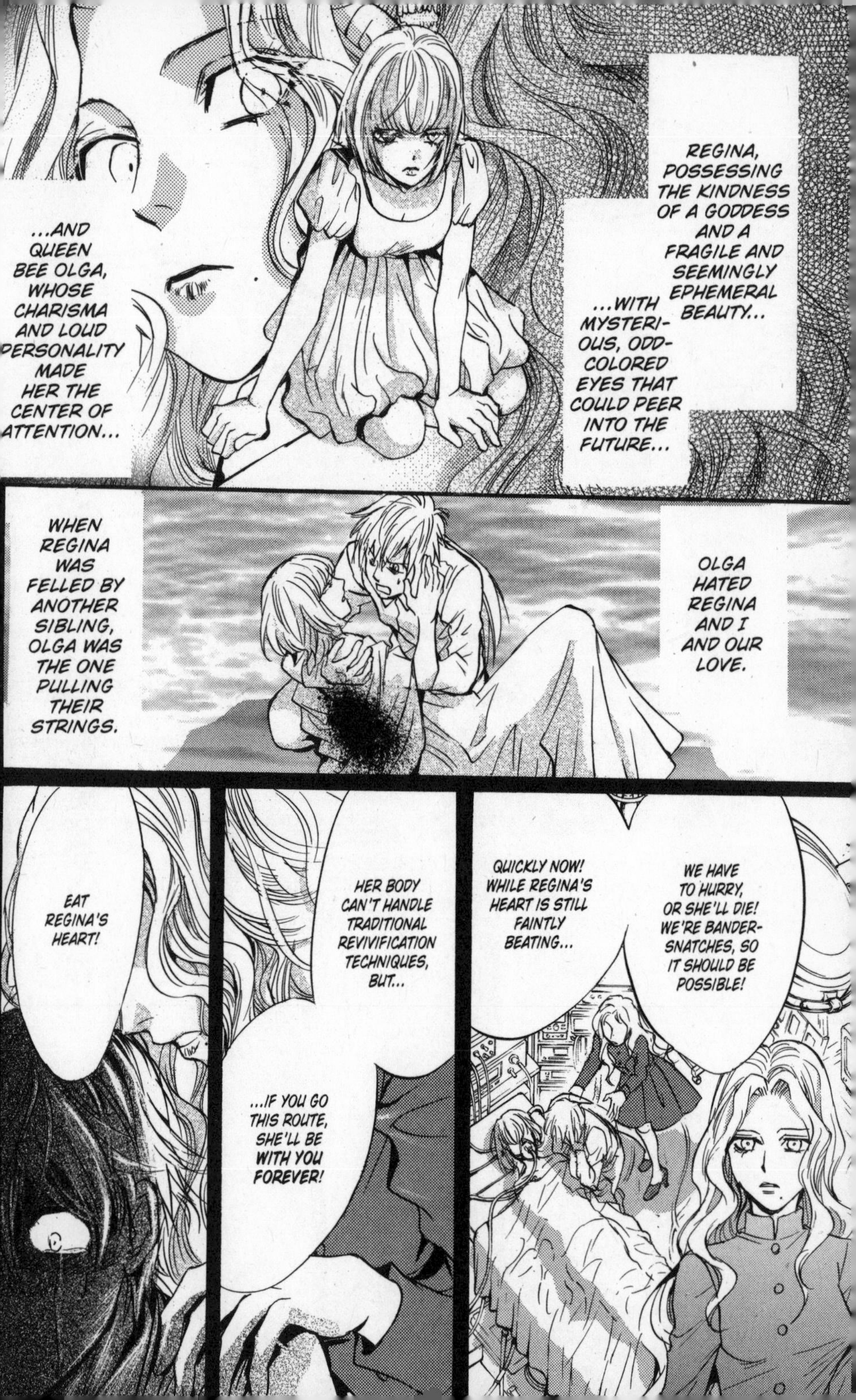
REGINA, POSSESSING THE KINDNESS OF A GODDESS AND A FRAGILE AND SEEMINGLY EPHEMERAL BEAUTY...
...WITH MYSTERI-OUS, ODD-COLORED EYES THAT COULD PEER INTO THE FUTURE...
...AND QUEEN BEE OLGA, WHOSE CHARISMA AND LOUD PERSONALITY MADE HER THE CENTER OF ATTENTION...
OLGA HATED REGINA AND I AND OUR LOVE.
WHEN REGINA WAS FELLED BY ANOTHER SIBLING, OLGA WAS THE ONE PULLING THEIR STRINGS.
WE HAVE TO HURRY, OR SHE'LL DIE! WE'RE BANDER-SNATCHES, SO IT SHOULD BE POSSIBLE!
QUICKLY NOW! WHILE REGINA'S HEART IS STILL FAINTLY BEATING...
HER BODY CAN'T HANDLE TRADITIONAL REVIVIFICATION TECHNIQUES, BUT...
...IF YOU GO THIS ROUTE, SHE'LL BE WITH YOU FOREVER!
EAT REGINA'S HEART!

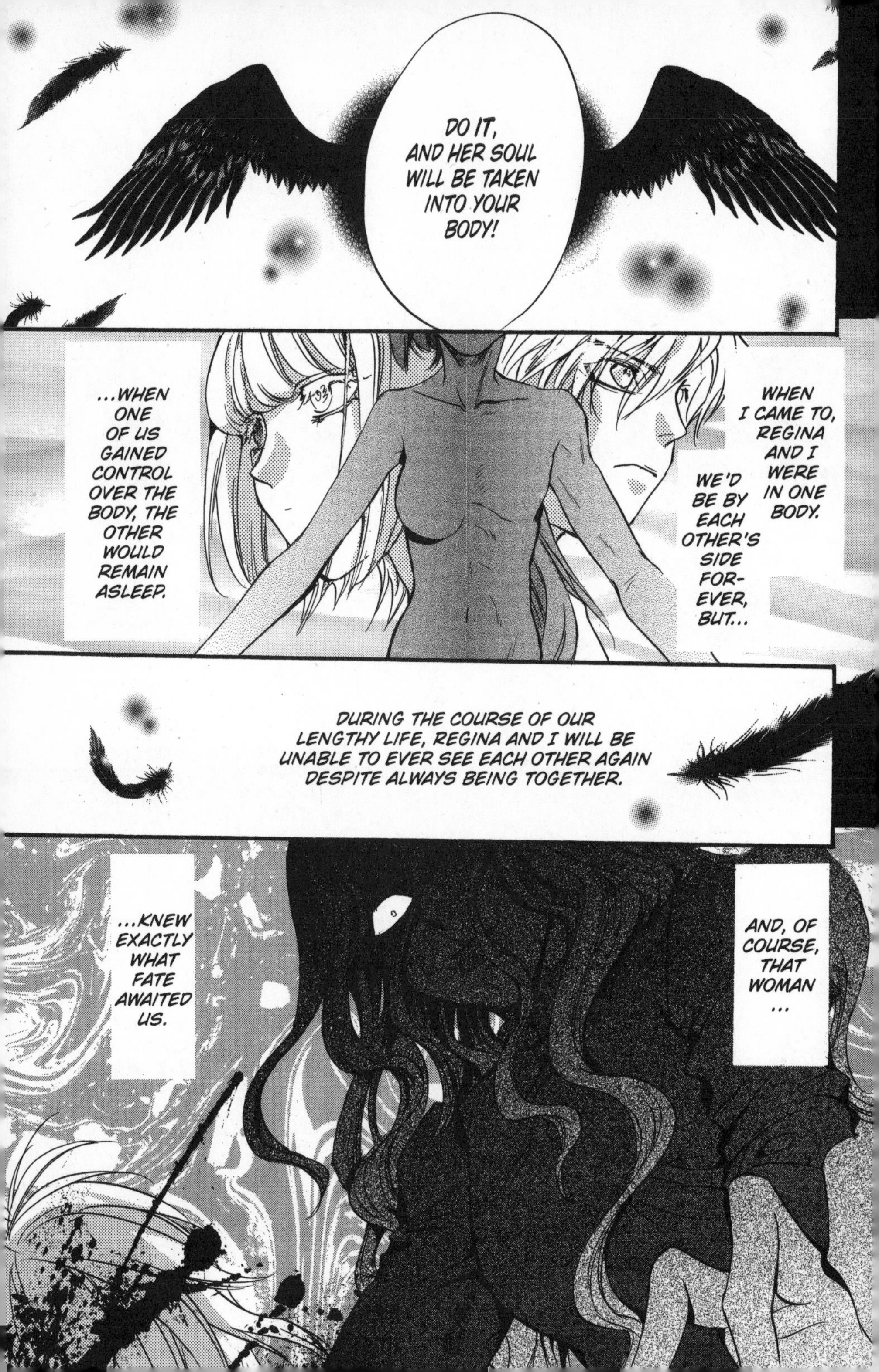
DO IT, AND HER SOUL WILL BE TAKEN INTO YOUR BODY!
WHEN I CAME TO, REGINA AND I WERE IN ONE BODY.
WE'D BE BY EACH OTHER'S SIDE FOR-EVER, BUT...
...WHEN ONE OF US GAINED CONTROL OVER THE BODY, THE OTHER WOULD REMAIN ASLEEP.
DURING THE COURSE OF OUR LENGTHY LIFE, REGINA AND I WILL BE UNABLE TO EVER SEE EACH OTHER AGAIN DESPITE ALWAYS BEING TOGETHER.
AND, OF COURSE, THAT WOMAN ...
...KNEW EXACTLY WHAT FATE AWAITED US.

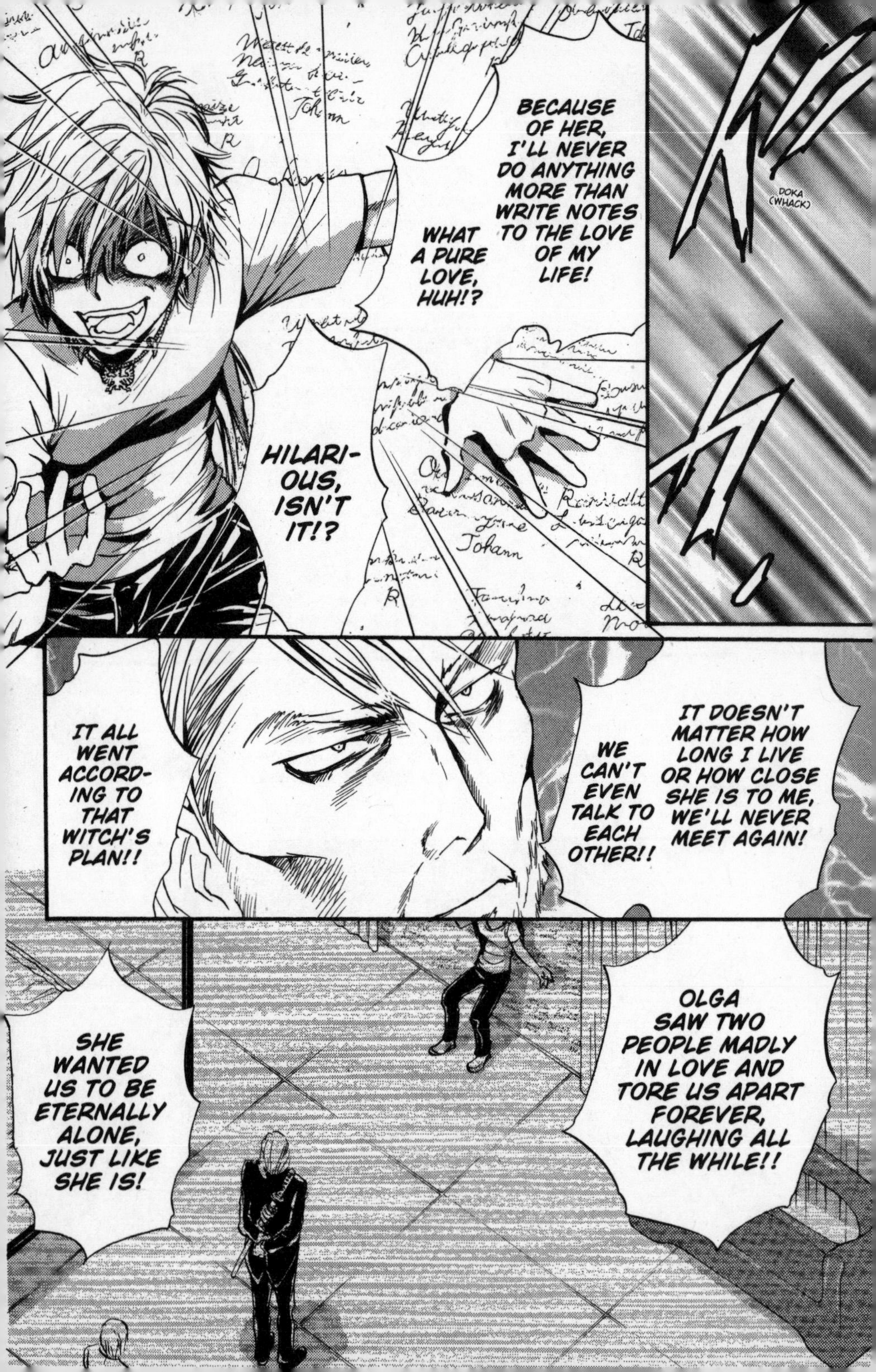
DOKA (WHACK)
BECAUSE OF HER, I'LL NEVER DO ANYTHING MORE THAN WRITE NOTES TO THE LOVE OF MY LIFE!
WHAT A PURE LOVE, HUH!?
HILARI-OUS, ISN'T IT!?
IT DOESN'T MATTER HOW LONG I LIVE OR HOW CLOSE SHE IS TO ME, WE'LL NEVER MEET AGAIN!
WE CAN'T EVEN TALK TO EACH OTHER!!
IT ALL WENT ACCORD-ING TO THAT WITCH'S PLAN!!
OLGA SAW TWO PEOPLE MADLY IN LOVE AND TORE US APART FOREVER, LAUGHING ALL THE WHILE!!
SHE WANTED US TO BE ETERNALLY ALONE, JUST LIKE SHE IS!

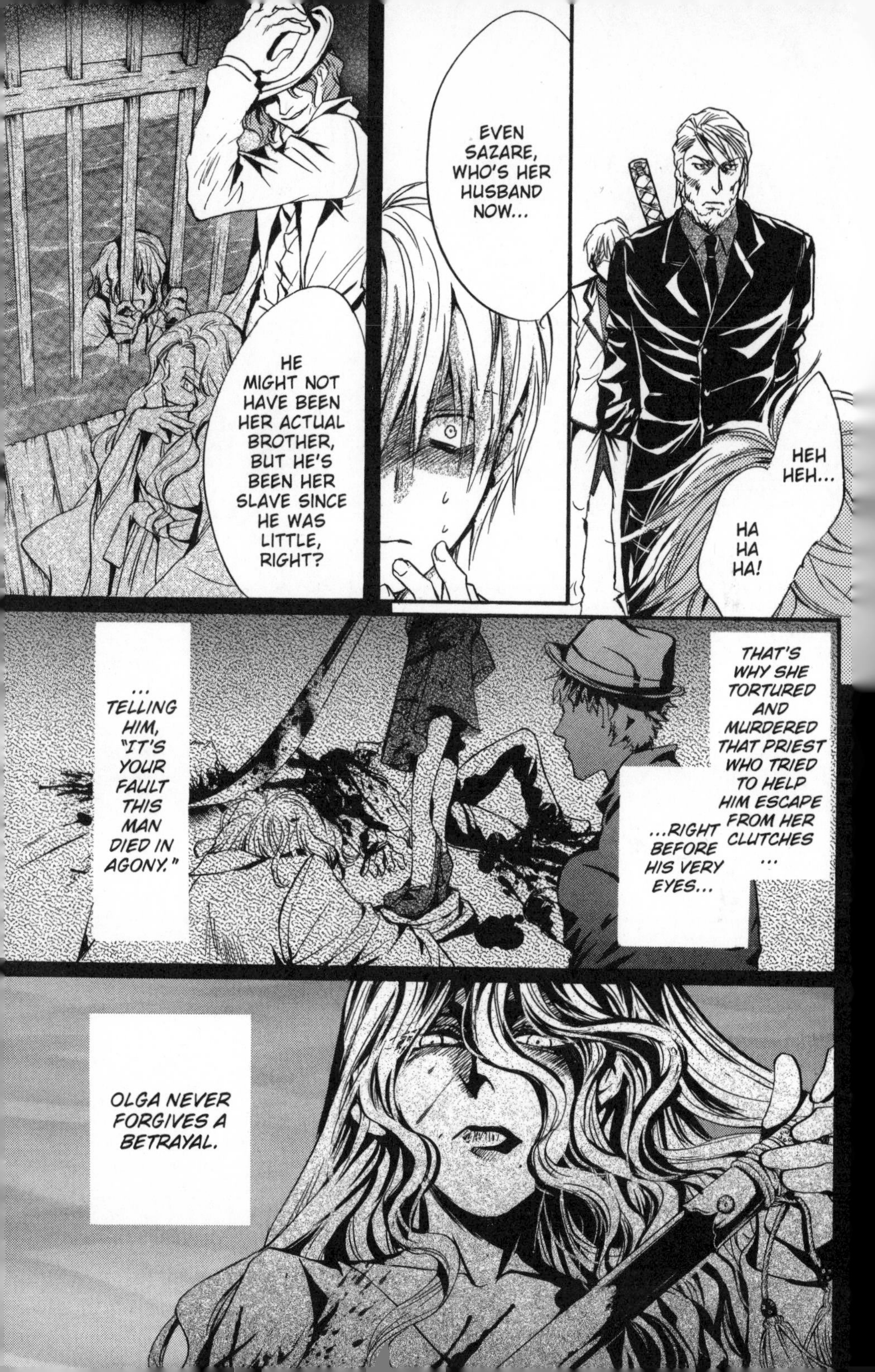
HEH HEH...
HA HA HA!
EVEN SAZARE, WHO'S HER HUSBAND NOW...
HE MIGHT NOT HAVE BEEN HER ACTUAL BROTHER, BUT HE'S BEEN HER SLAVE SINCE HE WAS LITTLE, RIGHT?
THAT'S WHY SHE TORTURED AND MURDERED THAT PRIEST WHO TRIED TO HELP HIM ESCAPE FROM HER CLUTCHES...
...RIGHT BEFORE HIS VERY EYES...
...TELLING HIM, "IT'S YOUR FAULT THIS MAN DIED IN AGONY."
OLGA NEVER FORGIVES A BETRAYAL.

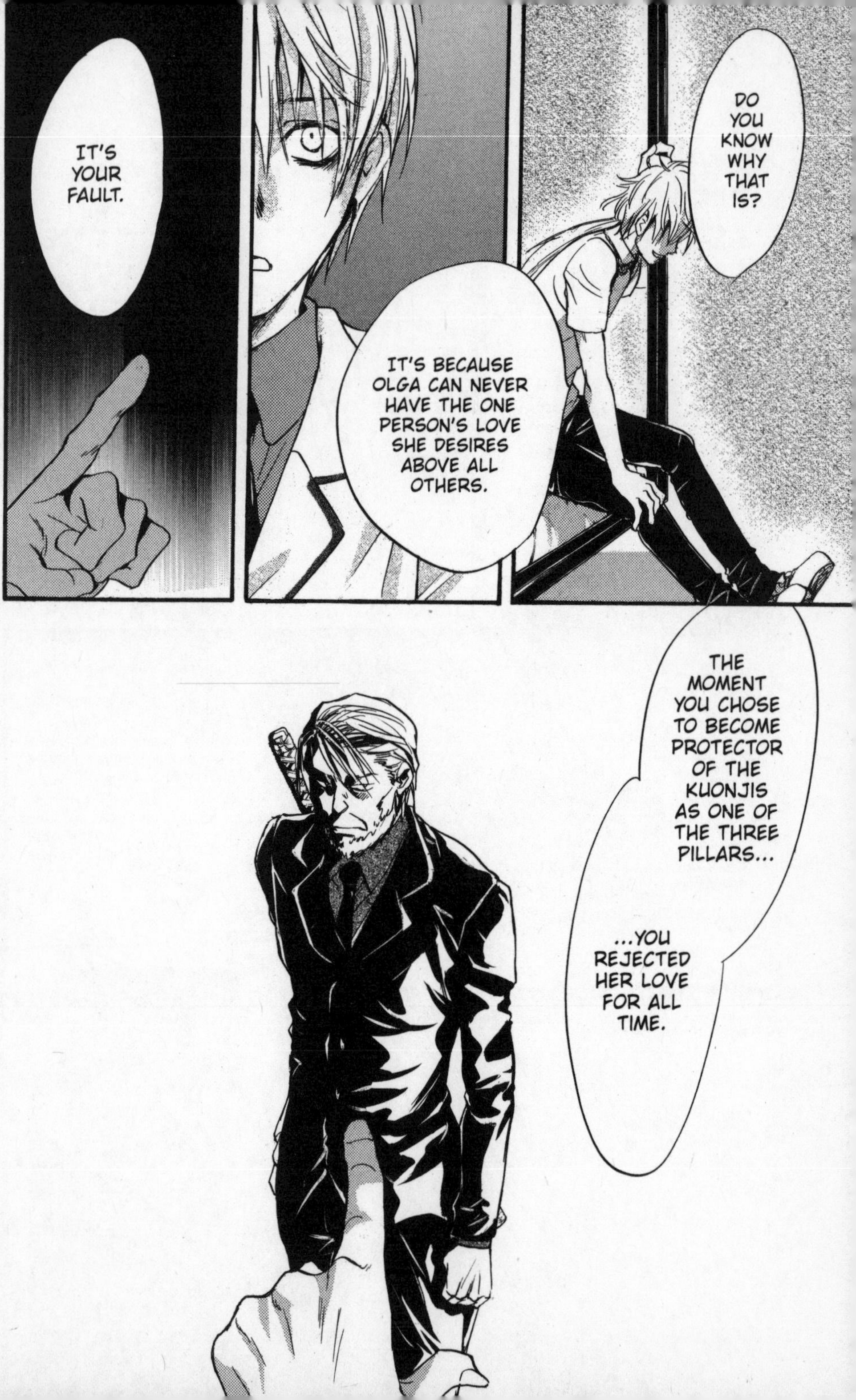
DO YOU KNOW WHY THAT IS?
IT'S BECAUSE OLGA CAN NEVER HAVE THE ONE PERSON'S LOVE SHE DESIRES ABOVE ALL OTHERS.
IT'S YOUR FAULT.
THE MOMENT YOU CHOSE TO BECOME PROTECTOR OF THE KUONJIS AS ONE OF THE THREE PILLARS...
...YOU REJECTED HER LOVE FOR ALL TIME.

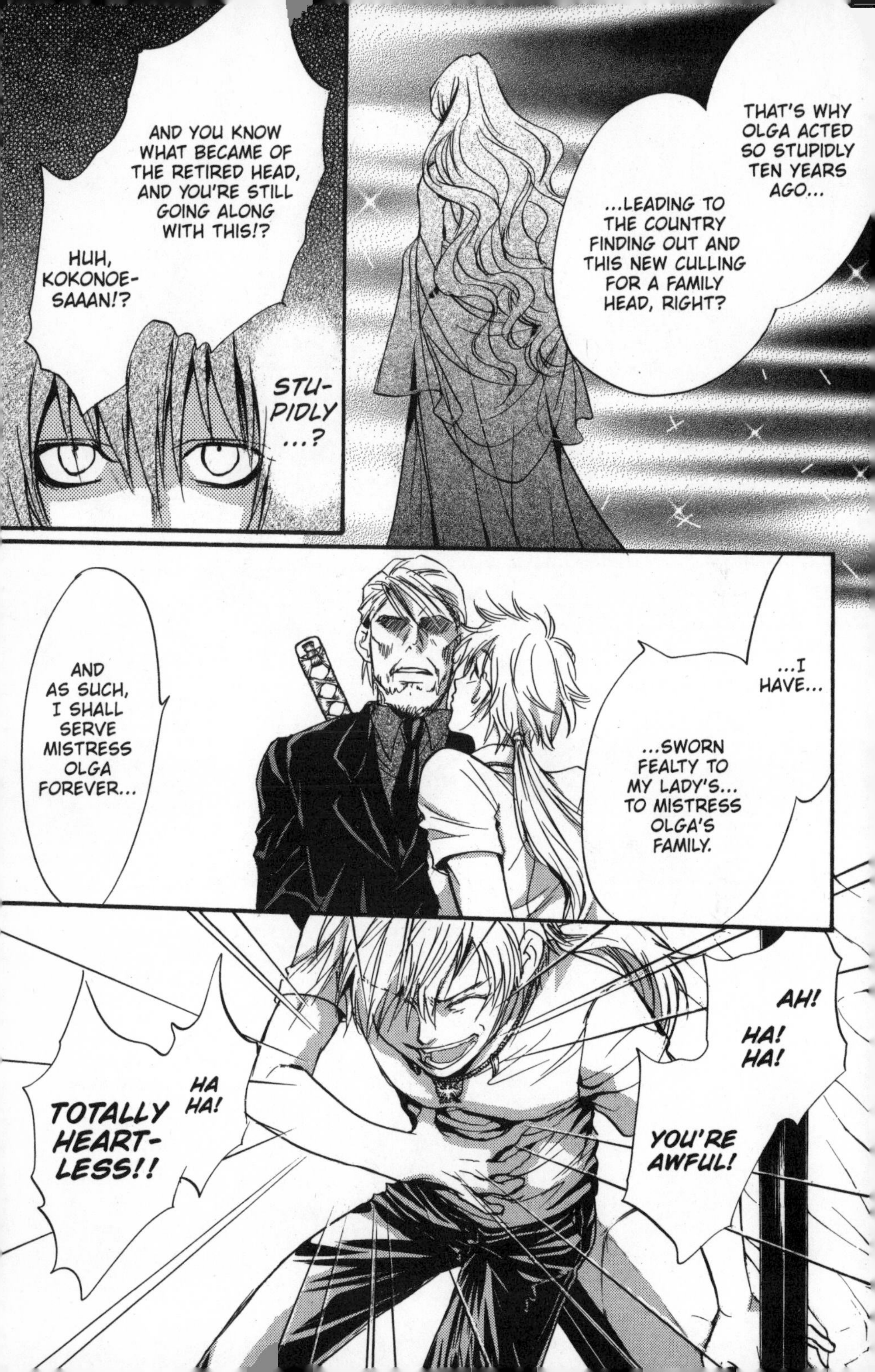
THAT'S WHY OLGA ACTED SO STUPIDLY TEN YEARS AGO...
...LEADING TO THE COUNTRY FINDING OUT AND THIS NEW CULLING FOR A FAMILY HEAD, RIGHT?
AND YOU KNOW WHAT BECAME OF THE RETIRED HEAD, AND YOU'RE STILL GOING ALONG WITH THIS!?
HUH, KOKONOE-SAAAN!?
STU-PIDLY ...?
...I HAVE...
...SWORN FEALTY TO MY LADY'S... TO MISTRESS OLGA'S FAMILY.
AND AS SUCH, I SHALL SERVE MISTRESS OLGA FOREVER...
AH! HA! HA!
YOU'RE AWFUL!
HA HA!
TOTALLY HEART-LESS!!

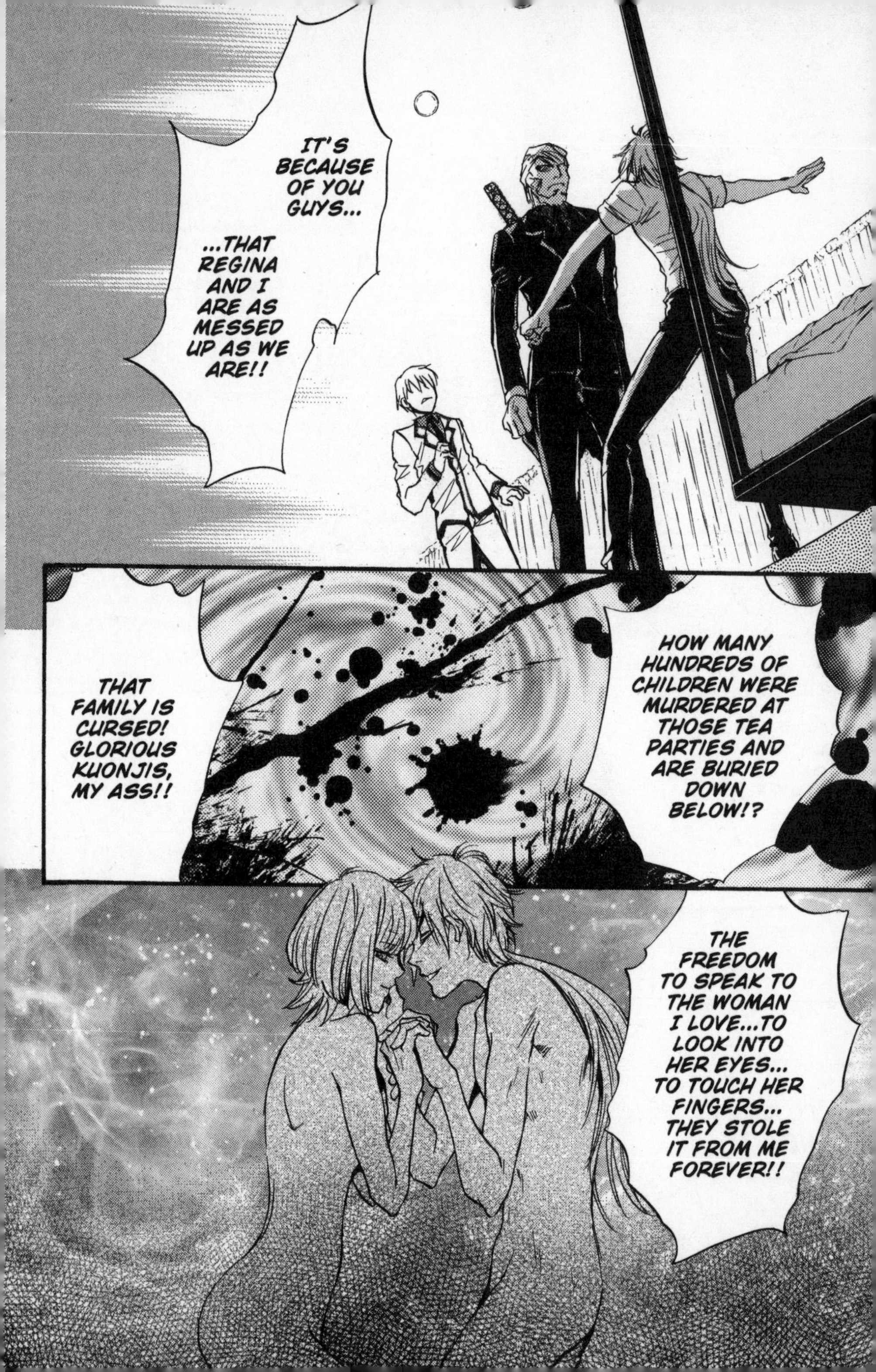
IT'S BECAUSE OF YOU GUYS...
...THAT REGINA AND I ARE AS MESSED UP AS WE ARE!!
HOW MANY HUNDREDS OF CHILDREN WERE MURDERED AT THOSE TEA PARTIES AND ARE BURIED DOWN BELOW!?
THAT FAMILY IS CURSED! GLORIOUS KUONJIS, MY ASS!!
THE FREEDOM TO SPEAK TO THE WOMAN I LOVE...TO LOOK INTO HER EYES... TO TOUCH HER FINGERS... THEY STOLE IT FROM ME FOREVER!!

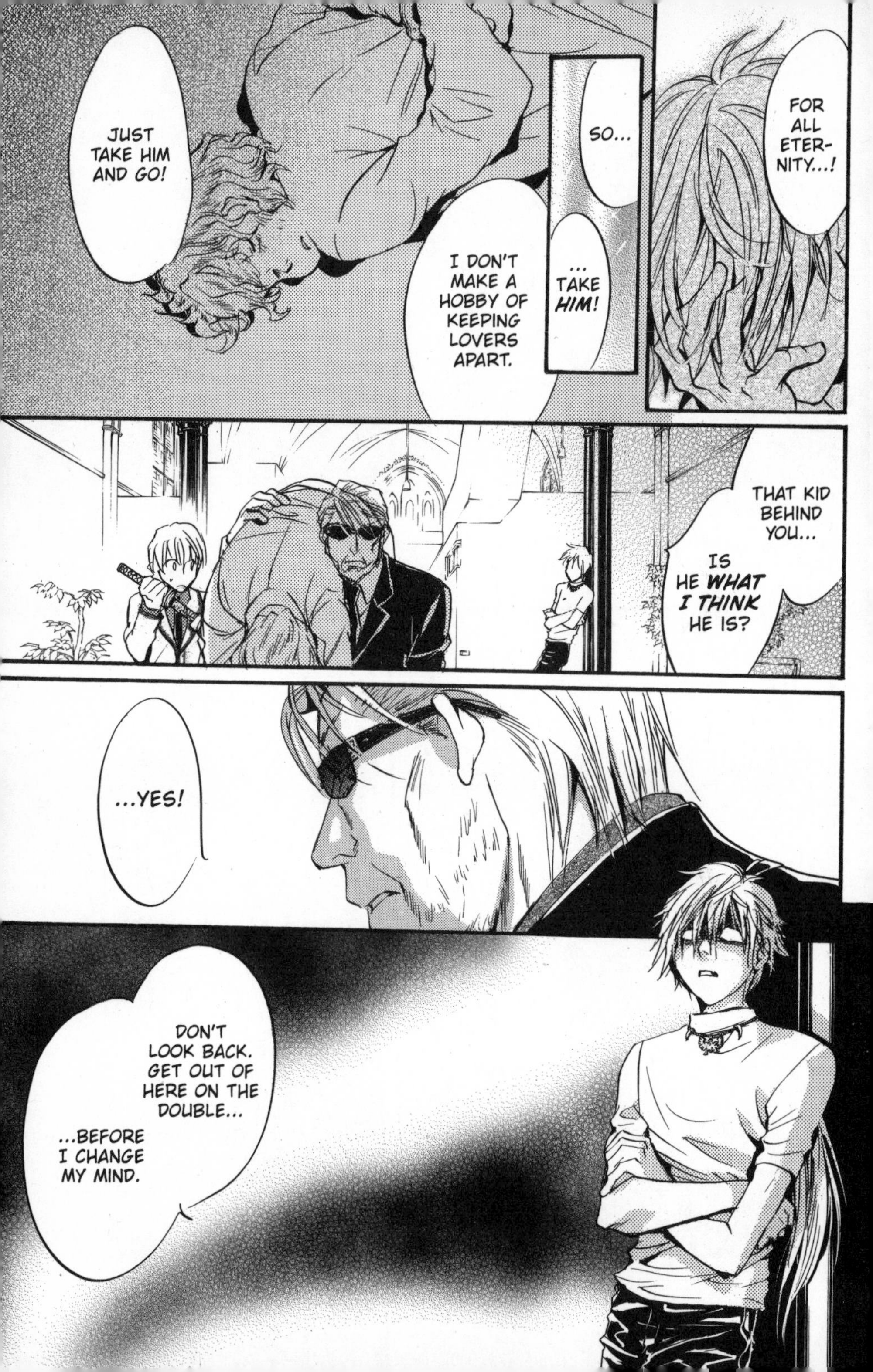
FOR ALL ETERNITY...!
SO...
...TAKE *HIM*!
JUST TAKE HIM AND GO!
I DON'T MAKE A HOBBY OF KEEPING LOVERS APART.
THAT KID BEHIND YOU...
IS HE ***WHAT I THINK*** HE IS?
...YES!
DON'T LOOK BACK. GET OUT OF HERE ON THE DOUBLE...
...BEFORE I CHANGE MY MIND.

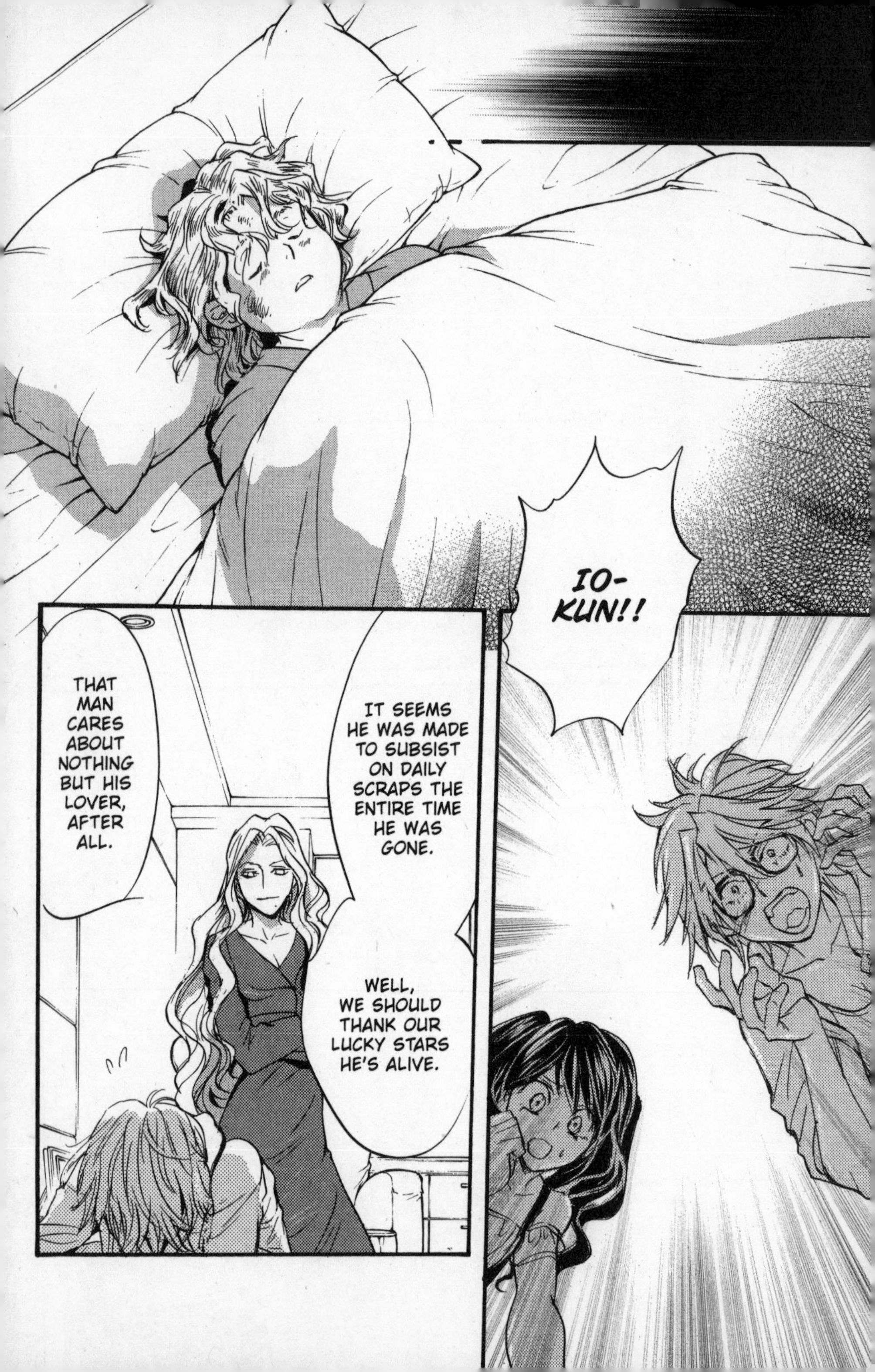
IO-KUN!!
IT SEEMS HE WAS MADE TO SUBSIST ON DAILY SCRAPS THE ENTIRE TIME HE WAS GONE.
THAT MAN CARES ABOUT NOTHING BUT HIS LOVER, AFTER ALL.
WELL, WE SHOULD THANK OUR LUCKY STARS HE'S ALIVE.

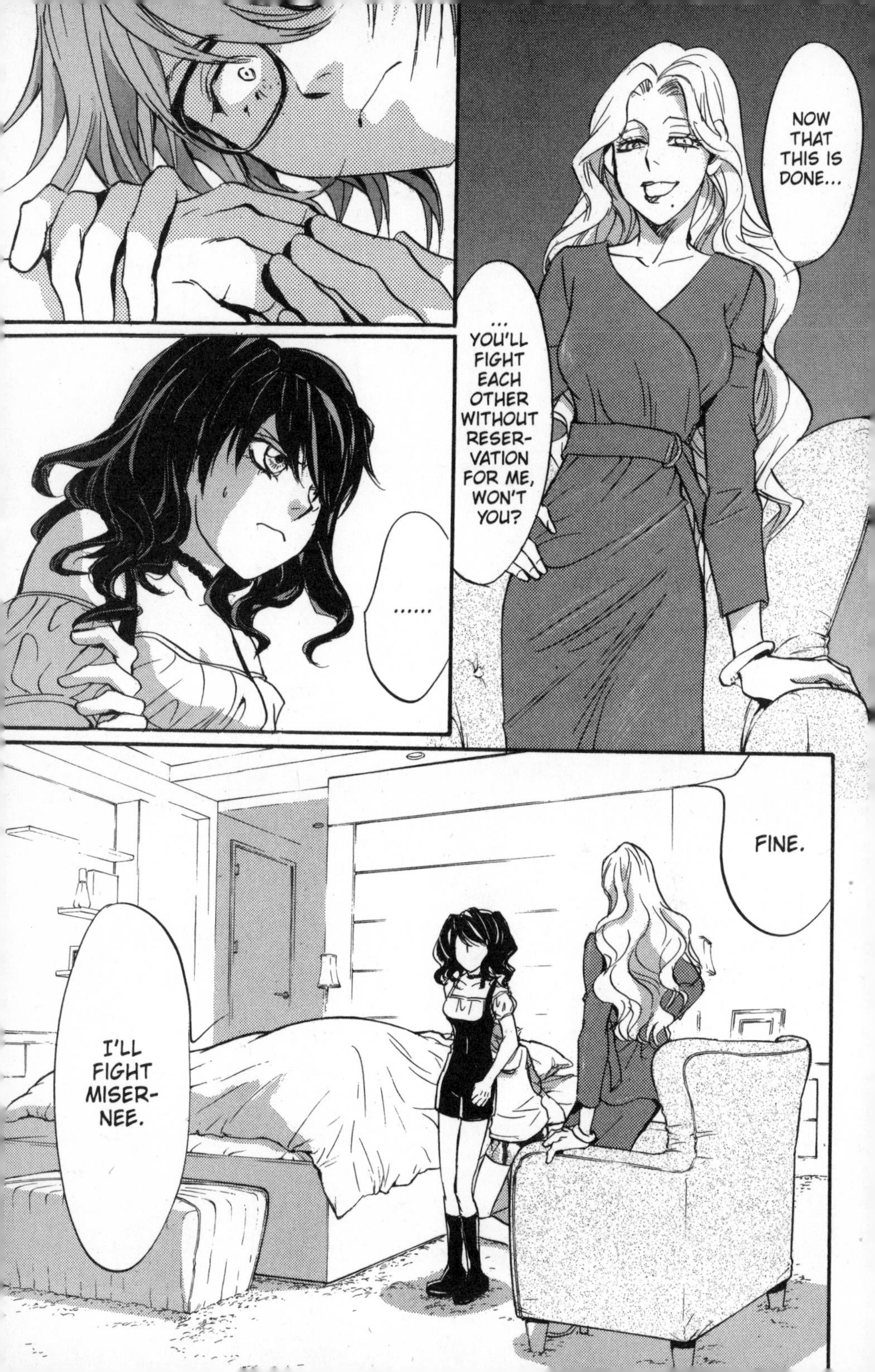
NOW THAT THIS IS DONE...
...YOU'LL FIGHT EACH OTHER WITHOUT RESERVATION FOR ME, WON'T YOU?
......
FINE.
I'LL FIGHT MISER-NEE.

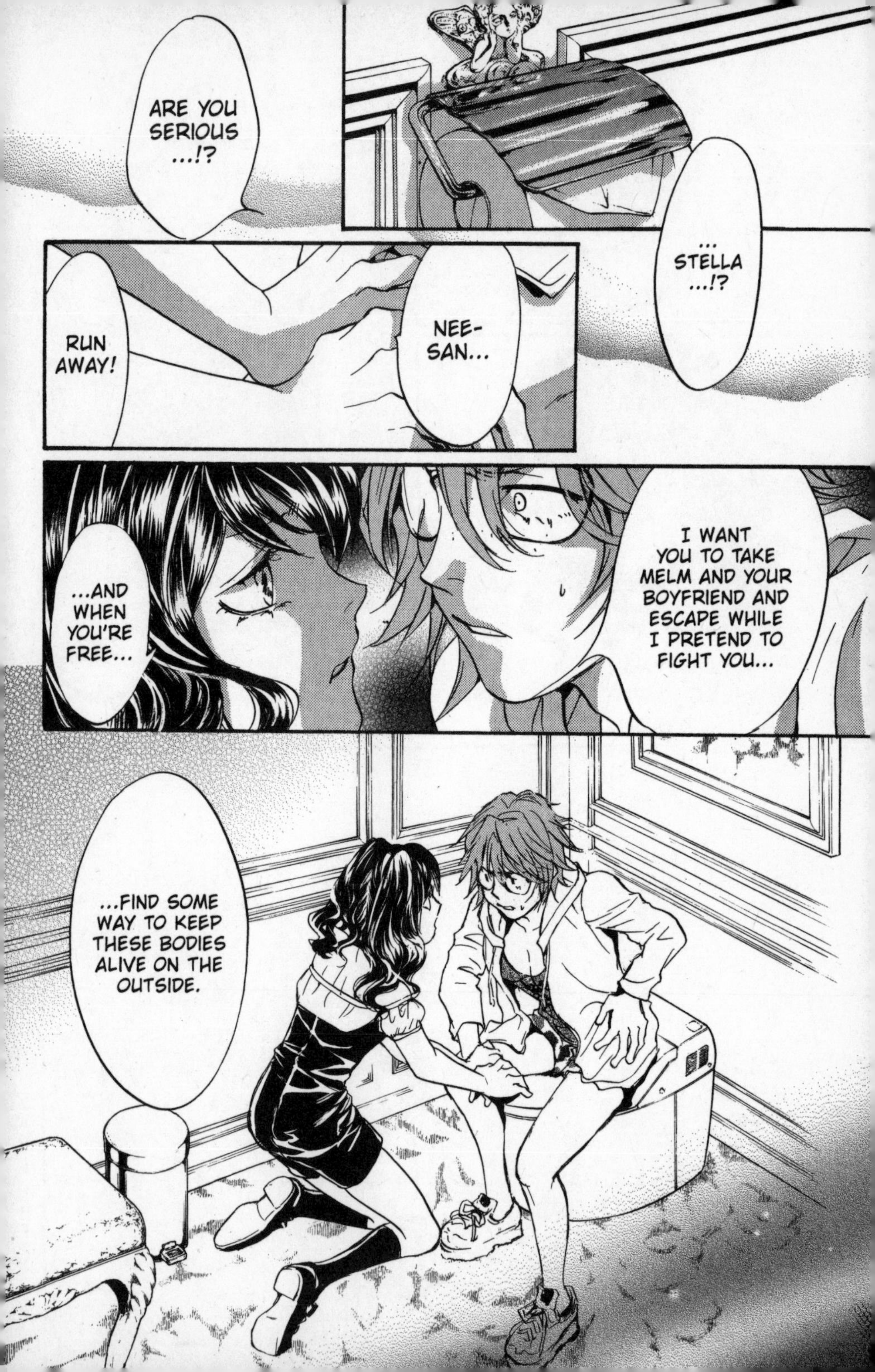
ARE YOU SERIOUS ...!?
... STELLA ...!?
NEE-SAN...
RUN AWAY!
I WANT YOU TO TAKE MELM AND YOUR BOYFRIEND AND ESCAPE WHILE I PRETEND TO FIGHT YOU...
...AND WHEN YOU'RE FREE...
...FIND SOME WAY TO KEEP THESE BODIES ALIVE ON THE OUTSIDE.

Alice in MURDERLAND

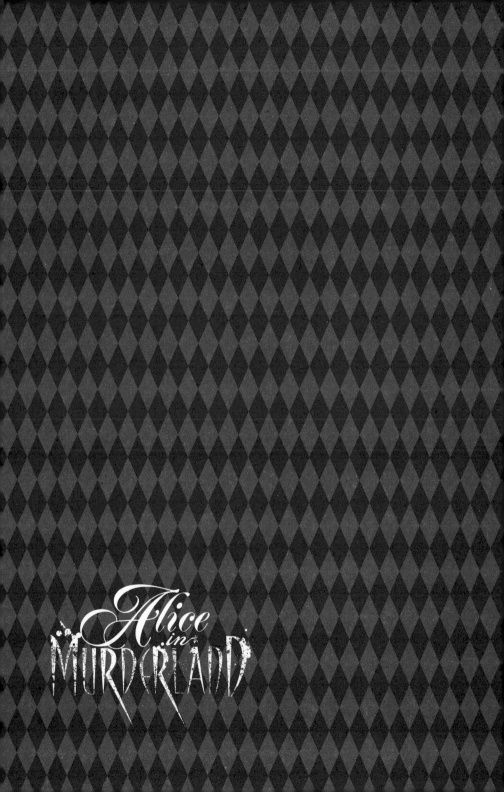

Alice in Murderland

Wonder 34

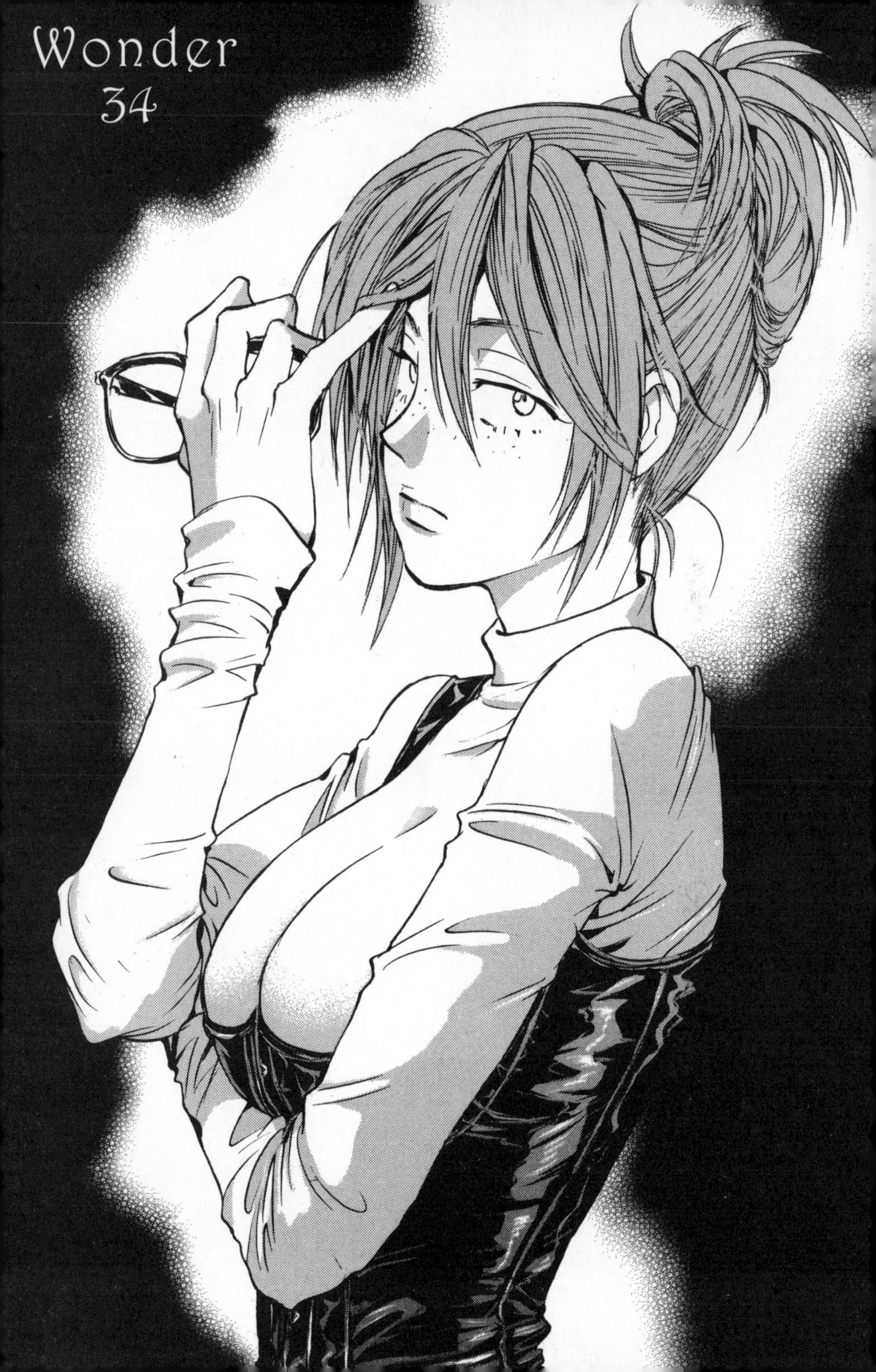

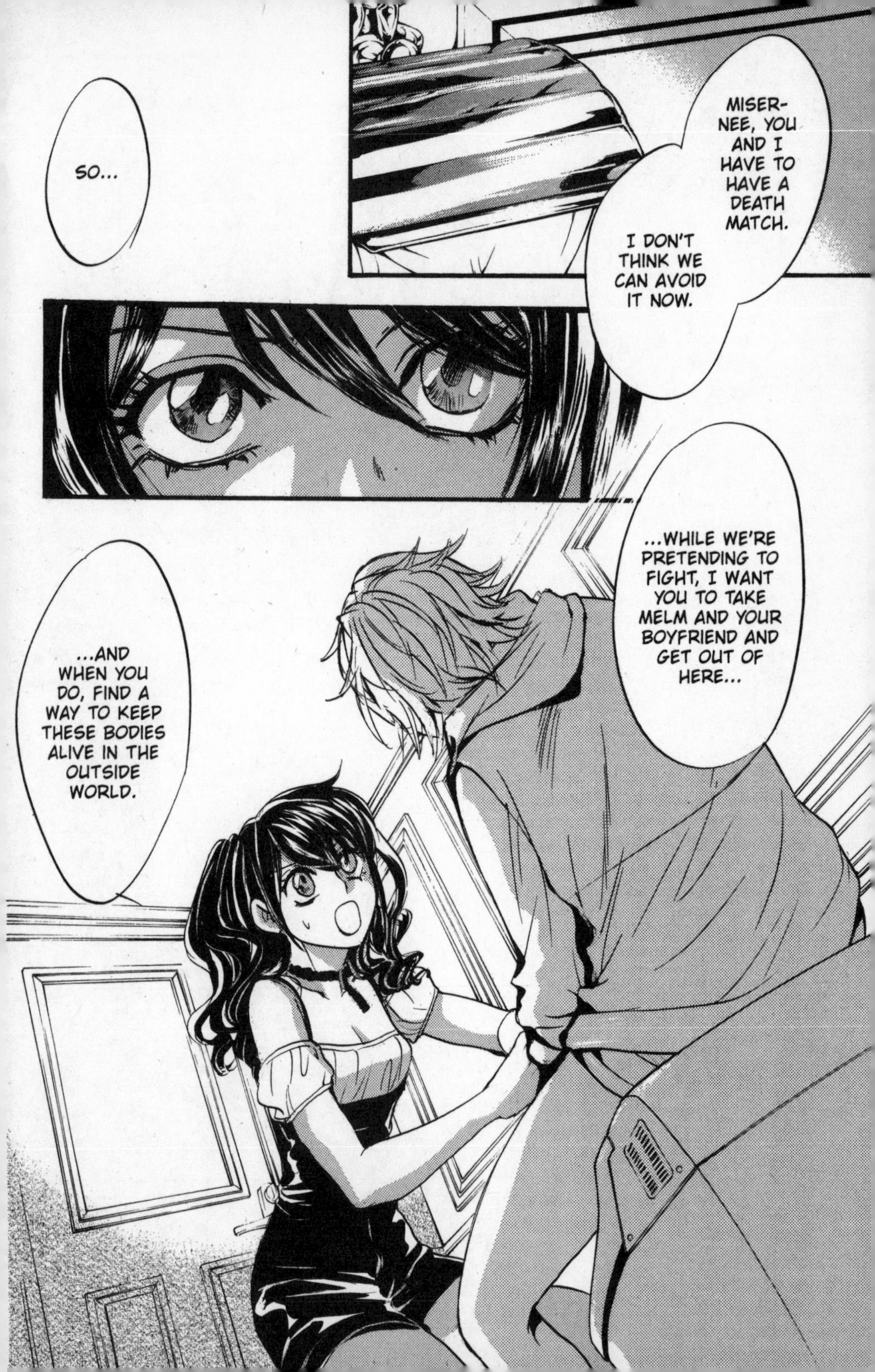
MISER-NEE, YOU AND I HAVE TO HAVE A DEATH MATCH.
I DON'T THINK WE CAN AVOID IT NOW.
SO...
...WHILE WE'RE PRETENDING TO FIGHT, I WANT YOU TO TAKE MELM AND YOUR BOYFRIEND AND GET OUT OF HERE...
...AND WHEN YOU DO, FIND A WAY TO KEEP THESE BODIES ALIVE IN THE OUTSIDE WORLD.

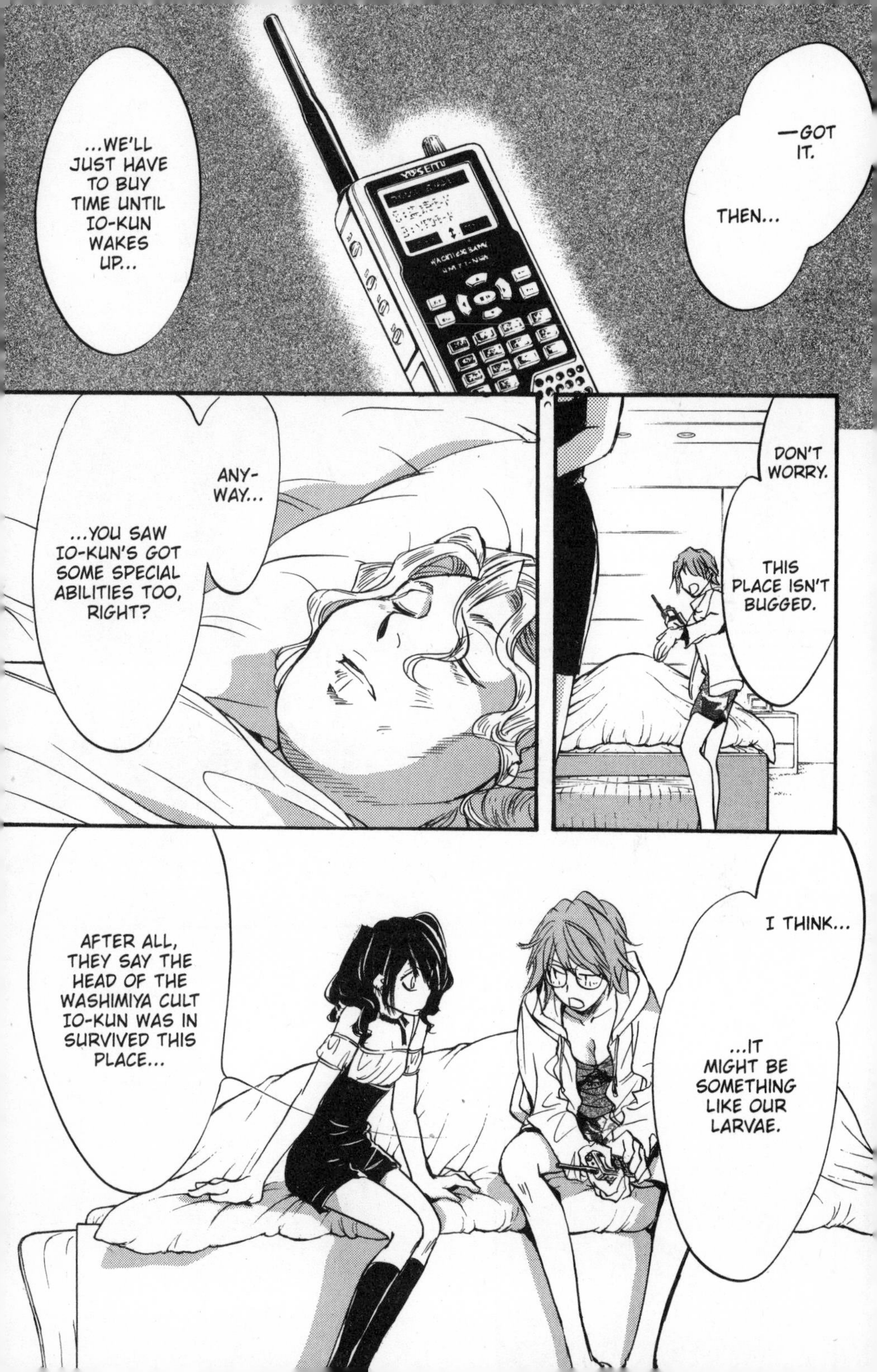
—GOT IT.
THEN...
...WE'LL JUST HAVE TO BUY TIME UNTIL IO-KUN WAKES UP...
DON'T WORRY.
THIS PLACE ISN'T BUGGED.
ANY-WAY...
...YOU SAW IO-KUN'S GOT SOME SPECIAL ABILITIES TOO, RIGHT?
I THINK...
...IT MIGHT BE SOMETHING LIKE OUR LARVAE.
AFTER ALL, THEY SAY THE HEAD OF THE WASHIMIYA CULT IO-KUN WAS IN SURVIVED THIS PLACE...

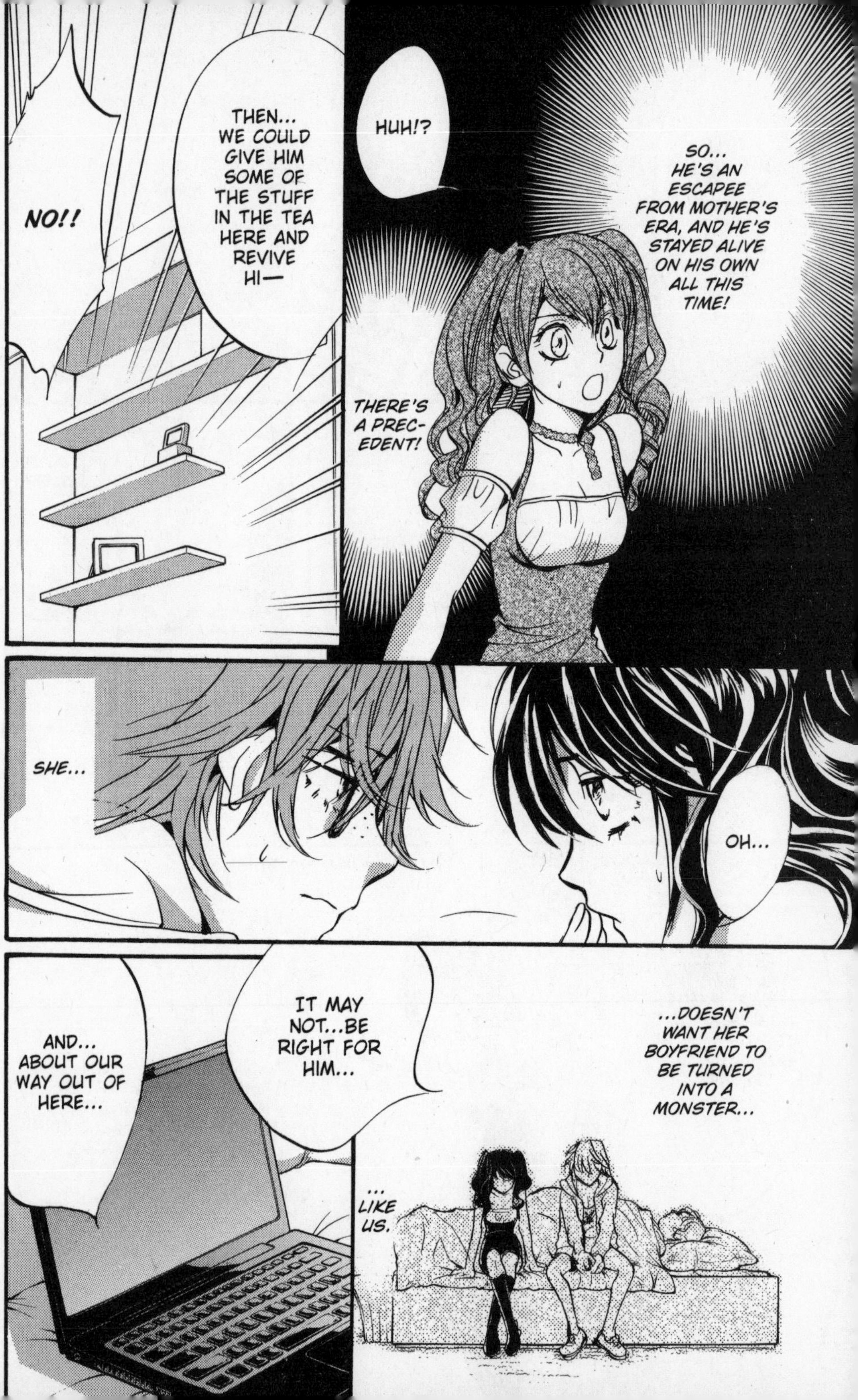
SO... HE'S AN ESCAPEE FROM MOTHER'S ERA, AND HE'S STAYED ALIVE ON HIS OWN ALL THIS TIME!
HUH!?
THERE'S A PREC-EDENT!
THEN... WE COULD GIVE HIM SOME OF THE STUFF IN THE TEA HERE AND REVIVE HI—
NO!!
OH...
SHE...
...DOESN'T WANT HER BOYFRIEND TO BE TURNED INTO A MONSTER...
...LIKE US.
IT MAY NOT...BE RIGHT FOR HIM...
AND... ABOUT OUR WAY OUT OF HERE...

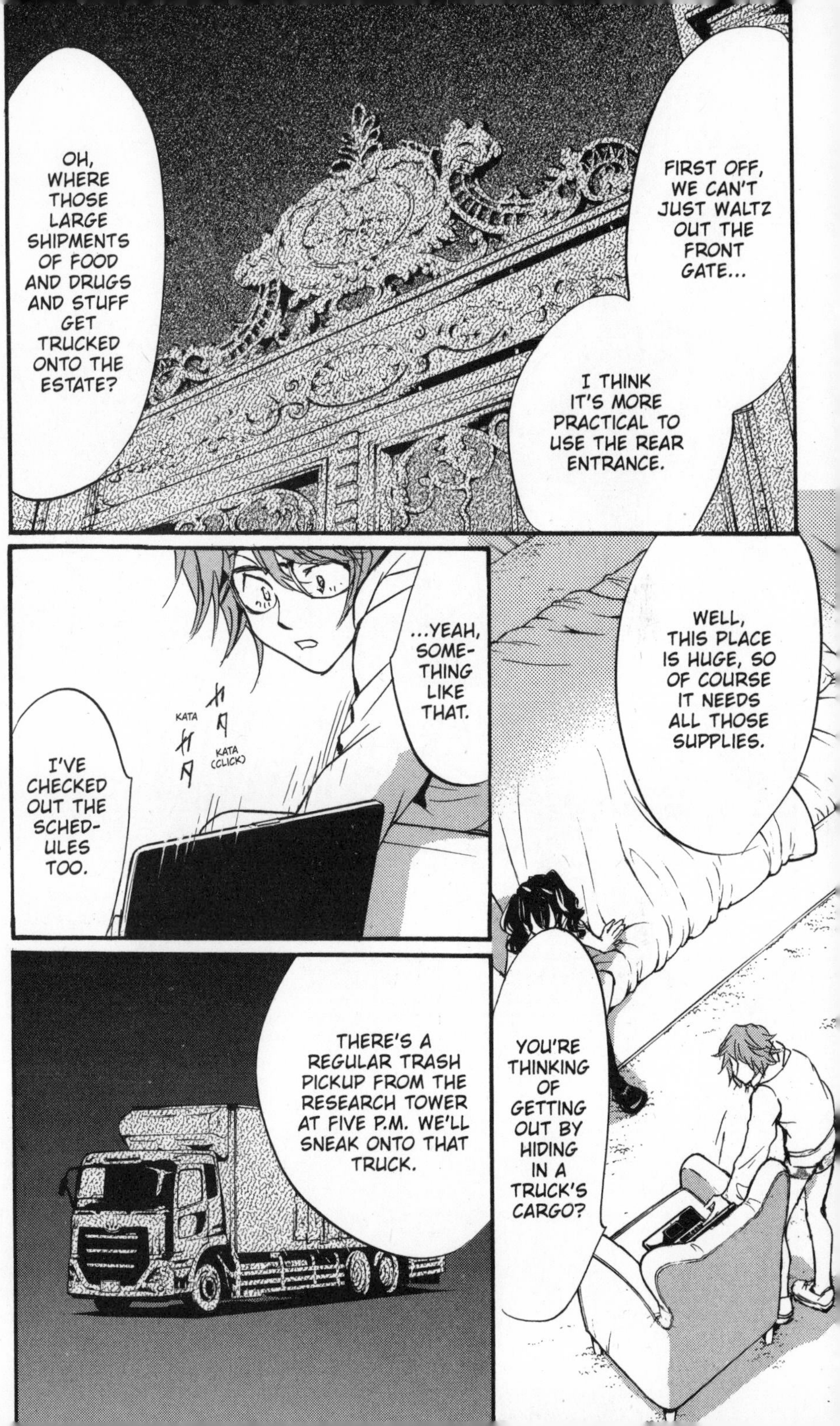
FIRST OFF, WE CAN'T JUST WALTZ OUT THE FRONT GATE...
I THINK IT'S MORE PRACTICAL TO USE THE REAR ENTRANCE.
OH, WHERE THOSE LARGE SHIPMENTS OF FOOD AND DRUGS AND STUFF GET TRUCKED ONTO THE ESTATE?
WELL, THIS PLACE IS HUGE, SO OF COURSE IT NEEDS ALL THOSE SUPPLIES.
...YEAH, SOMETHING LIKE THAT.
KATA KATA (CLICK)
I'VE CHECKED OUT THE SCHED-ULES TOO.
THERE'S A REGULAR TRASH PICKUP FROM THE RESEARCH TOWER AT FIVE P.M. WE'LL SNEAK ONTO THAT TRUCK.
YOU'RE THINKING OF GETTING OUT BY HIDING IN A TRUCK'S CARGO?

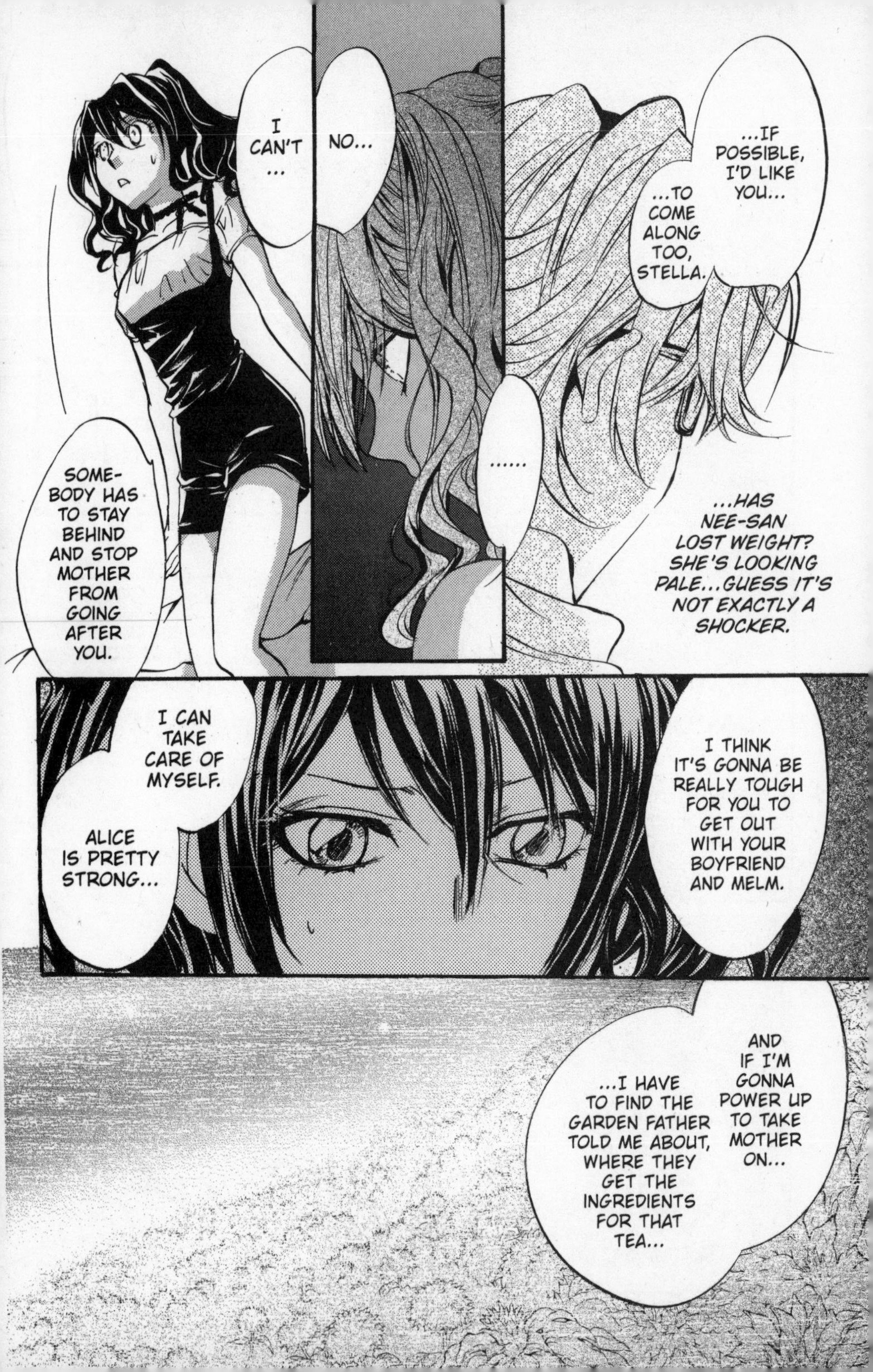
...IF POSSIBLE, I'D LIKE YOU...
...TO COME ALONG TOO, STELLA.
......
...HAS NEE-SAN LOST WEIGHT? SHE'S LOOKING PALE...GUESS IT'S NOT EXACTLY A SHOCKER.
NO...
I CAN'T ...
SOME-BODY HAS TO STAY BEHIND AND STOP MOTHER FROM GOING AFTER YOU.
I THINK IT'S GONNA BE REALLY TOUGH FOR YOU TO GET OUT WITH YOUR BOYFRIEND AND MELM.
I CAN TAKE CARE OF MYSELF.
ALICE IS PRETTY STRONG...
AND IF I'M GONNA POWER UP TO TAKE MOTHER ON...
...I HAVE TO FIND THE GARDEN FATHER TOLD ME ABOUT, WHERE THEY GET THE INGREDIENTS FOR THAT TEA...

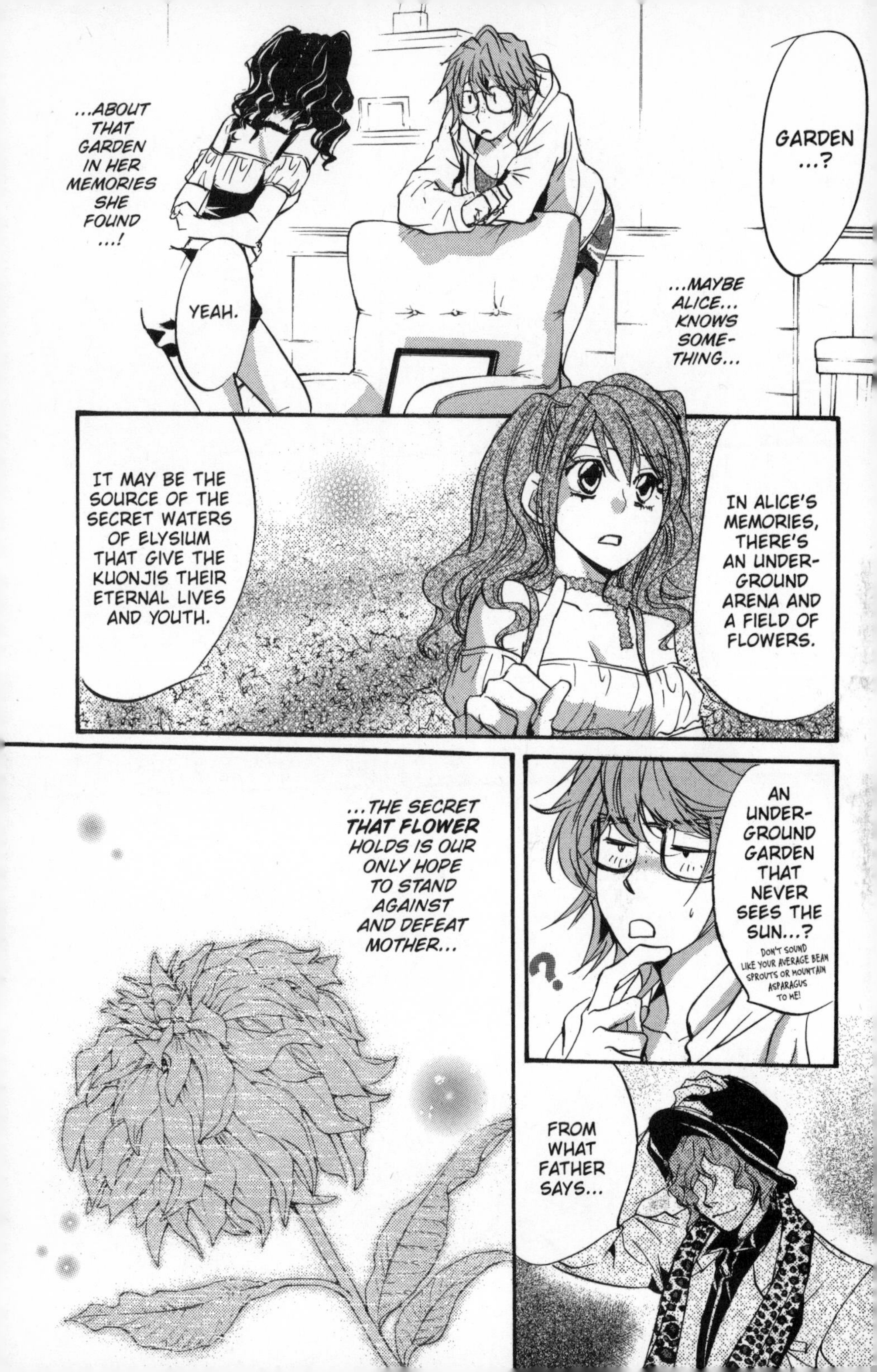
GARDEN ...?
...MAYBE ALICE... KNOWS SOMETHING...
...ABOUT THAT GARDEN IN HER MEMORIES SHE FOUND ...!
YEAH.
IN ALICE'S MEMORIES, THERE'S AN UNDERGROUND ARENA AND A FIELD OF FLOWERS.
IT MAY BE THE SOURCE OF THE SECRET WATERS OF ELYSIUM THAT GIVE THE KUONJIS THEIR ETERNAL LIVES AND YOUTH.
AN UNDERGROUND GARDEN THAT NEVER SEES THE SUN...?
DON'T SOUND LIKE YOUR AVERAGE BEAN SPROUTS OR MOUNTAIN ASPARAGUS TO ME!
FROM WHAT FATHER SAYS...
...THE SECRET *THAT FLOWER* HOLDS IS OUR ONLY HOPE TO STAND AGAINST AND DEFEAT MOTHER...

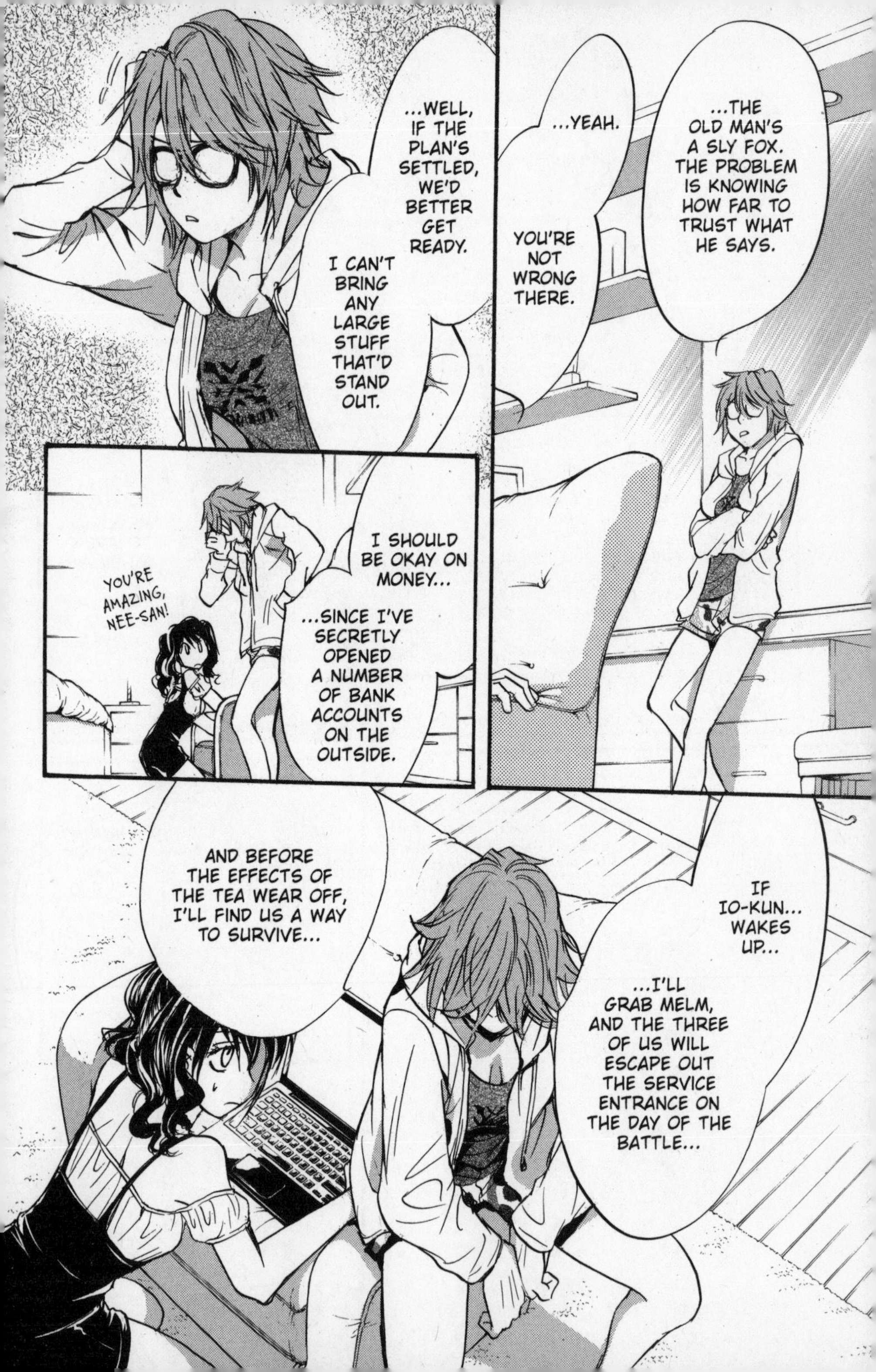
...THE OLD MAN'S A SLY FOX. THE PROBLEM IS KNOWING HOW FAR TO TRUST WHAT HE SAYS.
...YEAH.
YOU'RE NOT WRONG THERE.
...WELL, IF THE PLAN'S SETTLED, WE'D BETTER GET READY.
I CAN'T BRING ANY LARGE STUFF THAT'D STAND OUT.
I SHOULD BE OKAY ON MONEY...
...SINCE I'VE SECRETLY OPENED A NUMBER OF BANK ACCOUNTS ON THE OUTSIDE.
YOU'RE AMAZING, NEE-SAN!
IF IO-KUN... WAKES UP...
...I'LL GRAB MELM, AND THE THREE OF US WILL ESCAPE OUT THE SERVICE ENTRANCE ON THE DAY OF THE BATTLE...
AND BEFORE THE EFFECTS OF THE TEA WEAR OFF, I'LL FIND US A WAY TO SURVIVE...

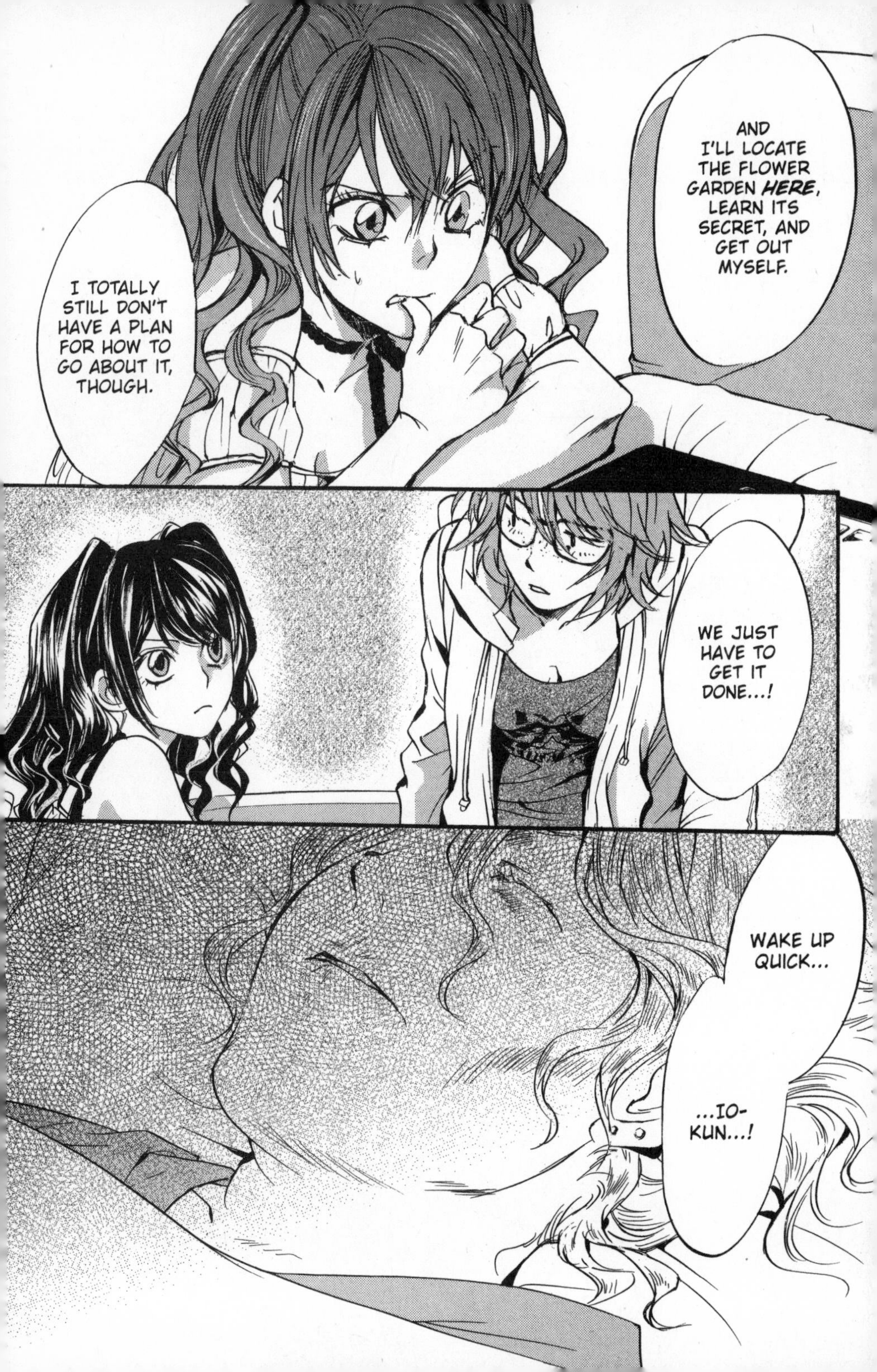
AND I'LL LOCATE THE FLOWER GARDEN *HERE*, LEARN ITS SECRET, AND GET OUT MYSELF.
I TOTALLY STILL DON'T HAVE A PLAN FOR HOW TO GO ABOUT IT, THOUGH.
WE JUST HAVE TO GET IT DONE...!
WAKE UP QUICK...
...IO-KUN...!

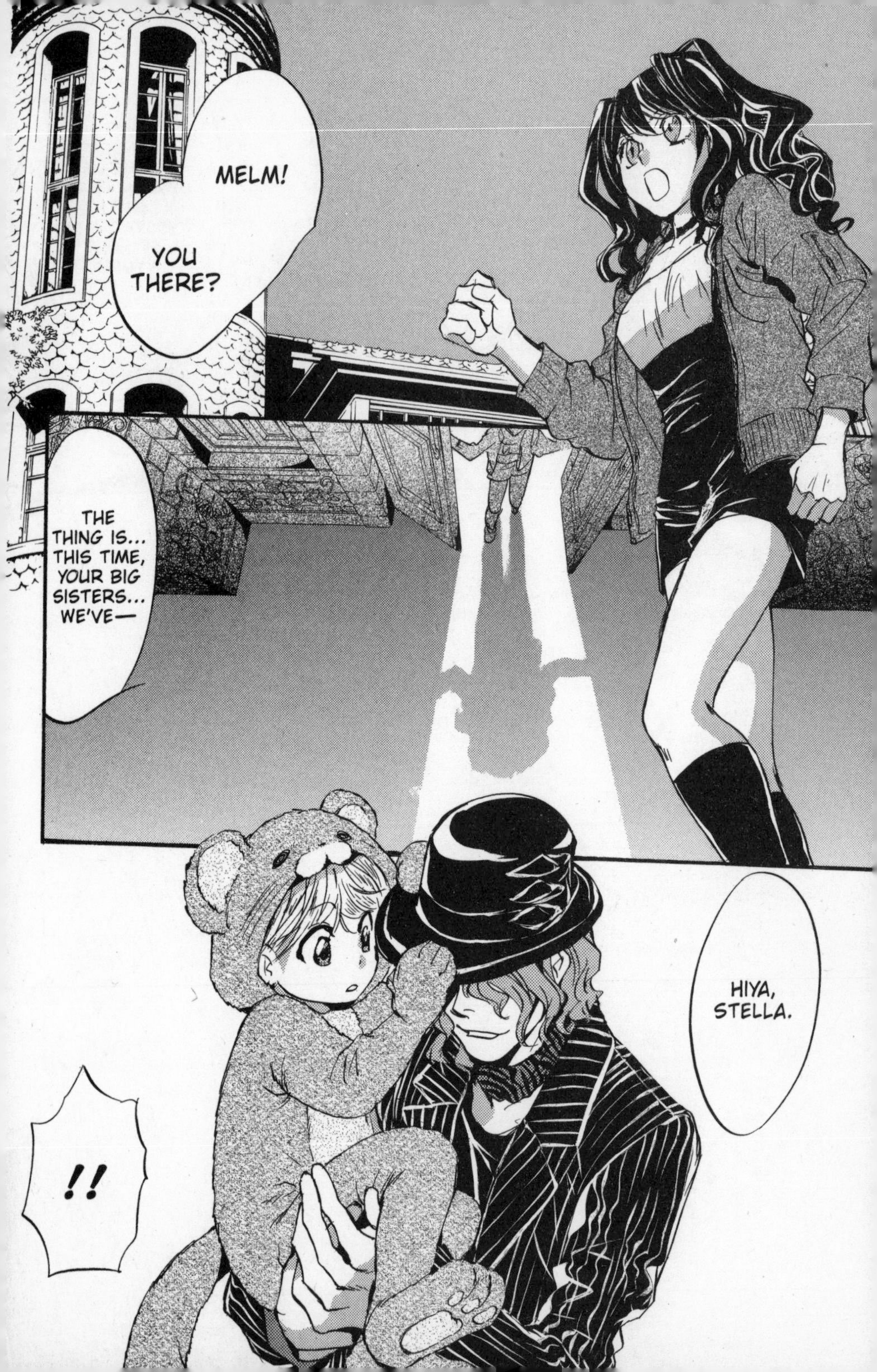
MELM!
YOU THERE?
THE THING IS... THIS TIME, YOUR BIG SISTERS... WE'VE—
HIYA, STELLA.
!!

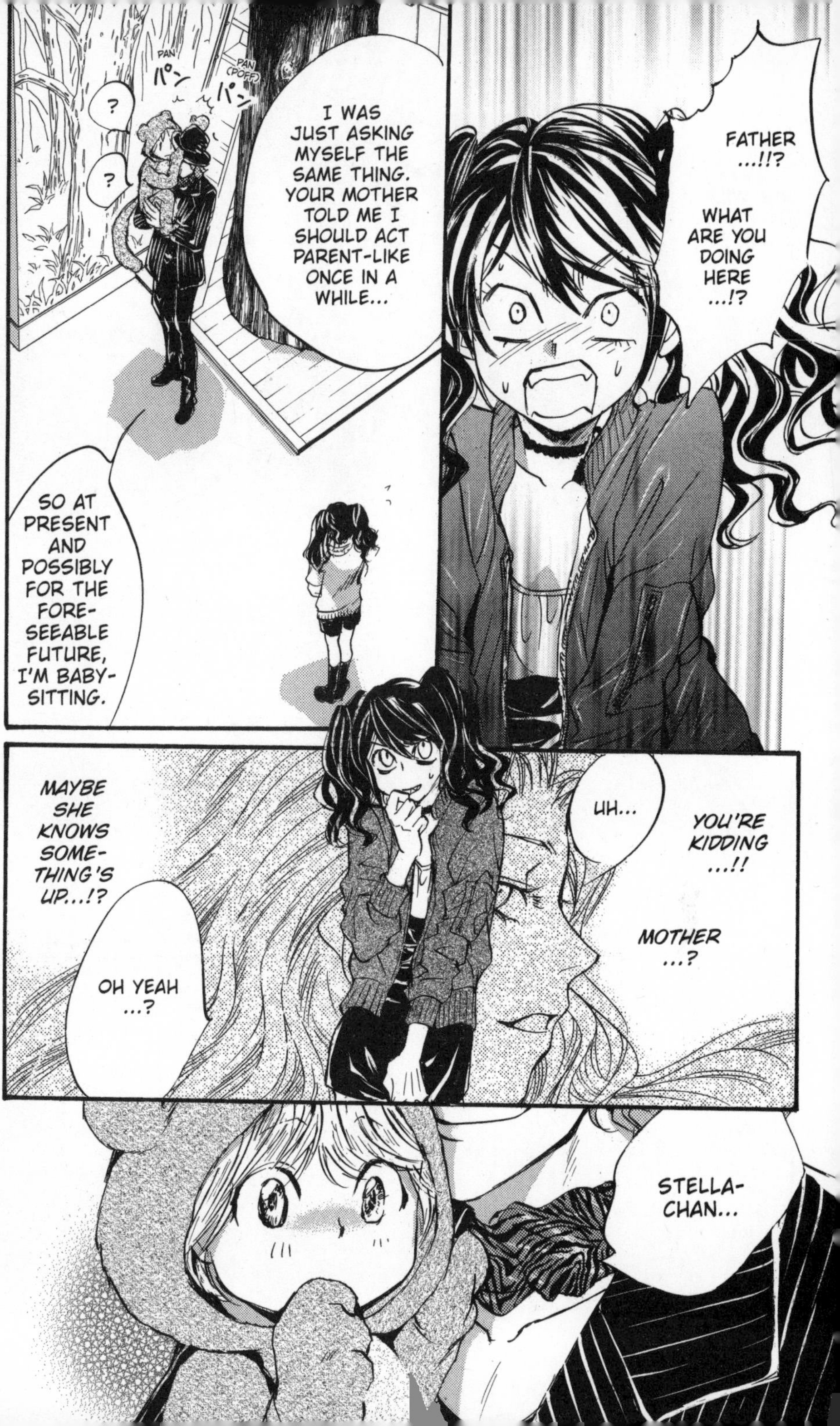
FATHER ...!!?
WHAT ARE YOU DOING HERE ...!?
PAN (POFF) パン
PAN パン
?
?
I WAS JUST ASKING MYSELF THE SAME THING. YOUR MOTHER TOLD ME I SHOULD ACT PARENT-LIKE ONCE IN A WHILE...
SO AT PRESENT AND POSSIBLY FOR THE FORE-SEEABLE FUTURE, I'M BABY-SITTING.
UH...
YOU'RE KIDDING ...!!
MOTHER ...?
MAYBE SHE KNOWS SOME-THING'S UP...!?
OH YEAH ...?
STELLA-CHAN...

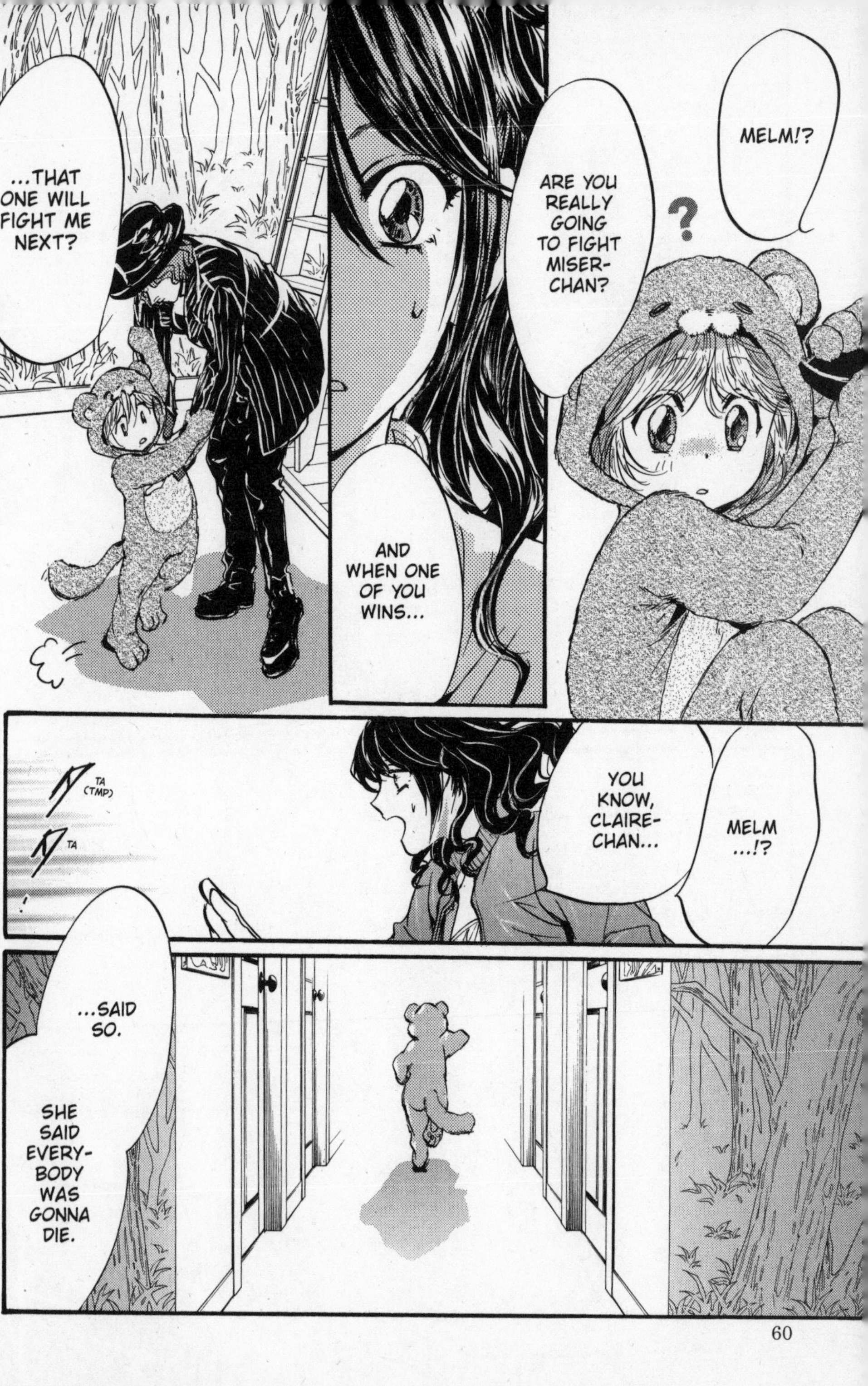
MELM!?
ARE YOU REALLY GOING TO FIGHT MISER-CHAN?
AND WHEN ONE OF YOU WINS...
...THAT ONE WILL FIGHT ME NEXT?
MELM ...!?
YOU KNOW, CLAIRE-CHAN...
TA (TMP)
TA
...SAID SO.
SHE SAID EVERY-BODY WAS GONNA DIE.

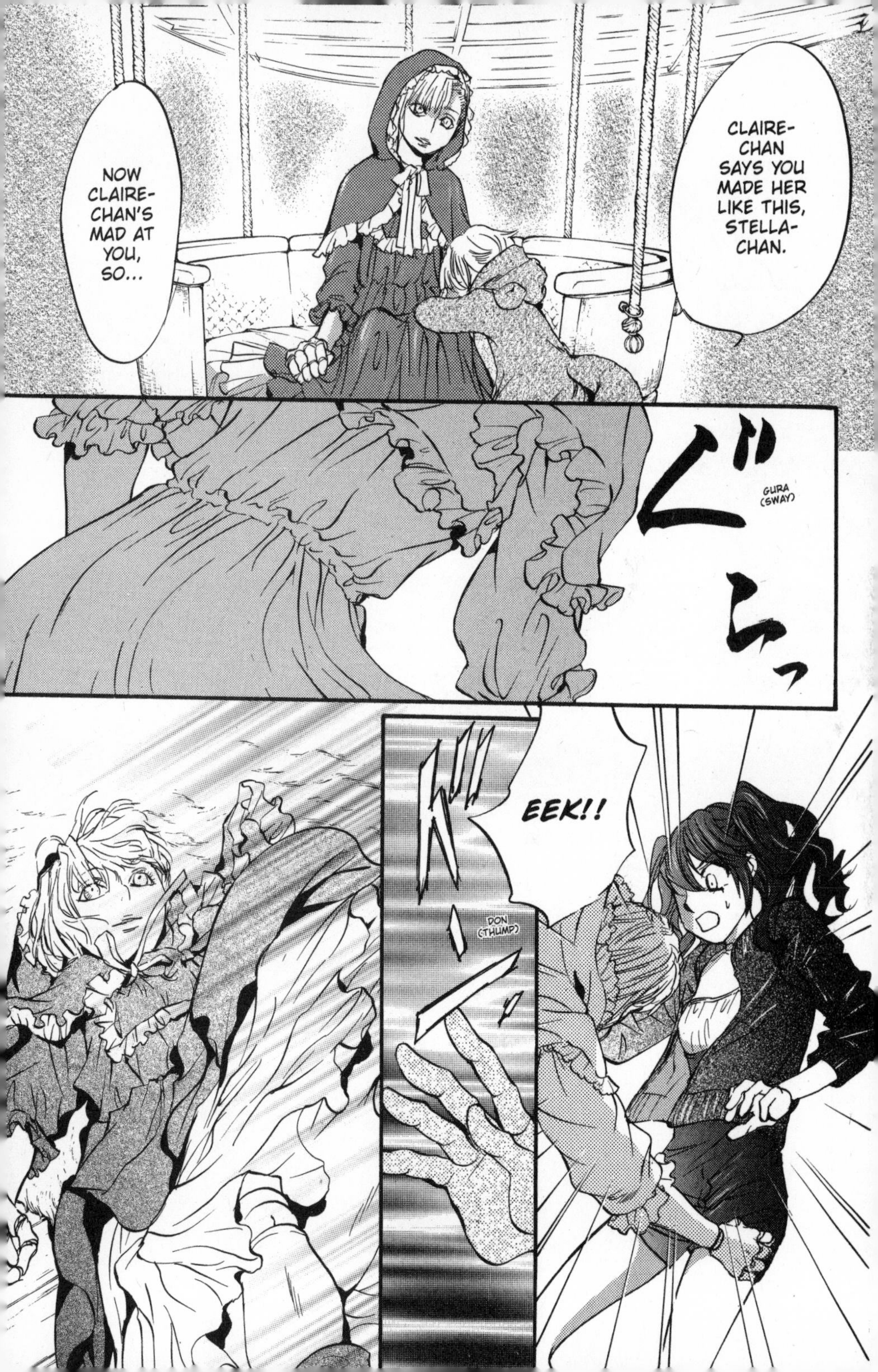
CLAIRE-CHAN SAYS YOU MADE HER LIKE THIS, STELLA-CHAN.
NOW CLAIRE-CHAN'S MAD AT YOU, SO...
ぐらっ
GURA (SWAY)
EEK!!
ドン
DON (THUMP)

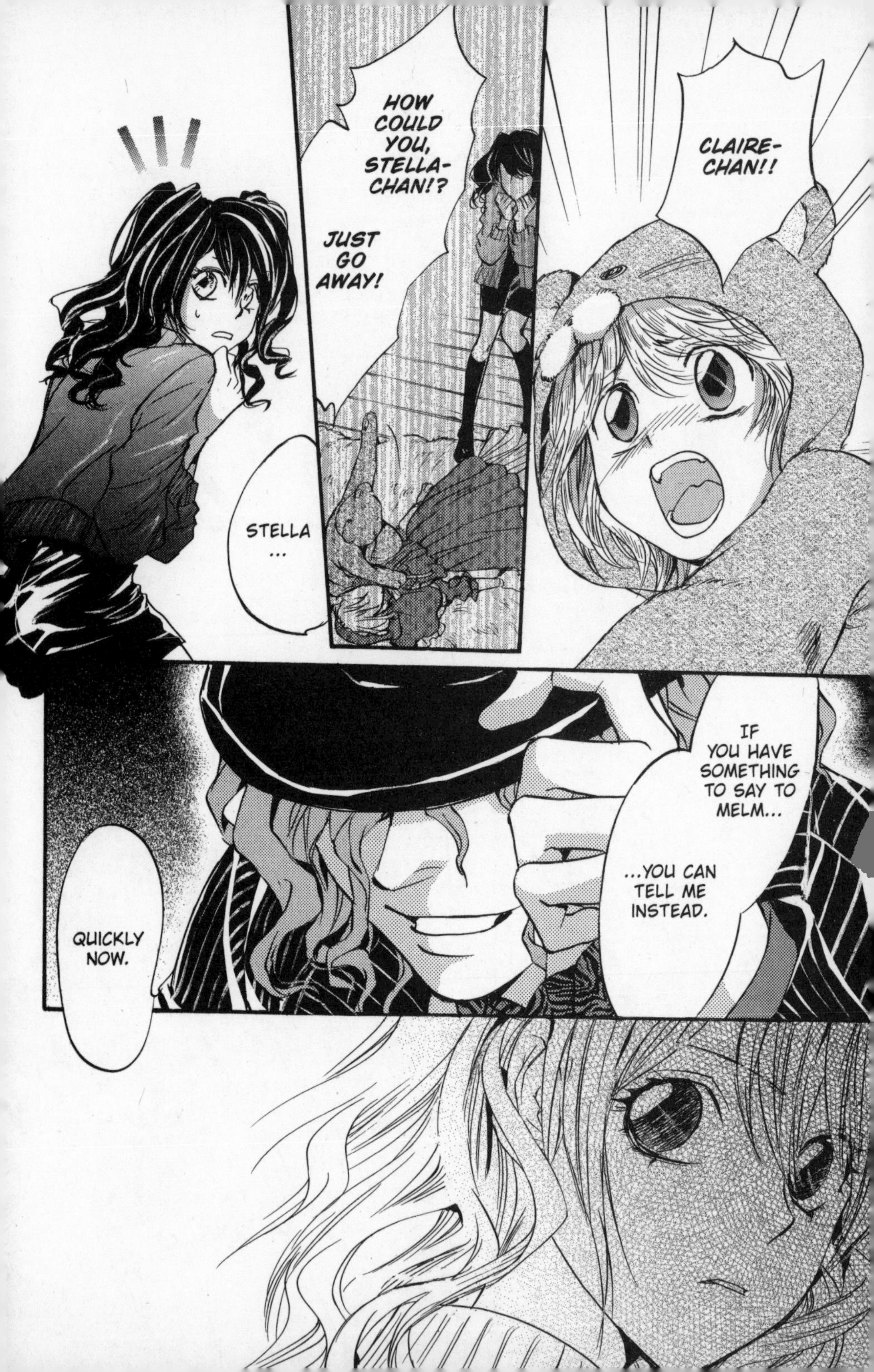
CLAIRE-CHAN!!
HOW COULD YOU, STELLA-CHAN!?
JUST GO AWAY!
STELLA...
IF YOU HAVE SOMETHING TO SAY TO MELM...
...YOU CAN TELL ME INSTEAD.
QUICKLY NOW.

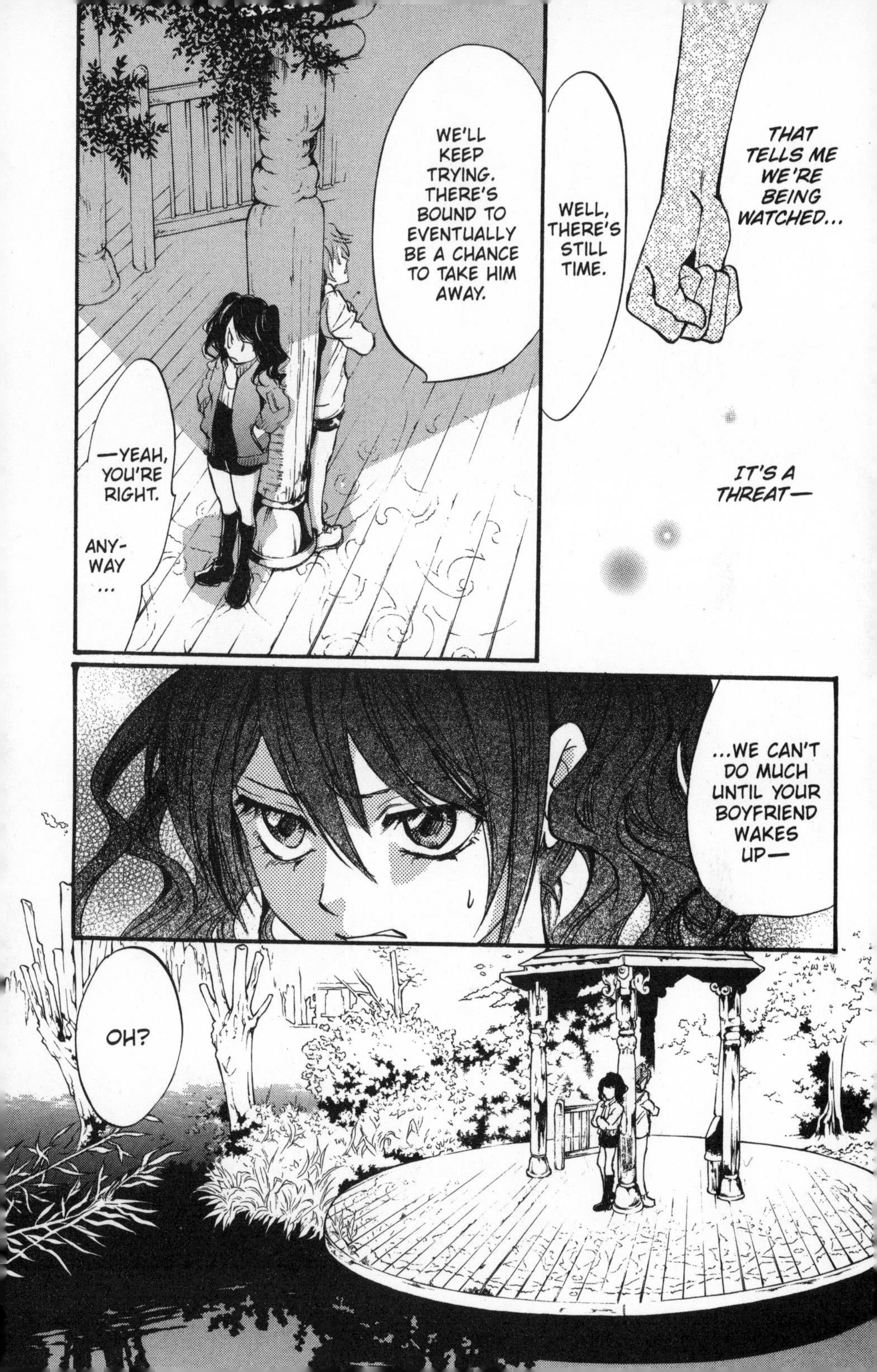
THAT TELLS ME WE'RE BEING WATCHED...
IT'S A THREAT—
WELL, THERE'S STILL TIME.
WE'LL KEEP TRYING. THERE'S BOUND TO EVENTUALLY BE A CHANCE TO TAKE HIM AWAY.
—YEAH, YOU'RE RIGHT.
ANY-WAY ...
...WE CAN'T DO MUCH UNTIL YOUR BOYFRIEND WAKES UP—
OH?

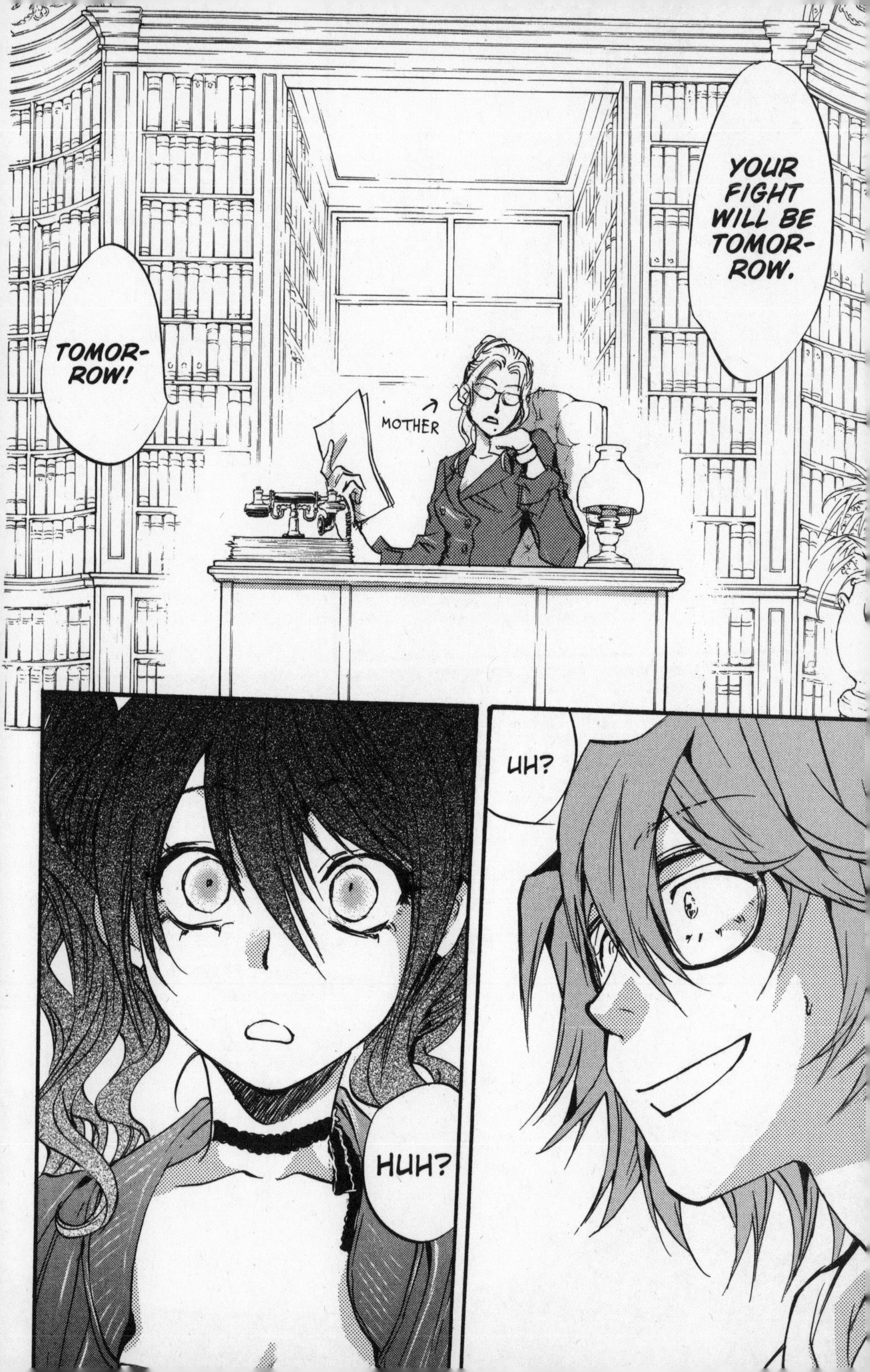
YOUR FIGHT WILL BE TOMOR-ROW.
MOTHER
TOMOR-ROW!
UH?
HUH?

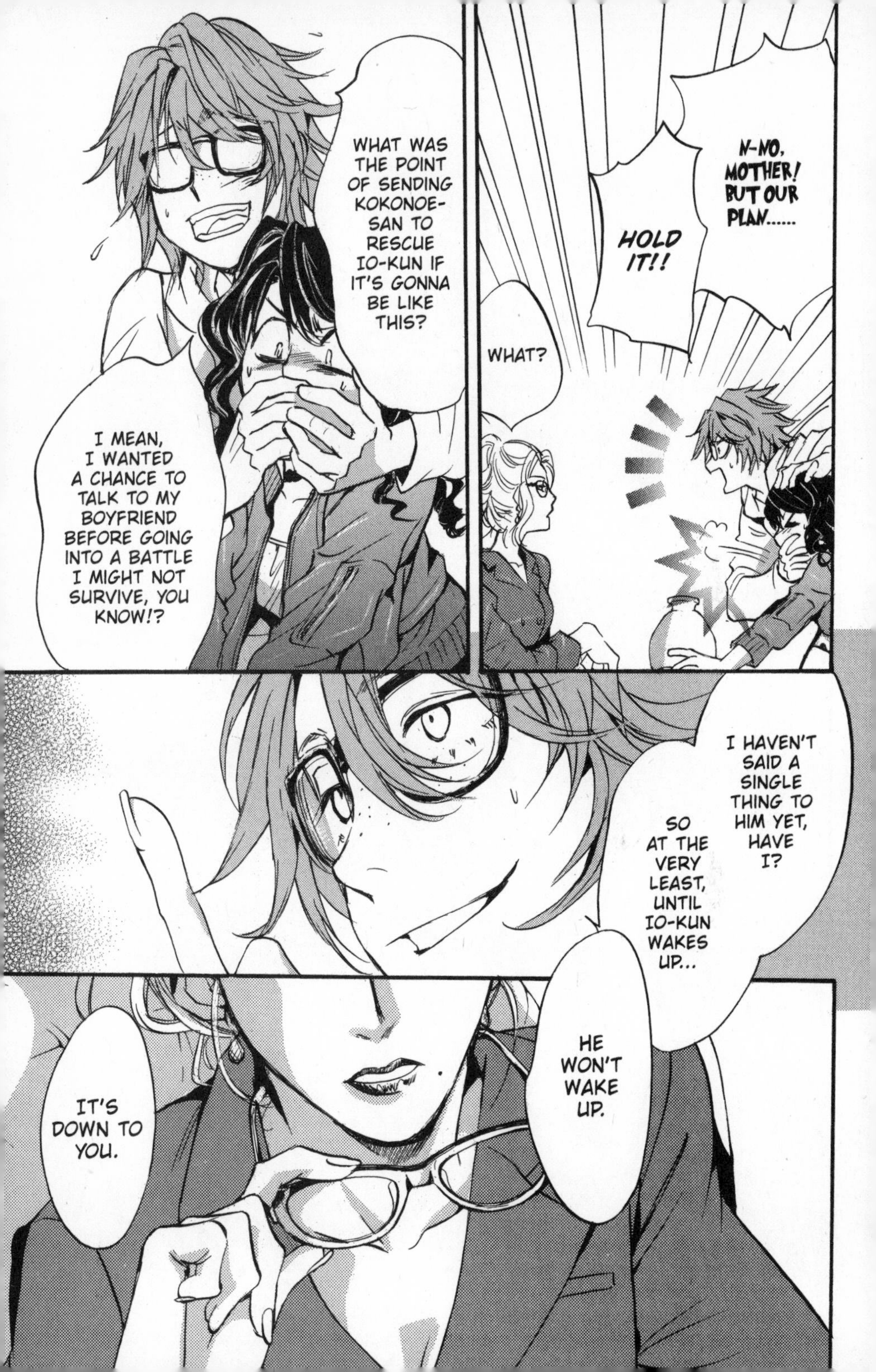
N-NO, MOTHER! BUT OUR PLAN......
HOLD IT!!
WHAT?
WHAT WAS THE POINT OF SENDING KOKONOE-SAN TO RESCUE IO-KUN IF IT'S GONNA BE LIKE THIS?
I MEAN, I WANTED A CHANCE TO TALK TO MY BOYFRIEND BEFORE GOING INTO A BATTLE I MIGHT NOT SURVIVE, YOU KNOW!?
I HAVEN'T SAID A SINGLE THING TO HIM YET, HAVE I?
SO AT THE VERY LEAST, UNTIL IO-KUN WAKES UP...
HE WON'T WAKE UP.
IT'S DOWN TO YOU.

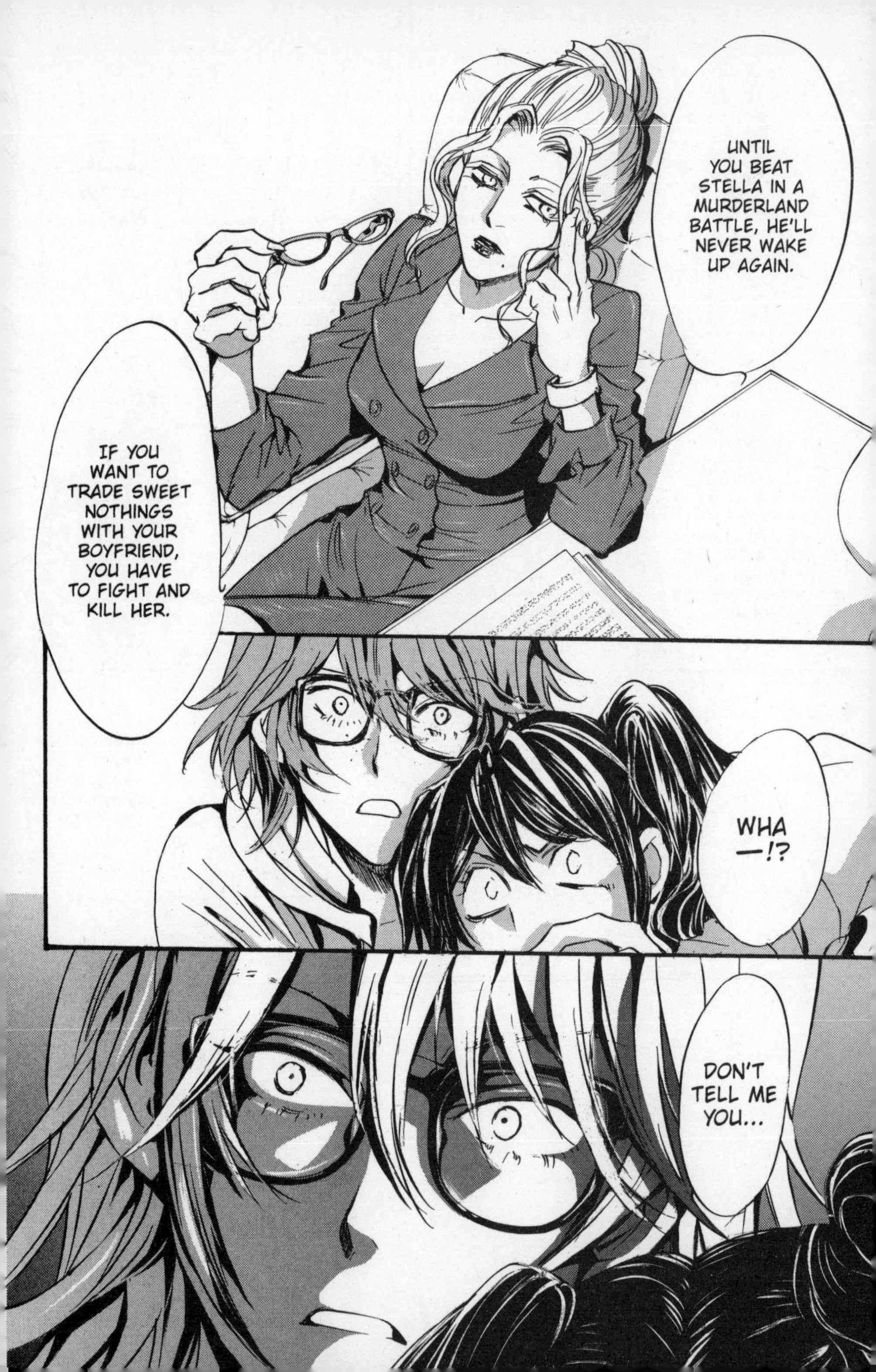
UNTIL YOU BEAT STELLA IN A MURDERLAND BATTLE, HE'LL NEVER WAKE UP AGAIN.
IF YOU WANT TO TRADE SWEET NOTHINGS WITH YOUR BOYFRIEND, YOU HAVE TO FIGHT AND KILL HER.
WHA—!?
DON'T TELL ME YOU...

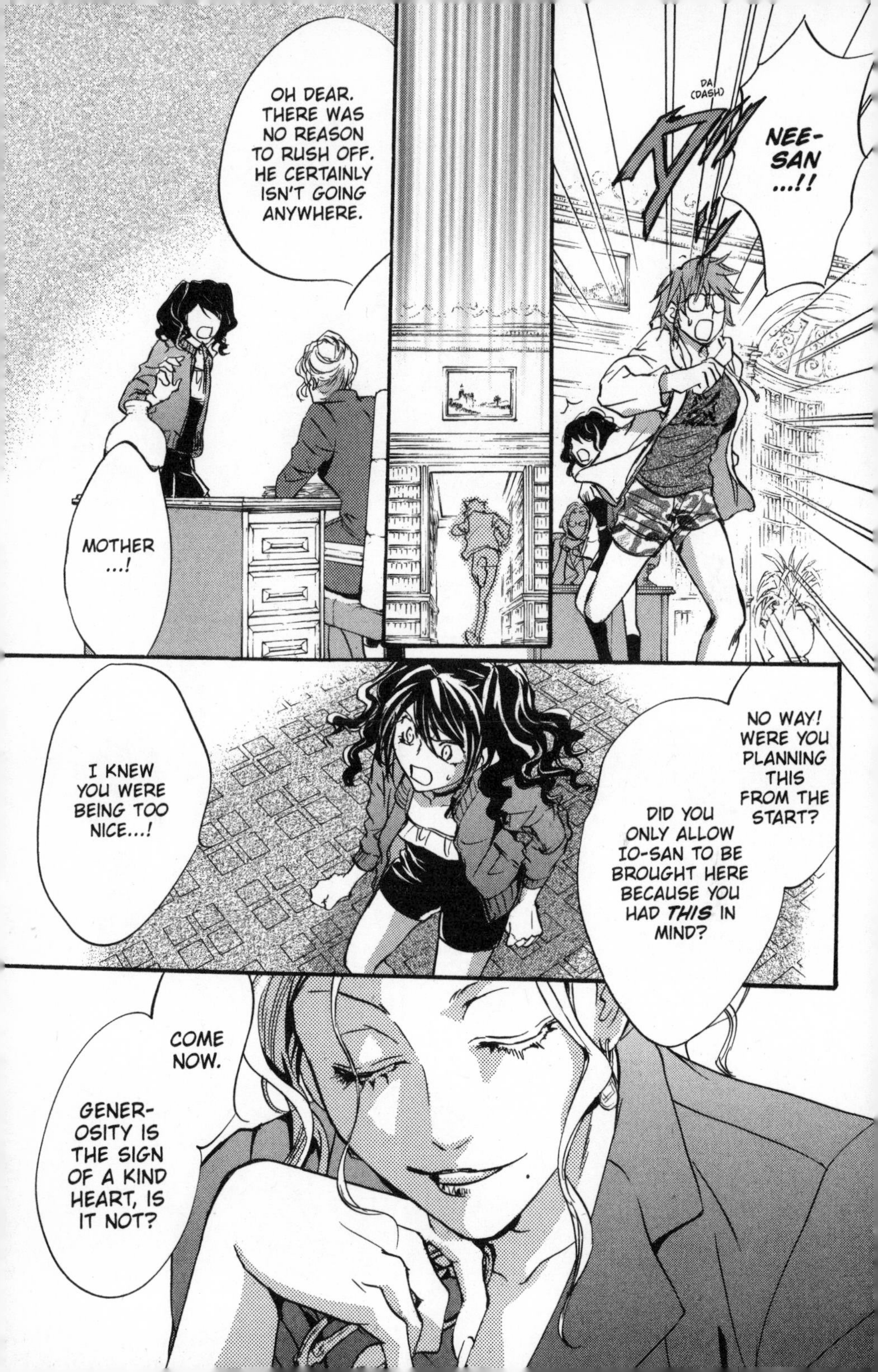
DA (DASH)
NEE-SAN ...!!
OH DEAR. THERE WAS NO REASON TO RUSH OFF. HE CERTAINLY ISN'T GOING ANYWHERE.
MOTHER ...!
NO WAY! WERE YOU PLANNING THIS FROM THE START?
DID YOU ONLY ALLOW IO-SAN TO BE BROUGHT HERE BECAUSE YOU HAD *THIS* IN MIND?
I KNEW YOU WERE BEING TOO NICE...!
COME NOW.
GENER-OSITY IS THE SIGN OF A KIND HEART, IS IT NOT?

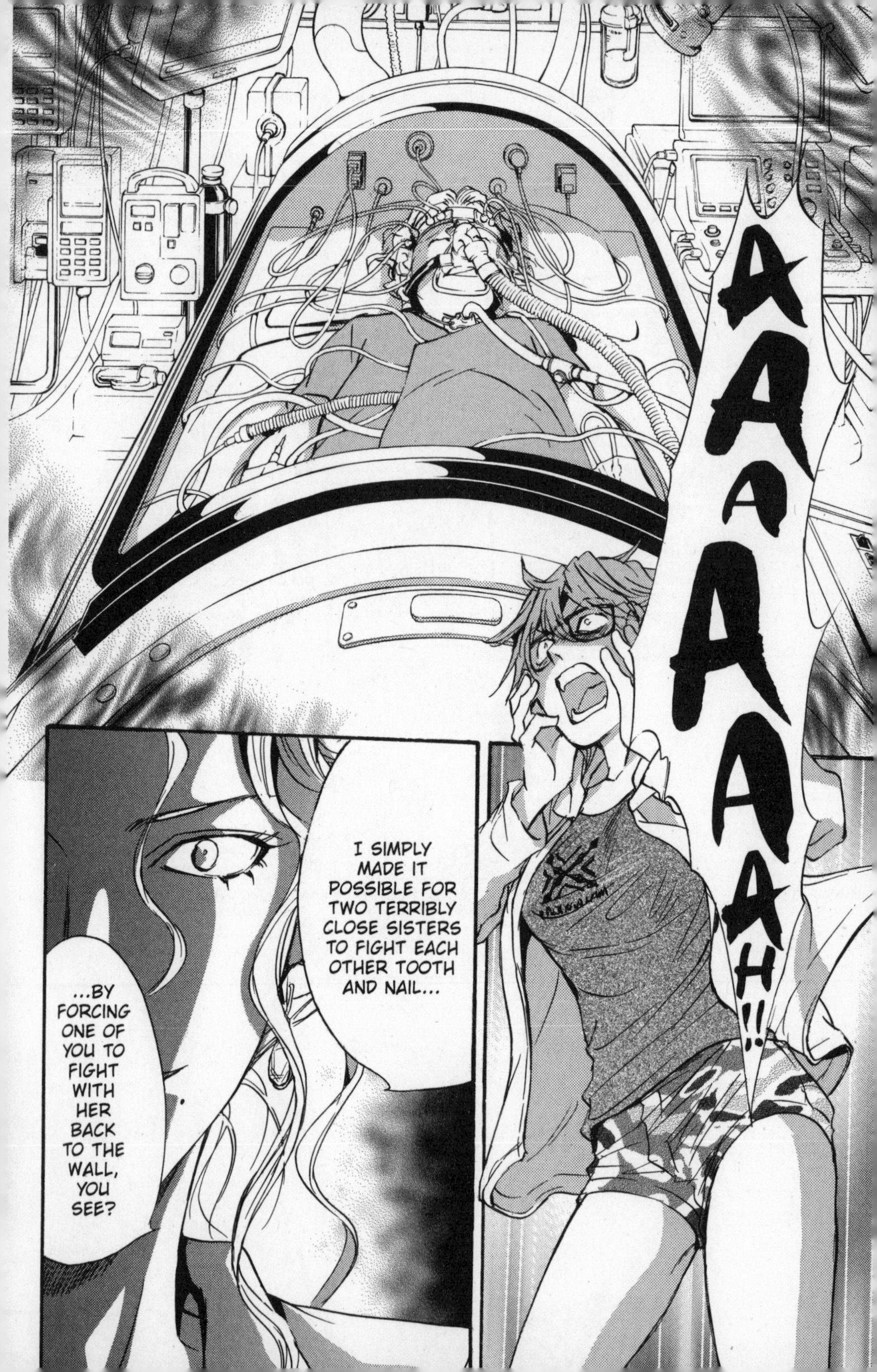
AAAAAAH!!
I SIMPLY MADE IT POSSIBLE FOR TWO TERRIBLY CLOSE SISTERS TO FIGHT EACH OTHER TOOTH AND NAIL...
...BY FORCING ONE OF YOU TO FIGHT WITH HER BACK TO THE WALL, YOU SEE?

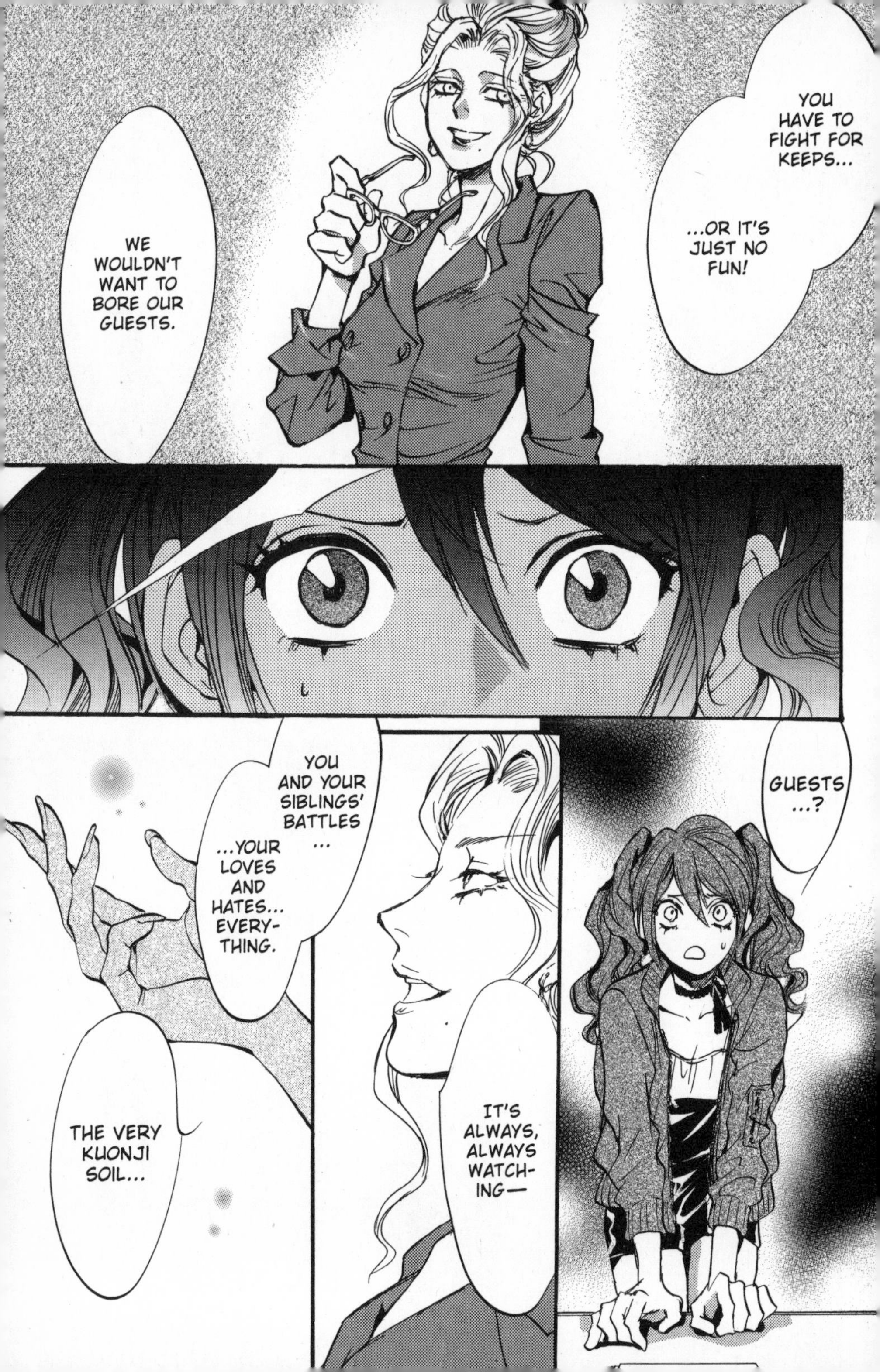
YOU HAVE TO FIGHT FOR KEEPS...
...OR IT'S JUST NO FUN!
WE WOULDN'T WANT TO BORE OUR GUESTS.
GUESTS ...?
YOU AND YOUR SIBLINGS' BATTLES ...
...YOUR LOVES AND HATES... EVERYTHING.
THE VERY KUONJI SOIL...
IT'S ALWAYS, ALWAYS WATCHING—

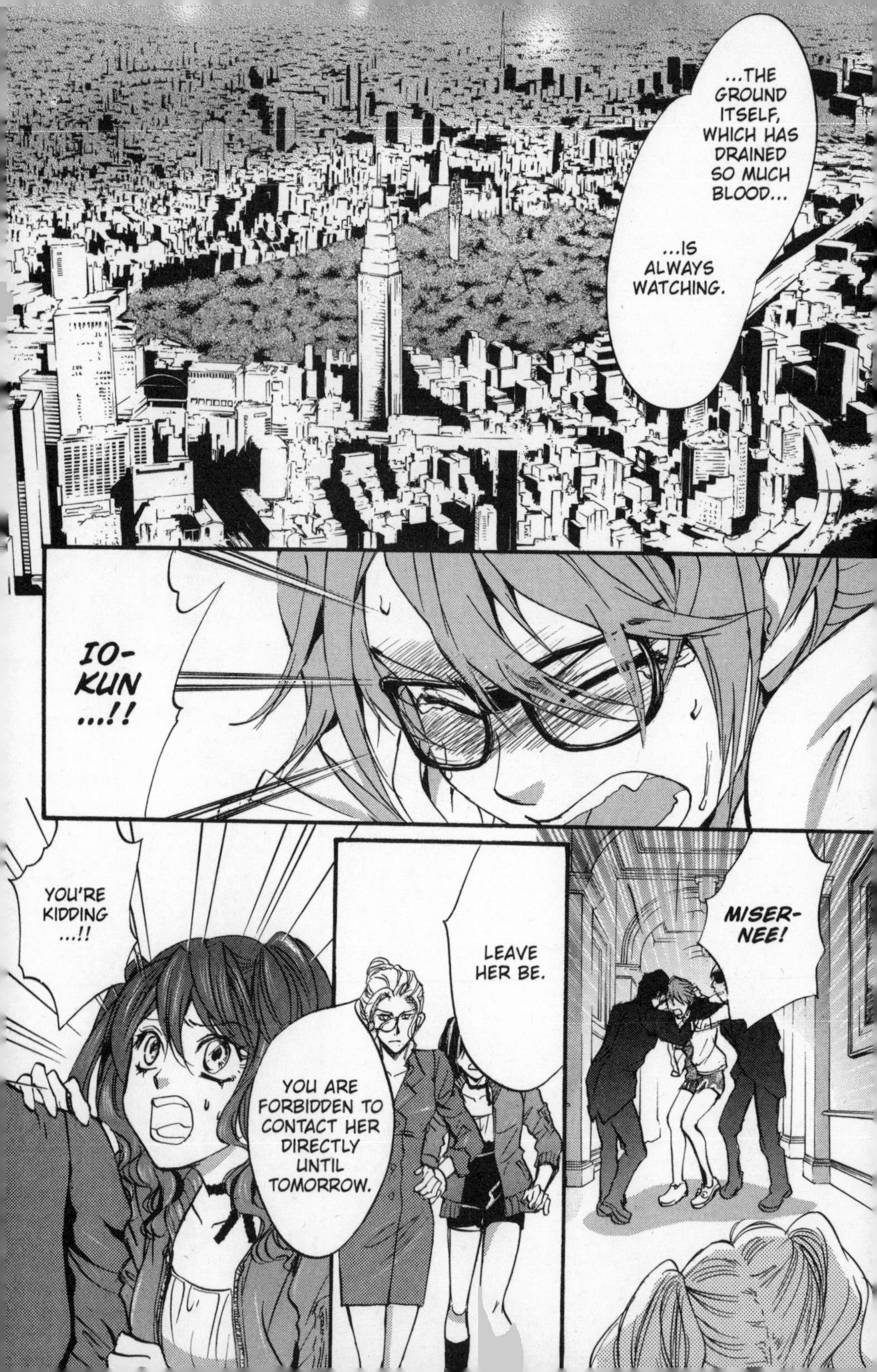

...THE GROUND ITSELF, WHICH HAS DRAINED SO MUCH BLOOD...
...IS ALWAYS WATCHING.
IO-KUN ...!!
MISER-NEE!
LEAVE HER BE.
YOU ARE FORBIDDEN TO CONTACT HER DIRECTLY UNTIL TOMORROW.
YOU'RE KIDDING ...!!

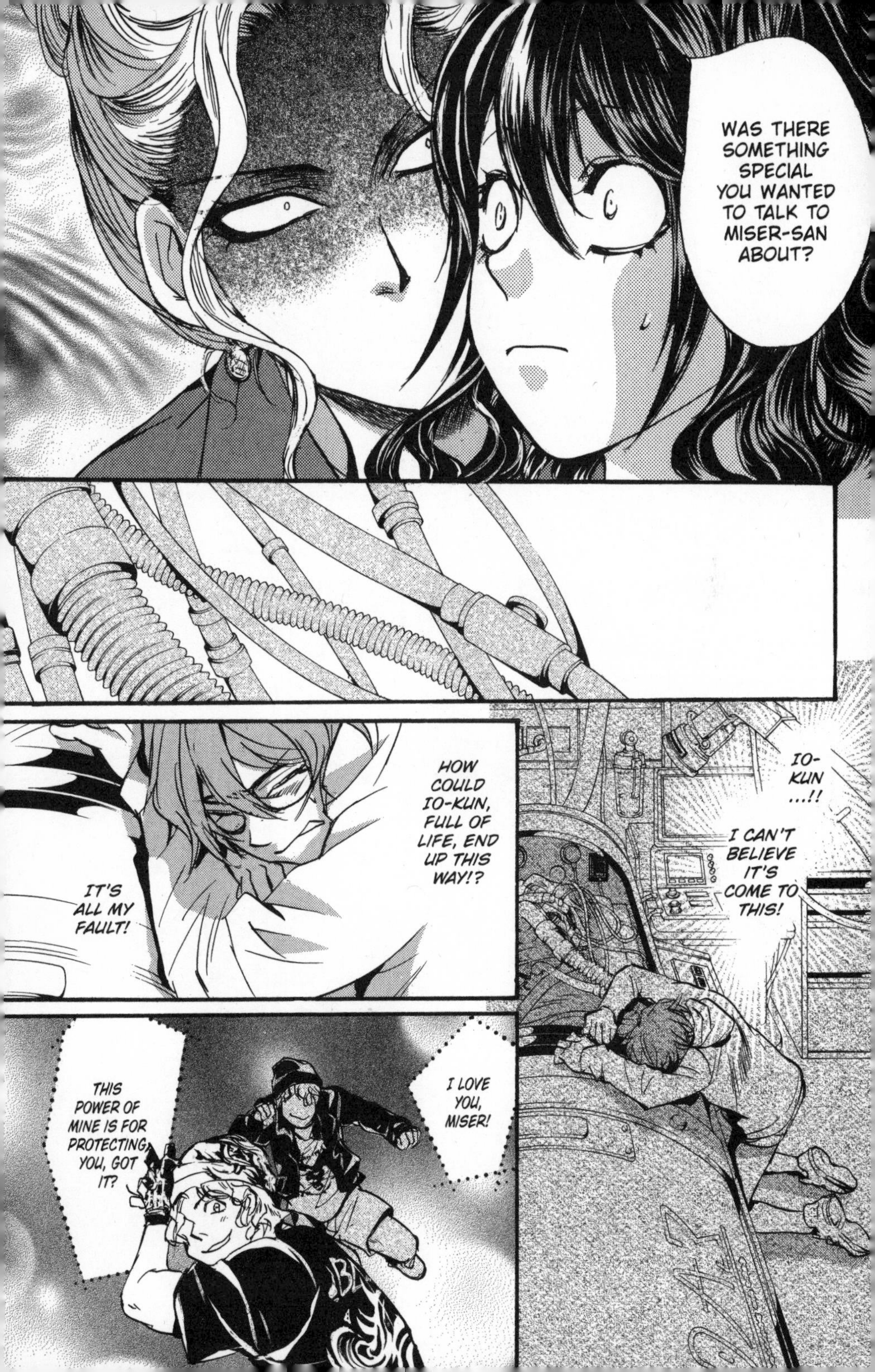
WAS THERE SOMETHING SPECIAL YOU WANTED TO TALK TO MISER-SAN ABOUT?
IO-KUN ...!!
I CAN'T BELIEVE IT'S COME TO THIS!
HOW COULD IO-KUN, FULL OF LIFE, END UP THIS WAY!?
IT'S ALL MY FAULT!
I LOVE YOU, MISER!
THIS POWER OF MINE IS FOR PROTECTING YOU, GOT IT?

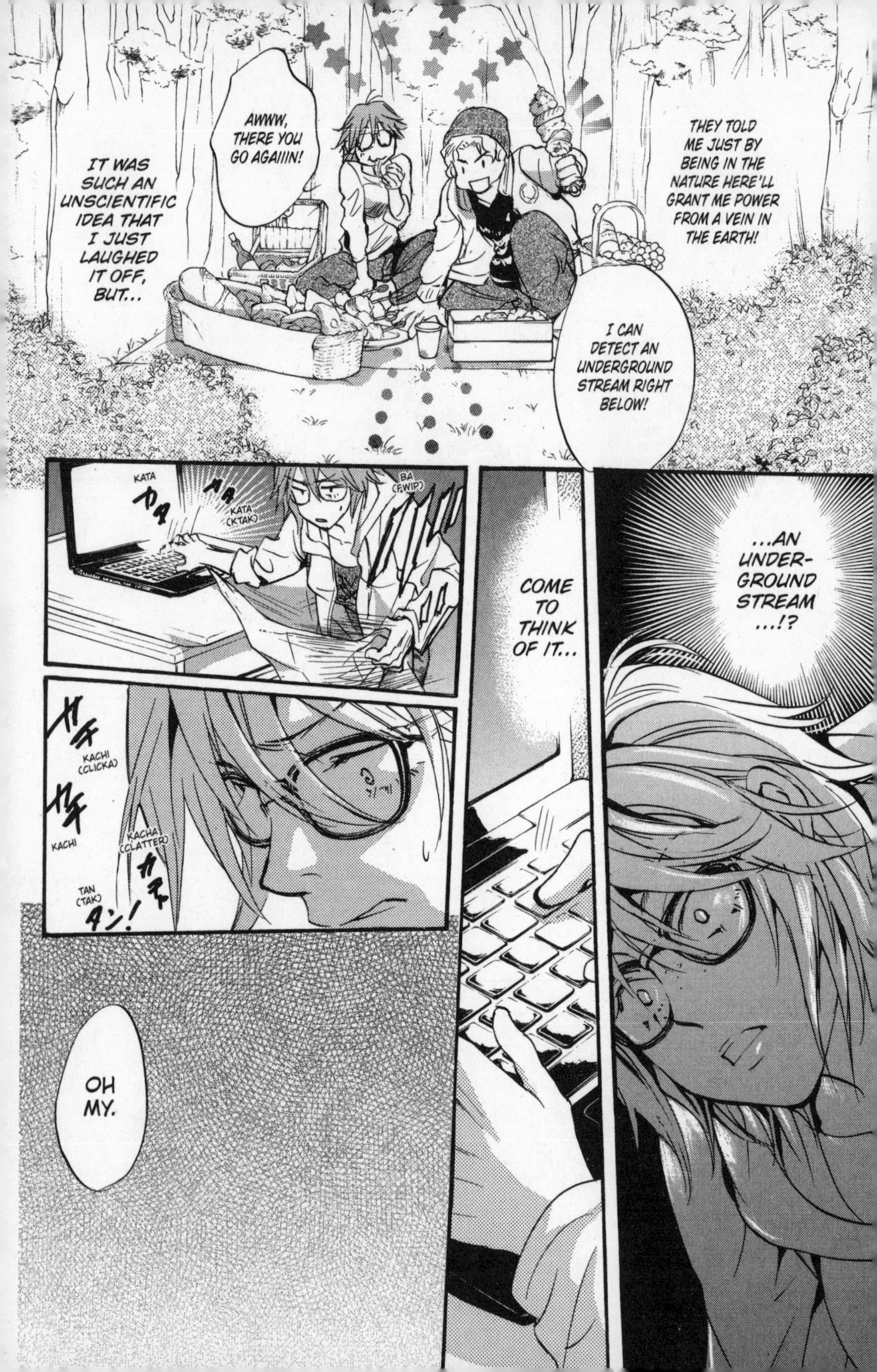
THEY TOLD ME JUST BY BEING IN THE NATURE HERE'LL GRANT ME POWER FROM A VEIN IN THE EARTH!
I CAN DETECT AN UNDERGROUND STREAM RIGHT BELOW!
AWWW, THERE YOU GO AGAIIIN!
IT WAS SUCH AN UNSCIENTIFIC IDEA THAT I JUST LAUGHED IT OFF, BUT...
...AN UNDER-GROUND STREAM ...!?
COME TO THINK OF IT...
BA (FWIP)
KATA
KATA (KTAK)
KACHI (CLICKA)
KACHI
KACHA (CLATTER)
TAN (TAK)
OH MY.

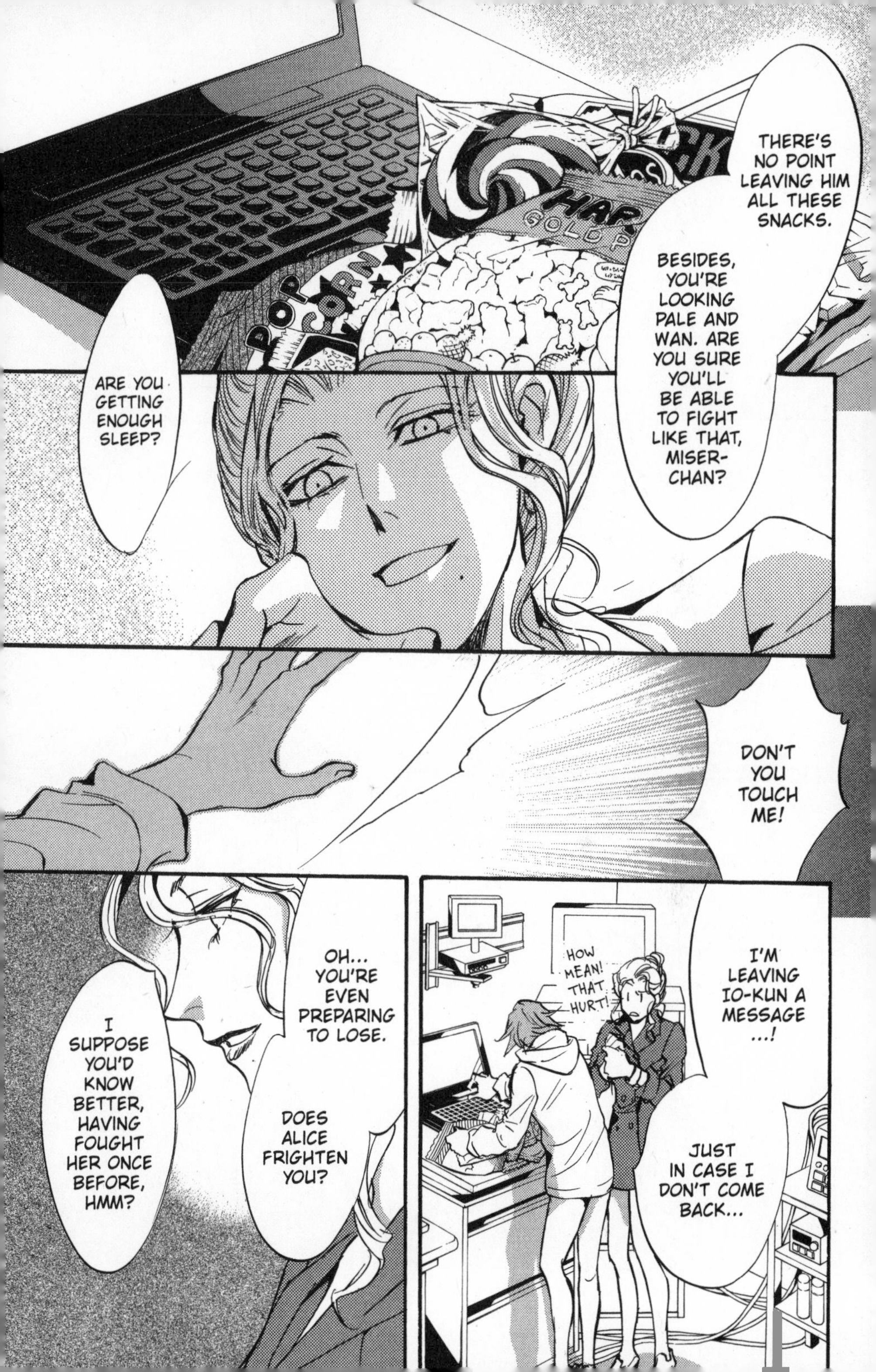
THERE'S NO POINT LEAVING HIM ALL THESE SNACKS.
BESIDES, YOU'RE LOOKING PALE AND WAN. ARE YOU SURE YOU'LL BE ABLE TO FIGHT LIKE THAT, MISER-CHAN?
ARE YOU GETTING ENOUGH SLEEP?
DON'T YOU TOUCH ME!
I'M LEAVING IO-KUN A MESSAGE ...!
HOW MEAN! THAT HURT!
JUST IN CASE I DON'T COME BACK...
OH... YOU'RE EVEN PREPARING TO LOSE.
DOES ALICE FRIGHTEN YOU?
I SUPPOSE YOU'D KNOW BETTER, HAVING FOUGHT HER ONCE BEFORE, HMM?

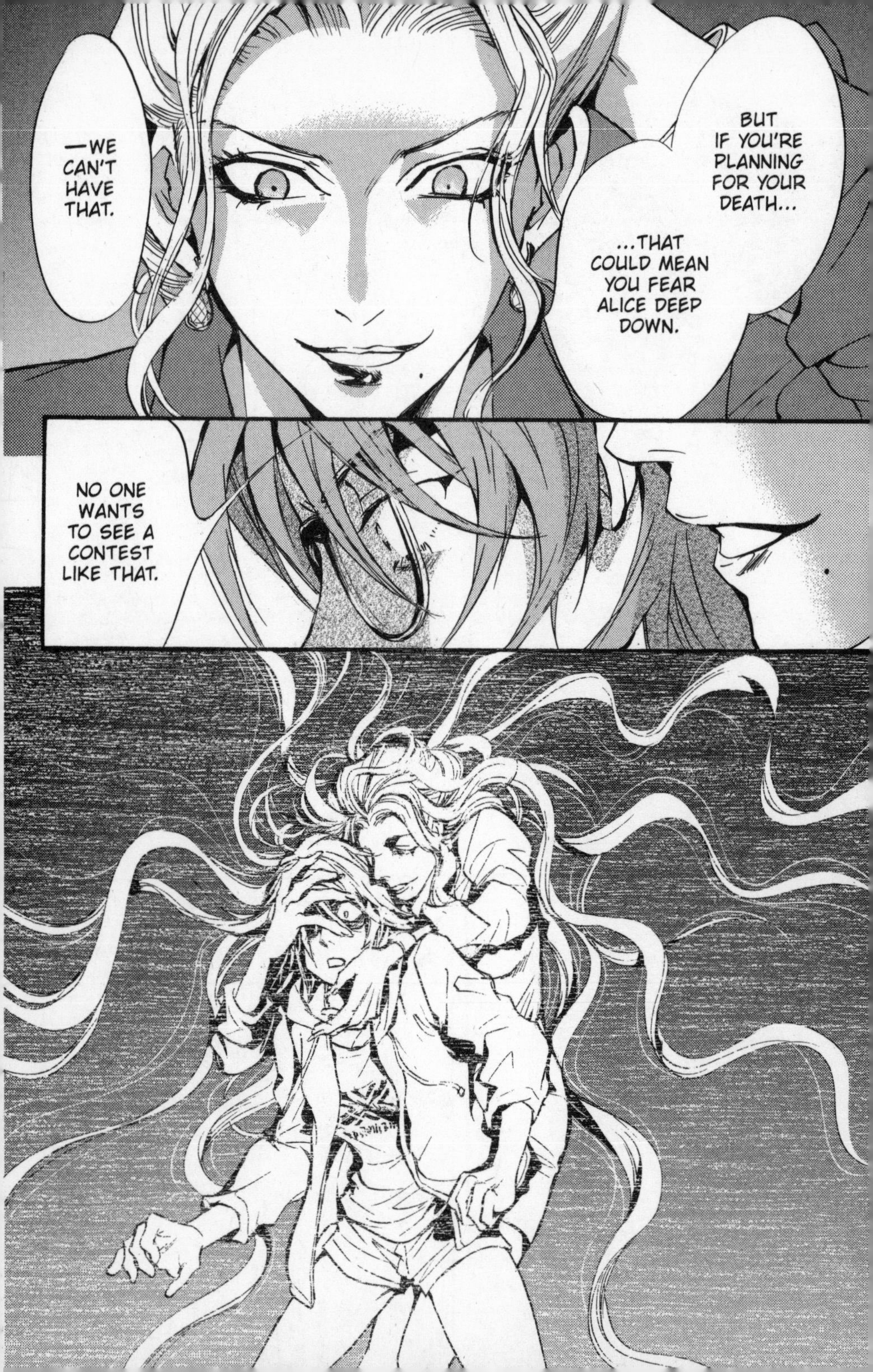
BUT IF YOU'RE PLANNING FOR YOUR DEATH...
...THAT COULD MEAN YOU FEAR ALICE DEEP DOWN.
—WE CAN'T HAVE THAT.
NO ONE WANTS TO SEE A CONTEST LIKE THAT.

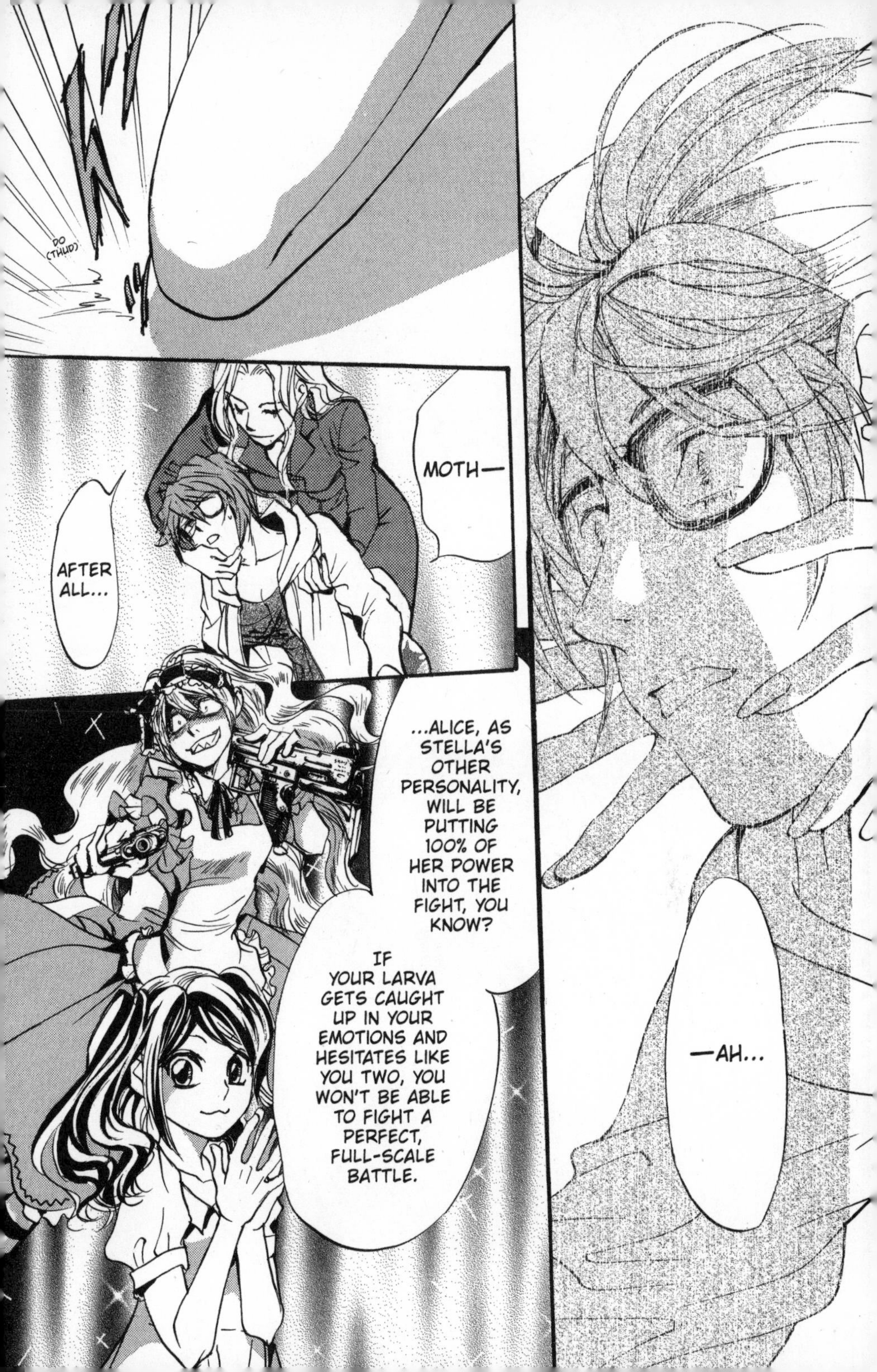
—AH...
DO (THUD)
MOTH—
AFTER ALL...
...ALICE, AS STELLA'S OTHER PERSONALITY, WILL BE PUTTING 100% OF HER POWER INTO THE FIGHT, YOU KNOW?
IF YOUR LARVA GETS CAUGHT UP IN YOUR EMOTIONS AND HESITATES LIKE YOU TWO, YOU WON'T BE ABLE TO FIGHT A PERFECT, FULL-SCALE BATTLE.

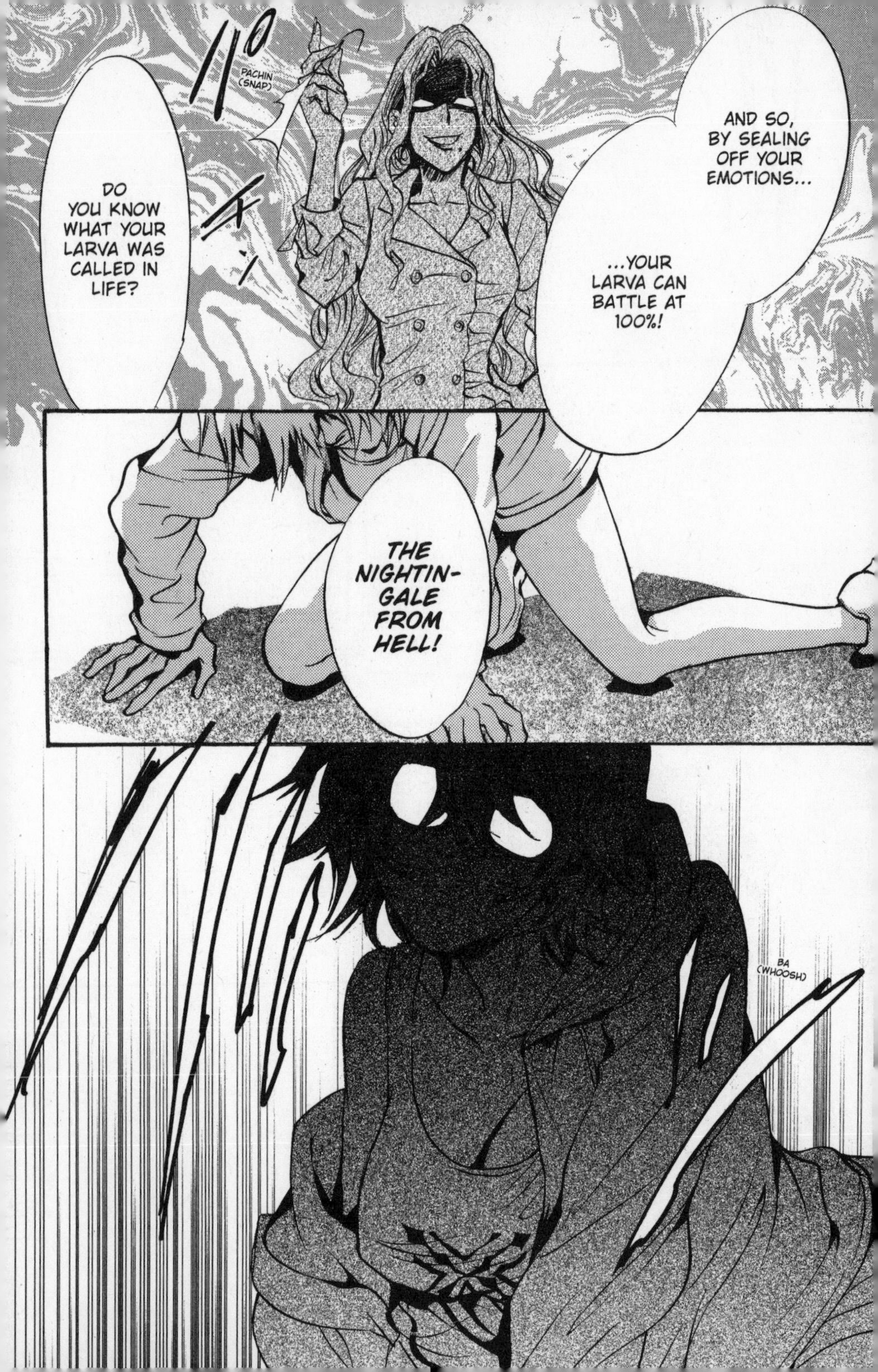
AND SO, BY SEALING OFF YOUR EMOTIONS...
...YOUR LARVA CAN BATTLE AT 100%!
PACHIN (SNAP)
DO YOU KNOW WHAT YOUR LARVA WAS CALLED IN LIFE?
THE NIGHTIN-GALE FROM HELL!
BA (WHOOSH)

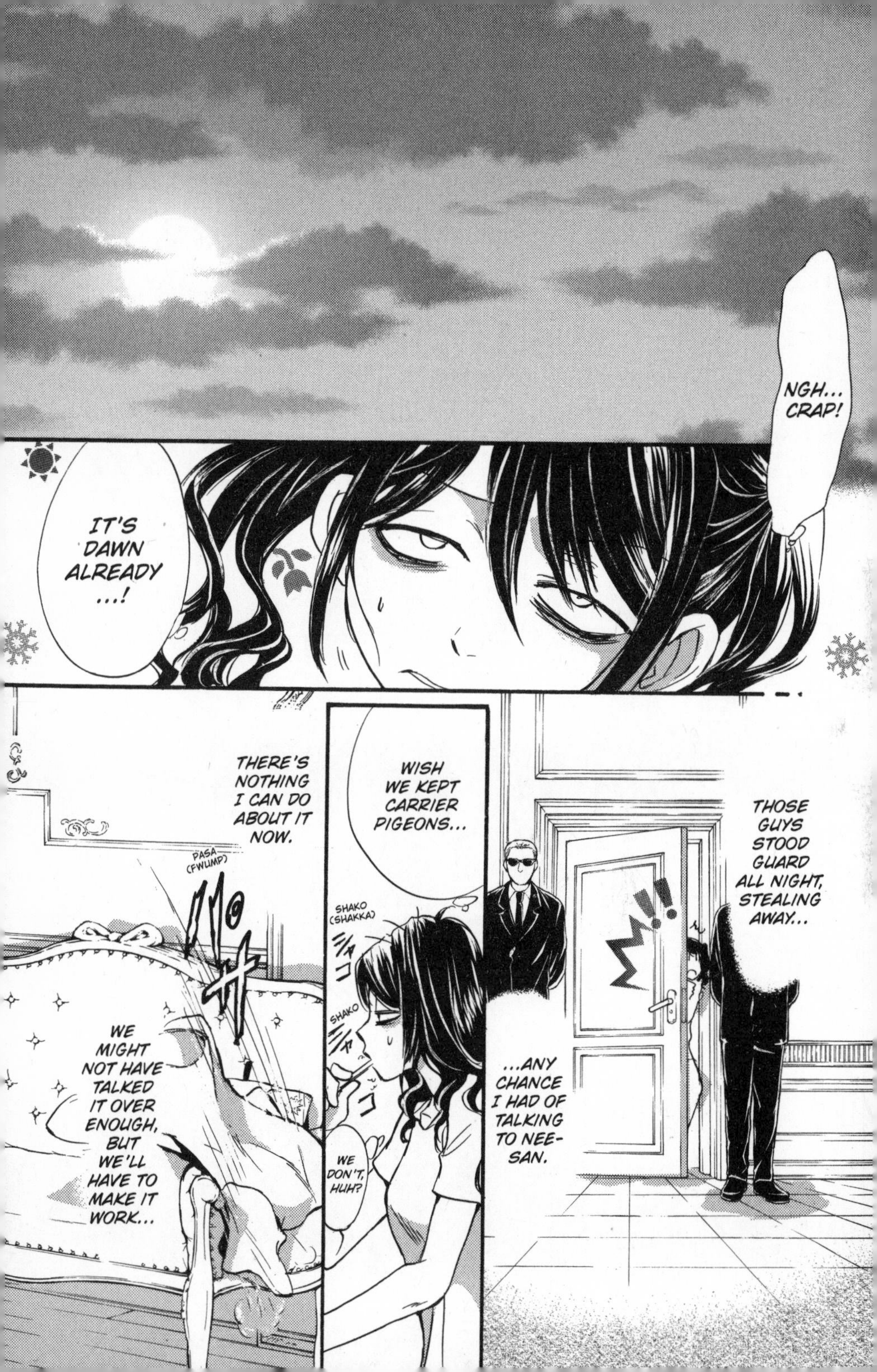
NGH... CRAP!
IT'S DAWN ALREADY ...!
THOSE GUYS STOOD GUARD ALL NIGHT, STEALING AWAY...
...ANY CHANCE I HAD OF TALKING TO NEE-SAN.
WISH WE KEPT CARRIER PIGEONS...
SHAKO (SHAKKA)
SHAKO
WE DON'T, HUH?
THERE'S NOTHING I CAN DO ABOUT IT NOW.
PASA (FWUMP)
WE MIGHT NOT HAVE TALKED IT OVER ENOUGH, BUT WE'LL HAVE TO MAKE IT WORK...

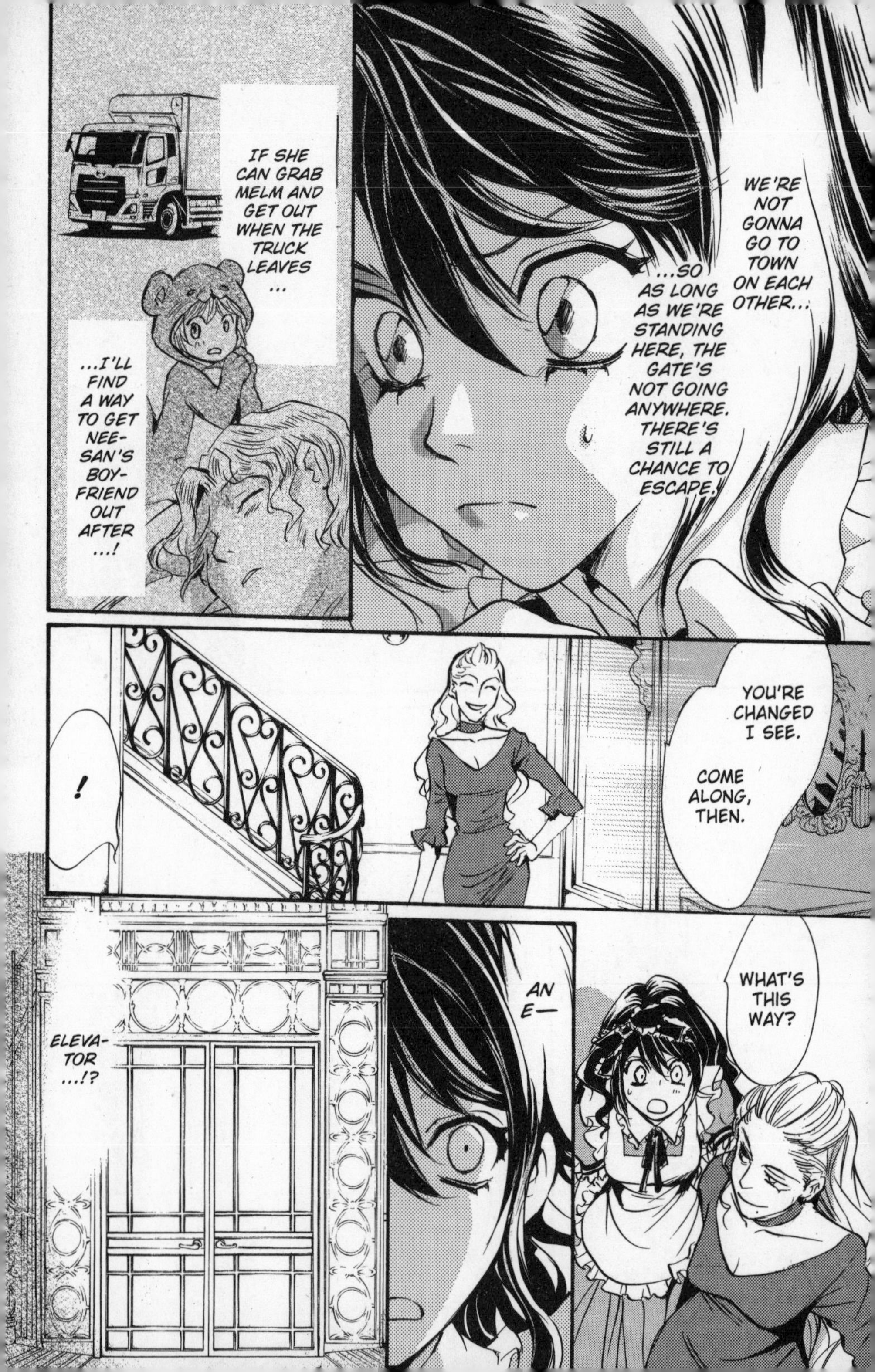
WE'RE NOT GONNA GO TO TOWN ON EACH OTHER...
...SO AS LONG AS WE'RE STANDING HERE, THE GATE'S NOT GOING ANYWHERE. THERE'S STILL A CHANCE TO ESCAPE.
IF SHE CAN GRAB MELM AND GET OUT WHEN THE TRUCK LEAVES ...
...I'LL FIND A WAY TO GET NEE-SAN'S BOY-FRIEND OUT AFTER ...!
YOU'RE CHANGED I SEE.
COME ALONG, THEN.
!
WHAT'S THIS WAY?
AN E—
ELEVA-TOR ...!?

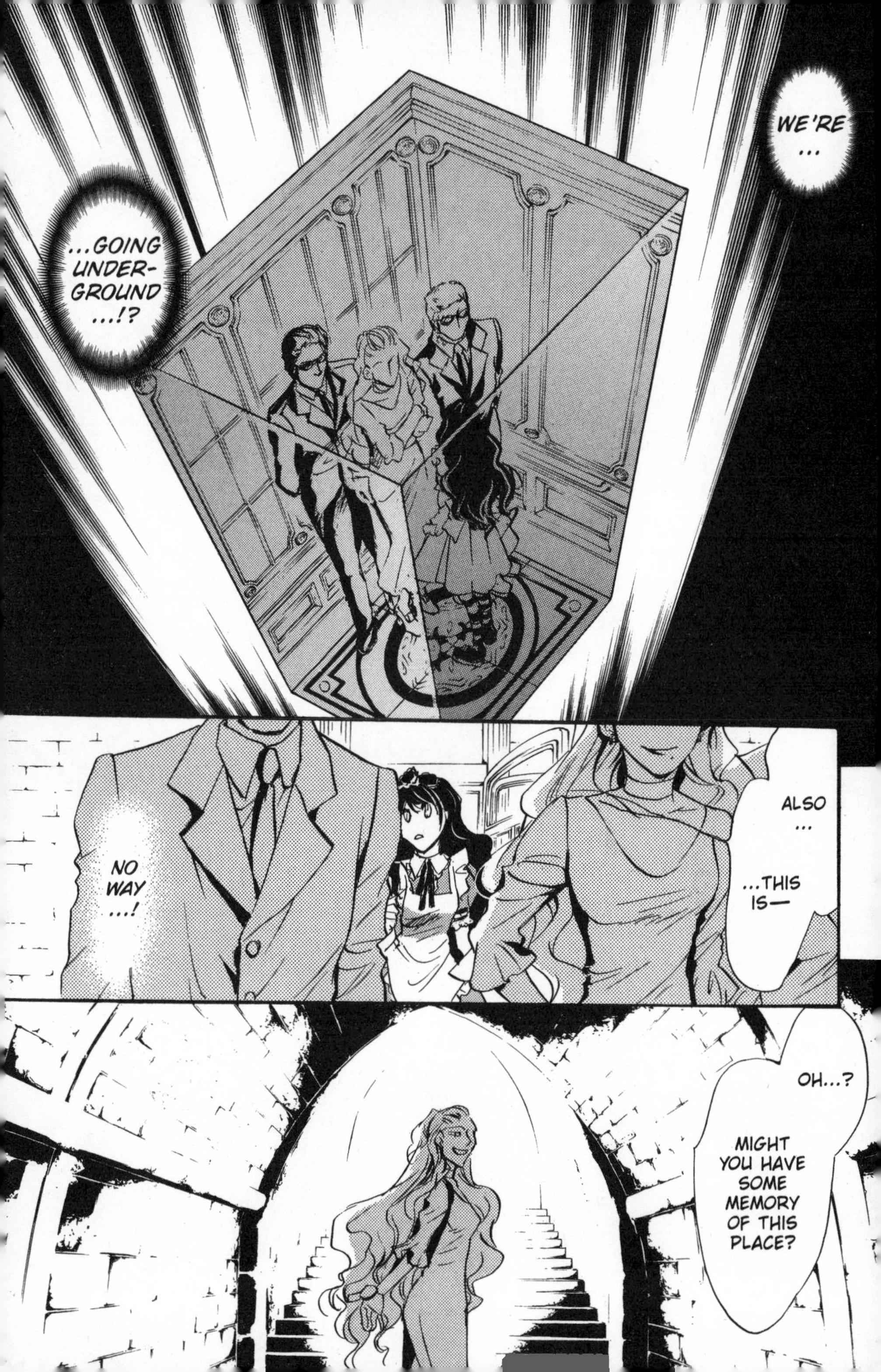
WE'RE ...
...GOING UNDER-GROUND ...!?
ALSO ...
...THIS IS—
NO WAY ...!
OH...?
MIGHT YOU HAVE SOME MEMORY OF THIS PLACE?

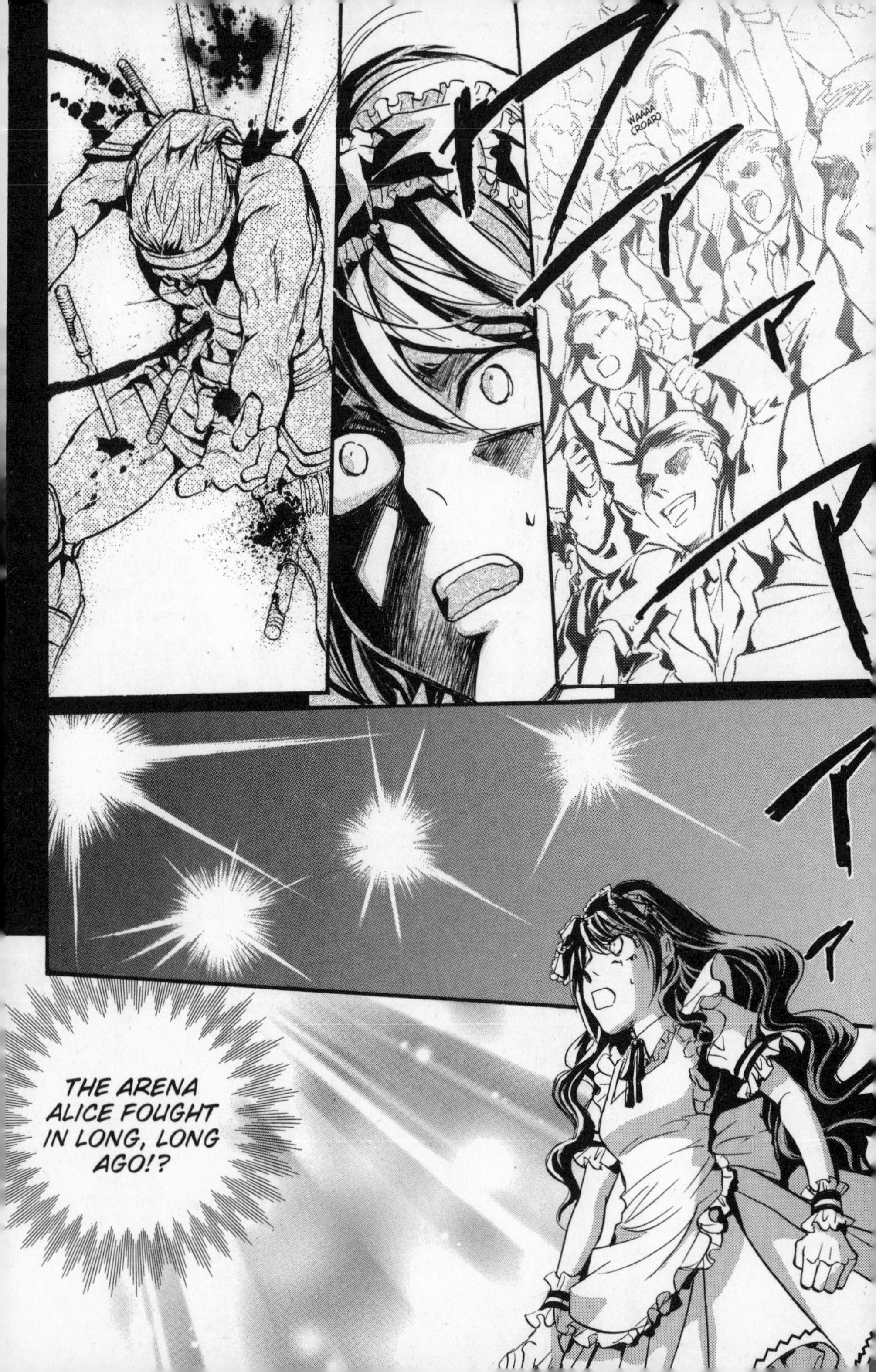
WAAAA
(ROAR)
THE ARENA ALICE FOUGHT IN LONG, LONG AGO!?

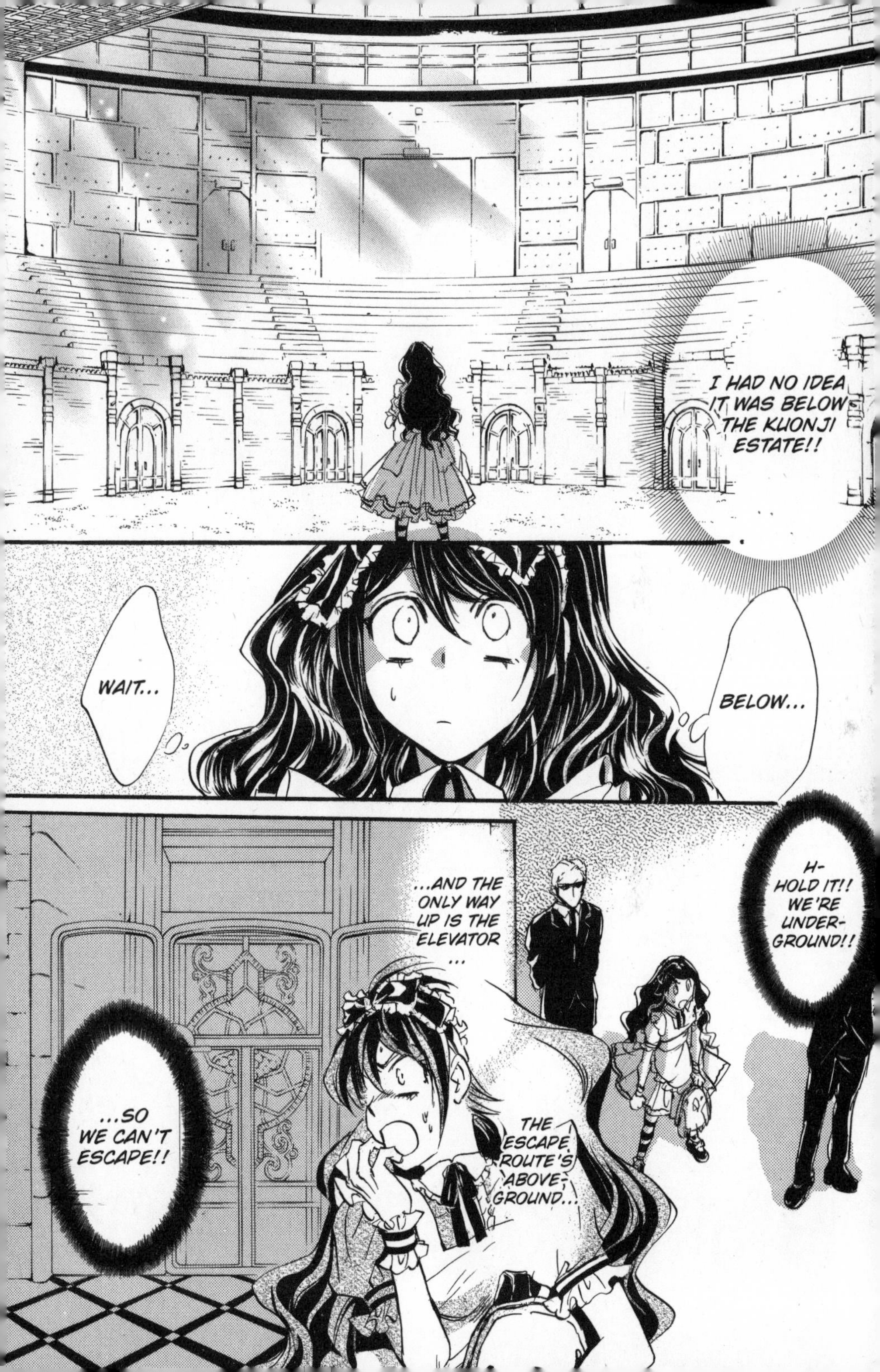
I HAD NO IDEA IT WAS BELOW THE KUONJI ESTATE!!
BELOW...
WAIT...
H-HOLD IT!! WE'RE UNDER-GROUND!!
...AND THE ONLY WAY UP IS THE ELEVATOR...
THE ESCAPE ROUTE'S ABOVE-GROUND...
...SO WE CAN'T ESCAPE!!

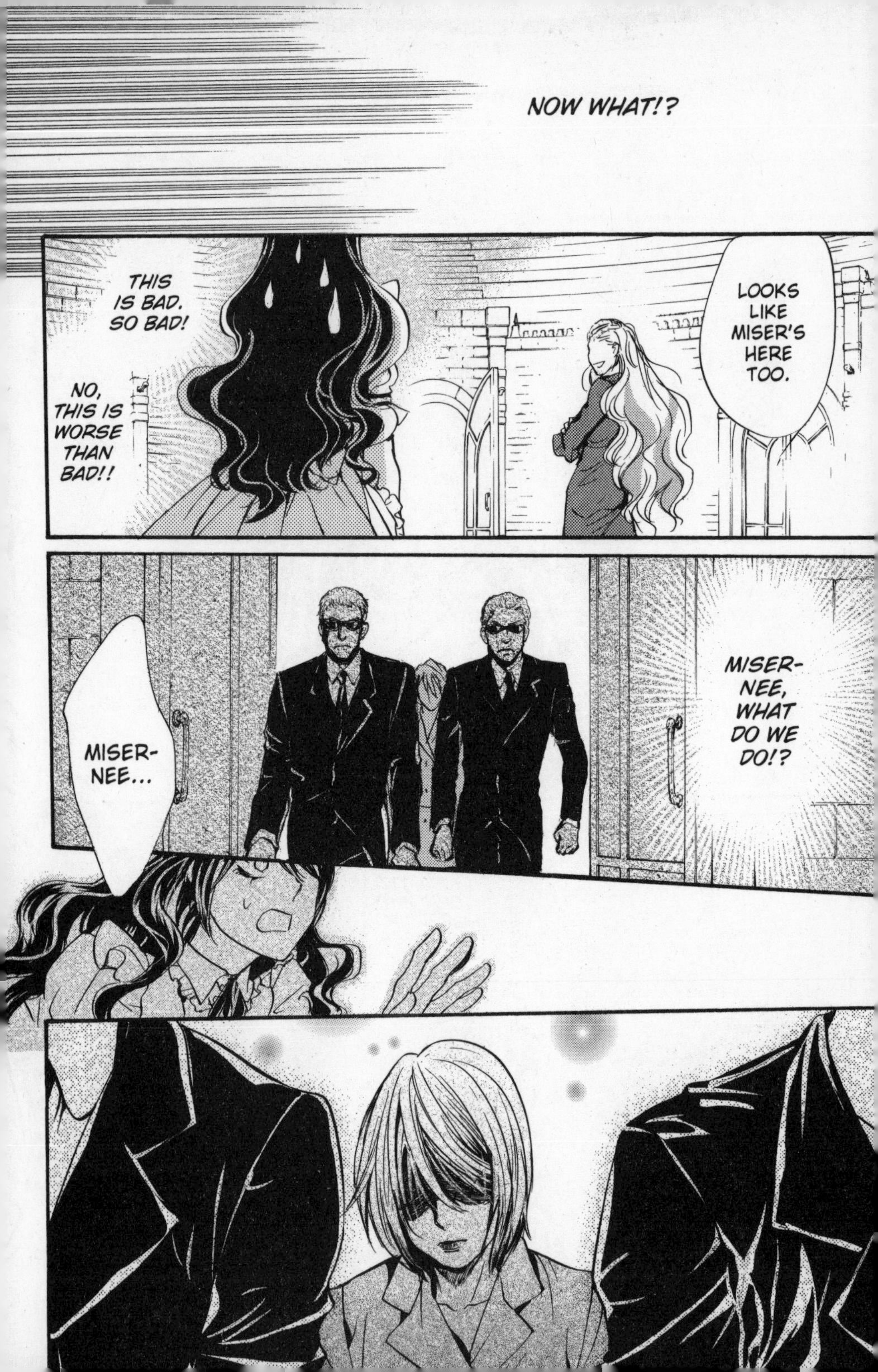
NOW WHAT!?
LOOKS LIKE MISER'S HERE TOO.
THIS IS BAD. SO BAD!
NO, THIS IS WORSE THAN BAD!!
MISER-NEE, WHAT DO WE DO!?
MISER-NEE...

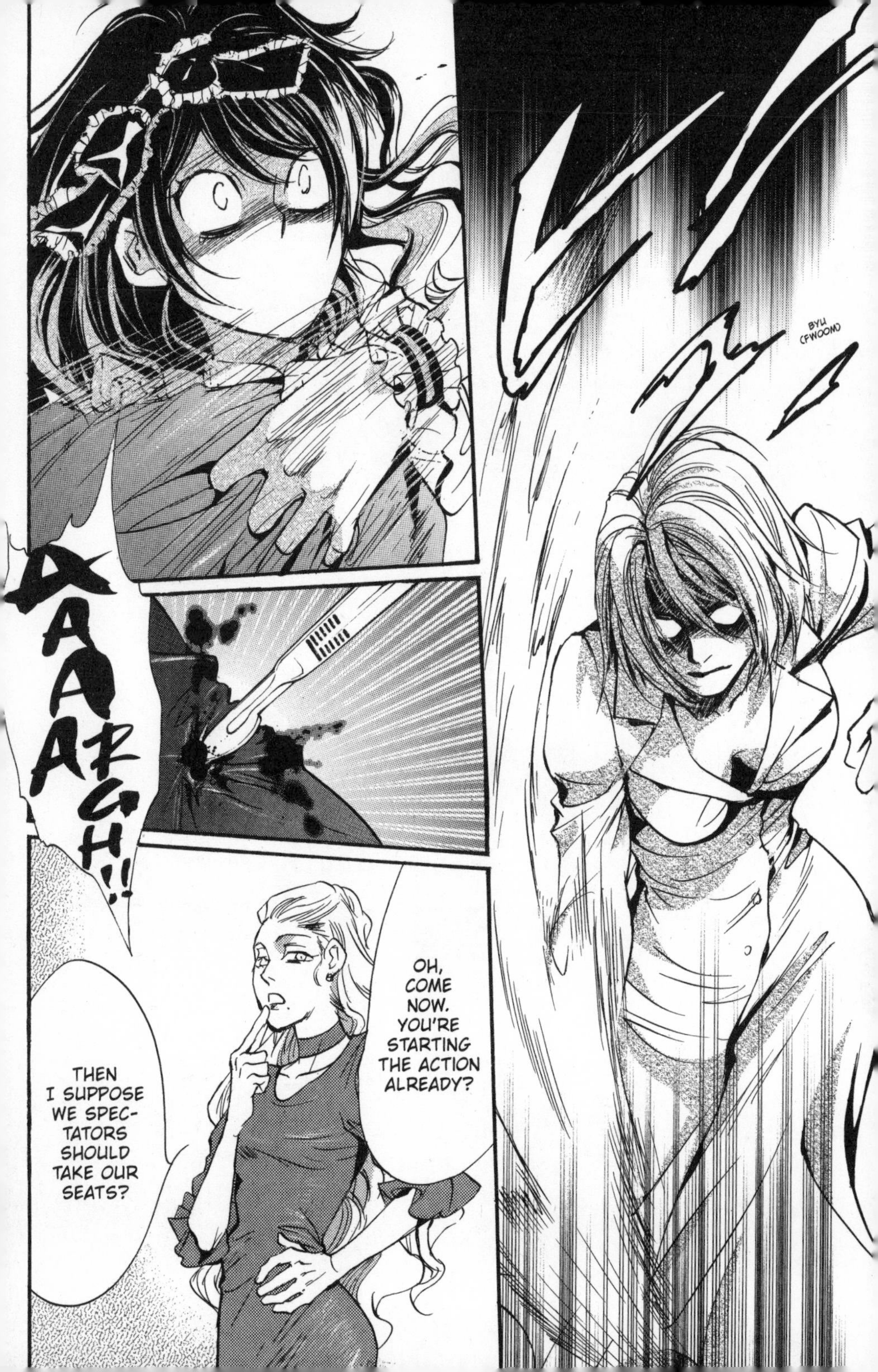
BYU (FWOOM)
DAAAARGH!!
OH, COME NOW. YOU'RE STARTING THE ACTION ALREADY?
THEN I SUPPOSE WE SPEC-TATORS SHOULD TAKE OUR SEATS?

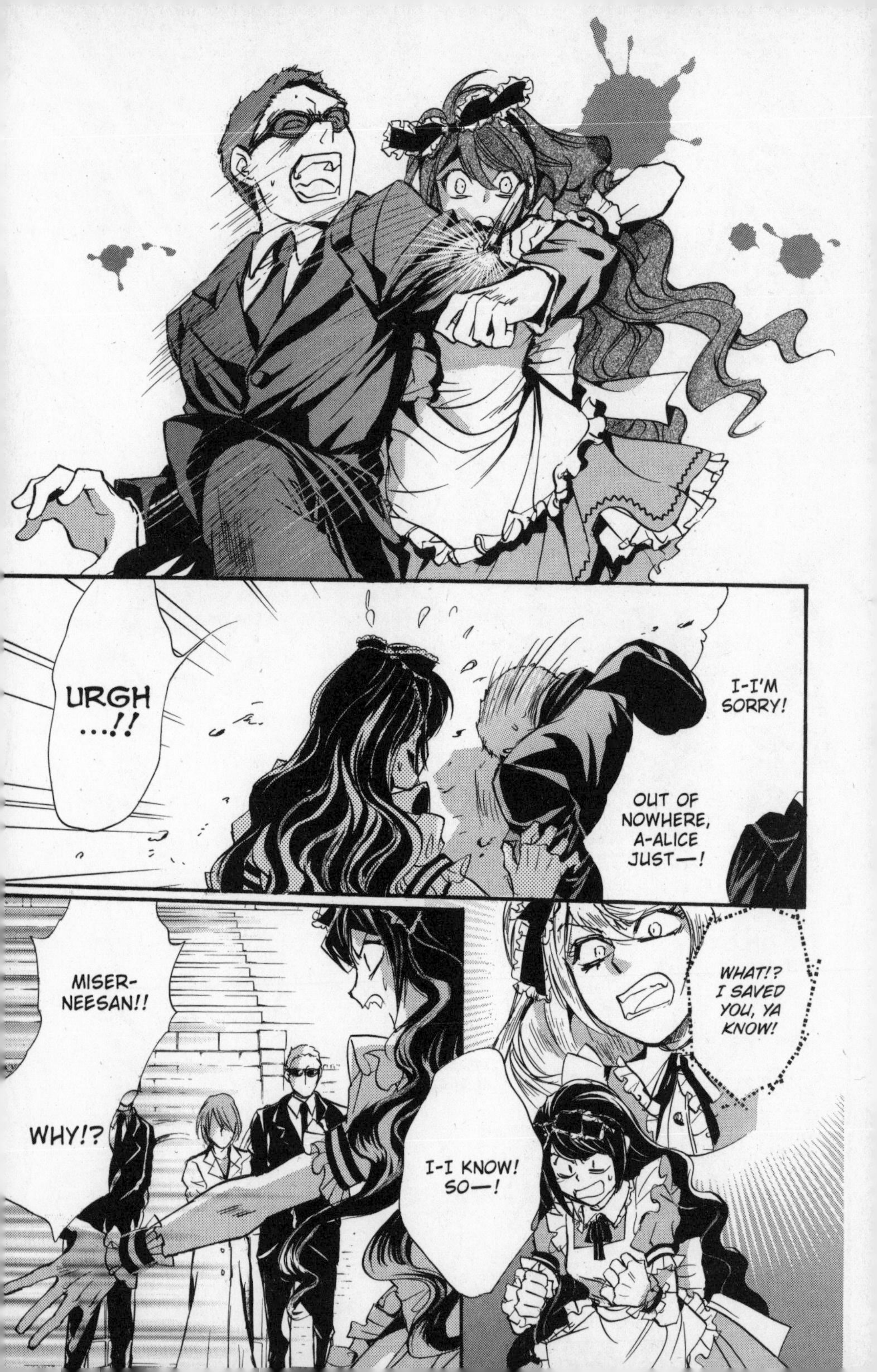
I-I'M SORRY!
OUT OF NOWHERE, A-ALICE JUST—!
URGH ...!!
WHAT!? I SAVED YOU, YA KNOW!
I-I KNOW! SO—!
MISER-NEESAN!!
WHY!?

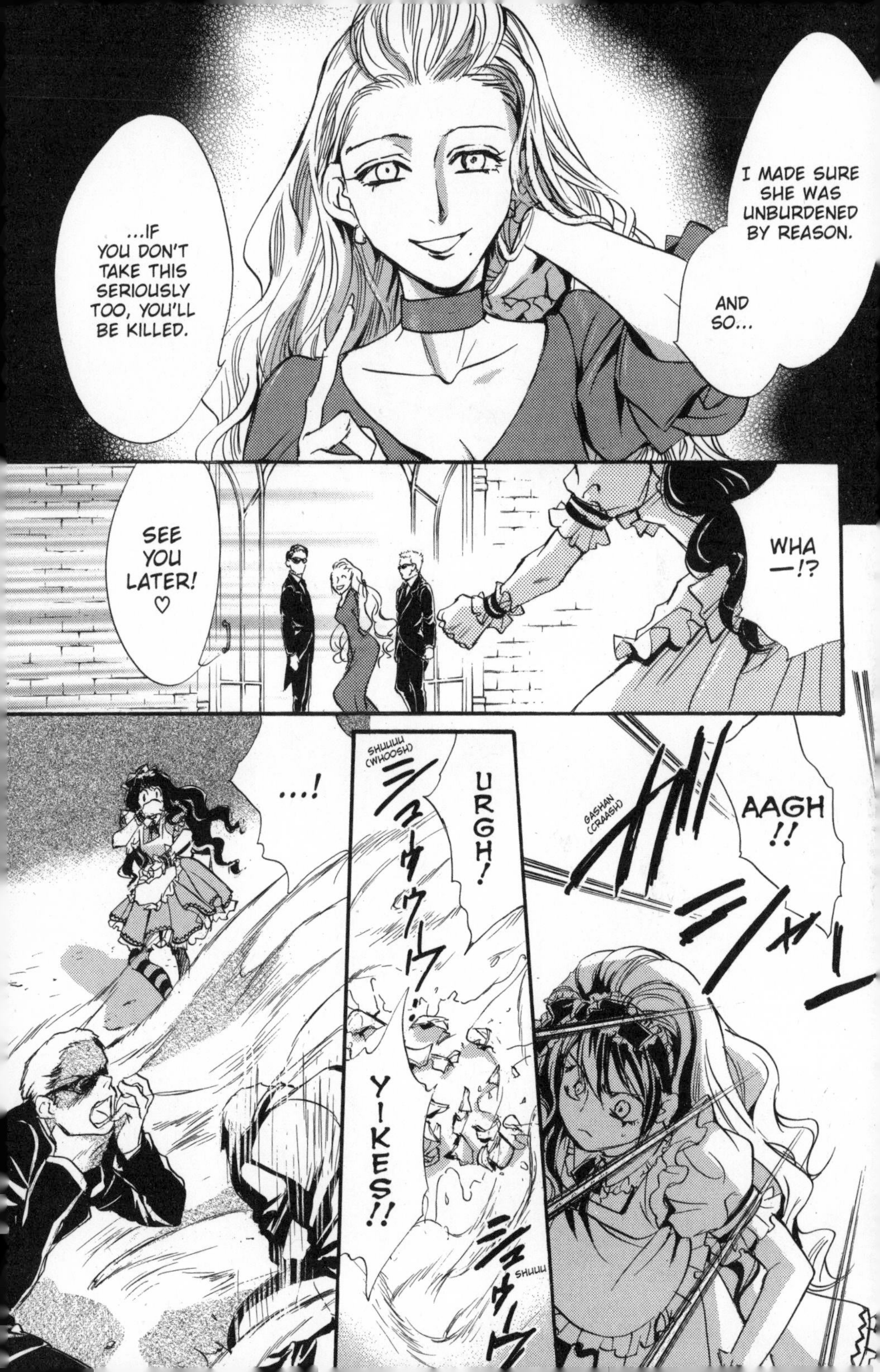

I MADE SURE SHE WAS UNBURDENED BY REASON.
AND SO...
...IF YOU DON'T TAKE THIS SERIOUSLY TOO, YOU'LL BE KILLED.
WHA—!?
SEE YOU LATER! ♡
GASHAN (CRAASH)
AAGH!!
SHUUU
SHUUUU (WHOOSH)
URGH!
YIKES!!
...!

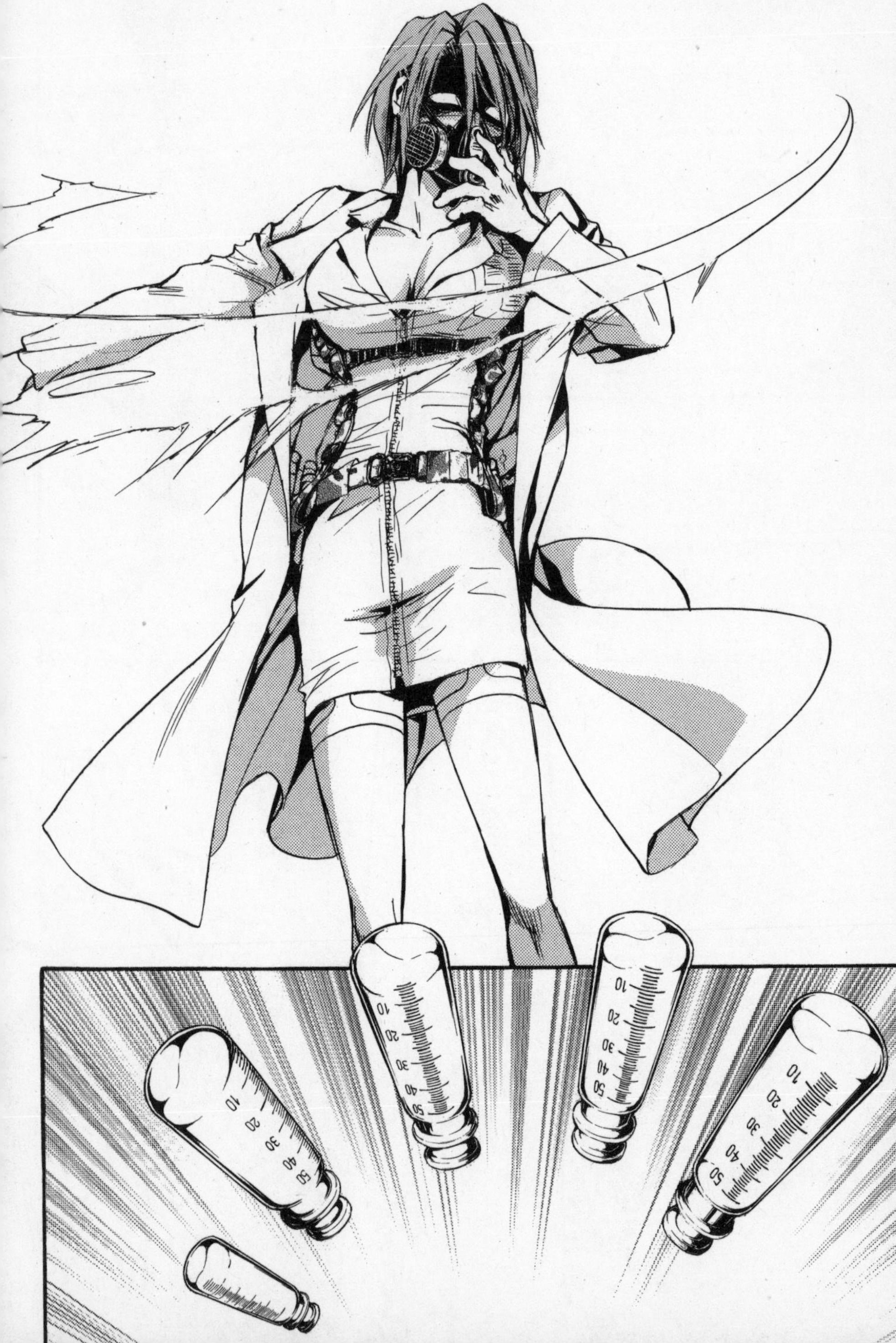

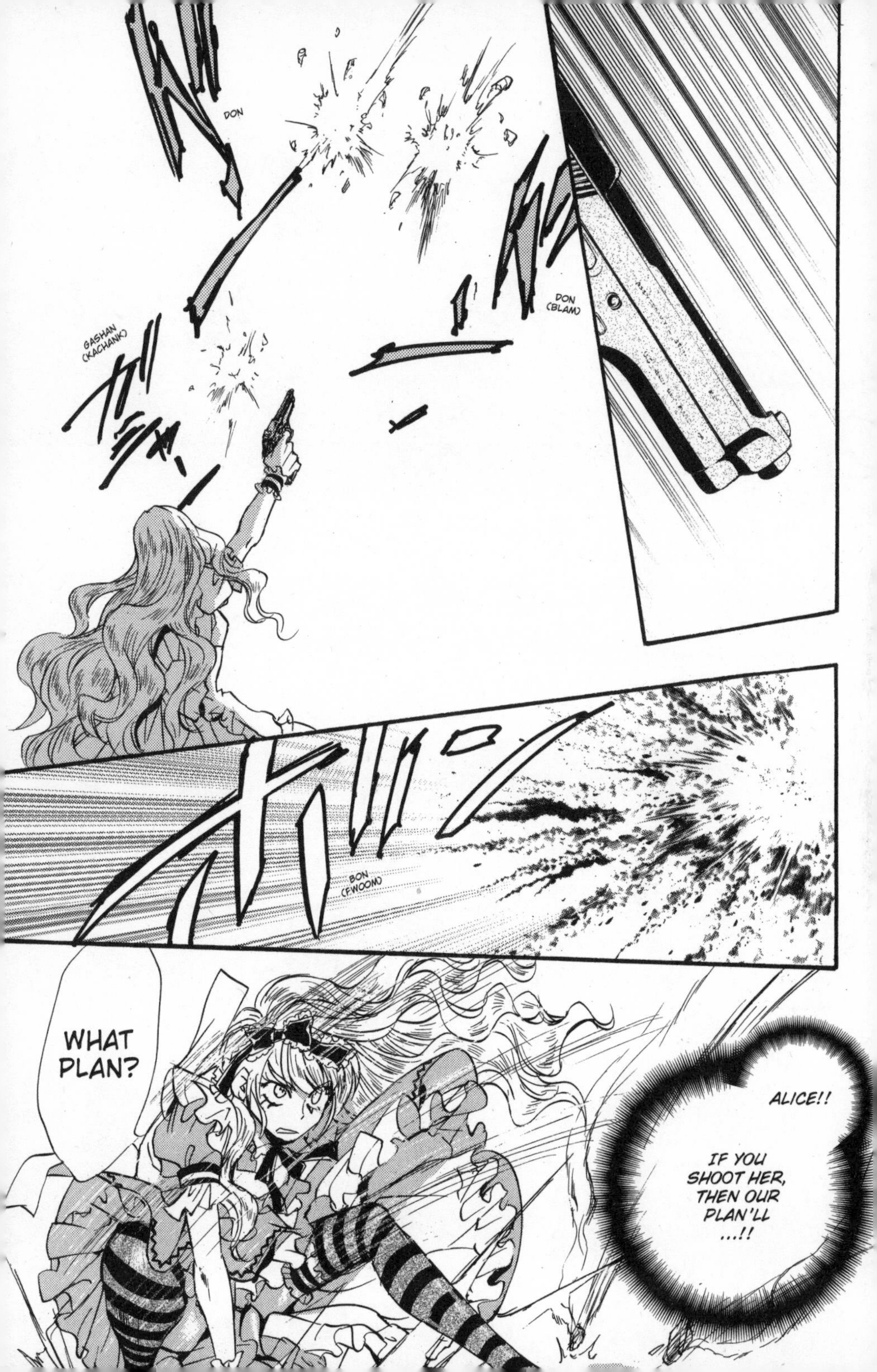
DON
DON (BLAM)
GASHAN (KACHANK)
BON (FWOOM)
ALICE!!
IF YOU SHOOT HER, THEN OUR PLAN'LL ...!!
WHAT PLAN?

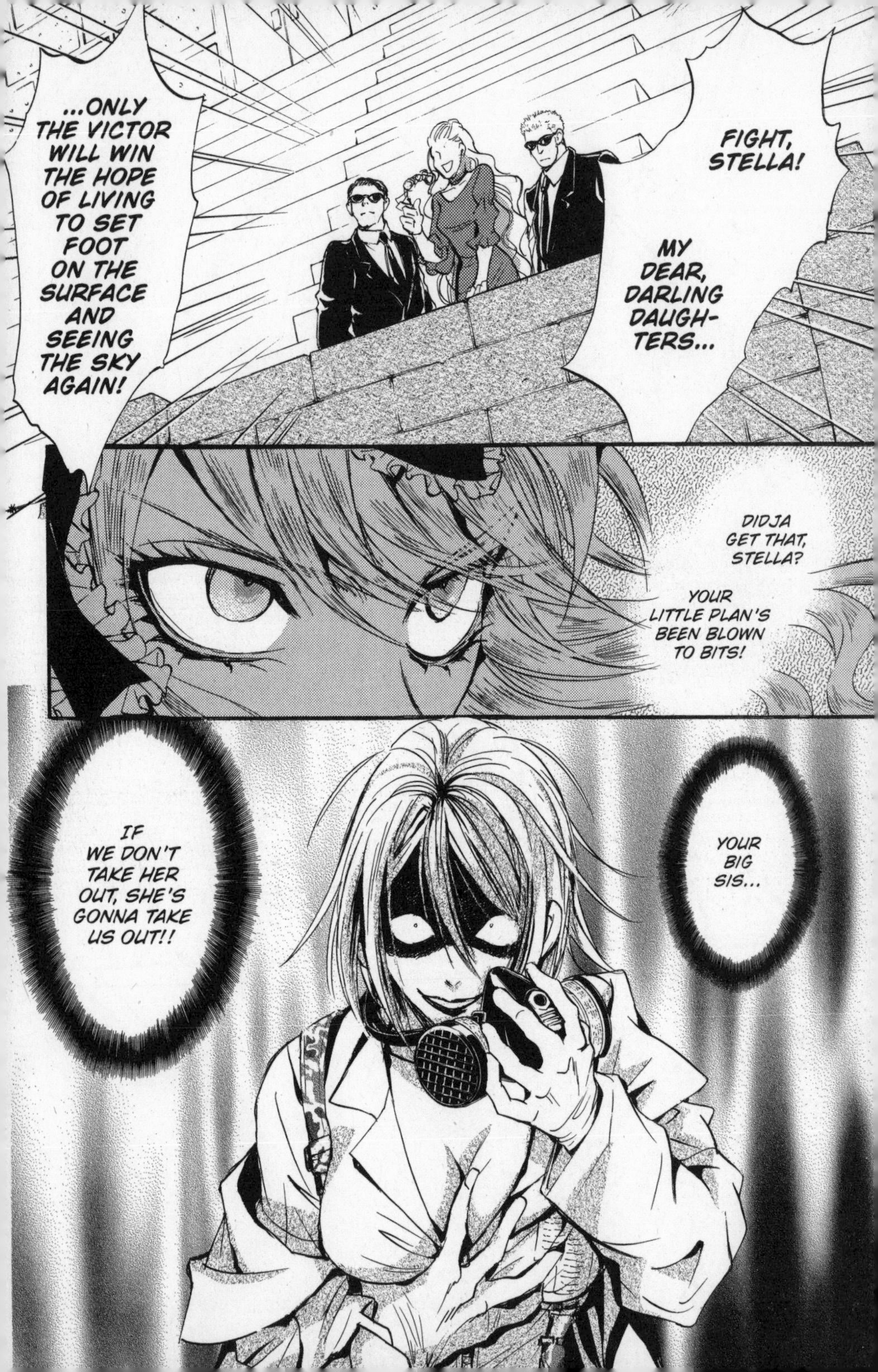
FIGHT, STELLA!
MY DEAR, DARLING DAUGHTERS...
...ONLY THE VICTOR WILL WIN THE HOPE OF LIVING TO SET FOOT ON THE SURFACE AND SEEING THE SKY AGAIN!
DIDJA GET THAT, STELLA?
YOUR LITTLE PLAN'S BEEN BLOWN TO BITS!
YOUR BIG SIS...
IF WE DON'T TAKE HER OUT, SHE'S GONNA TAKE US OUT!!

Alice in MURDERLAND

Alice in Murderland

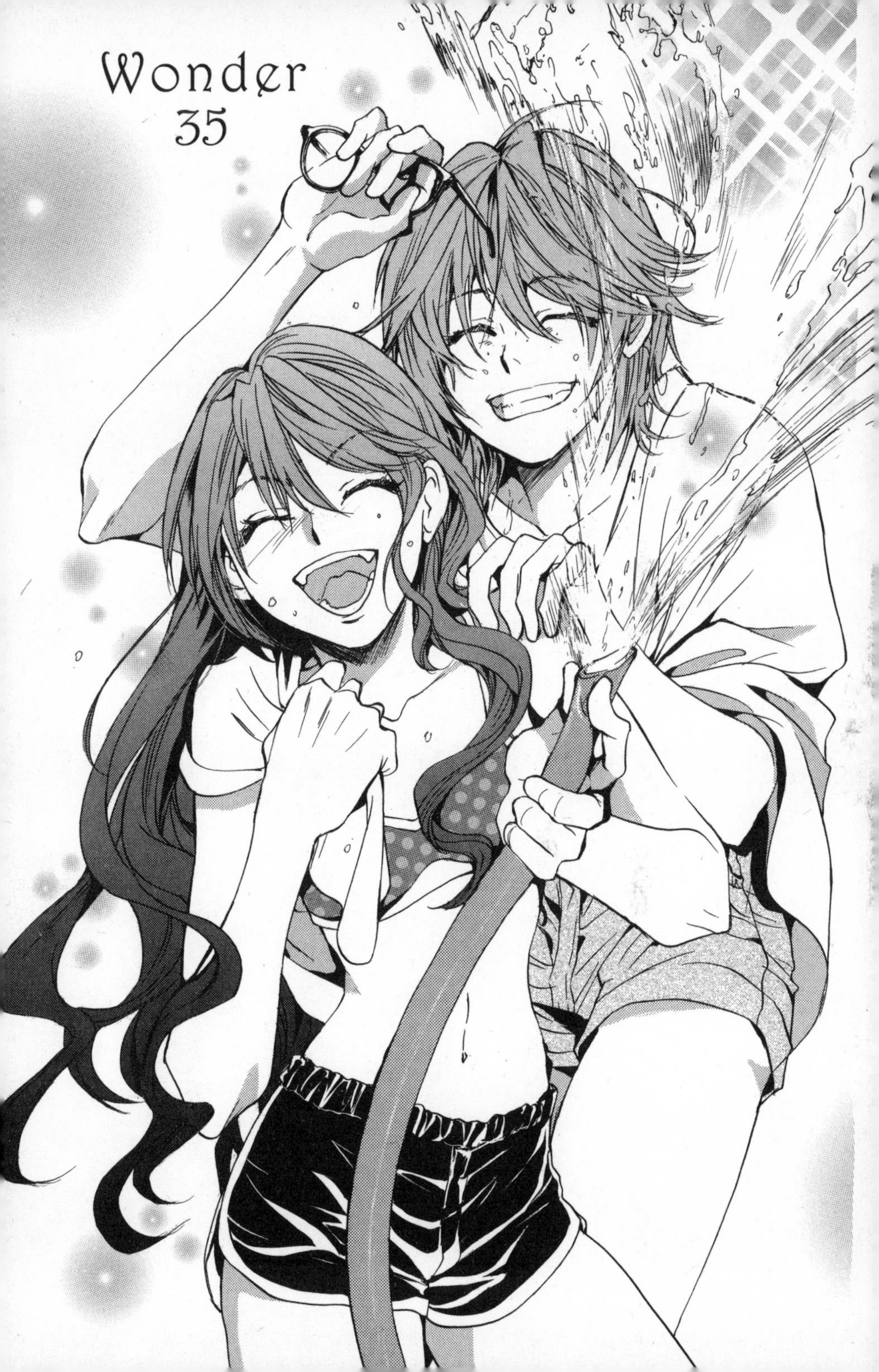
Wonder
35

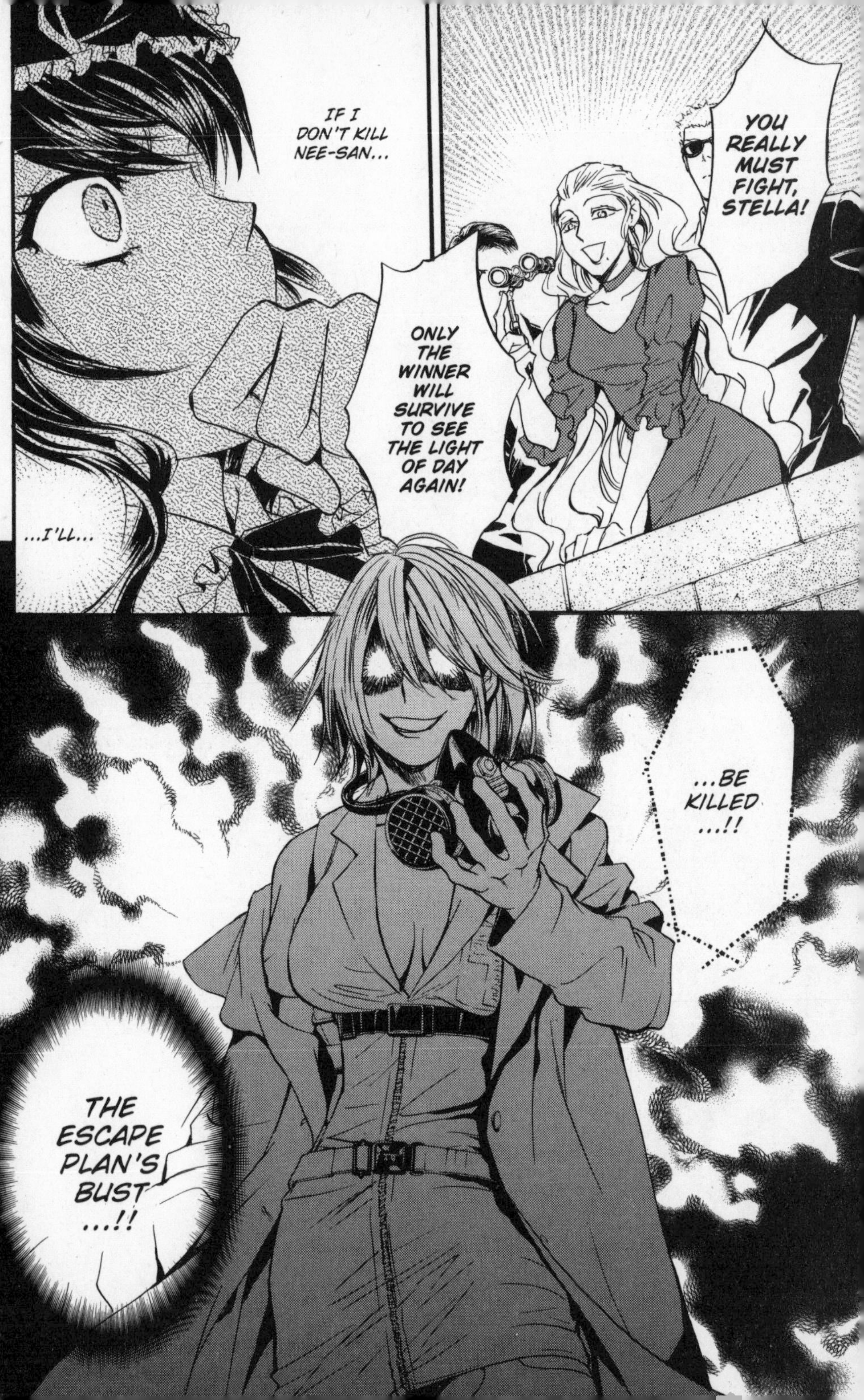
YOU REALLY MUST FIGHT, STELLA!
ONLY THE WINNER WILL SURVIVE TO SEE THE LIGHT OF DAY AGAIN!
IF I DON'T KILL NEE-SAN...
...I'LL...
...BE KILLED...!!
THE ESCAPE PLAN'S BUST...!!

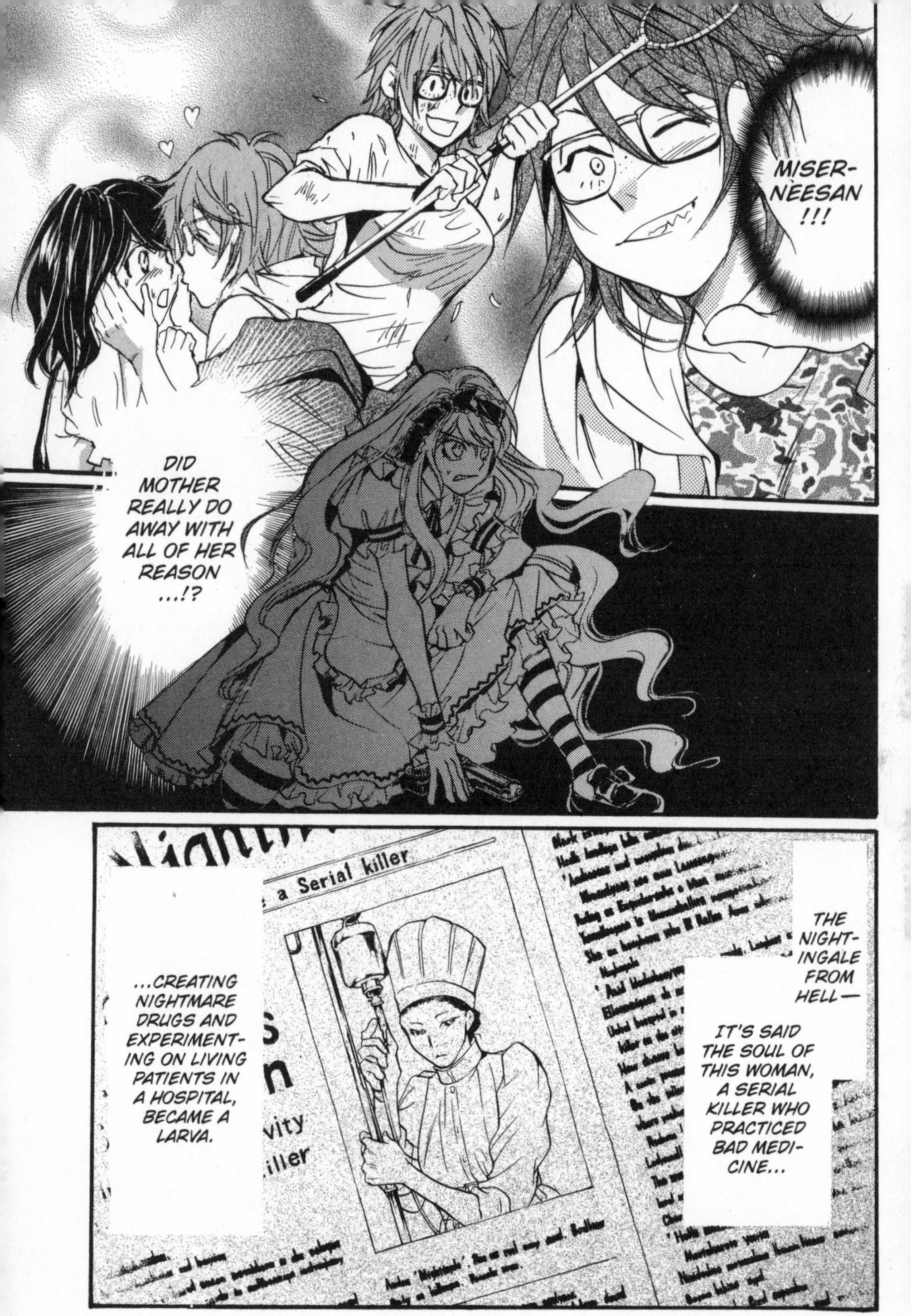
MISER-NEESAN!!!
DID MOTHER REALLY DO AWAY WITH ALL OF HER REASON...!?
THE NIGHT-INGALE FROM HELL—
IT'S SAID THE SOUL OF THIS WOMAN, A SERIAL KILLER WHO PRACTICED BAD MEDI-CINE...
...CREATING NIGHTMARE DRUGS AND EXPERIMENT-ING ON LIVING PATIENTS IN A HOSPITAL, BECAME A LARVA.
a Serial killer

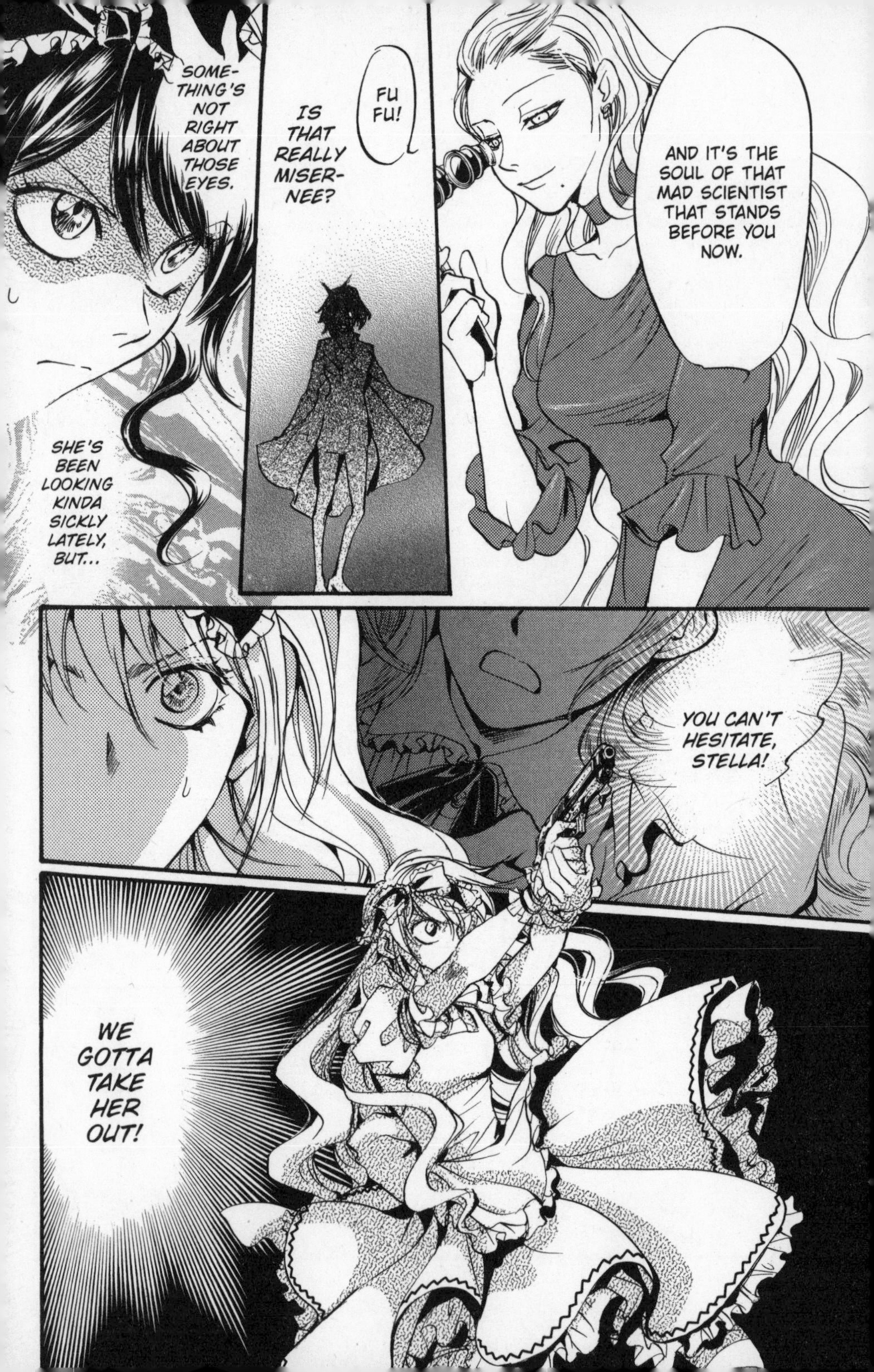
AND IT'S THE SOUL OF THAT MAD SCIENTIST THAT STANDS BEFORE YOU NOW.
FU FU!
IS THAT REALLY MISERNEE?
SOMETHING'S NOT RIGHT ABOUT THOSE EYES.
SHE'S BEEN LOOKING KINDA SICKLY LATELY, BUT...
YOU CAN'T HESITATE, STELLA!
WE GOTTA TAKE HER OUT!

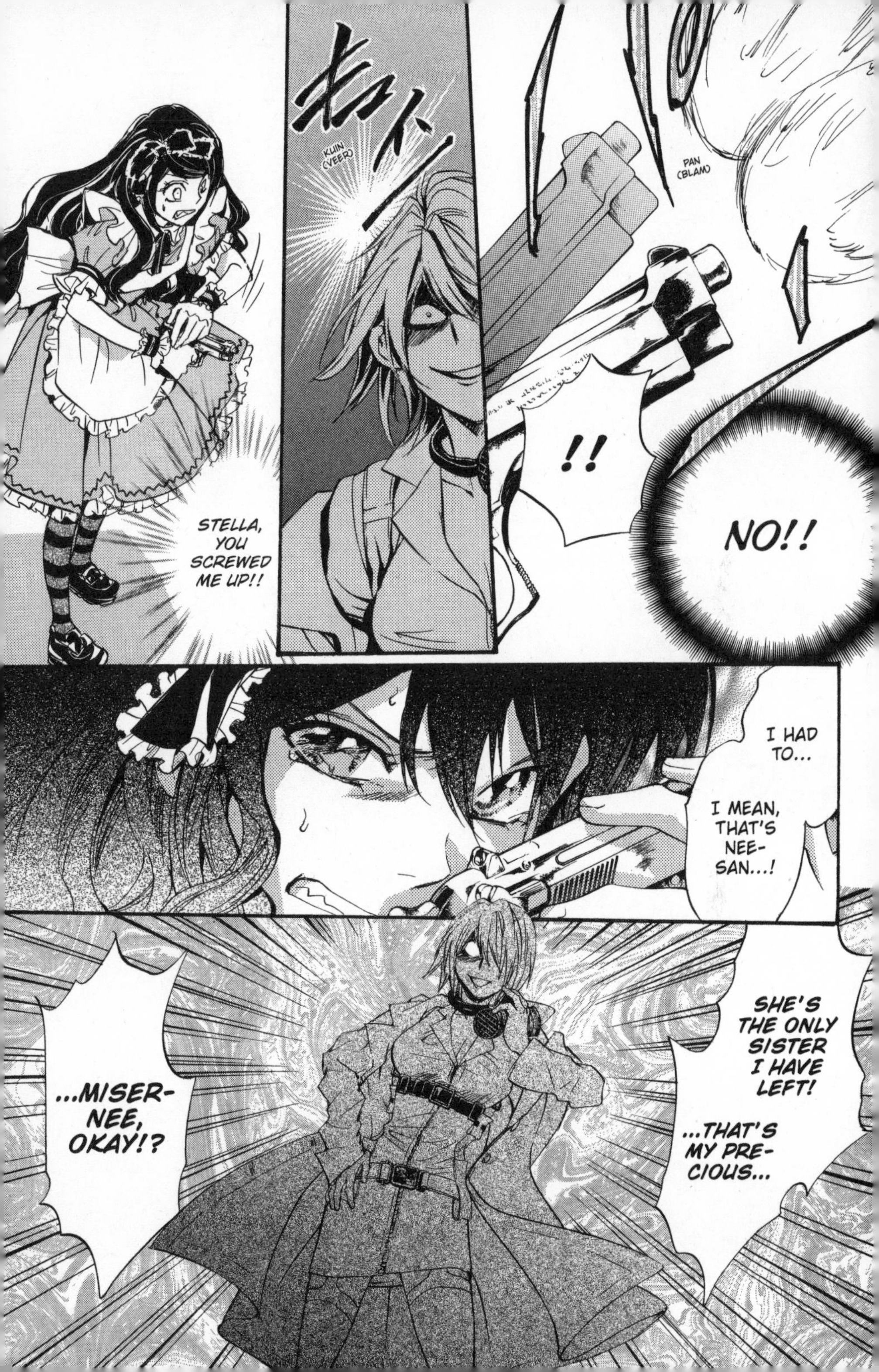
PAN (BLAM)
!!
NO!!
KUIN (VEER)
STELLA, YOU SCREWED ME UP!!
I HAD TO...
I MEAN, THAT'S NEE-SAN...!
SHE'S THE ONLY SISTER I HAVE LEFT!
...THAT'S MY PRECIOUS...
...MISER-NEE, OKAY!?

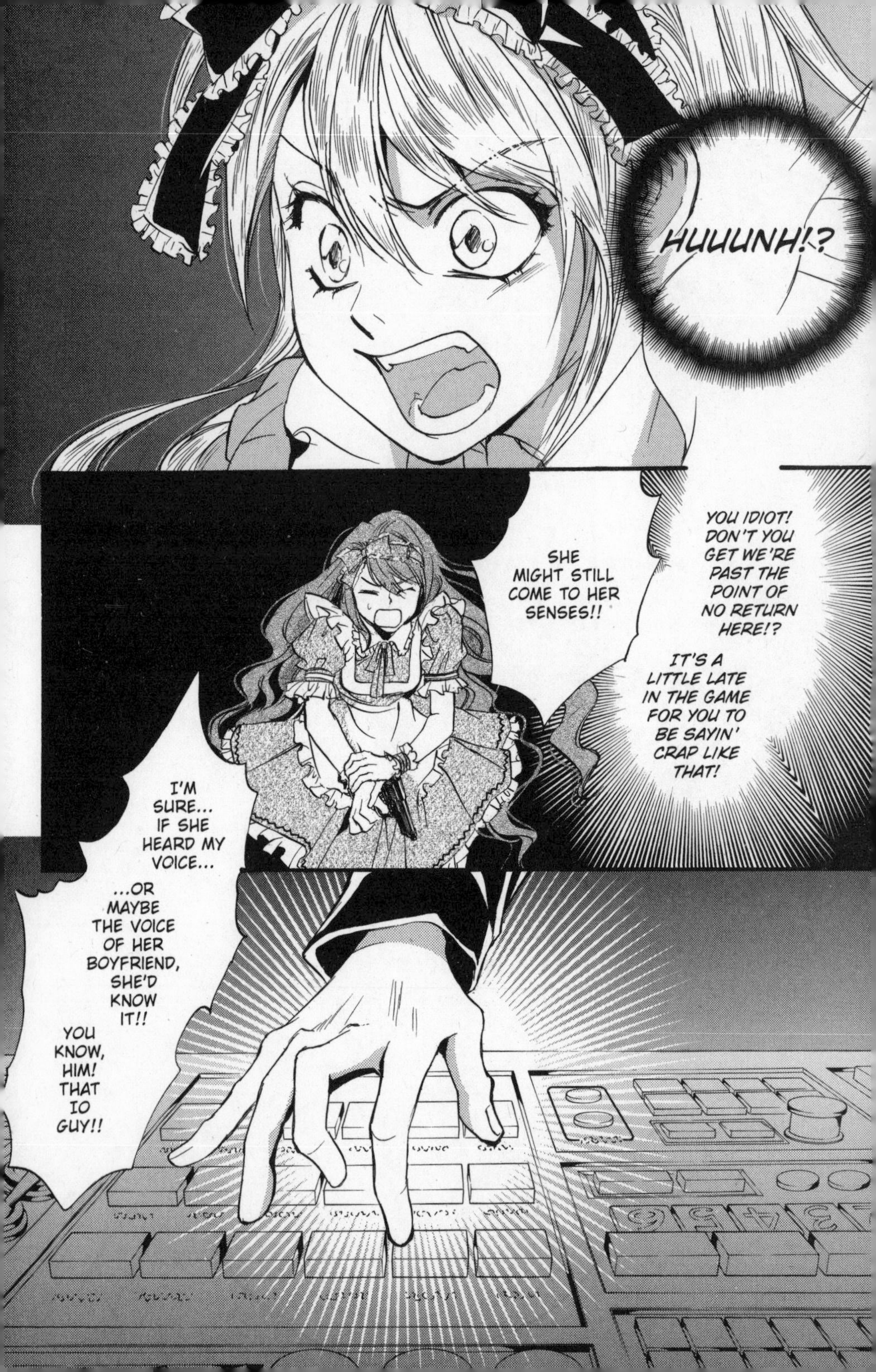
HUUUNH!?
YOU IDIOT! DON'T YOU GET WE'RE PAST THE POINT OF NO RETURN HERE!?
IT'S A LITTLE LATE IN THE GAME FOR YOU TO BE SAYIN' CRAP LIKE THAT!
SHE MIGHT STILL COME TO HER SENSES!!
I'M SURE... IF SHE HEARD MY VOICE...
...OR MAYBE THE VOICE OF HER BOYFRIEND, SHE'D KNOW IT!!
YOU KNOW, HIM! THAT IO GUY!!

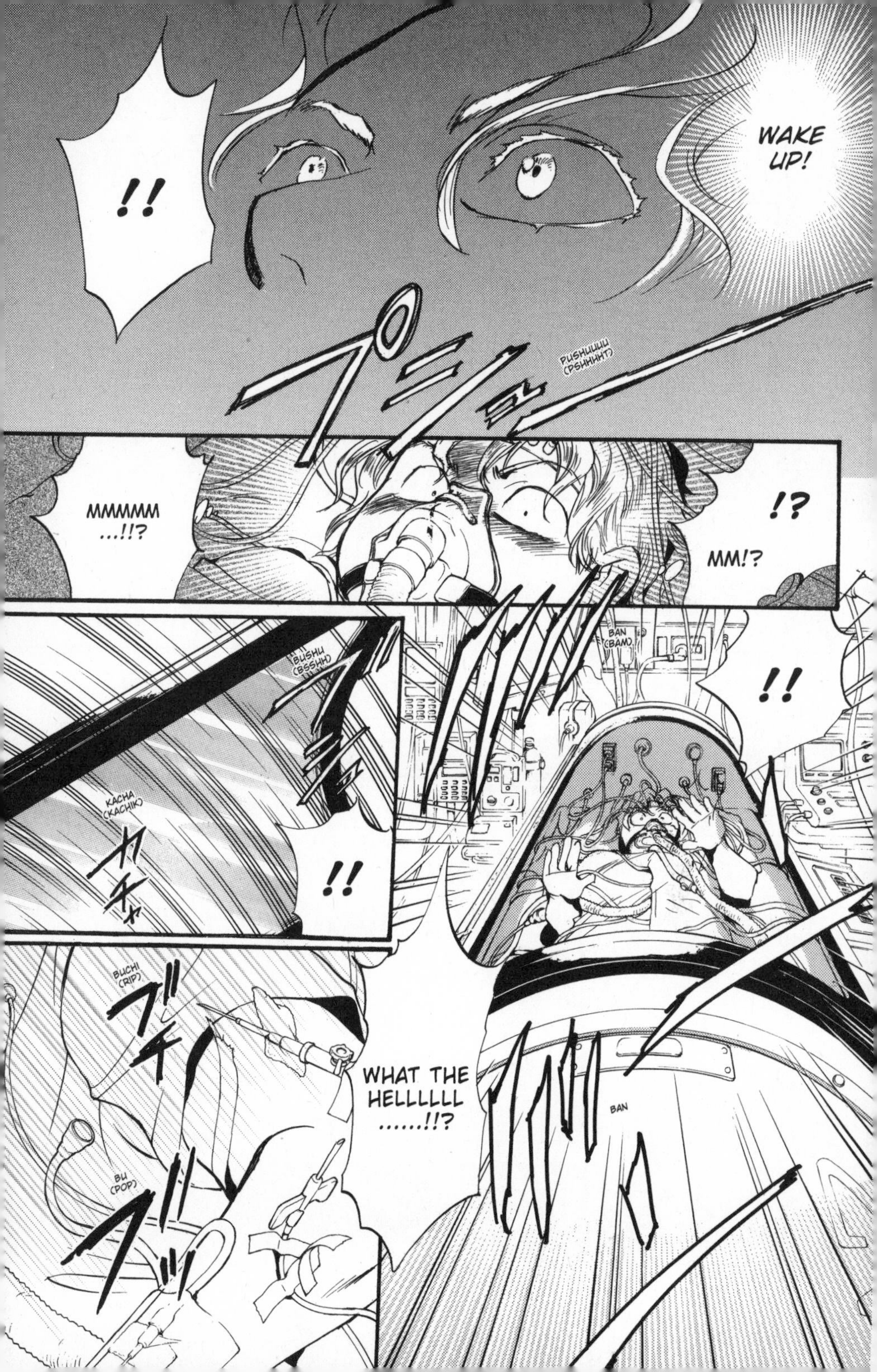
WAKE UP!
!!
PUSHUUUU (PSHHHHT)
!?
MM!?
MMMMM ...!!?
BAN (BAM)
!!
BUSHU (BSSHH)
KACHA (KACHIK)
!!
BAN
WHAT THE HELLLLLLL ......!!?
BUCHI (RIP)
BU (POP)

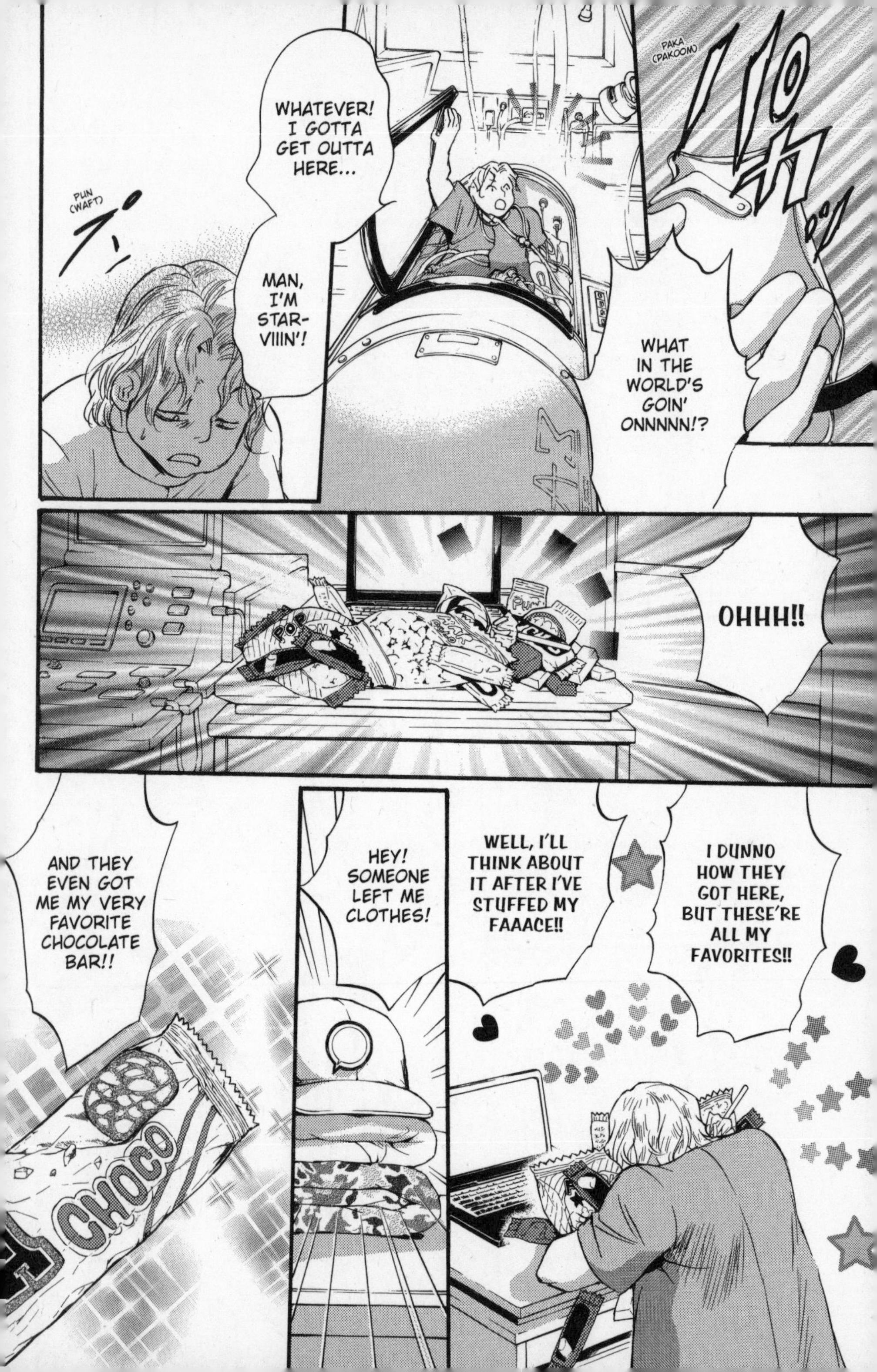
PAKA (PAKOOM)
WHAT IN THE WORLD'S GOIN' ONNNNN!?
WHATEVER! I GOTTA GET OUTTA HERE...
MAN, I'M STAR-VIIIN'!
PUN (WAFT)
OHHH!!
I DUNNO HOW THEY GOT HERE, BUT THESE'RE ALL MY FAVORITES!!
WELL, I'LL THINK ABOUT IT AFTER I'VE STUFFED MY FAAACE!!
HEY! SOMEONE LEFT ME CLOTHES!
AND THEY EVEN GOT ME MY VERY FAVORITE CHOCOLATE BAR!!
CHOCO

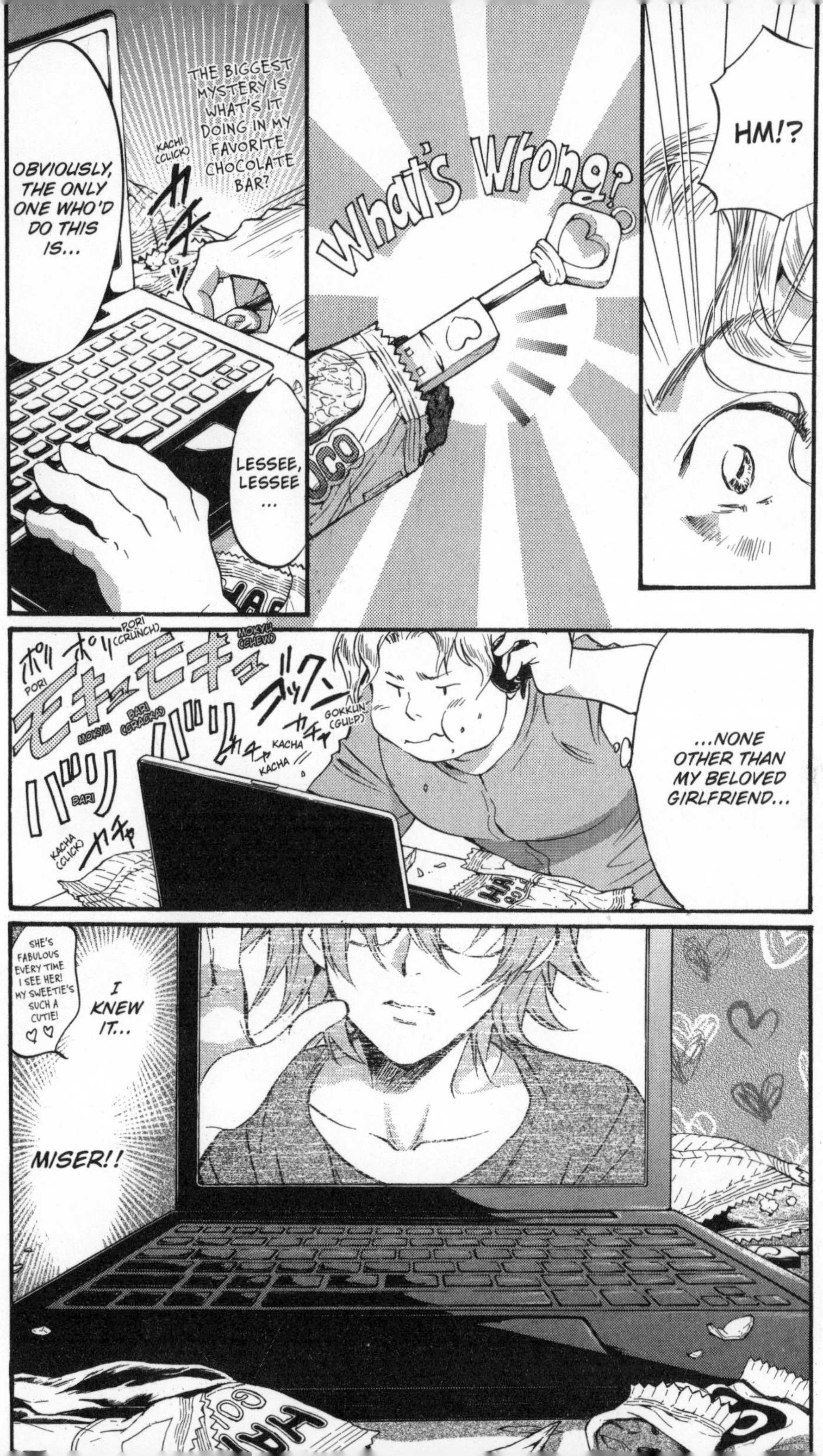
HM!?
What's Wrong?
THE BIGGEST MYSTERY IS WHAT'S IT DOING IN MY FAVORITE CHOCOLATE BAR?
OBVIOUSLY, THE ONLY ONE WHO'D DO THIS IS...
KACHI (CLICK)
LESSEE, LESSEE ...
...NONE OTHER THAN MY BELOVED GIRLFRIEND...
GOKKUN (GULP)
KACHA KACHA
MOKYU (CHEW)
PORI (CRUNCH)
PORI
MOKYU
BARI (CRACK)
BARI
KACHA (CLICK)
SHE'S FABULOUS EVERY TIME I SEE HER! MY SWEETIE'S SUCH A CUTIE! ♡ ♡
I KNEW IT...
MISER!!

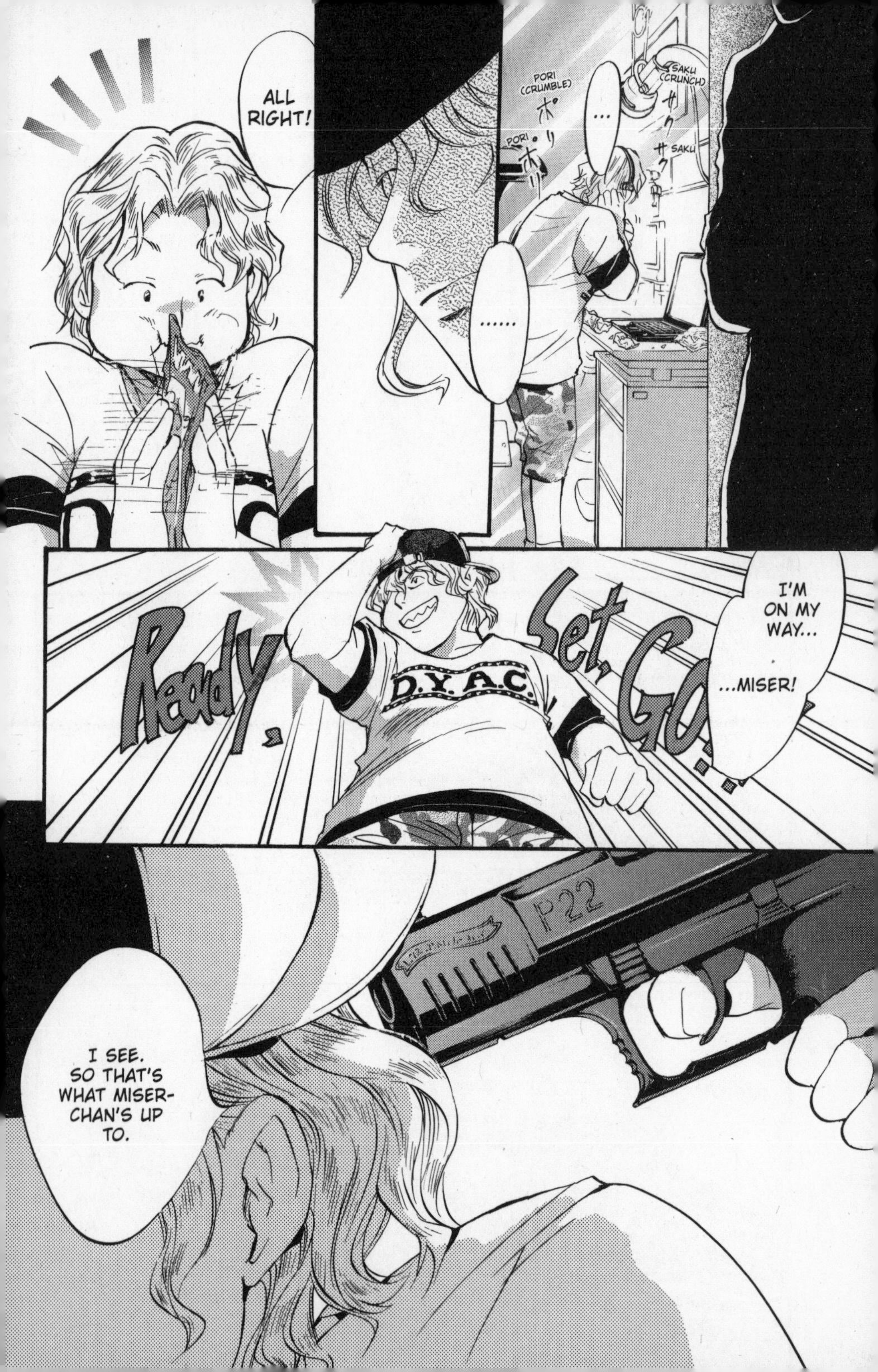
PORI (CRUMBLE)
ポリ
PORI
ポリ
SAKU (CRUNCH)
サク
SAKU
サク
...
......
ALL RIGHT!
I'M ON MY WAY...
...MISER!
Ready, Set, GO!!
D.Y.A.C.
P22
I SEE. SO THAT'S WHAT MISER-CHAN'S UP TO.

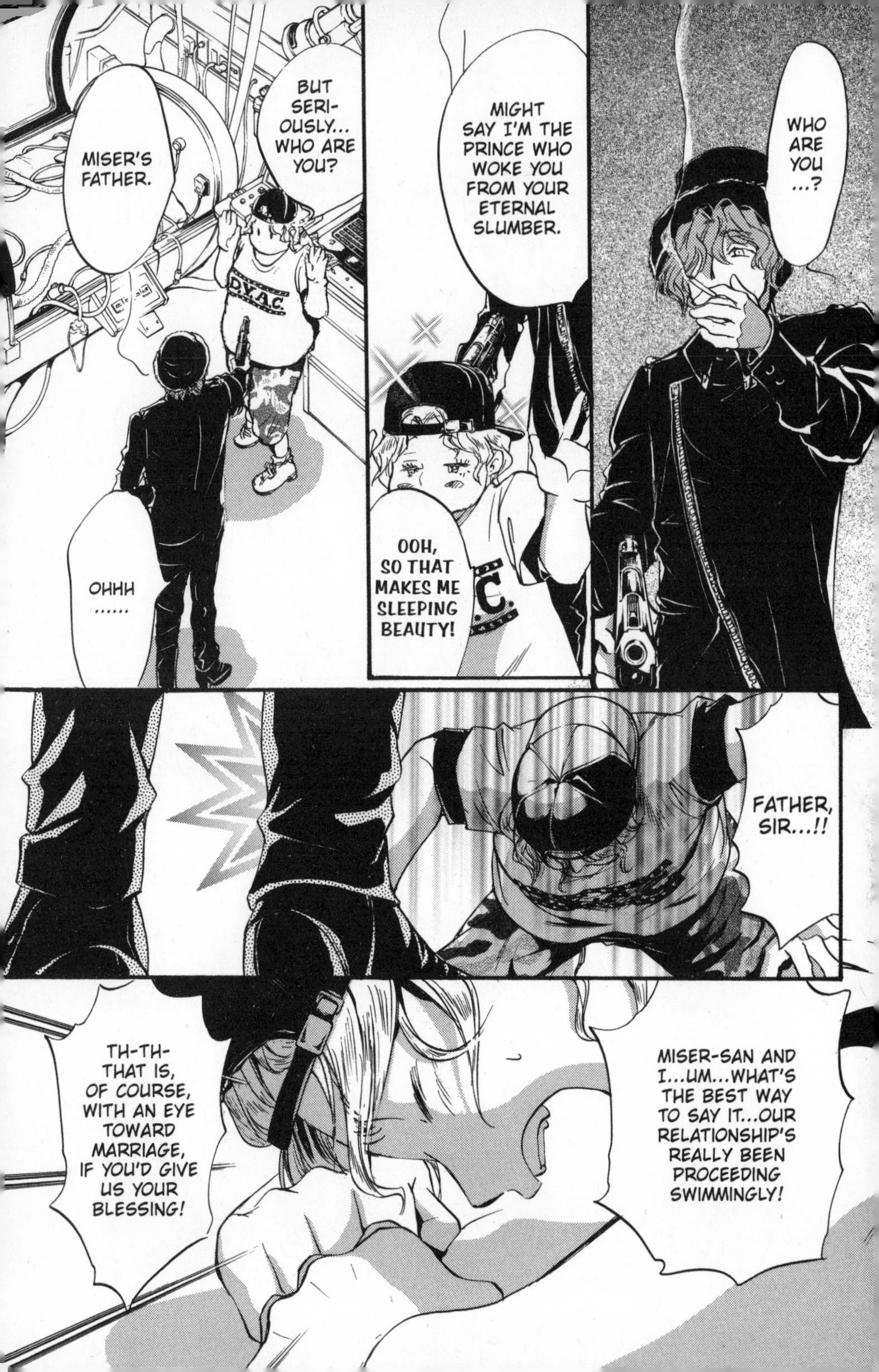
WHO ARE YOU ...?
MIGHT SAY I'M THE PRINCE WHO WOKE YOU FROM YOUR ETERNAL SLUMBER.
OOH, SO THAT MAKES ME SLEEPING BEAUTY!
BUT SERI-OUSLY... WHO ARE YOU?
MISER'S FATHER.
OHHH ......
FATHER, SIR...!!
MISER-SAN AND I...UM...WHAT'S THE BEST WAY TO SAY IT...OUR RELATIONSHIP'S REALLY BEEN PROCEEDING SWIMMINGLY!
TH-TH-THAT IS, OF COURSE, WITH AN EYE TOWARD MARRIAGE, IF YOU'D GIVE US YOUR BLESSING!

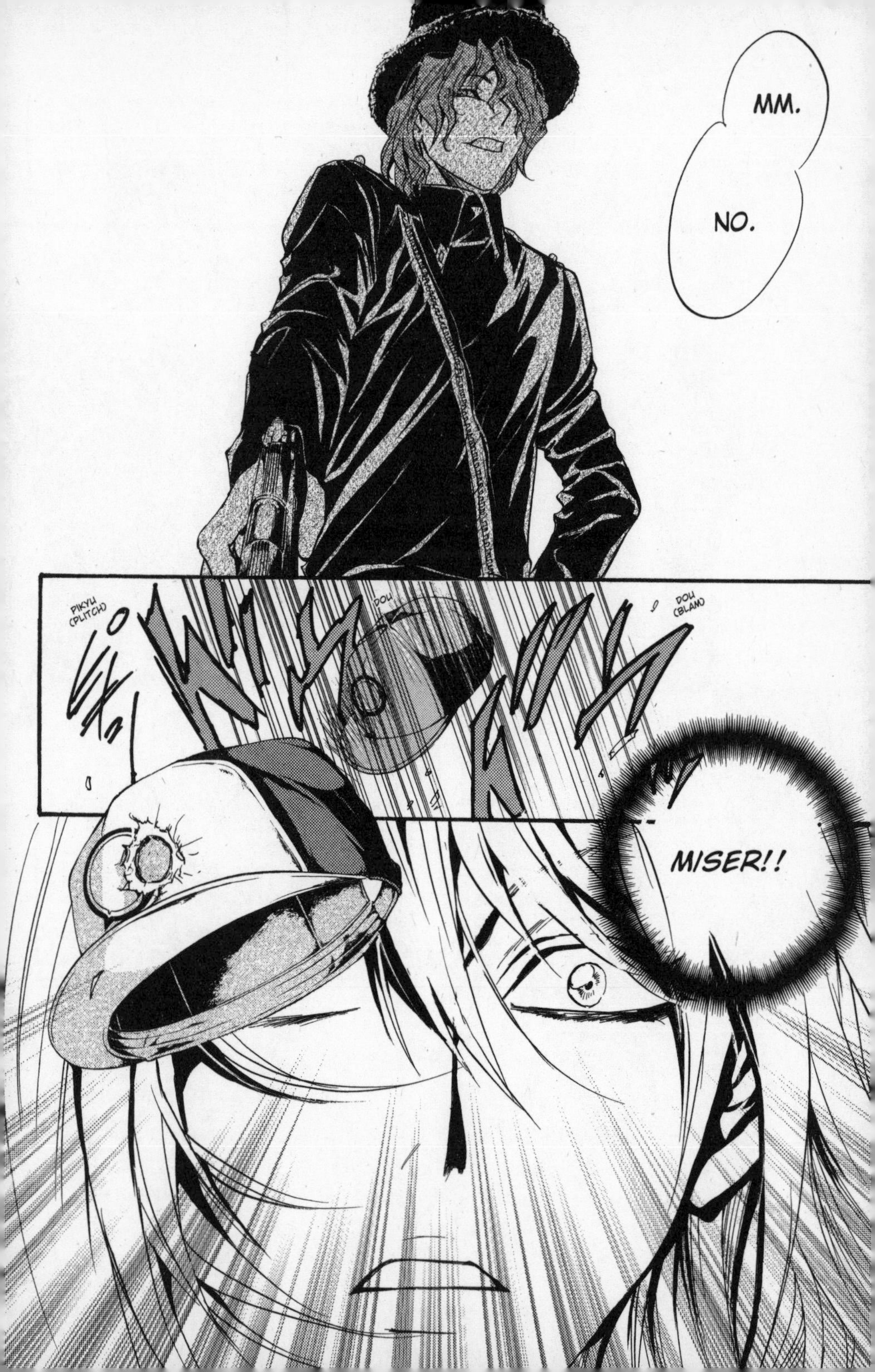
MM.
NO.
DOU (BLAM)
DOU
PIKYU (PLITCH)
MISER!!

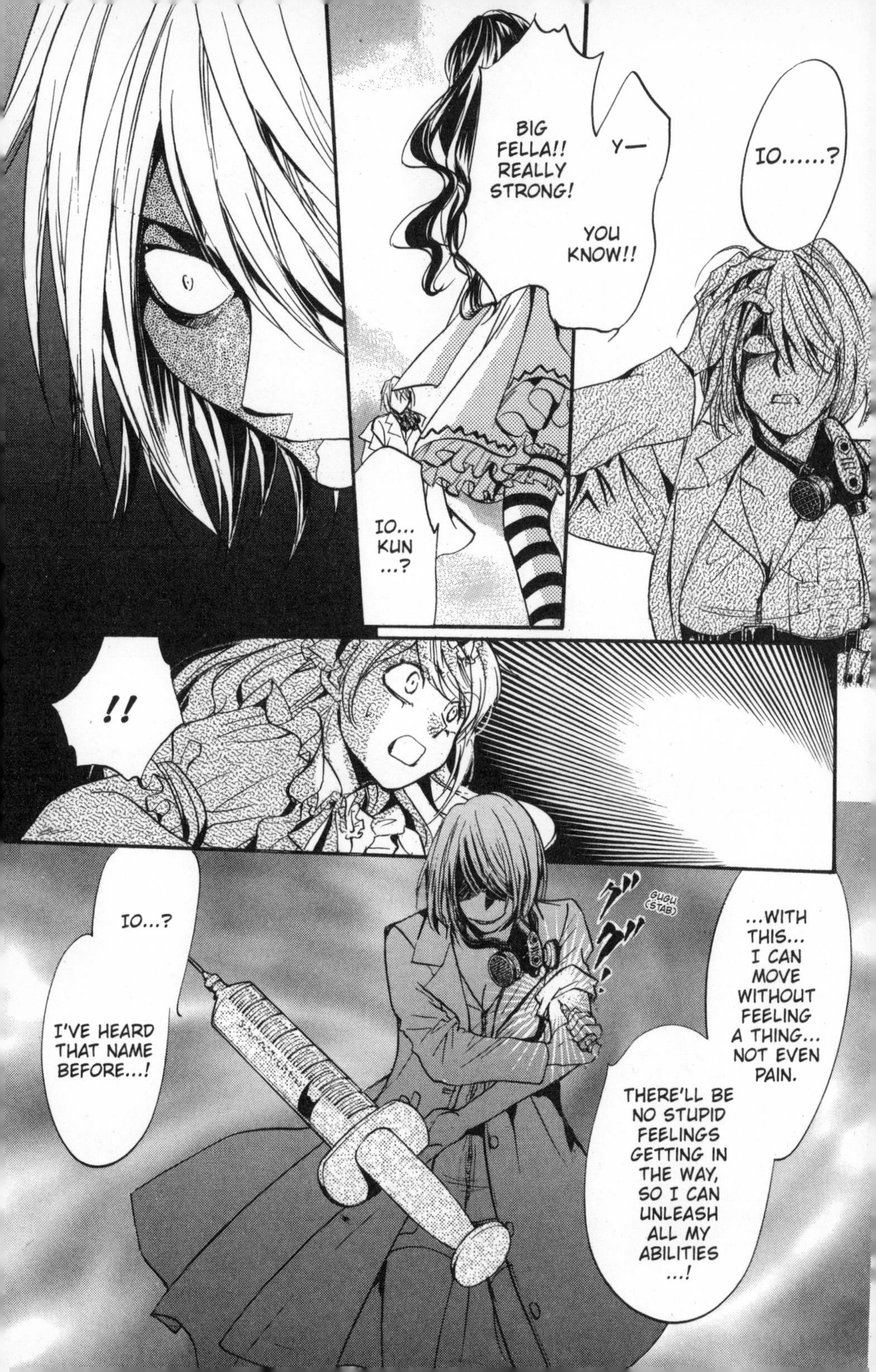
IO......?
Y— YOU KNOW!!
BIG FELLA!! REALLY STRONG!
IO... KUN ...?
!!
GUGU (STAB)
...WITH THIS... I CAN MOVE WITHOUT FEELING A THING... NOT EVEN PAIN.
THERE'LL BE NO STUPID FEELINGS GETTING IN THE WAY, SO I CAN UNLEASH ALL MY ABILITIES ...!
IO...? I'VE HEARD THAT NAME BEFORE...!

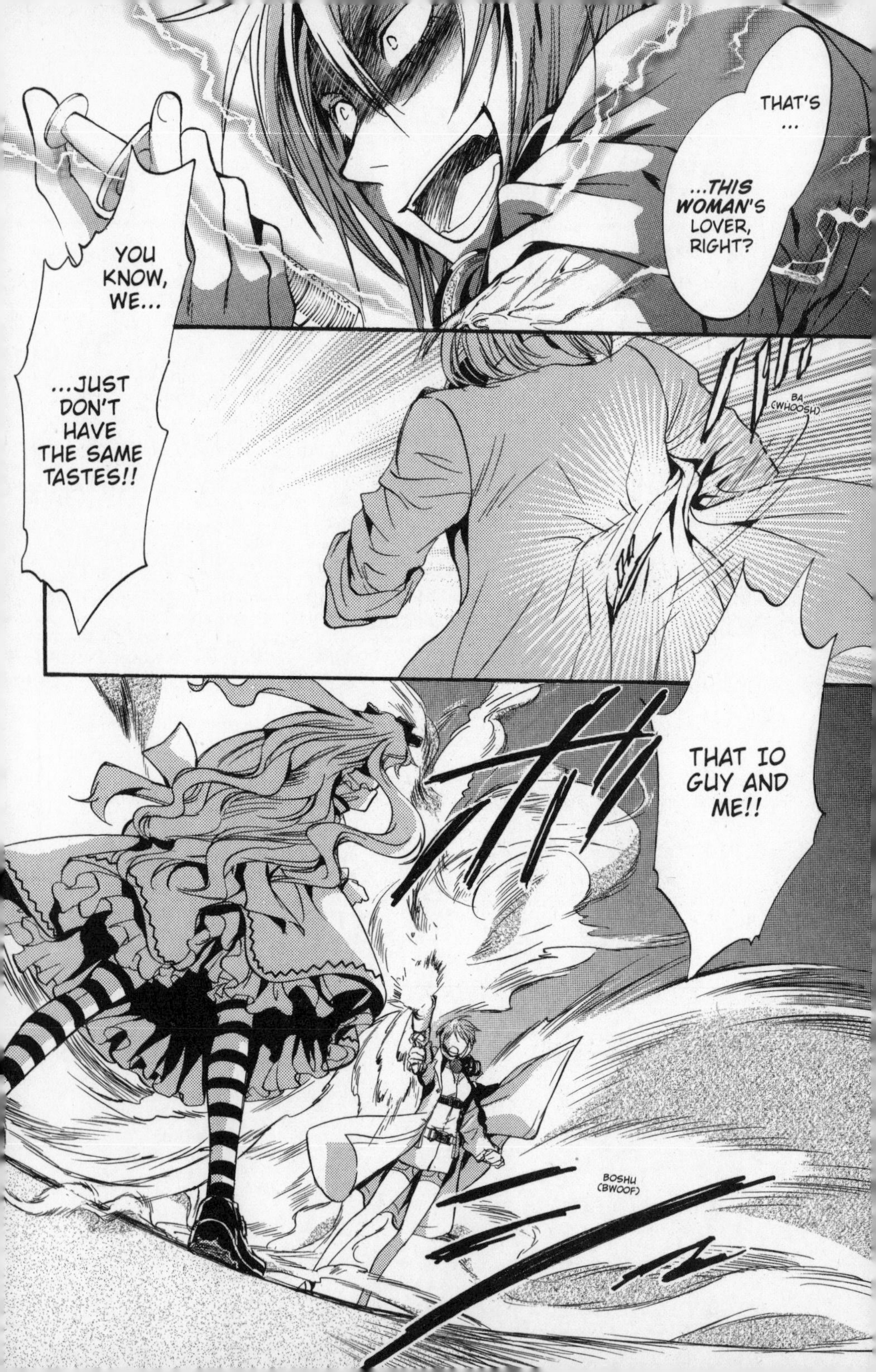
THAT'S ...
...*THIS WOMAN*'S LOVER, RIGHT?
YOU KNOW, WE...
...JUST DON'T HAVE THE SAME TASTES!!
BA (WHOOSH)
THAT IO GUY AND ME!!
BOSHU (BWOOF)

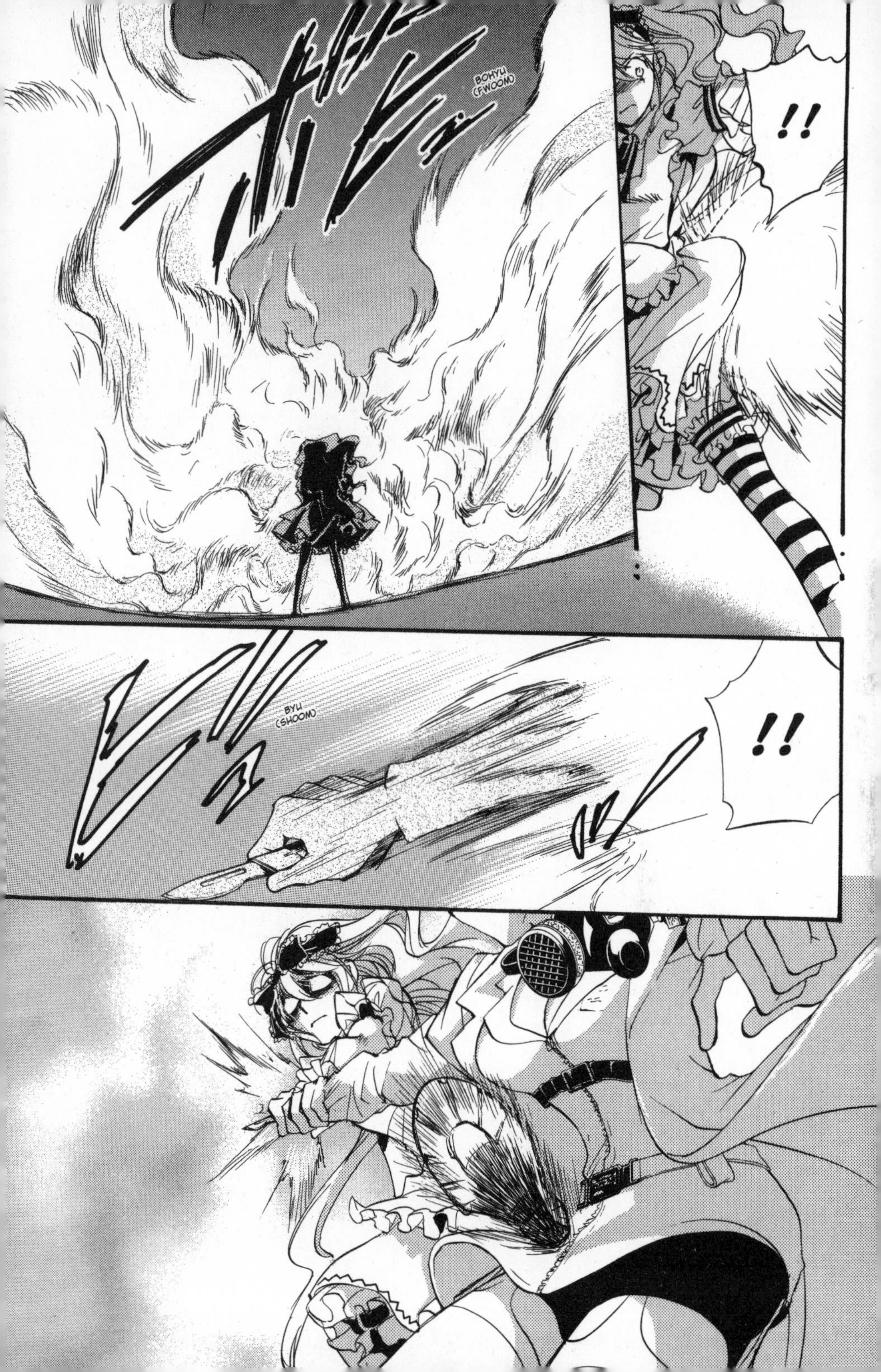
!!
BOHYU
(FWOOM)
!!
BYU
(SHOOM)

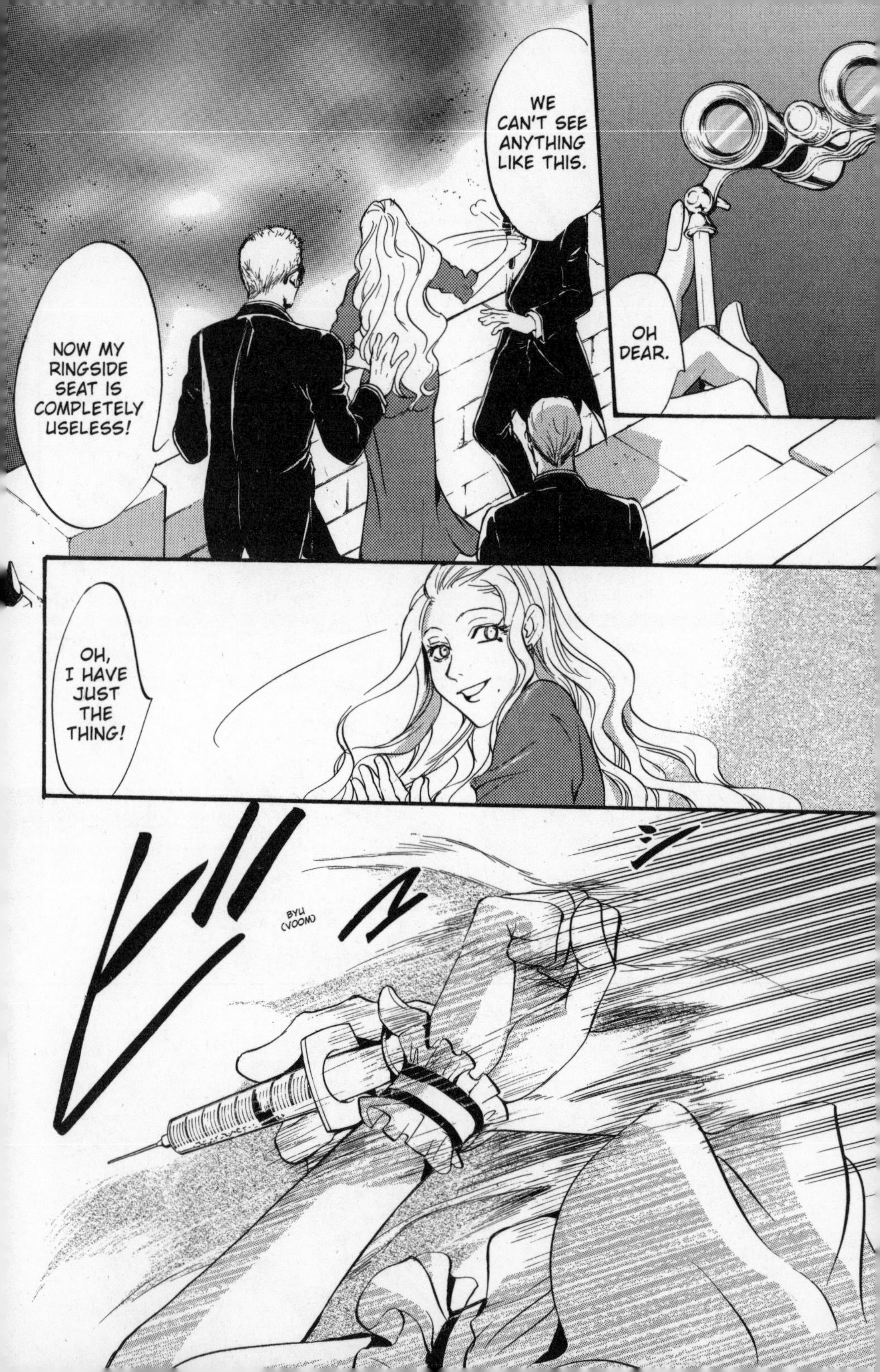
OH DEAR.
WE CAN'T SEE ANYTHING LIKE THIS.
NOW MY RINGSIDE SEAT IS COMPLETELY USELESS!
OH, I HAVE JUST THE THING!
BYU (VOOM)

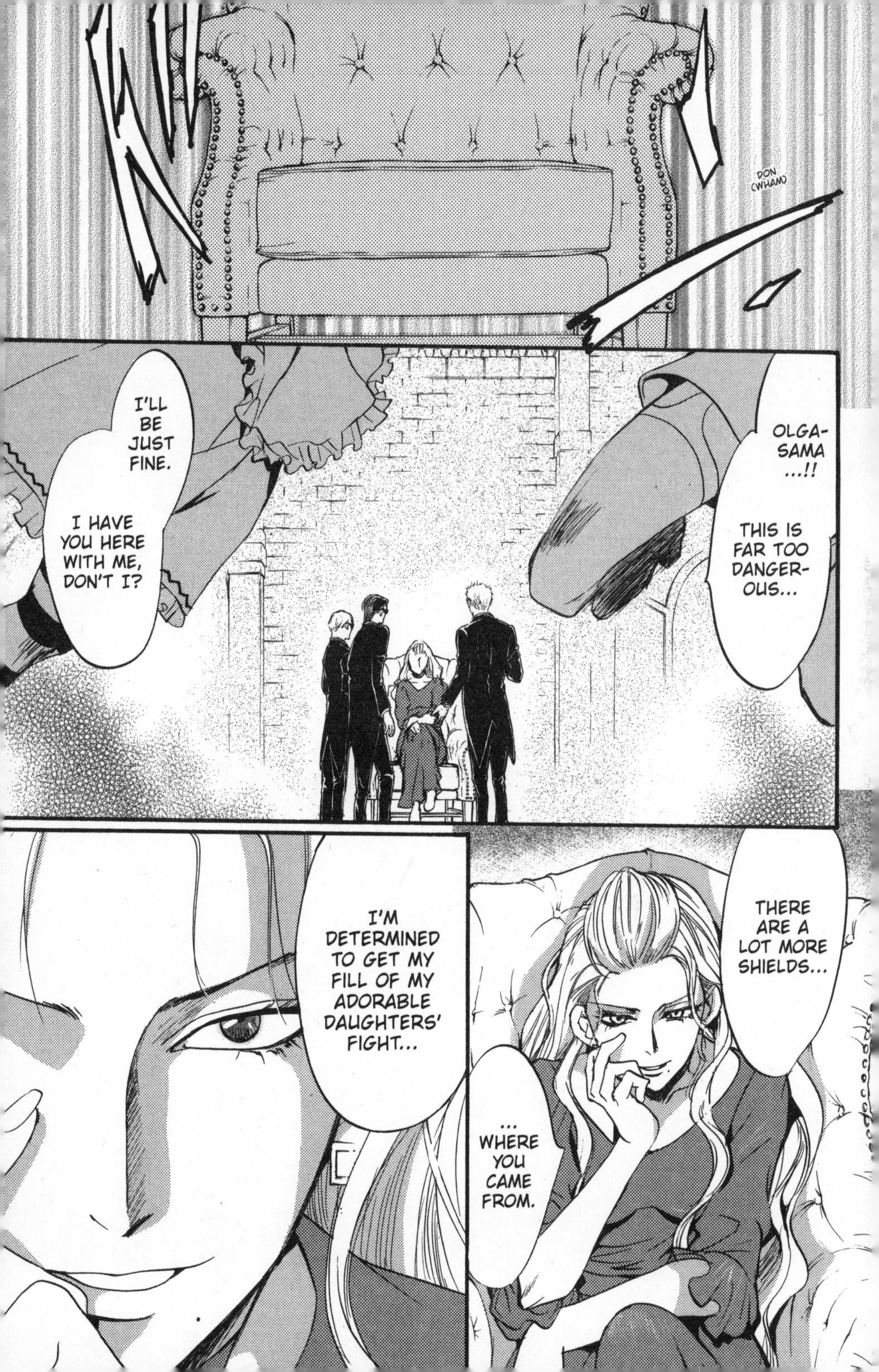
DON (WHAM)
OLGA-SAMA...!!
THIS IS FAR TOO DANGER-OUS...
I'LL BE JUST FINE.
I HAVE YOU HERE WITH ME, DON'T I?
THERE ARE A LOT MORE SHIELDS...
... WHERE YOU CAME FROM.
I'M DETERMINED TO GET MY FILL OF MY ADORABLE DAUGHTERS' FIGHT...

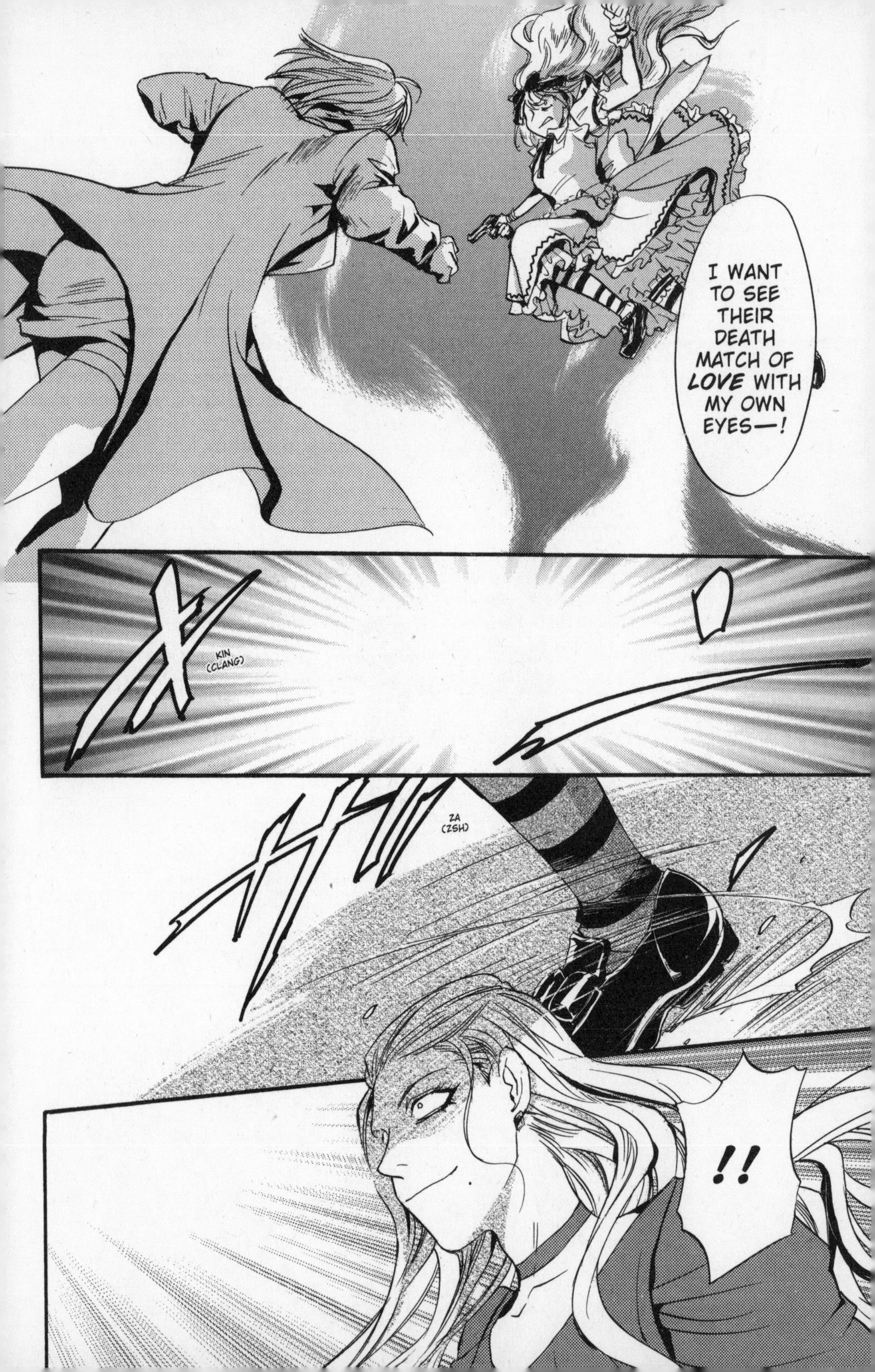
I WANT TO SEE THEIR DEATH MATCH OF LOVE WITH MY OWN EYES—!
KIN (CLANG)
ZA (ZSH)
!!

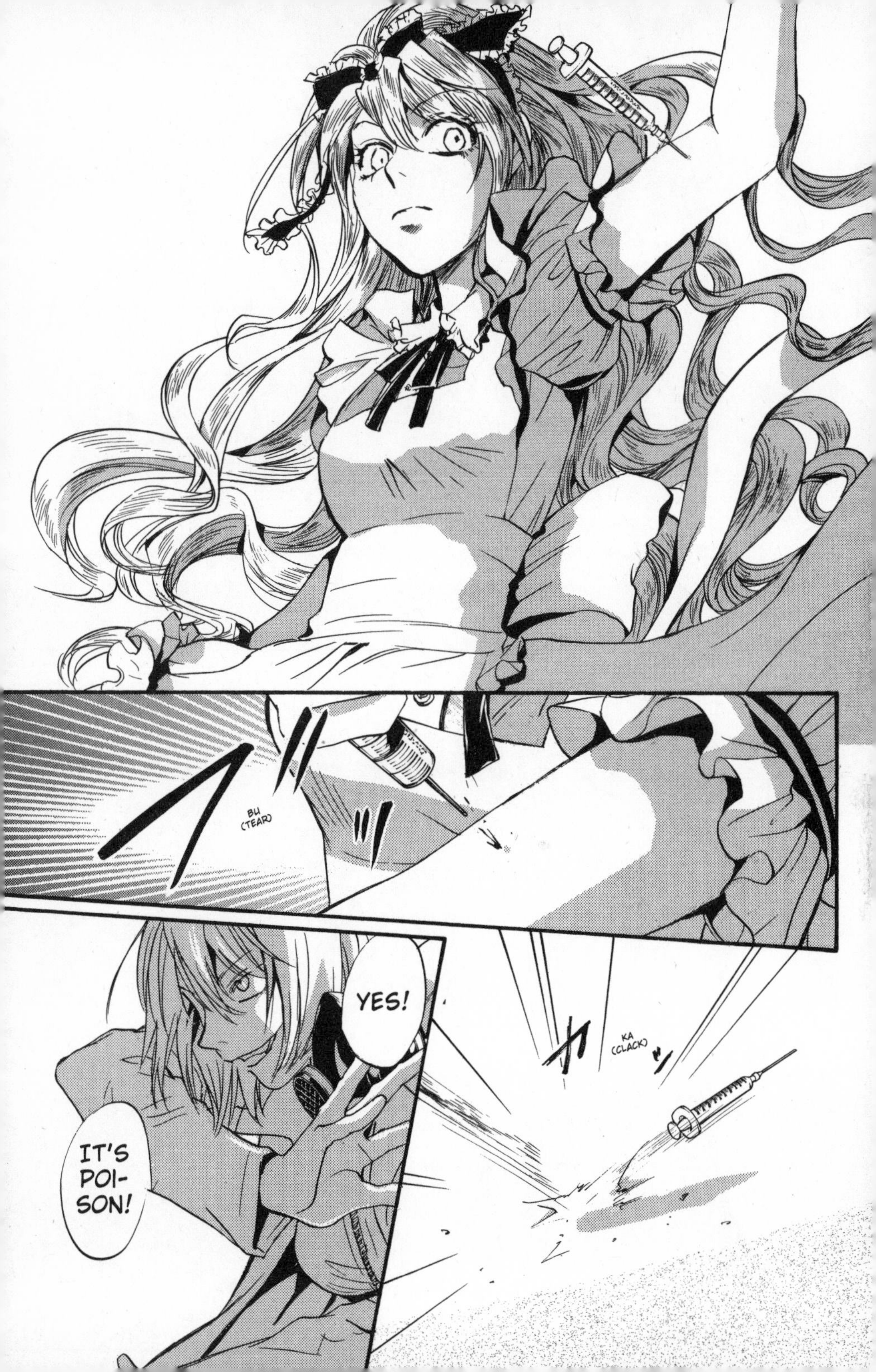
BU (TEAR)
YES!
IT'S POI- SON!
KA (CLACK)

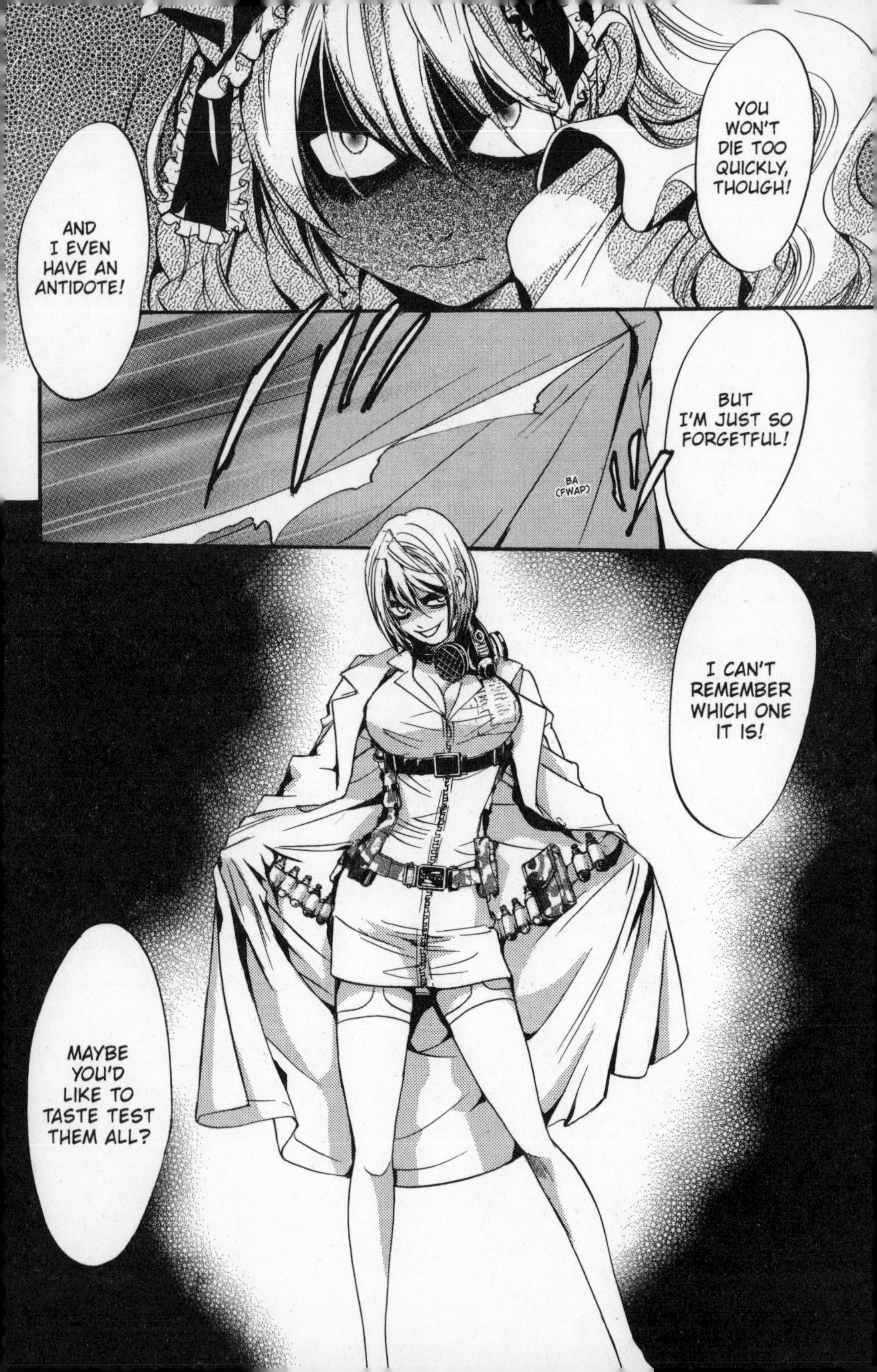
YOU WON'T DIE TOO QUICKLY, THOUGH!
AND I EVEN HAVE AN ANTIDOTE!
BUT I'M JUST SO FORGETFUL!
BA (FWAP)
I CAN'T REMEMBER WHICH ONE IT IS!
MAYBE YOU'D LIKE TO TASTE TEST THEM ALL?

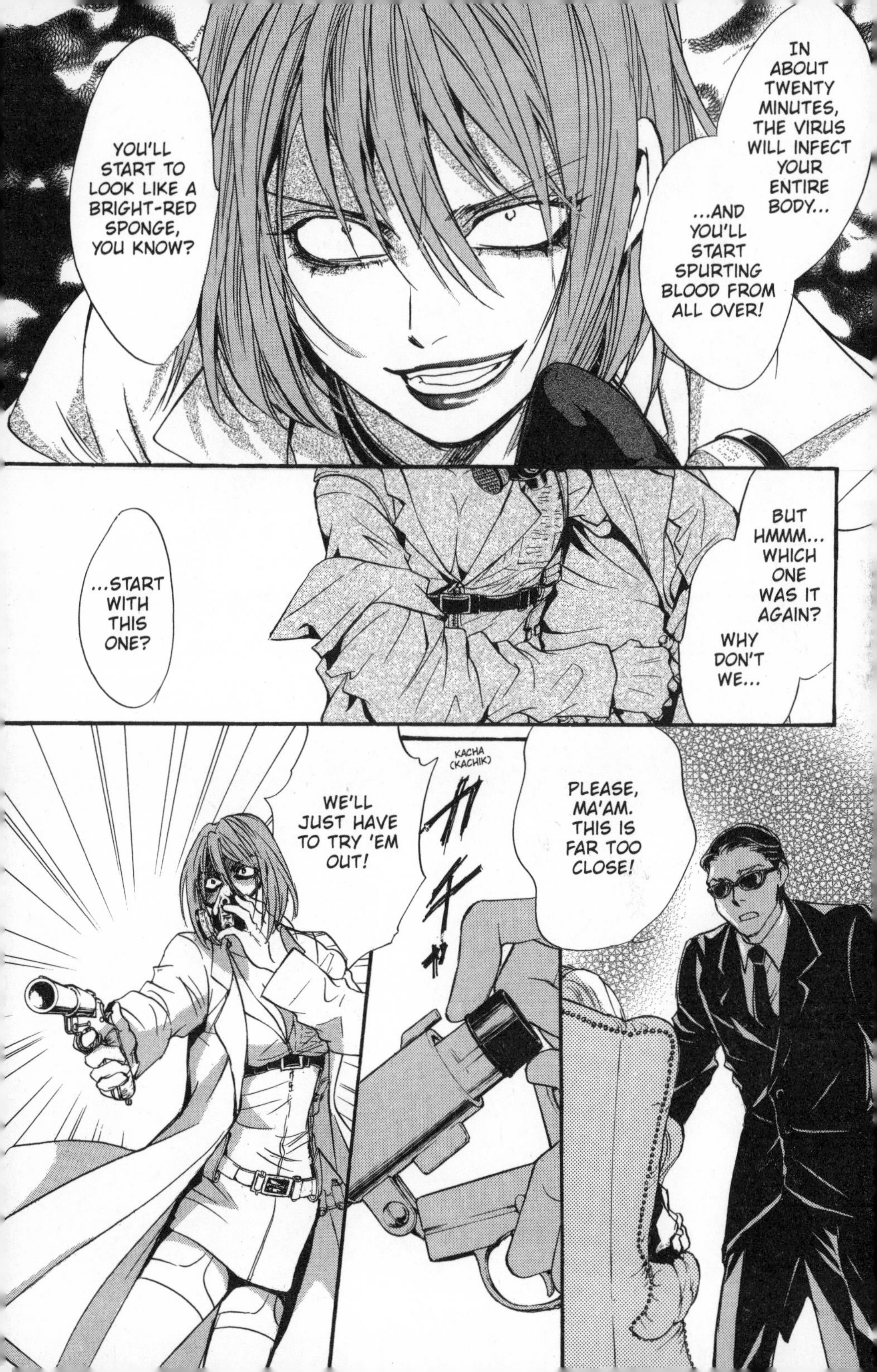
IN ABOUT TWENTY MINUTES, THE VIRUS WILL INFECT YOUR ENTIRE BODY...
...AND YOU'LL START SPURTING BLOOD FROM ALL OVER!
YOU'LL START TO LOOK LIKE A BRIGHT-RED SPONGE, YOU KNOW?
BUT HMMM... WHICH ONE WAS IT AGAIN?
WHY DON'T WE...
...START WITH THIS ONE?
PLEASE, MA'AM. THIS IS FAR TOO CLOSE!
KACHA (KACHIK)
WE'LL JUST HAVE TO TRY 'EM OUT!

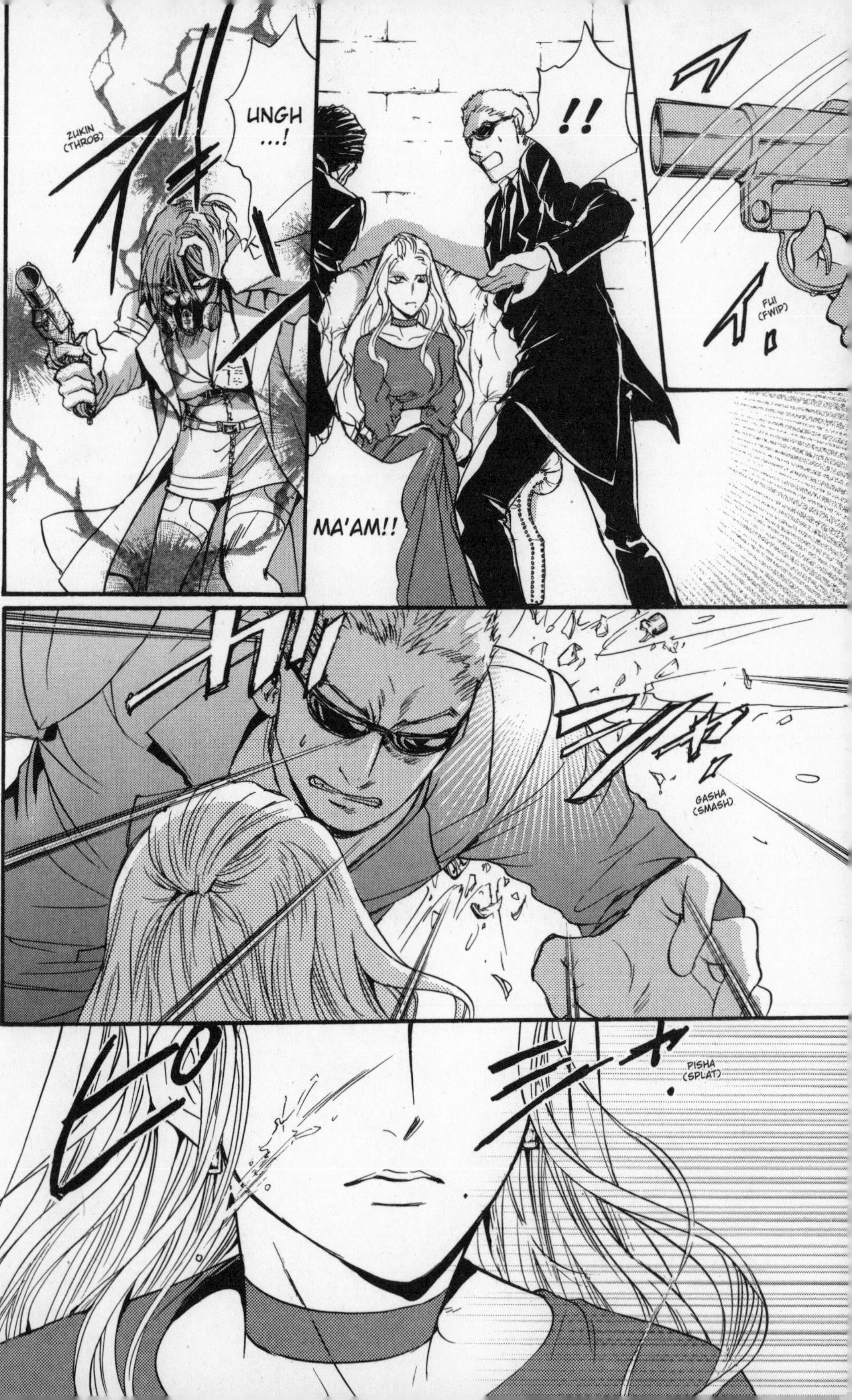
FUI (FWIP)
!!
MA'AM!!
ZUKIN (THROB)
UNGH ...!
GASHA (SMASH)
PISHA (SPLAT)

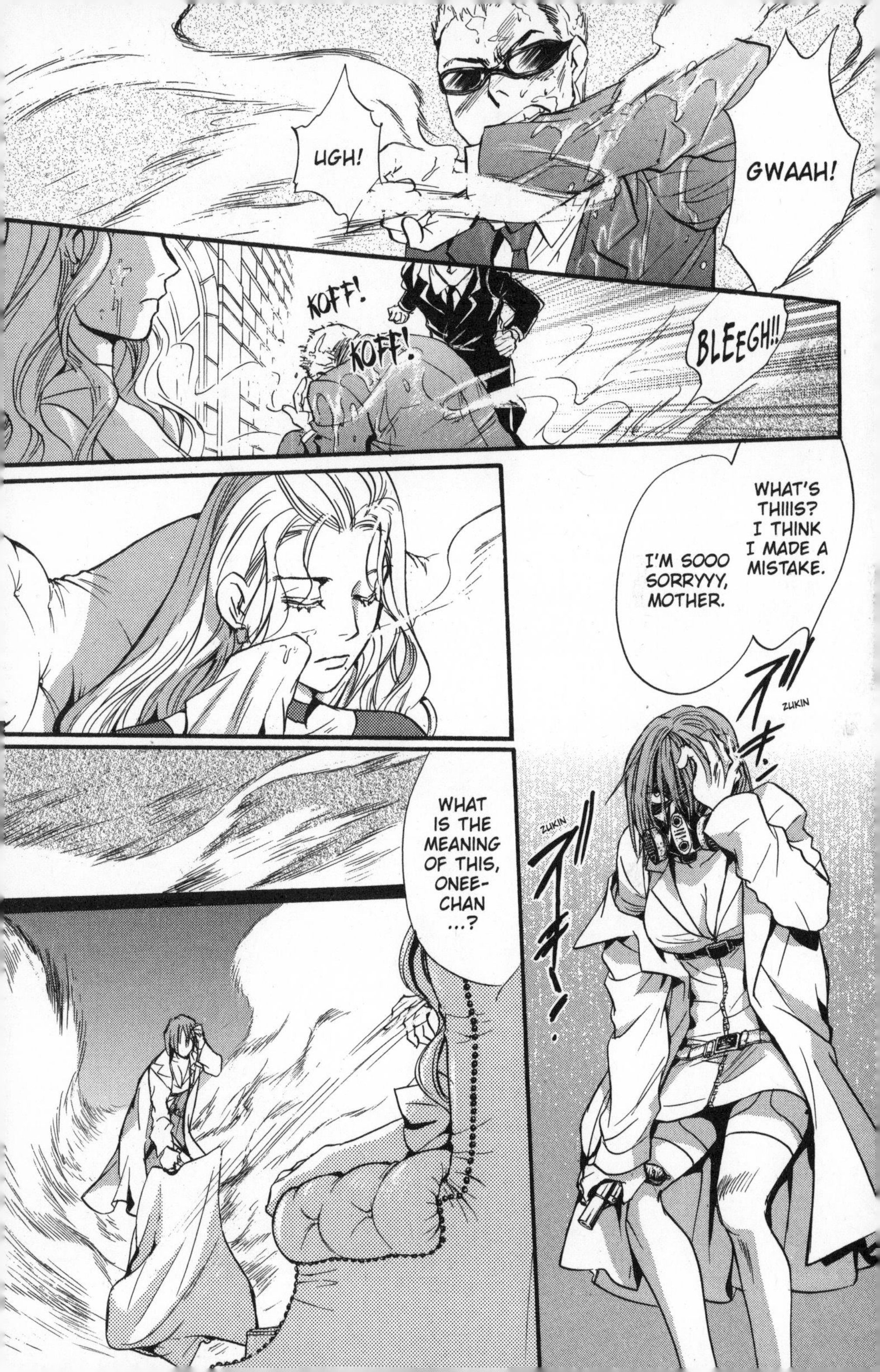
GWAAH!
UGH!
BLEEGH!!
KOFF!
KOFF!
WHAT'S THIIIS? I THINK I MADE A MISTAKE.
I'M SOOO SORRYYY, MOTHER.
ZUKIN
ZUKIN
WHAT IS THE MEANING OF THIS, ONEE-CHAN ...?

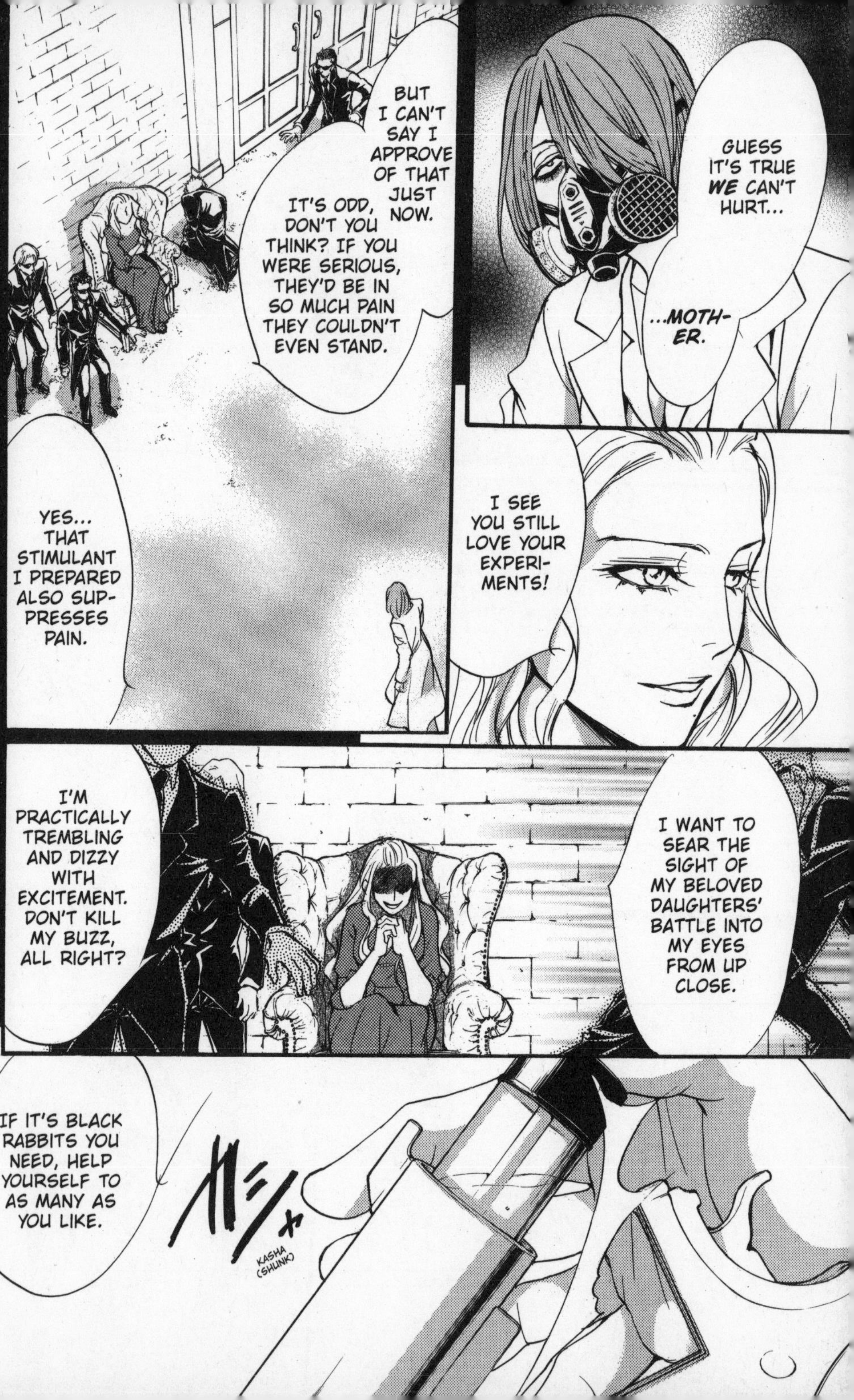
GUESS IT'S TRUE *WE* CAN'T HURT...
...*MOTHER.*
I SEE YOU STILL LOVE YOUR EXPERIMENTS!
BUT I CAN'T SAY I APPROVE OF THAT JUST NOW.
IT'S ODD, DON'T YOU THINK? IF YOU WERE SERIOUS, THEY'D BE IN SO MUCH PAIN THEY COULDN'T EVEN STAND.
YES... THAT STIMULANT I PREPARED ALSO SUPPRESSES PAIN.
I WANT TO SEAR THE SIGHT OF MY BELOVED DAUGHTERS' BATTLE INTO MY EYES FROM UP CLOSE.
I'M PRACTICALLY TREMBLING AND DIZZY WITH EXCITEMENT. DON'T KILL MY BUZZ, ALL RIGHT?
カシャ
KASHA (SHUNK)
IF IT'S BLACK RABBITS YOU NEED, HELP YOURSELF TO AS MANY AS YOU LIKE.

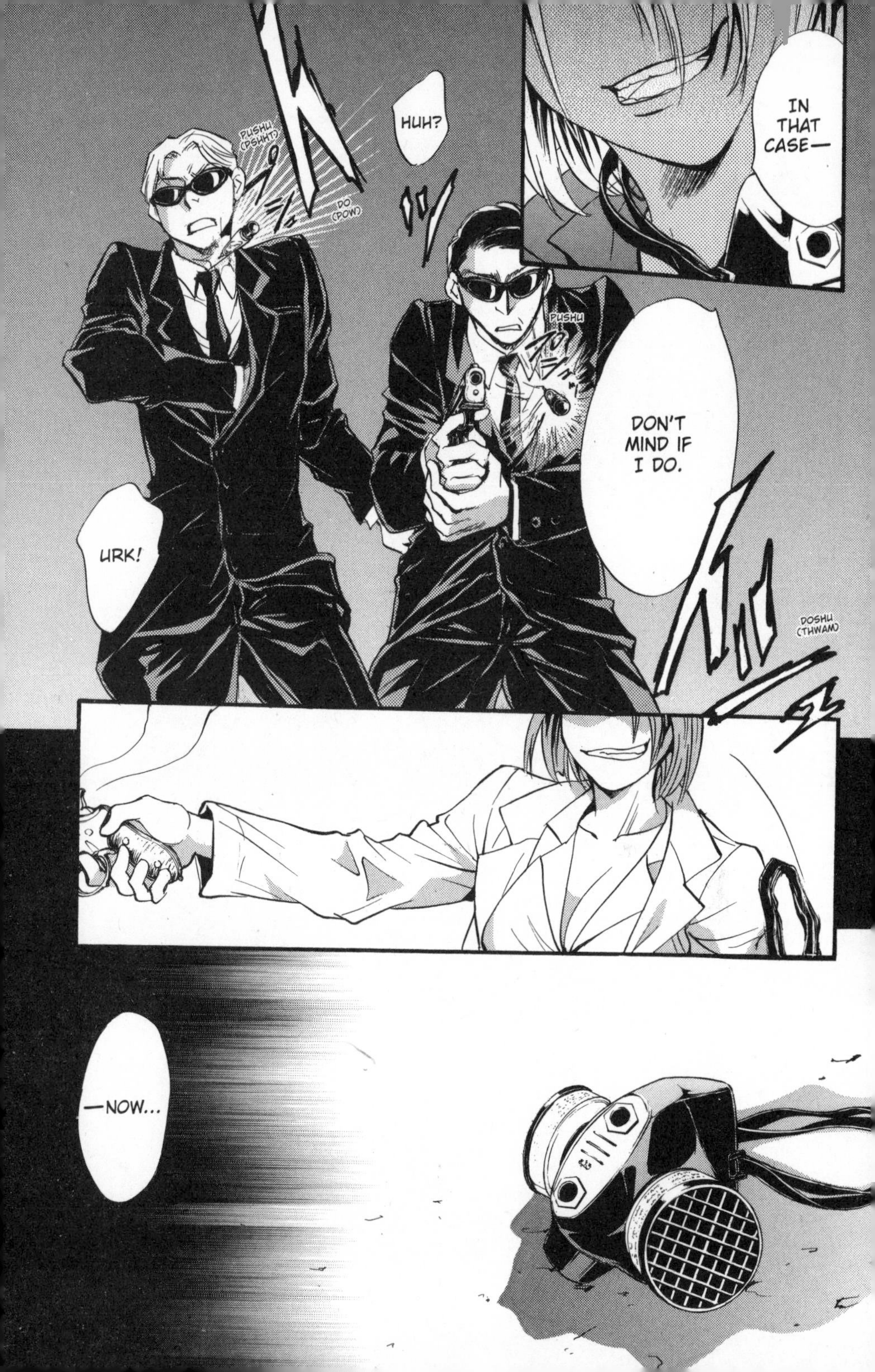
IN THAT CASE—
HUH?
DON'T MIND IF I DO.
PUSHU
PUSHU (PSHHT)
DO (POW)
URK!
DOSHU (THWAM)
—NOW...

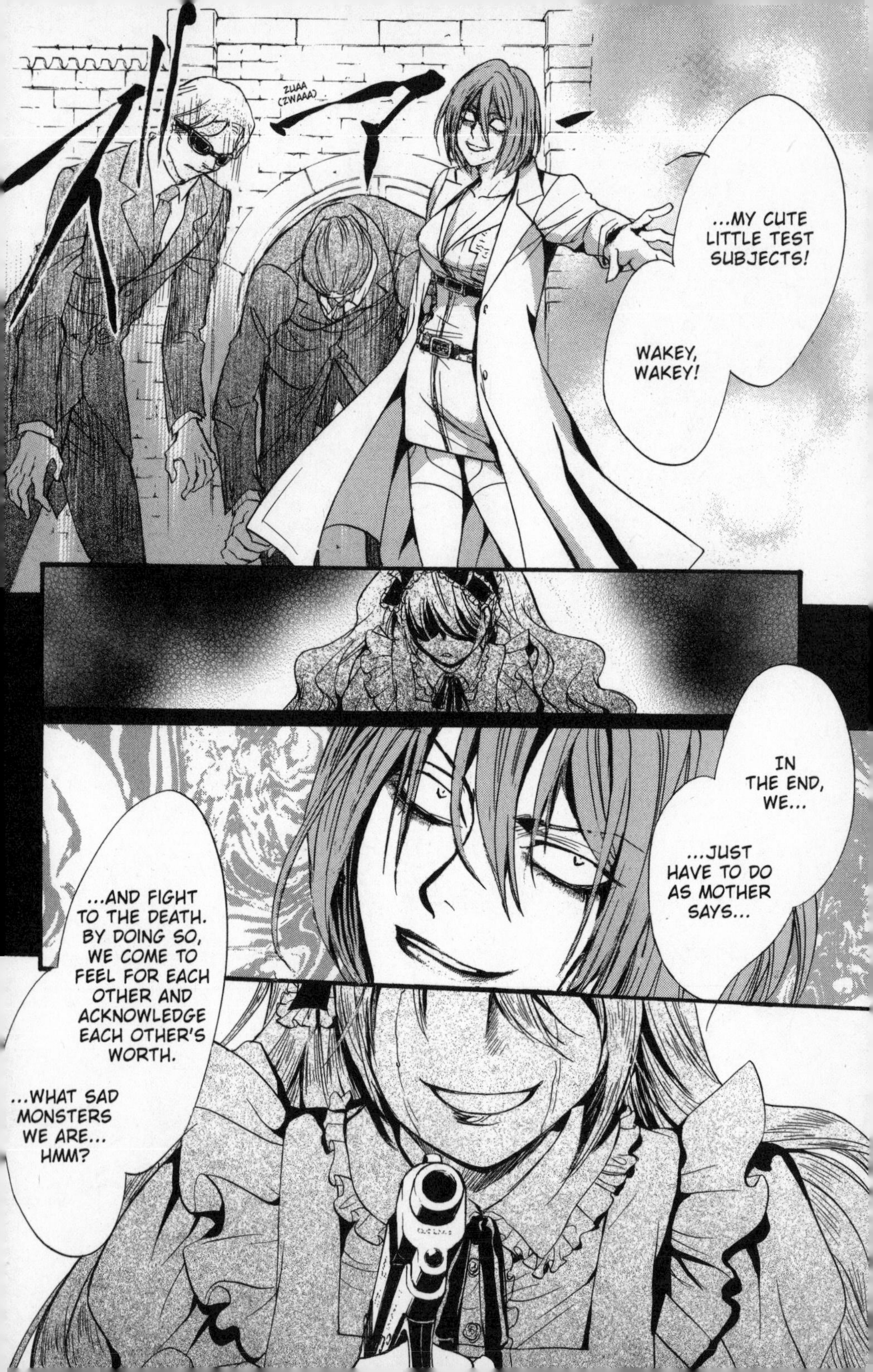
...MY CUTE LITTLE TEST SUBJECTS!
WAKEY, WAKEY!
ZUAA (ZWAAA)
IN THE END, WE...
...JUST HAVE TO DO AS MOTHER SAYS...
...AND FIGHT TO THE DEATH. BY DOING SO, WE COME TO FEEL FOR EACH OTHER AND ACKNOWLEDGE EACH OTHER'S WORTH.
...WHAT SAD MONSTERS WE ARE... HMM?

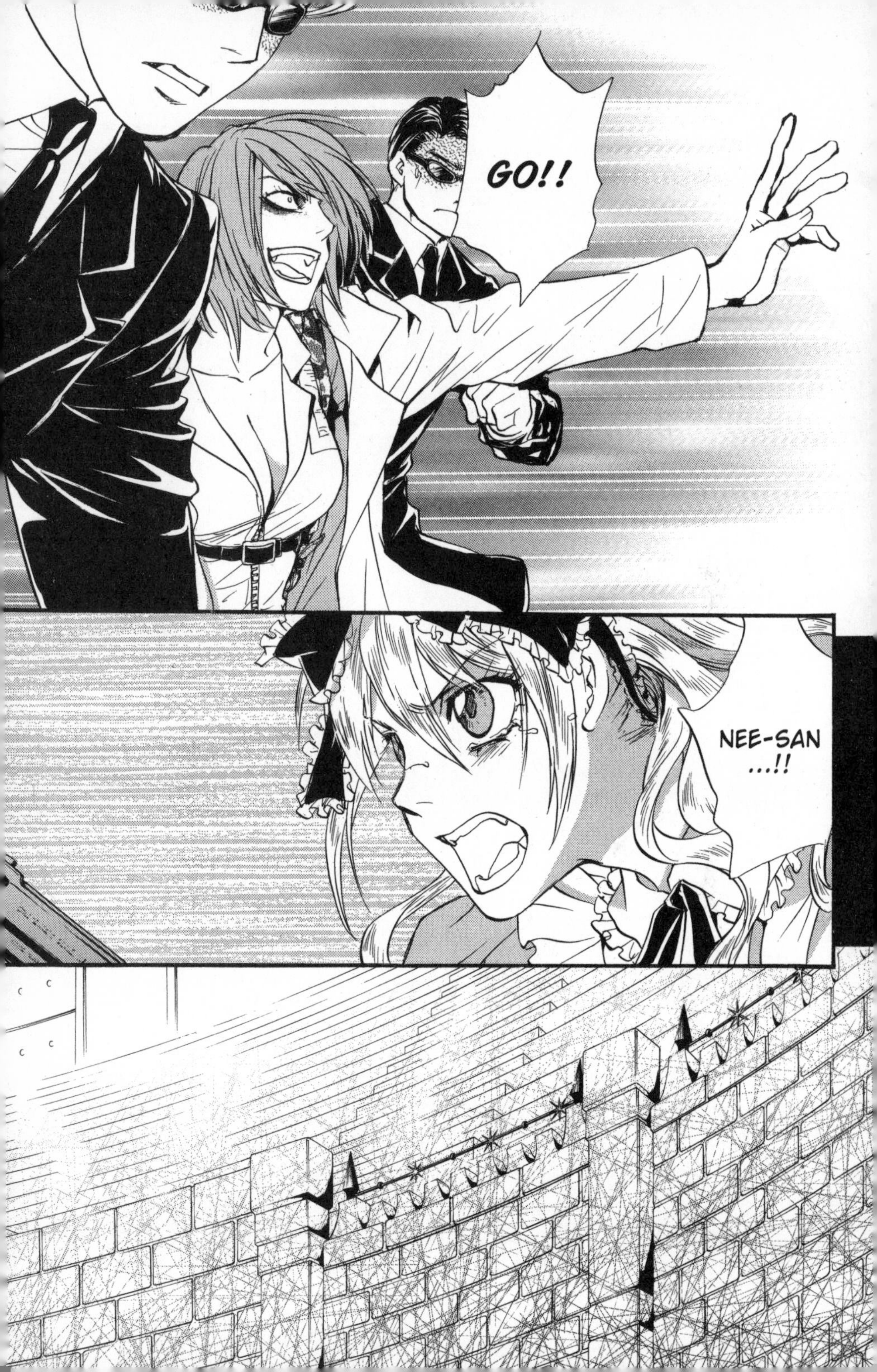
GO!!
NEE-SAN ...!!

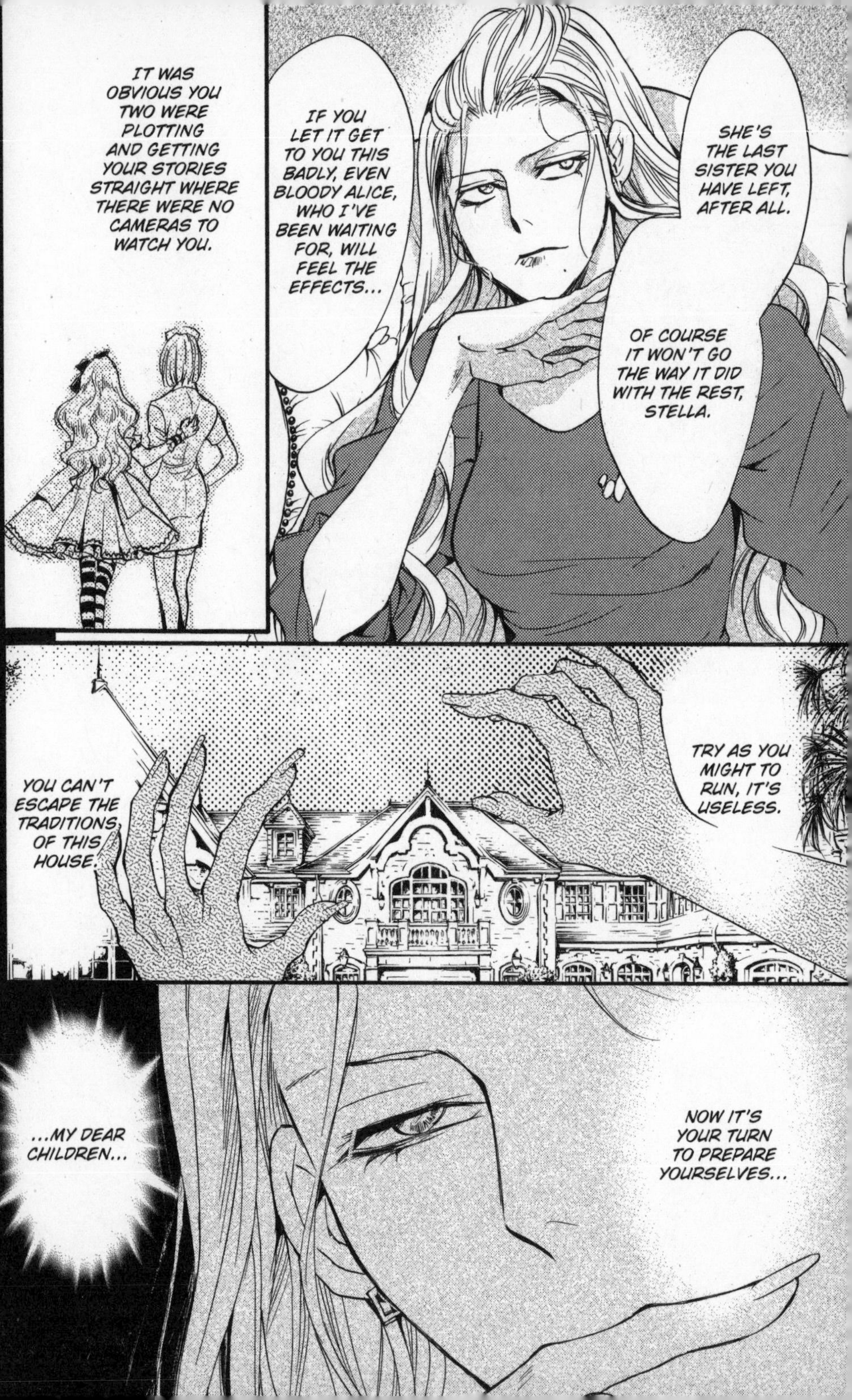
SHE'S THE LAST SISTER YOU HAVE LEFT, AFTER ALL.
IF YOU LET IT GET TO YOU THIS BADLY, EVEN BLOODY ALICE, WHO I'VE BEEN WAITING FOR, WILL FEEL THE EFFECTS...
OF COURSE IT WON'T GO THE WAY IT DID WITH THE REST, STELLA.
IT WAS OBVIOUS YOU TWO WERE PLOTTING AND GETTING YOUR STORIES STRAIGHT WHERE THERE WERE NO CAMERAS TO WATCH YOU.
TRY AS YOU MIGHT TO RUN, IT'S USELESS.
YOU CAN'T ESCAPE THE TRADITIONS OF THIS HOUSE.
NOW IT'S YOUR TURN TO PREPARE YOURSELVES...
...MY DEAR CHILDREN...

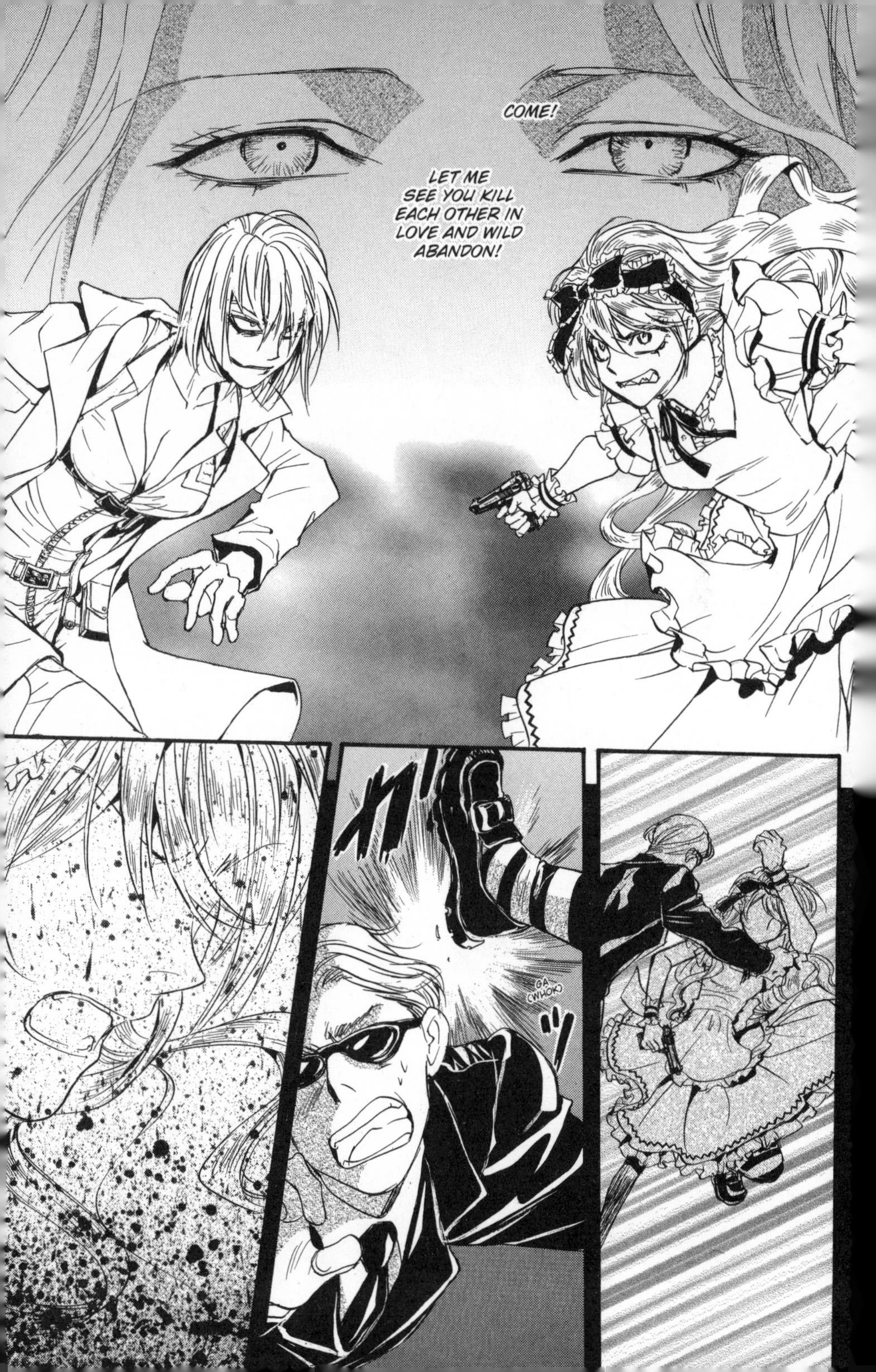
COME!
LET ME SEE YOU KILL EACH OTHER IN LOVE AND WILD ABANDON!
GA (WHOK)

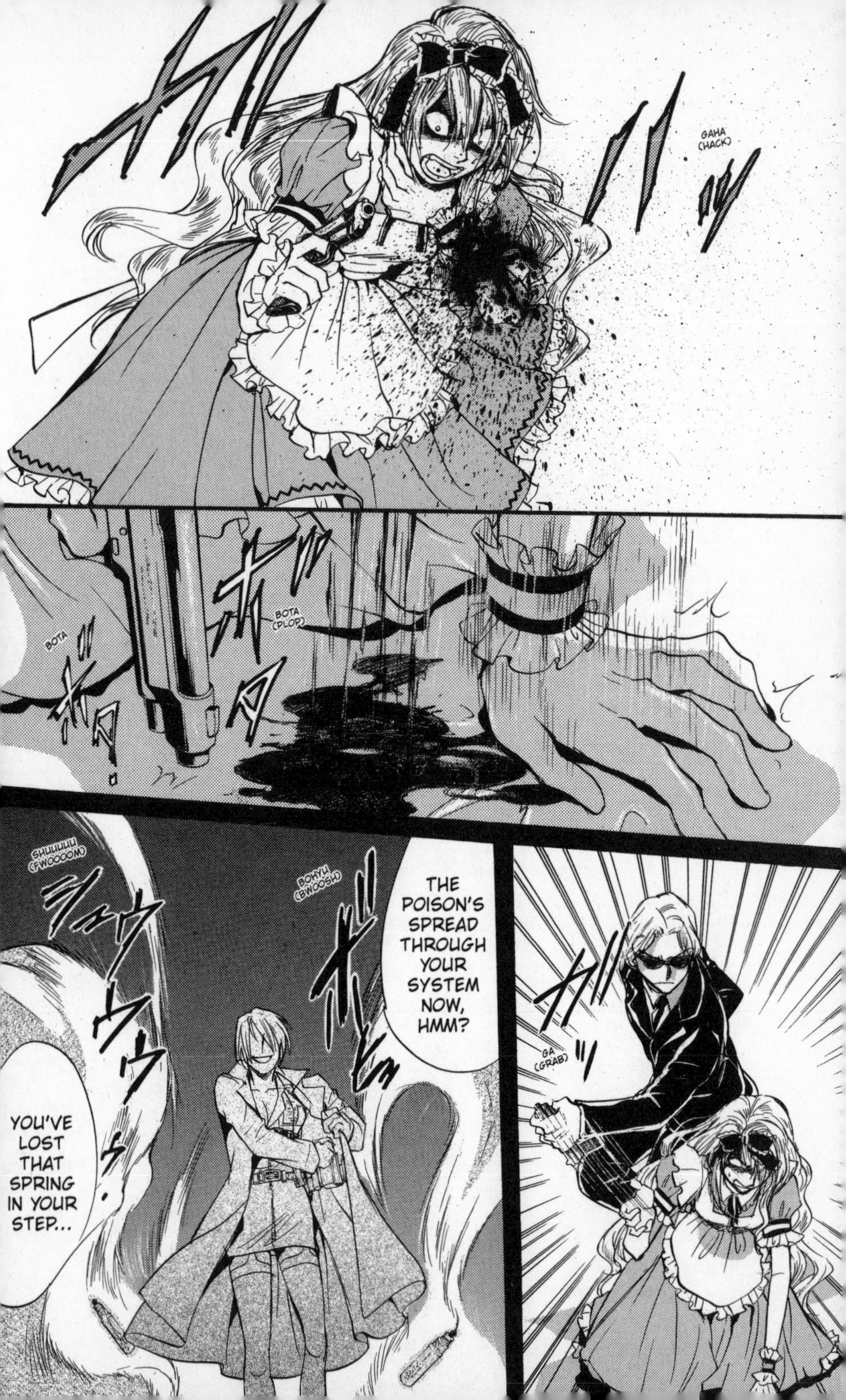
GAHA (HACK)
BOTA (PLOP)
BOTA
GA (GRAB)
THE POISON'S SPREAD THROUGH YOUR SYSTEM NOW, HMM?
BOHYU (BWOOSH)
SHUUUUU (FWOOOOM)
YOU'VE LOST THAT SPRING IN YOUR STEP...

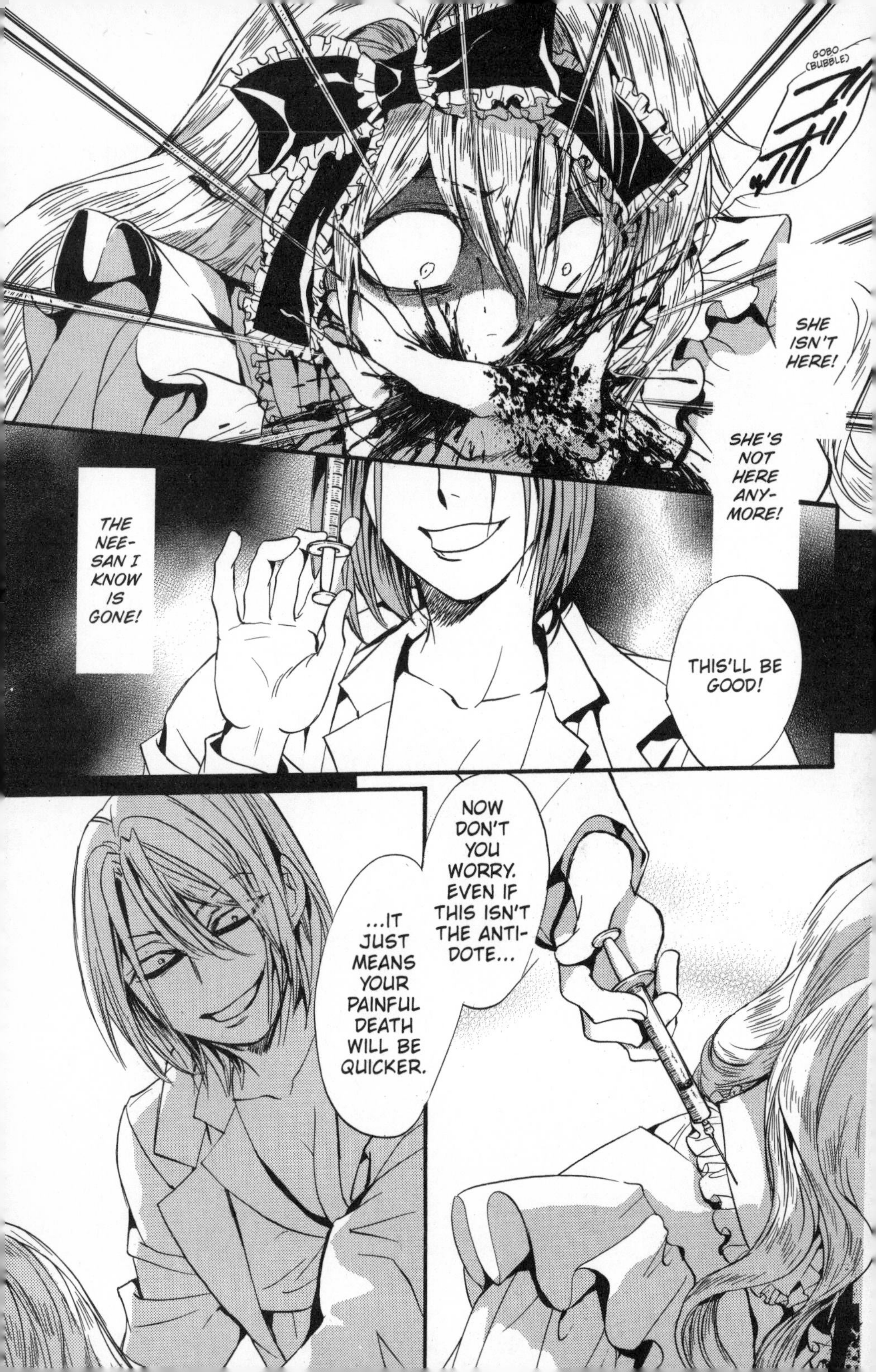
GOBO (BUBBLE)
SHE ISN'T HERE!
SHE'S NOT HERE ANYMORE!
THIS'LL BE GOOD!
THE NEE-SAN I KNOW IS GONE!
NOW DON'T YOU WORRY. EVEN IF THIS ISN'T THE ANTI-DOTE...
...IT JUST MEANS YOUR PAINFUL DEATH WILL BE QUICKER.

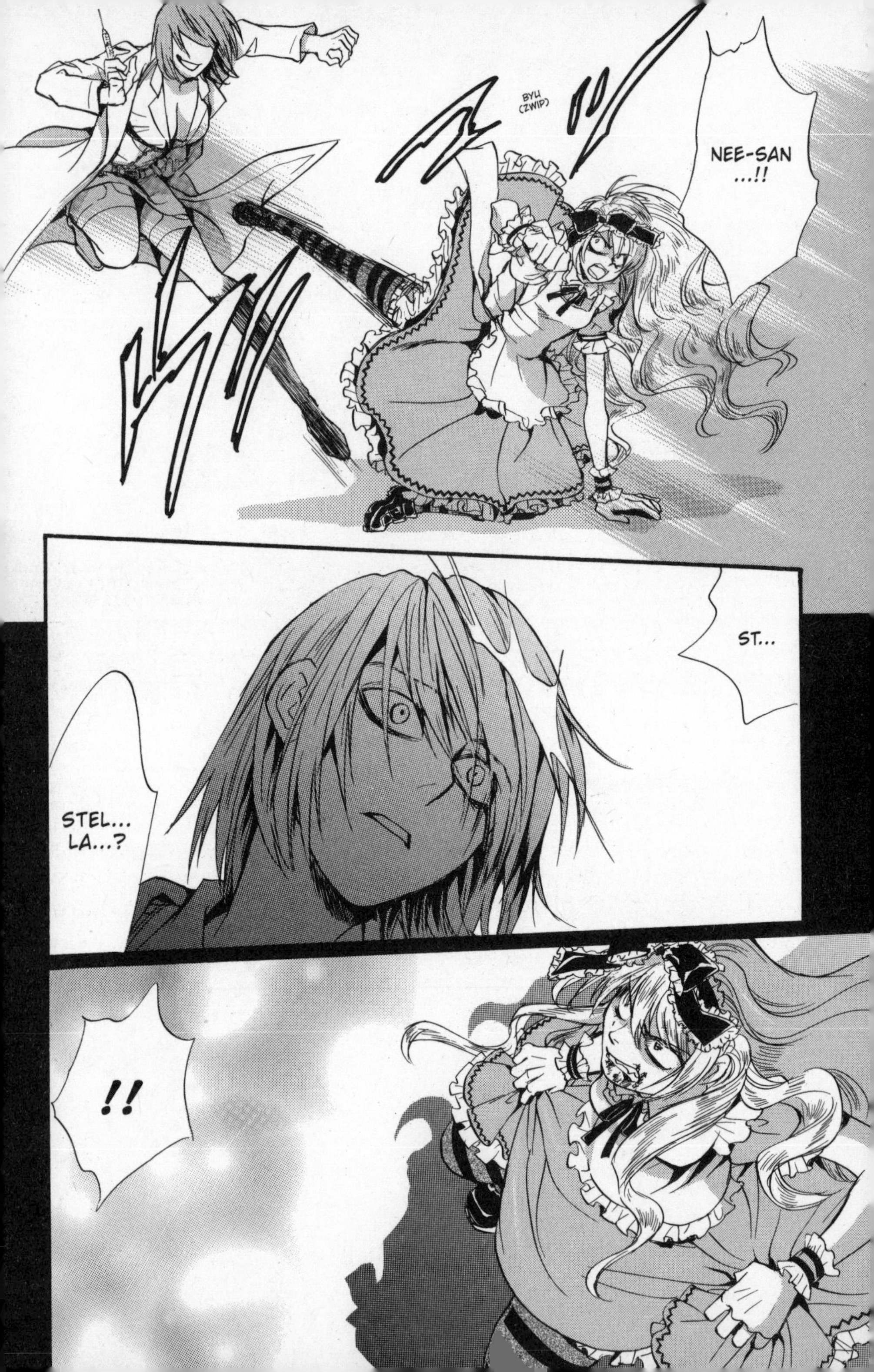
NEE-SAN ...!!
BYU (ZWIP)
ST...
STEL... LA...?
!!

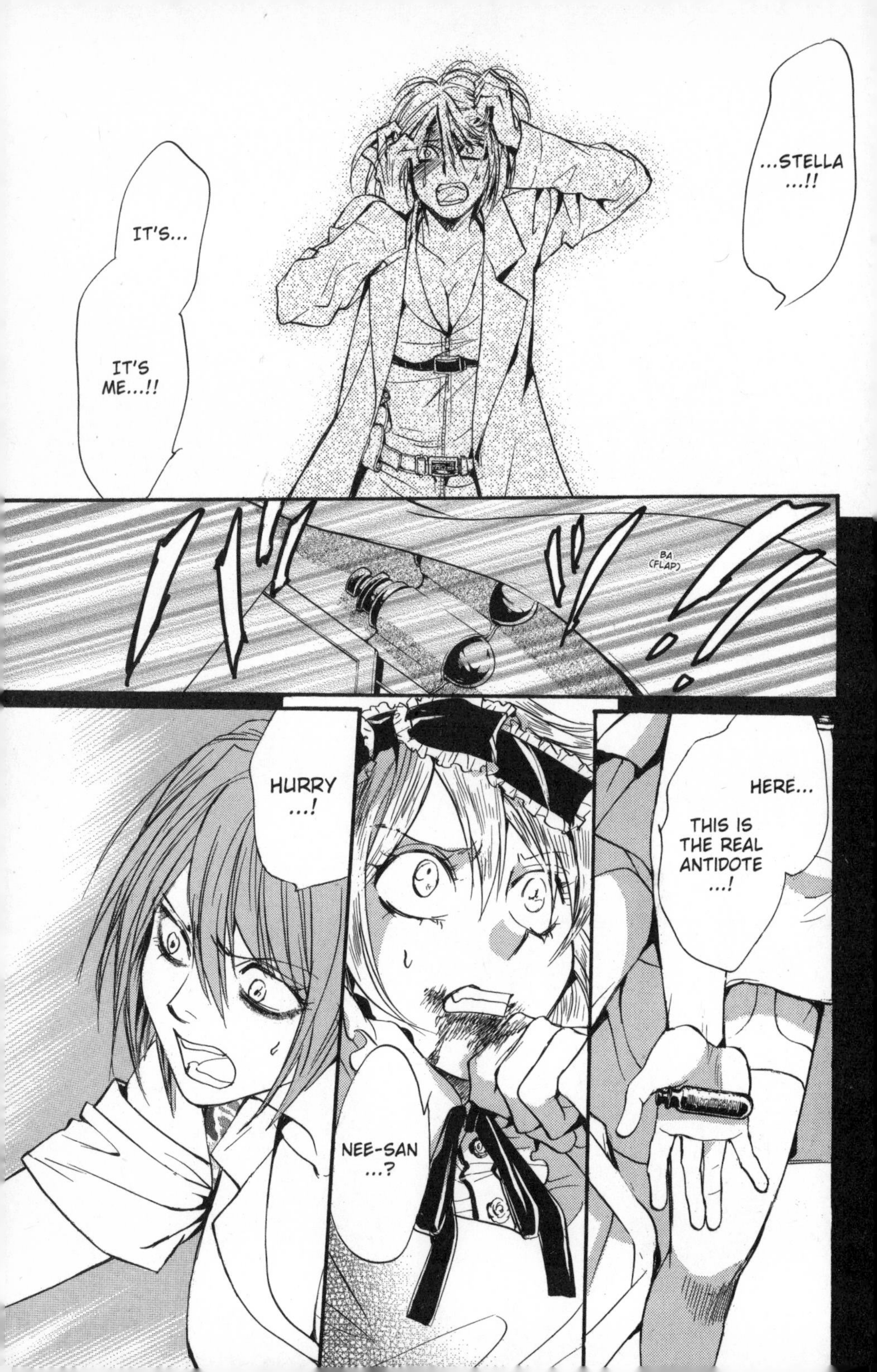
...STELLA ...!!
IT'S...
IT'S ME...!!
BA (FLAP)
HERE...
THIS IS THE REAL ANTIDOTE ...!
NEE-SAN ...?
HURRY ...!

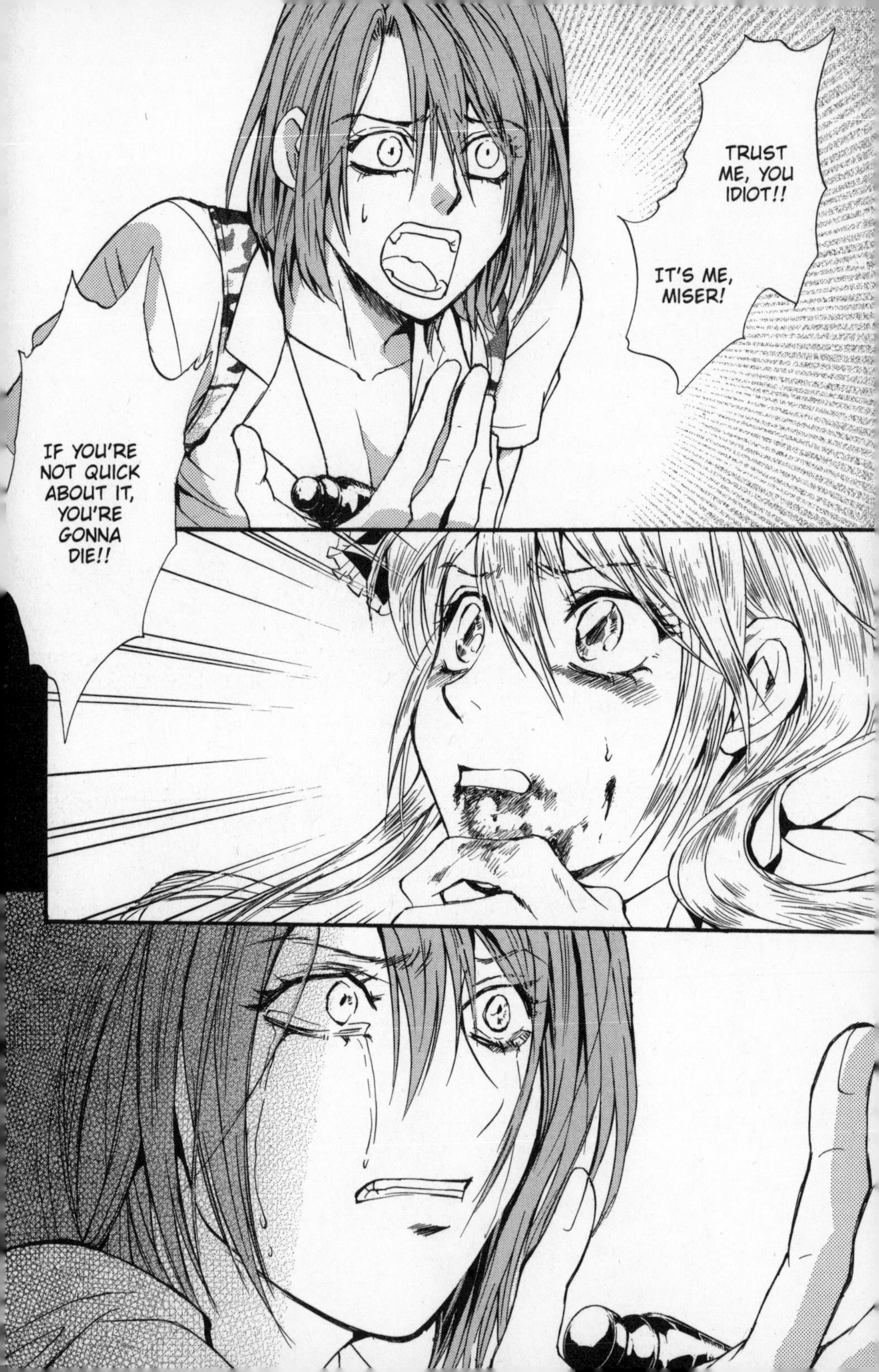
TRUST ME, YOU IDIOT!!
IT'S ME, MISER!
IF YOU'RE NOT QUICK ABOUT IT, YOU'RE GONNA DIE!!

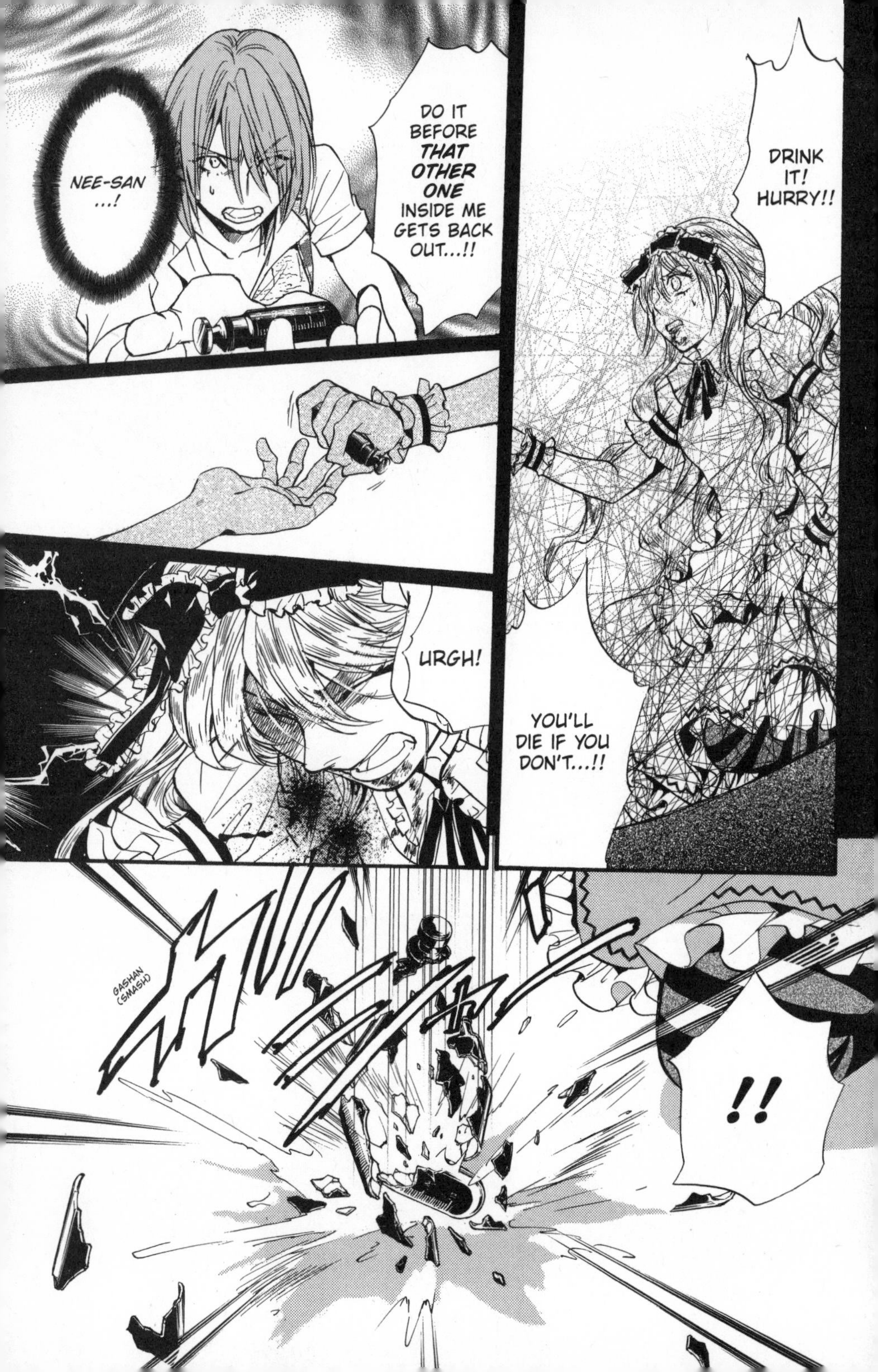
DRINK IT! HURRY!!
YOU'LL DIE IF YOU DON'T...!!
DO IT BEFORE THAT OTHER ONE INSIDE ME GETS BACK OUT...!!
NEE-SAN ...!
URGH!
!!
GASHAN (SMASH)

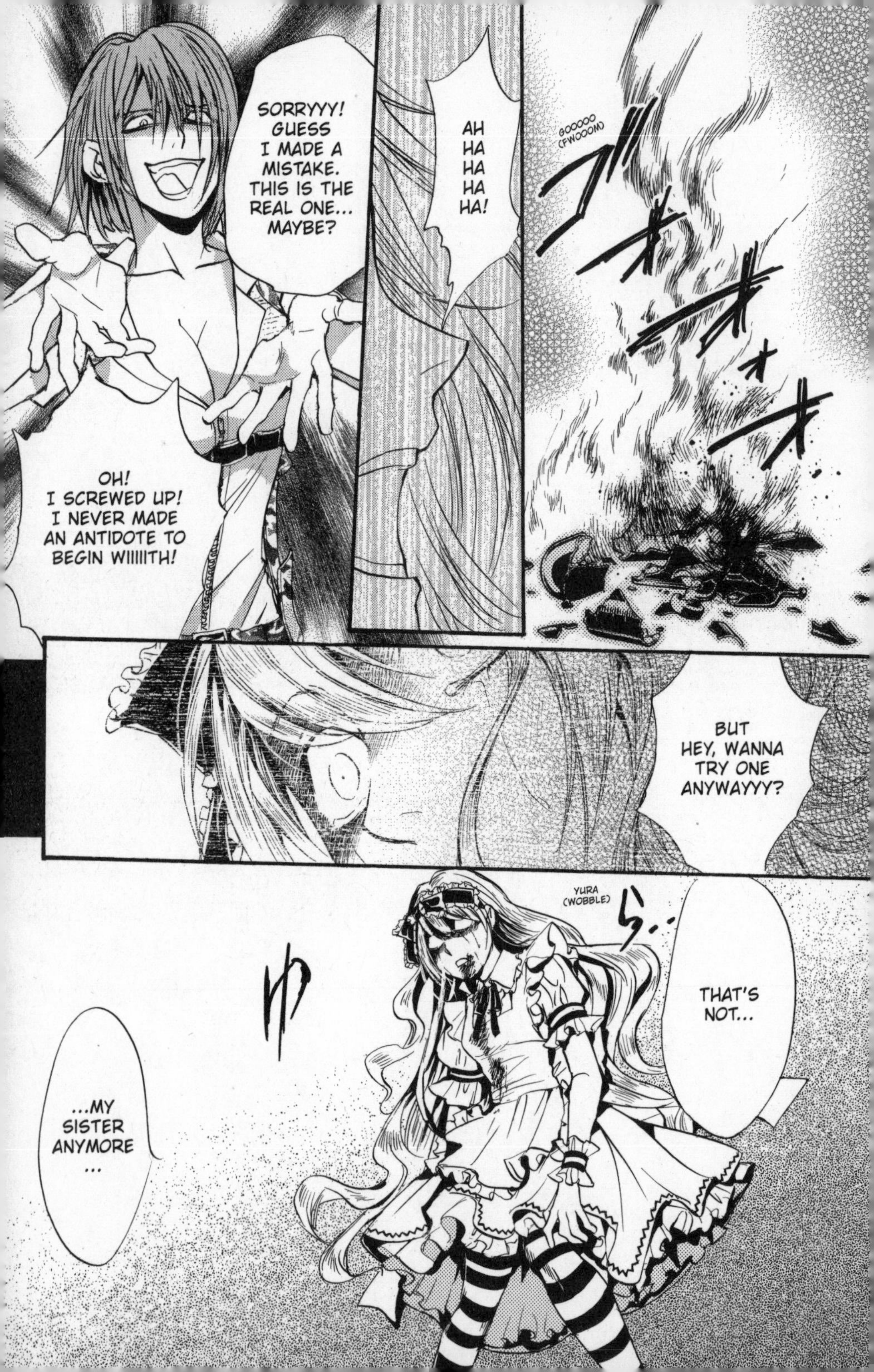
GOOOOO (FWOOOM)
AH HA HA HA HA!
SORRYYY! GUESS I MADE A MISTAKE. THIS IS THE REAL ONE... MAYBE?
OH! I SCREWED UP! I NEVER MADE AN ANTIDOTE TO BEGIN WIIIIITH!
BUT HEY, WANNA TRY ONE ANYWAYYY?
YURA (WOBBLE)
THAT'S NOT...
...MY SISTER ANYMORE ...

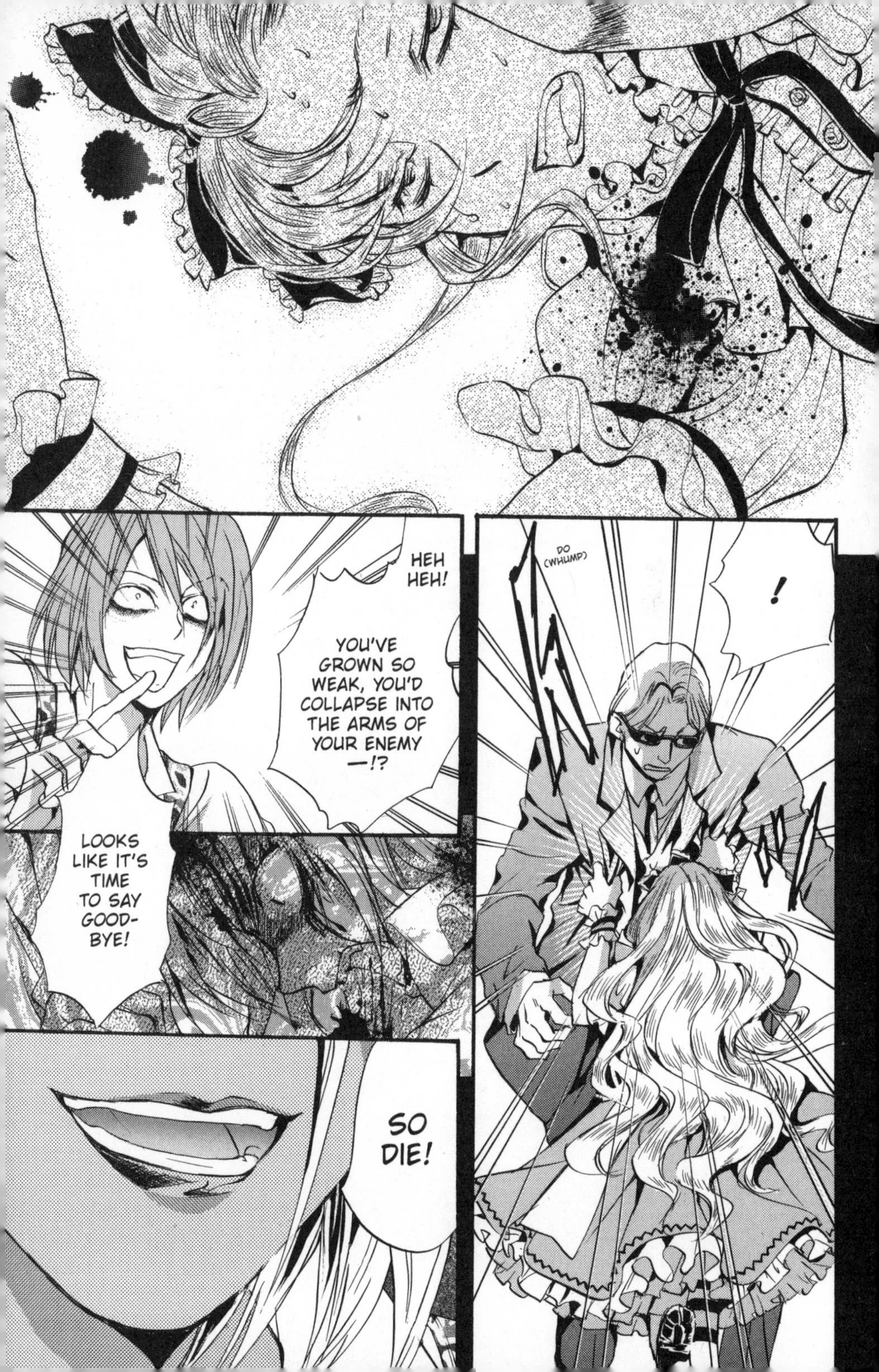
DO (WHUMP)
!
HEH HEH!
YOU'VE GROWN SO WEAK, YOU'D COLLAPSE INTO THE ARMS OF YOUR ENEMY —!?
LOOKS LIKE IT'S TIME TO SAY GOOD-BYE!
SO DIE!

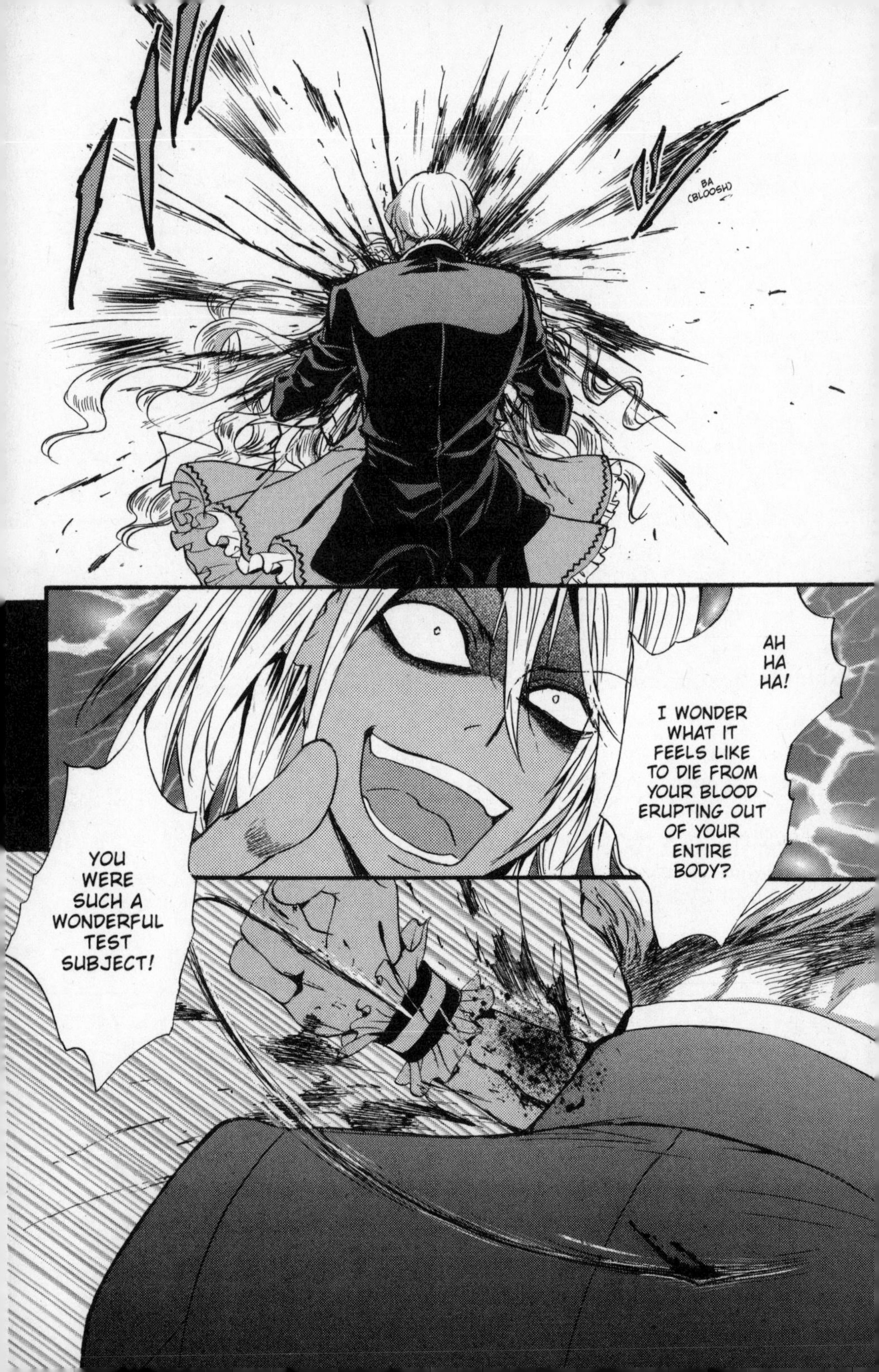
BA (BLOOSH)
AH HA HA!
I WONDER WHAT IT FEELS LIKE TO DIE FROM YOUR BLOOD ERUPTING OUT OF YOUR ENTIRE BODY?
YOU WERE SUCH A WONDERFUL TEST SUBJECT!

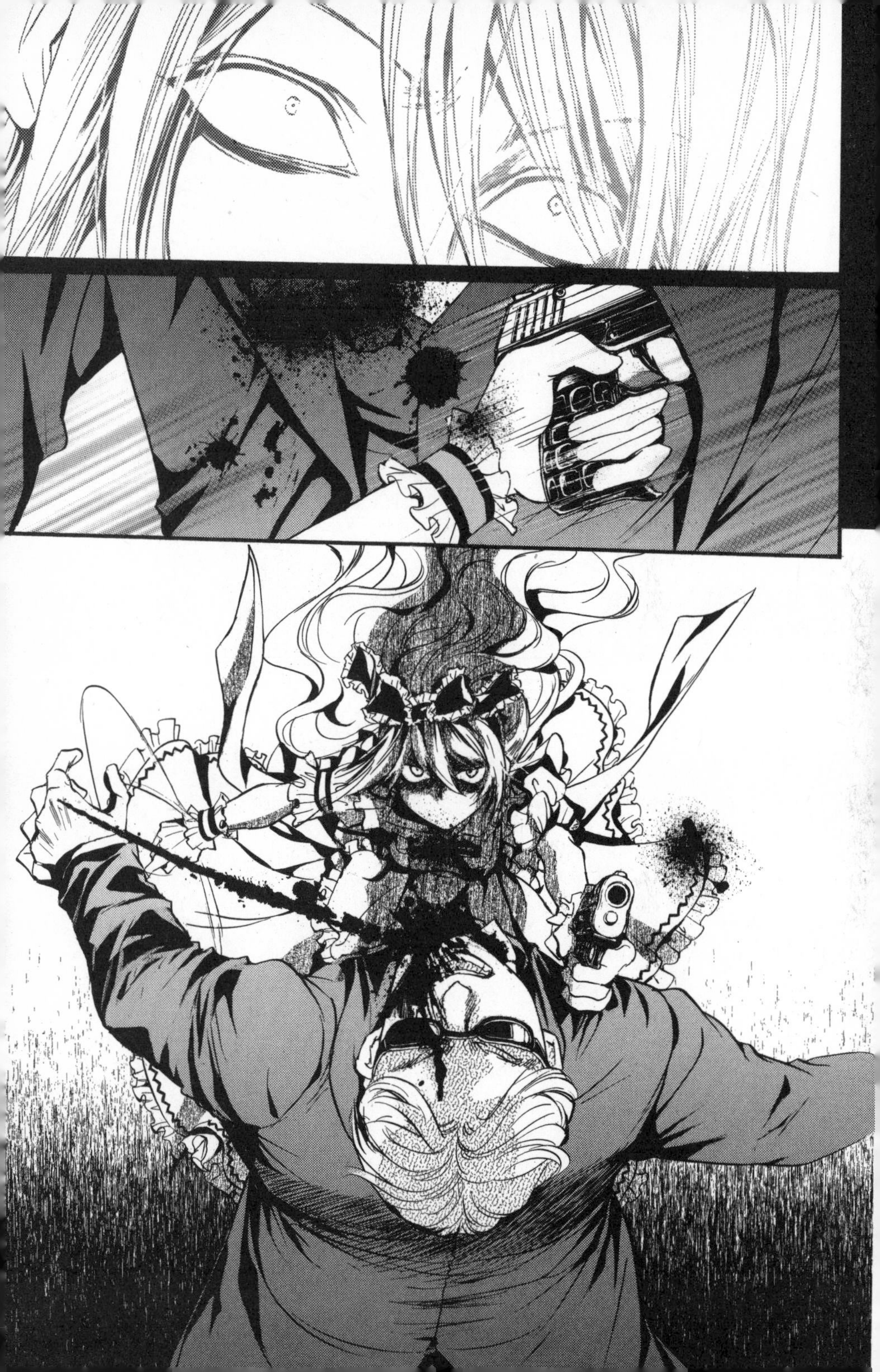

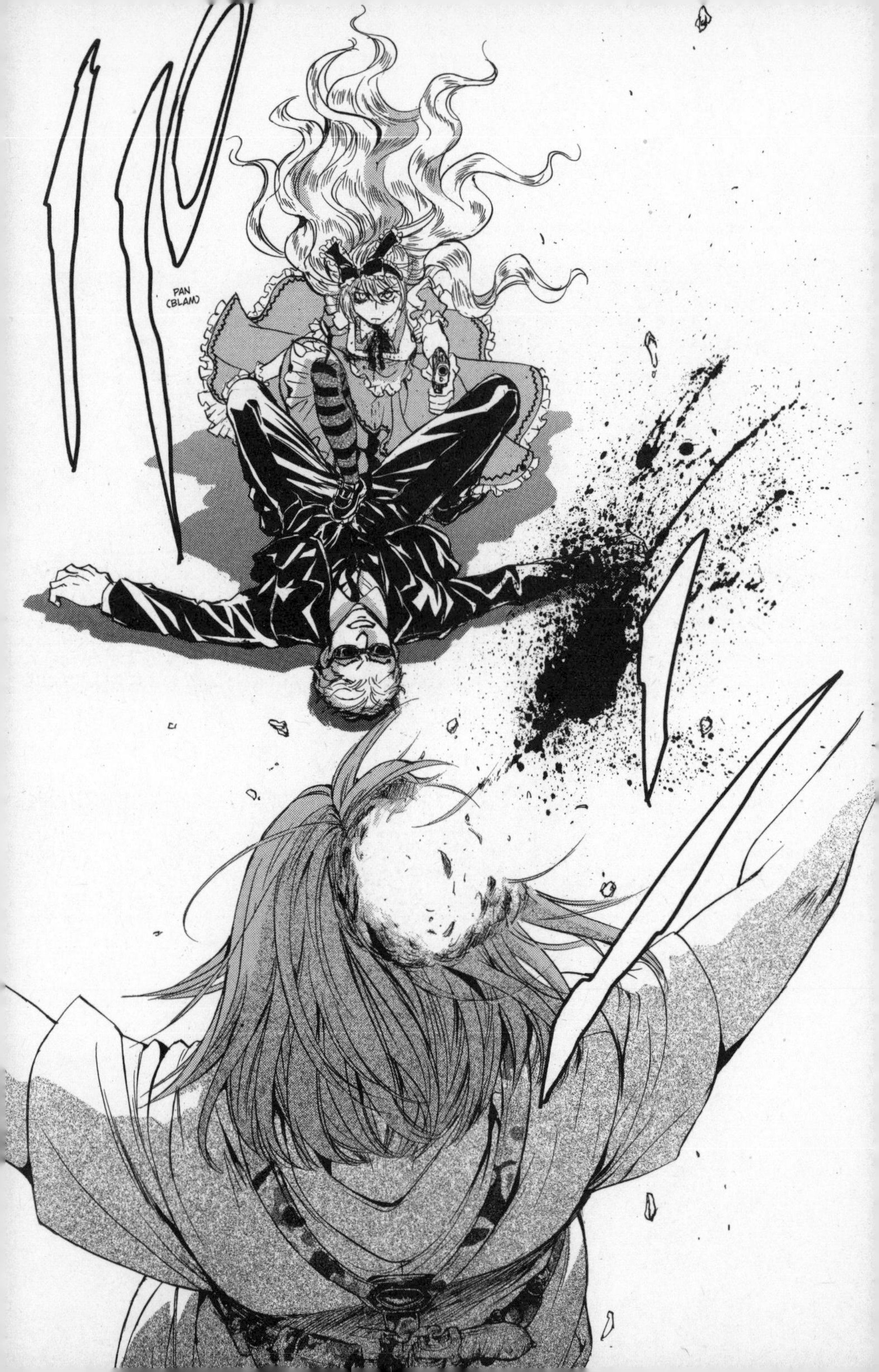
PAN
(BLAM)

Alice in Murderland

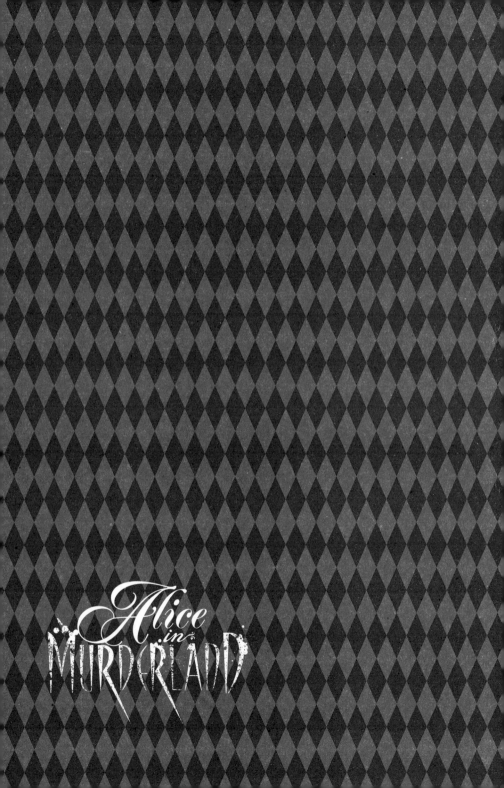

Alice in Murderland

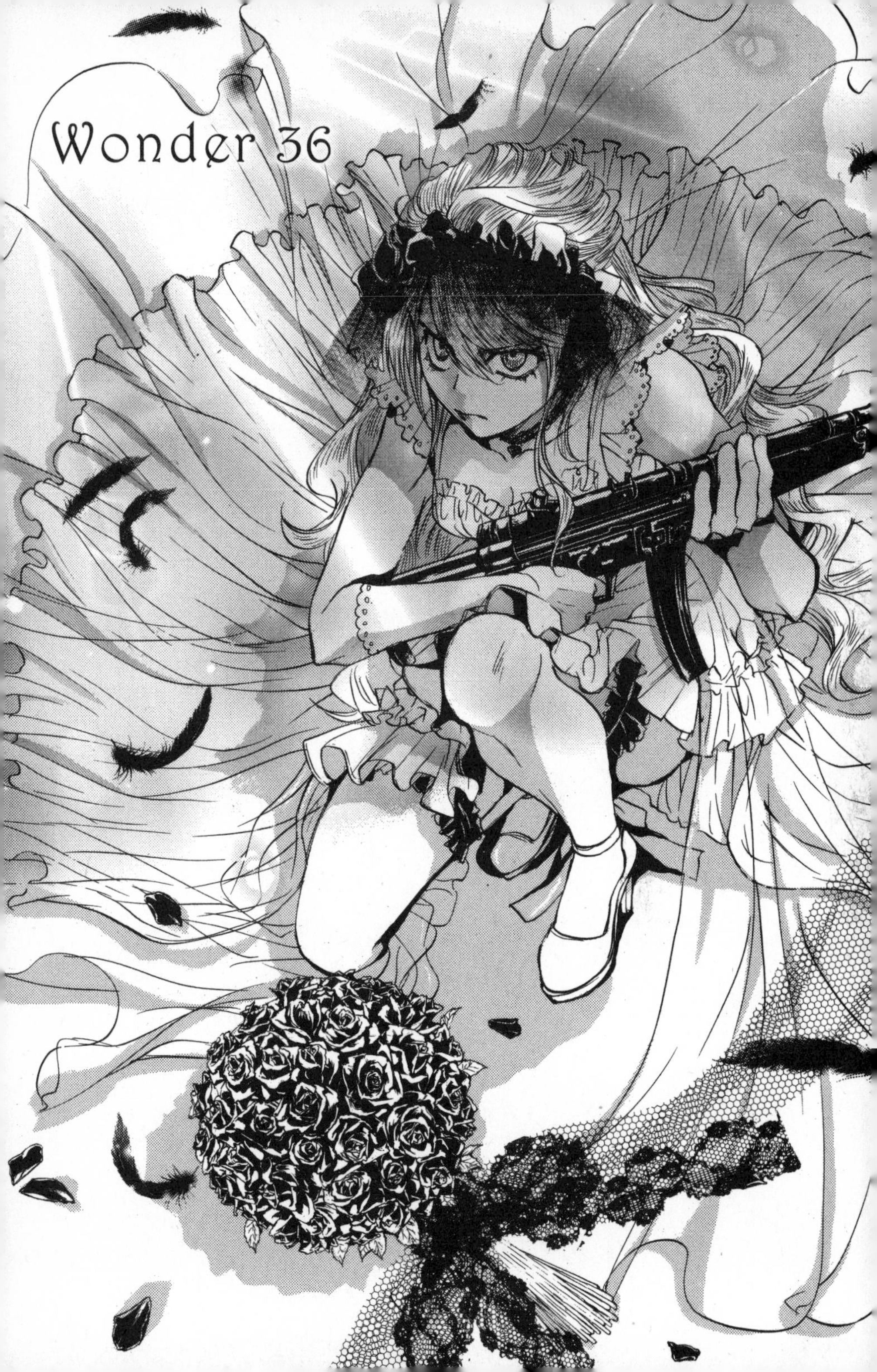
Wonder 36

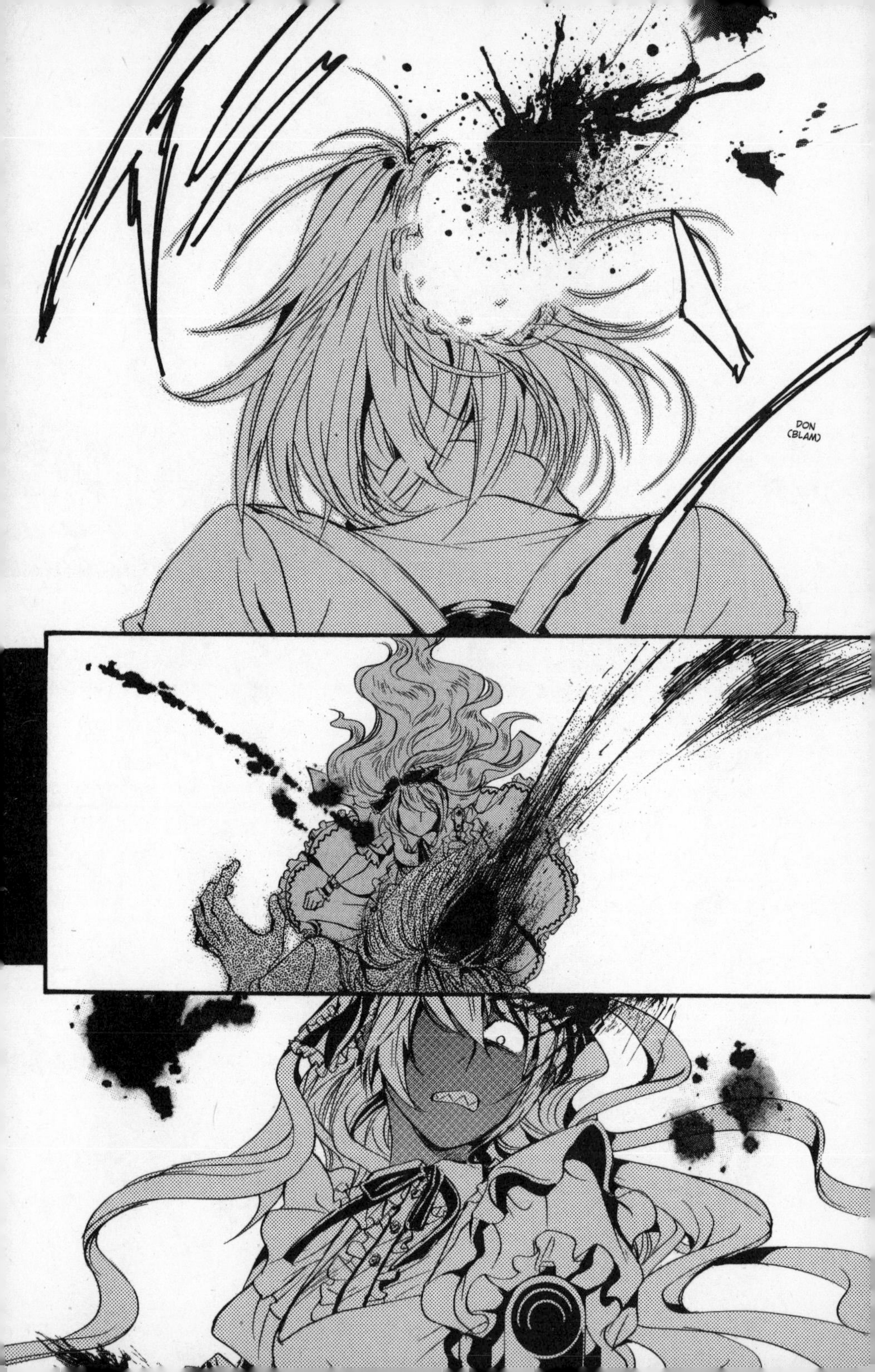
DON
(BLAM)

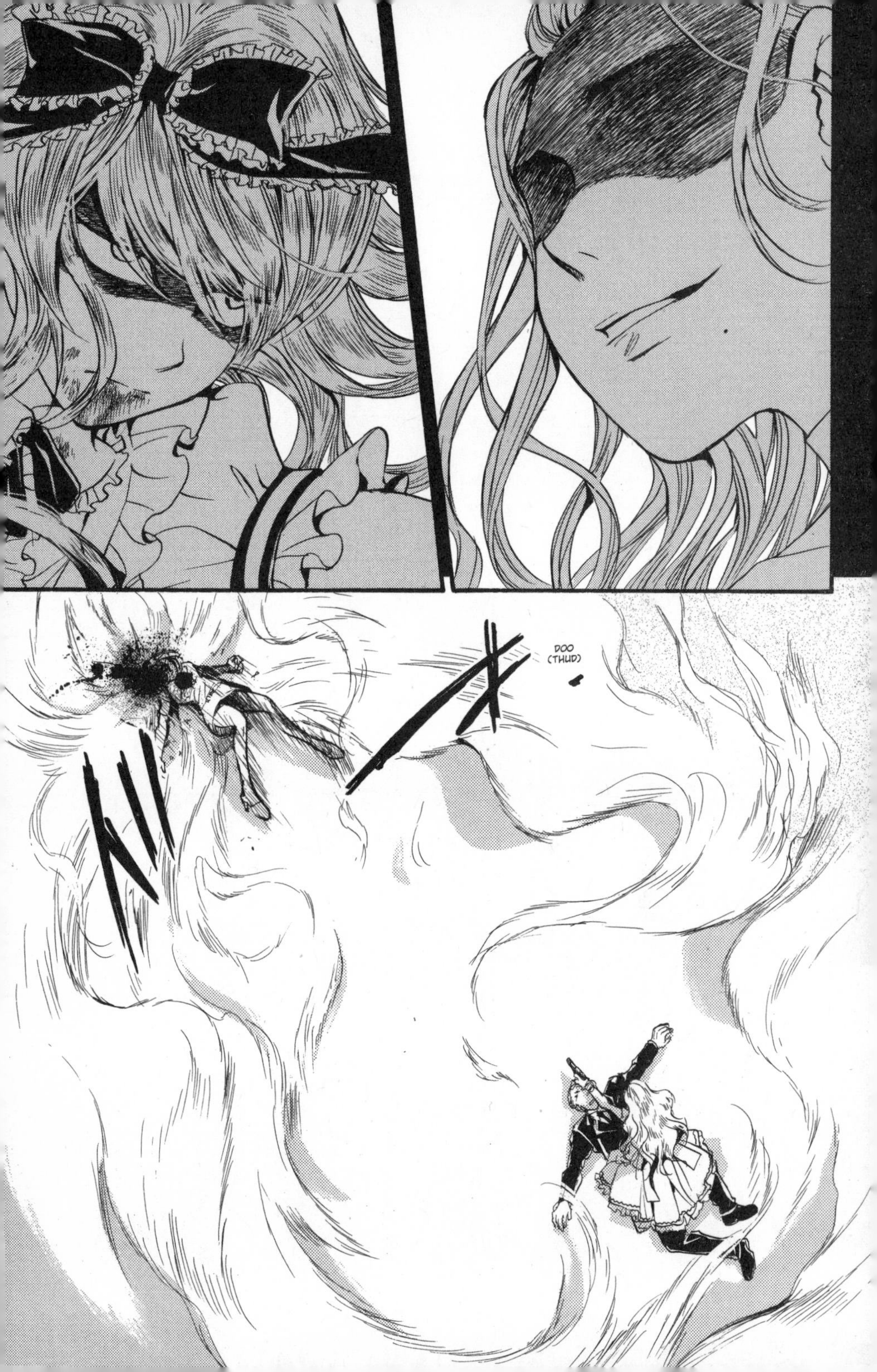
DOO
(THUD)

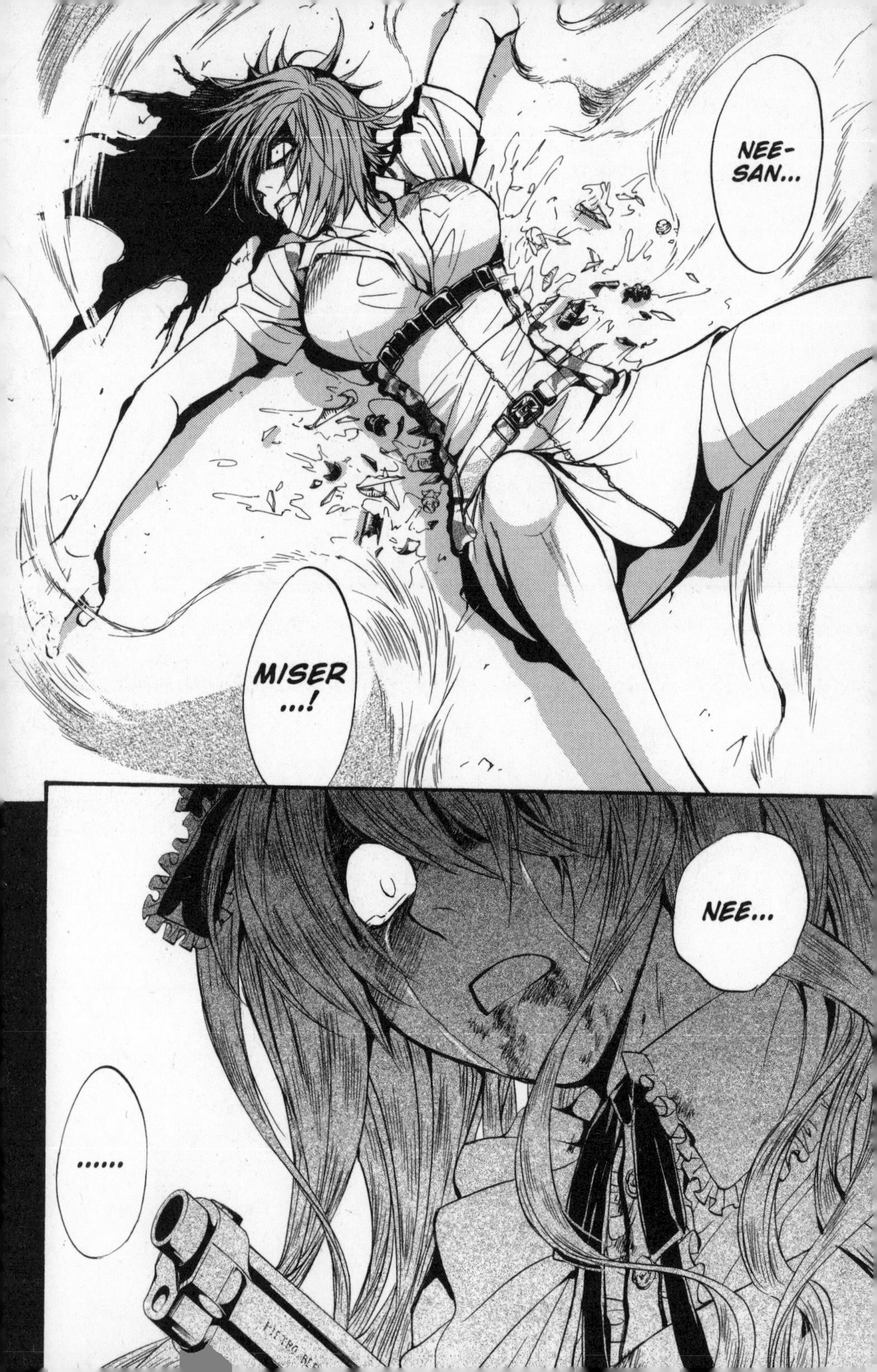
NEE-SAN...
MISER ...!
NEE...
......

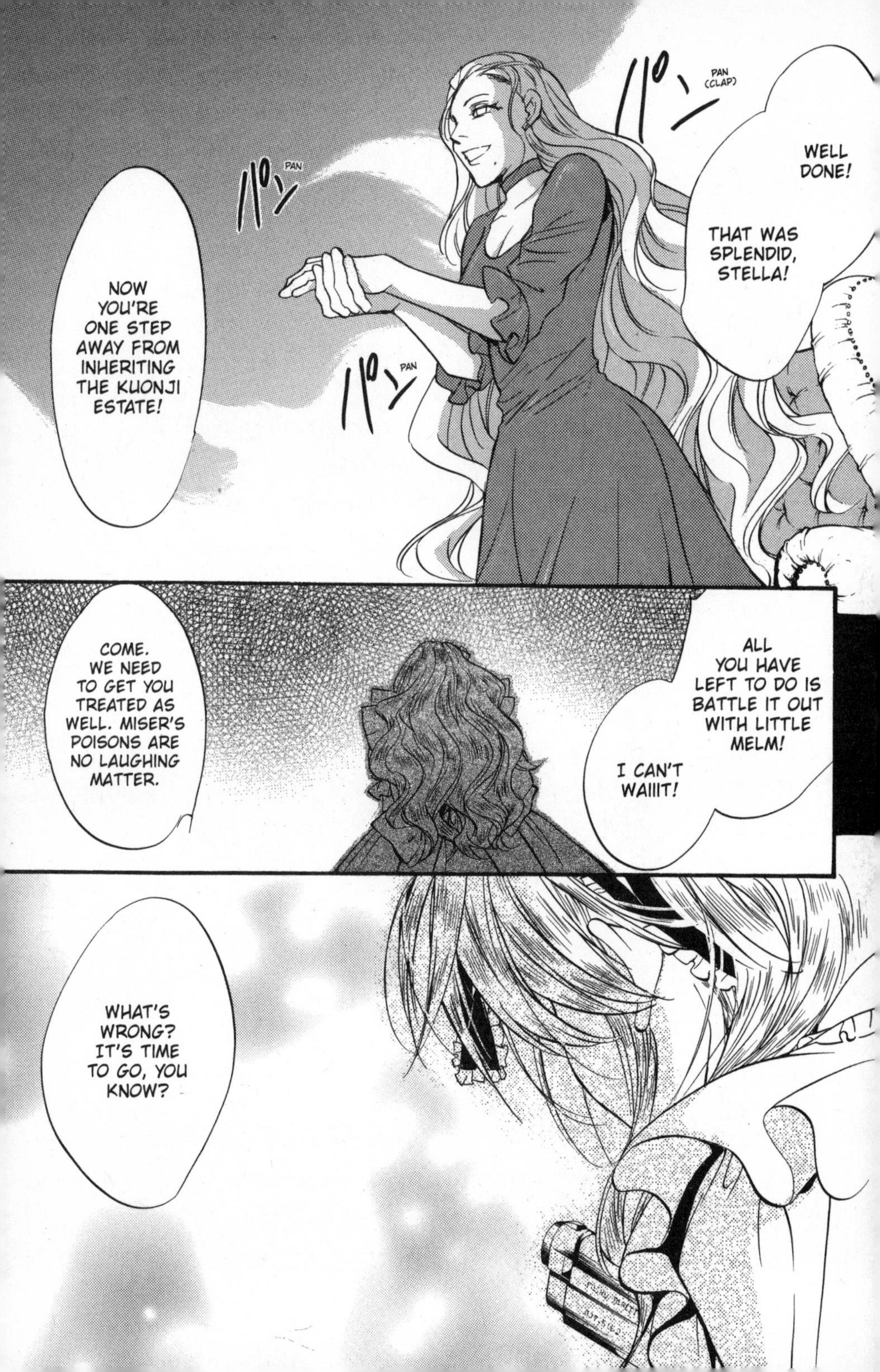
PAN (CLAP)
WELL DONE!
THAT WAS SPLENDID, STELLA!
PAN
PAN
NOW YOU'RE ONE STEP AWAY FROM INHERITING THE KUONJI ESTATE!
ALL YOU HAVE LEFT TO DO IS BATTLE IT OUT WITH LITTLE MELM!
I CAN'T WAIIIT!
COME. WE NEED TO GET YOU TREATED AS WELL. MISER'S POISONS ARE NO LAUGHING MATTER.
WHAT'S WRONG? IT'S TIME TO GO, YOU KNOW?

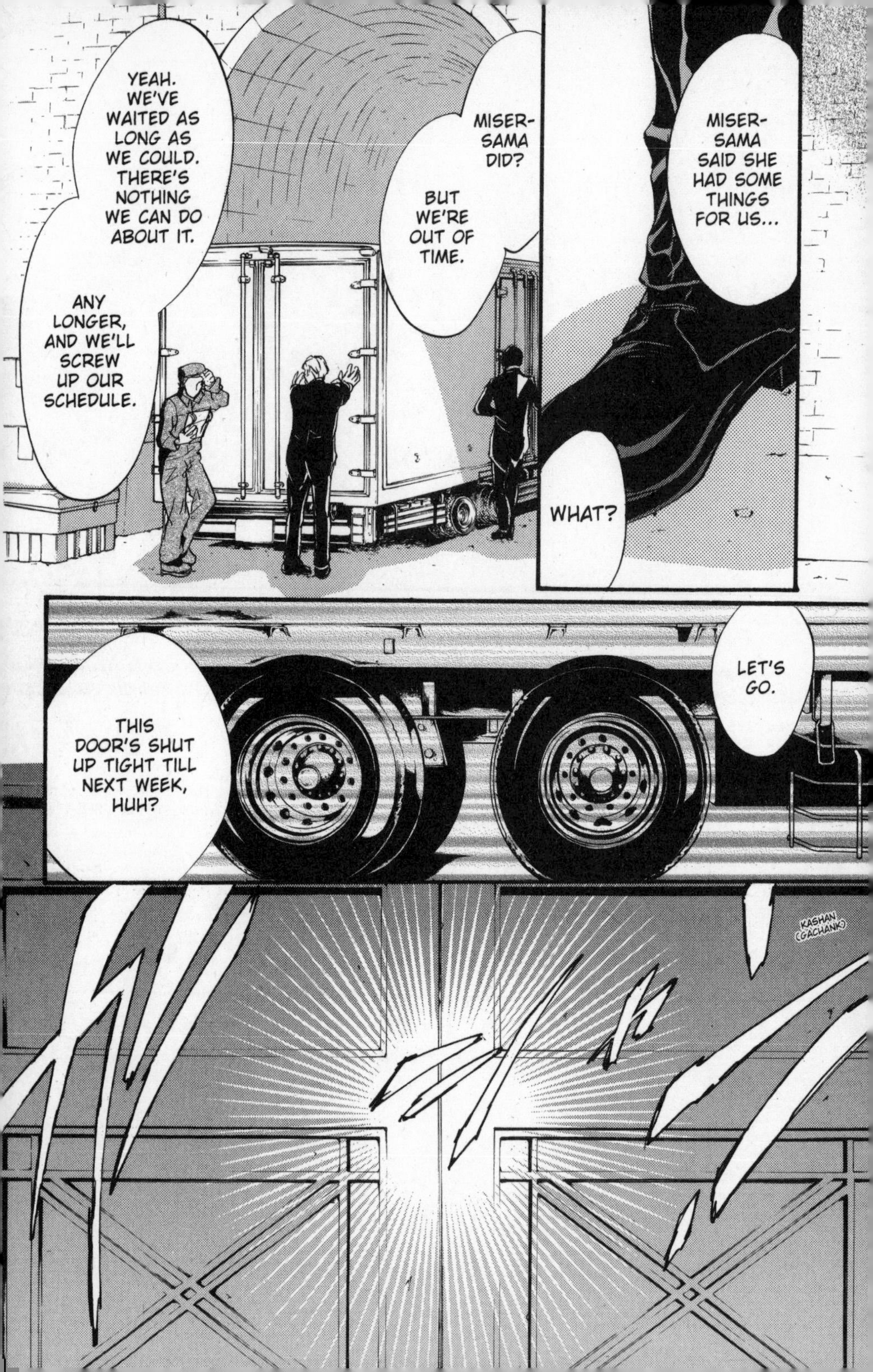
MISER-SAMA SAID SHE HAD SOME THINGS FOR US...
WHAT?
MISER-SAMA DID?
BUT WE'RE OUT OF TIME.
YEAH. WE'VE WAITED AS LONG AS WE COULD. THERE'S NOTHING WE CAN DO ABOUT IT.
ANY LONGER, AND WE'LL SCREW UP OUR SCHEDULE.
LET'S GO.
THIS DOOR'S SHUT UP TIGHT TILL NEXT WEEK, HUH?
KASHAN (GACHANK)

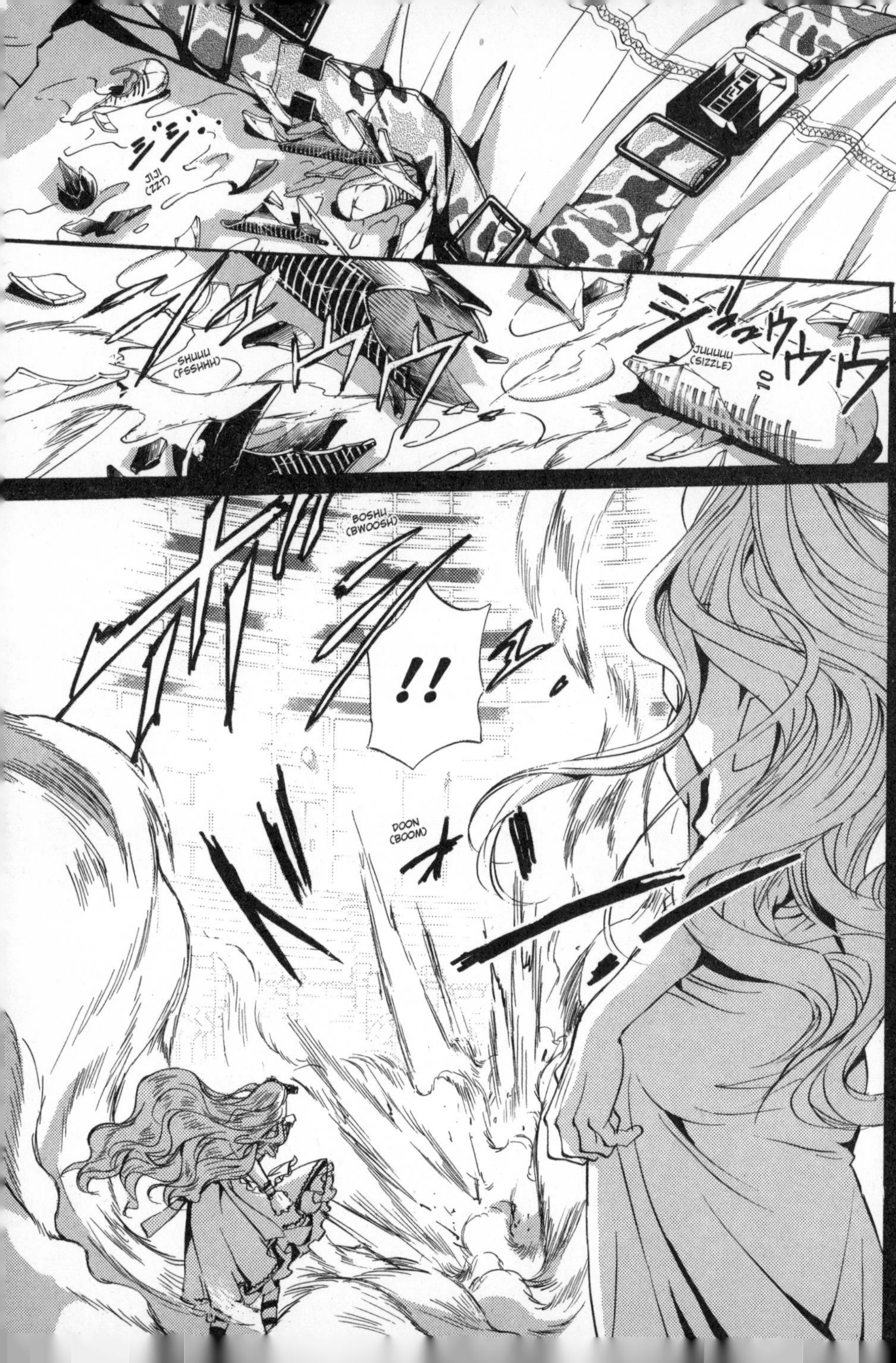
JIJI
(ZZZ)
JUUUUU
(SIZZLE)
SHUUU
(FSSHHH)
BOSHU
(BWOOSH)
!!
DOON
(BOOM)

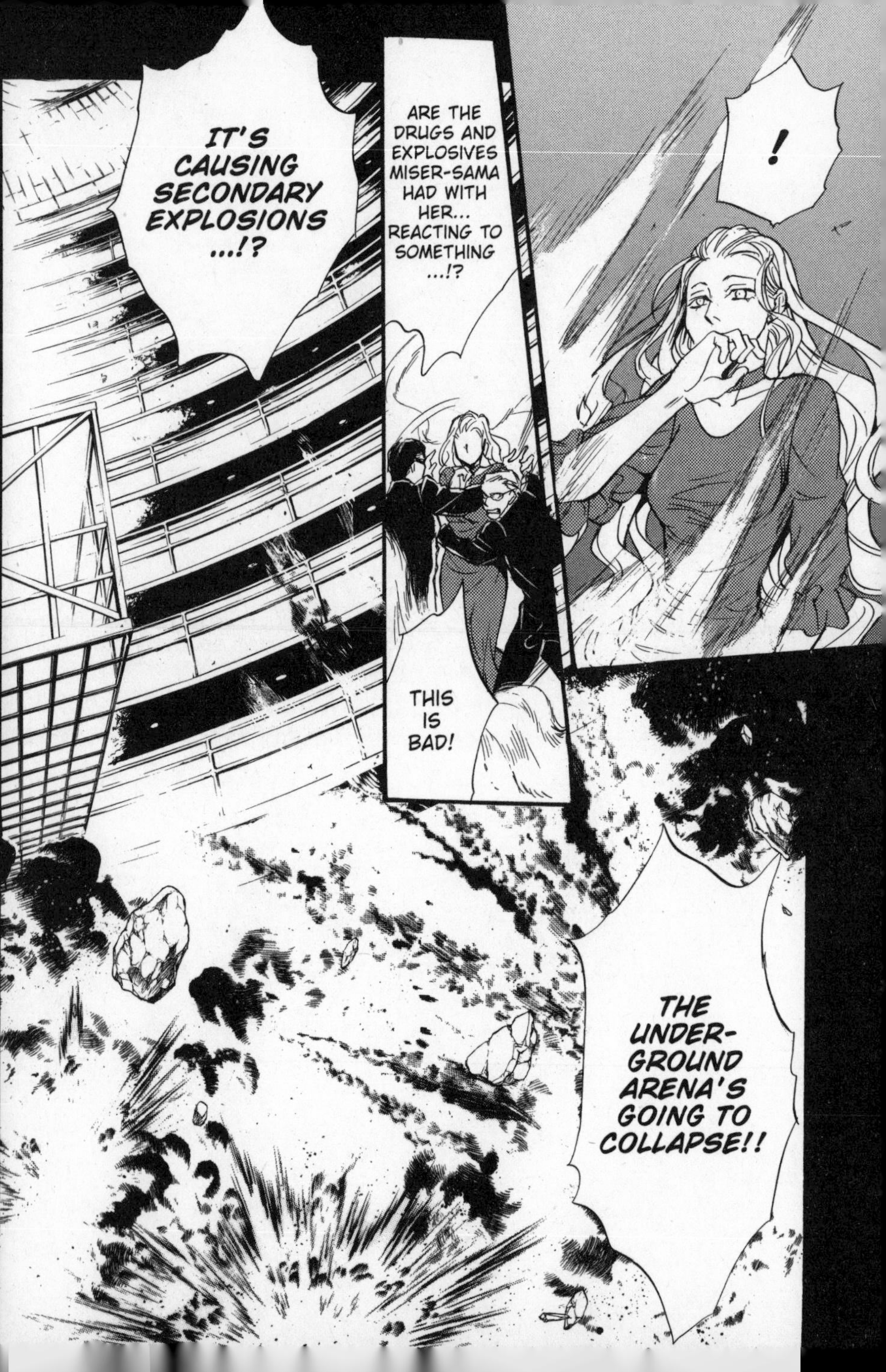
!
ARE THE DRUGS AND EXPLOSIVES MISER-SAMA HAD WITH HER... REACTING TO SOMETHING ...!?
THIS IS BAD!
IT'S CAUSING SECONDARY EXPLOSIONS ...!?
THE UNDER-GROUND ARENA'S GOING TO COLLAPSE!!

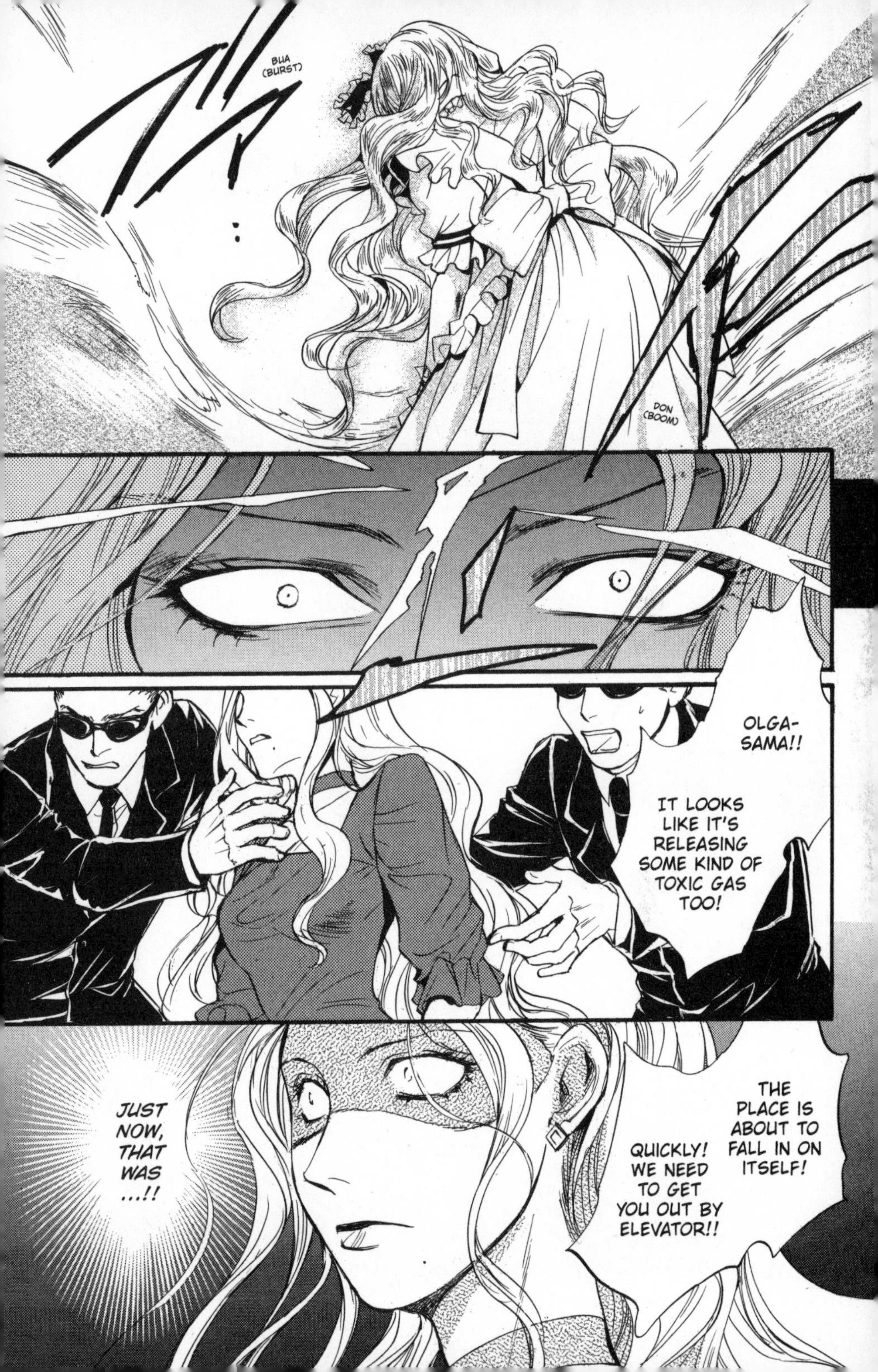
BUA (BURST)
DON (BOOM)
OLGA-SAMA!!
IT LOOKS LIKE IT'S RELEASING SOME KIND OF TOXIC GAS TOO!
THE PLACE IS ABOUT TO FALL IN ON ITSELF!
QUICKLY! WE NEED TO GET YOU OUT BY ELEVATOR!!
JUST NOW, THAT WAS ...!!

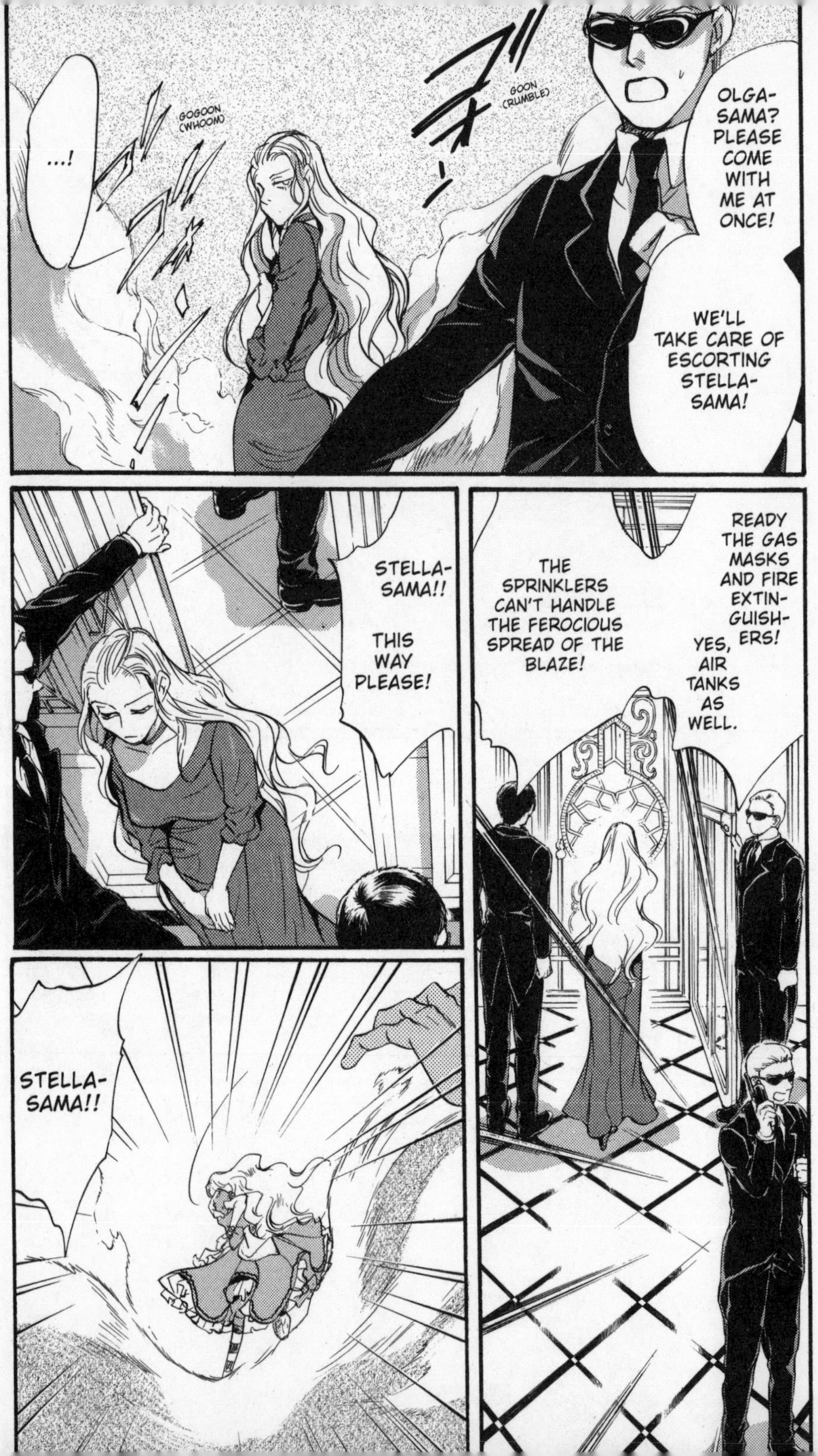
OLGA-SAMA? PLEASE COME WITH ME AT ONCE!
WE'LL TAKE CARE OF ESCORTING STELLA-SAMA!
GOON (RUMBLE)
GOGOON (WHOOM)
...!
READY THE GAS MASKS AND FIRE EXTINGUISHERS!
YES, AIR TANKS AS WELL.
THE SPRINKLERS CAN'T HANDLE THE FEROCIOUS SPREAD OF THE BLAZE!
STELLA-SAMA!!
THIS WAY PLEASE!
STELLA-SAMA!!

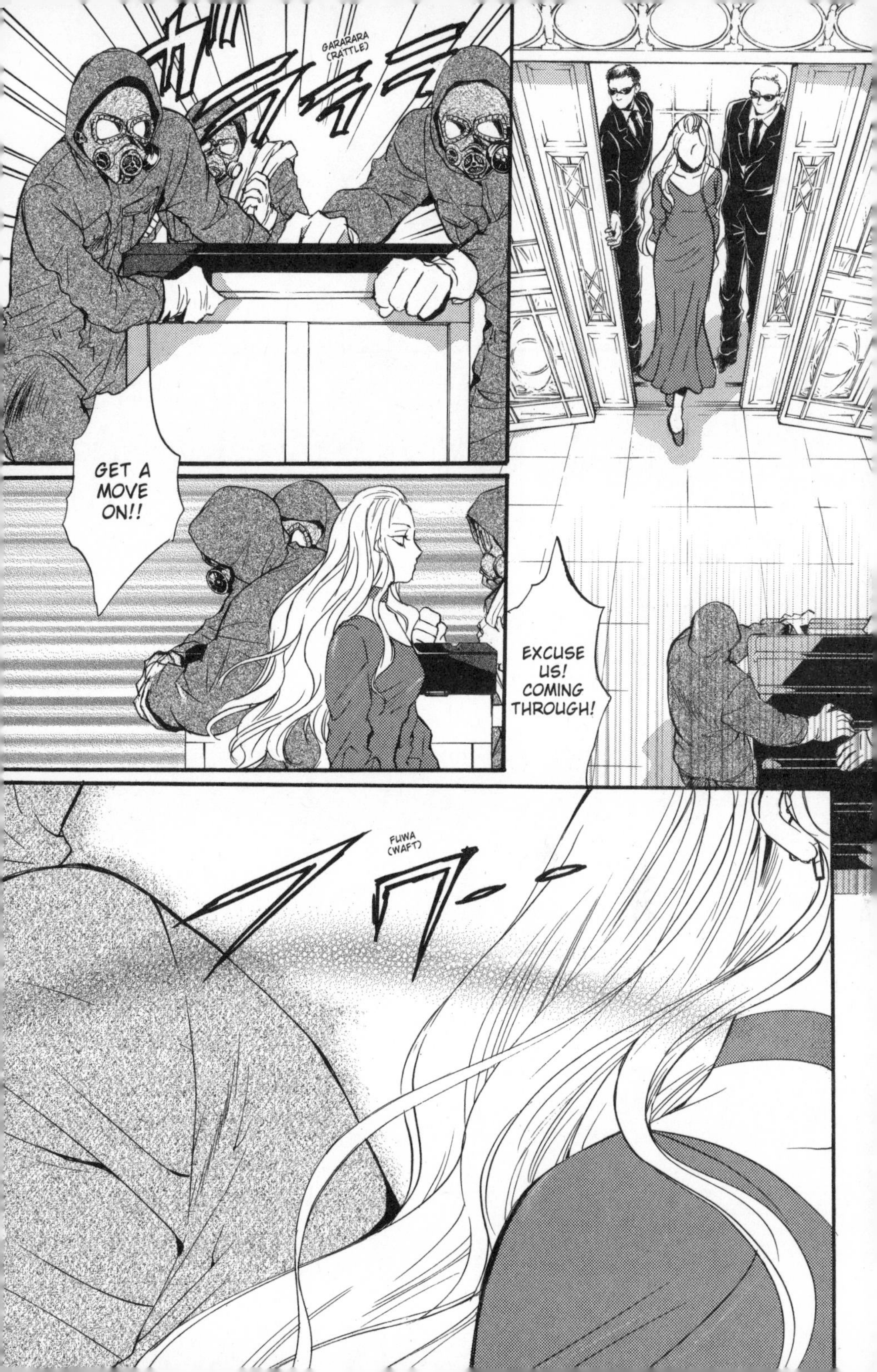
EXCUSE US! COMING THROUGH!
GARARARA (RATTLE)
GET A MOVE ON!!
FUWA (WAFT)

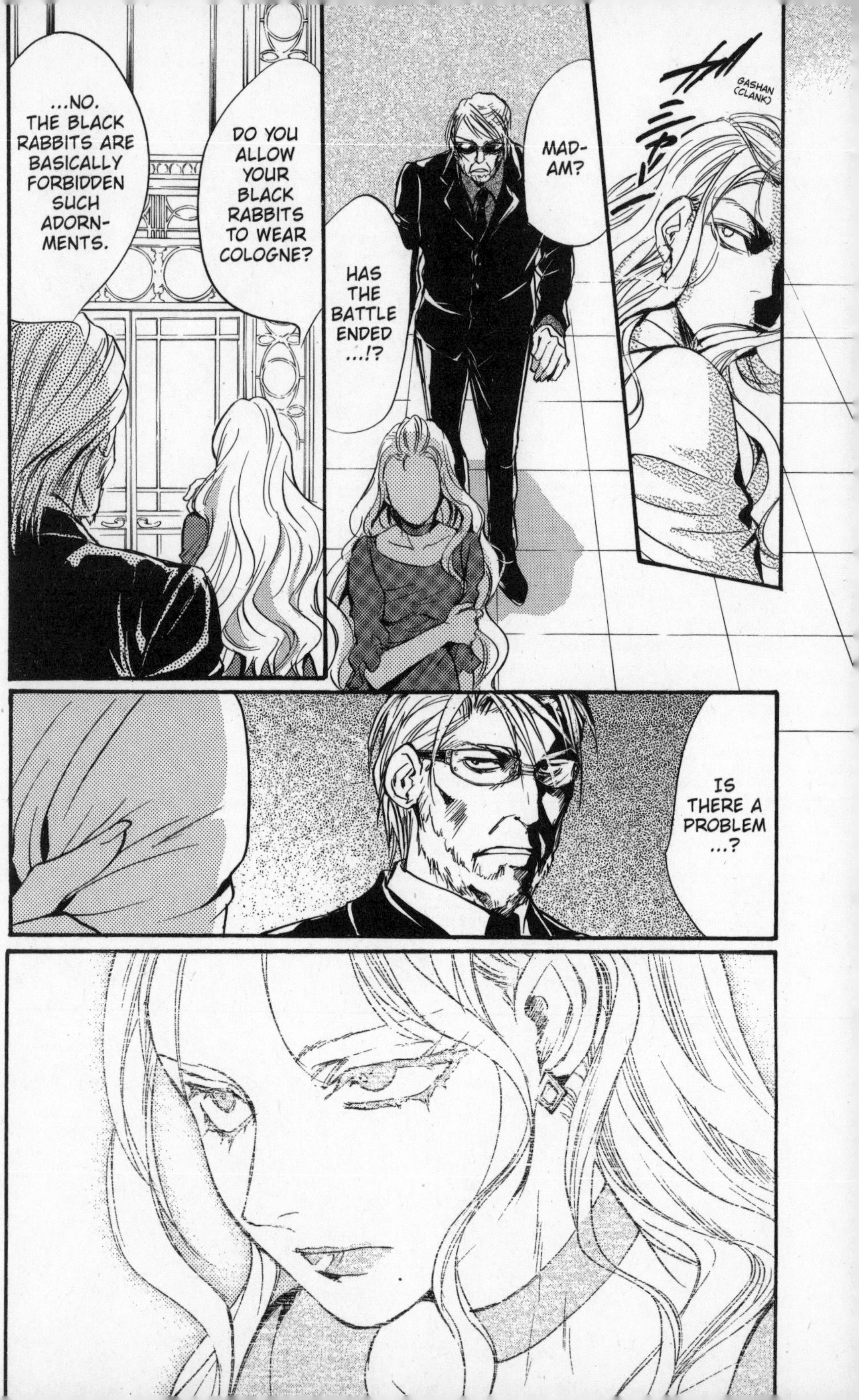
GASHAN (CLANK)
MAD-AM?
HAS THE BATTLE ENDED ...!?
DO YOU ALLOW YOUR BLACK RABBITS TO WEAR COLOGNE?
...NO. THE BLACK RABBITS ARE BASICALLY FORBIDDEN SUCH ADORN-MENTS.
IS THERE A PROBLEM ...?

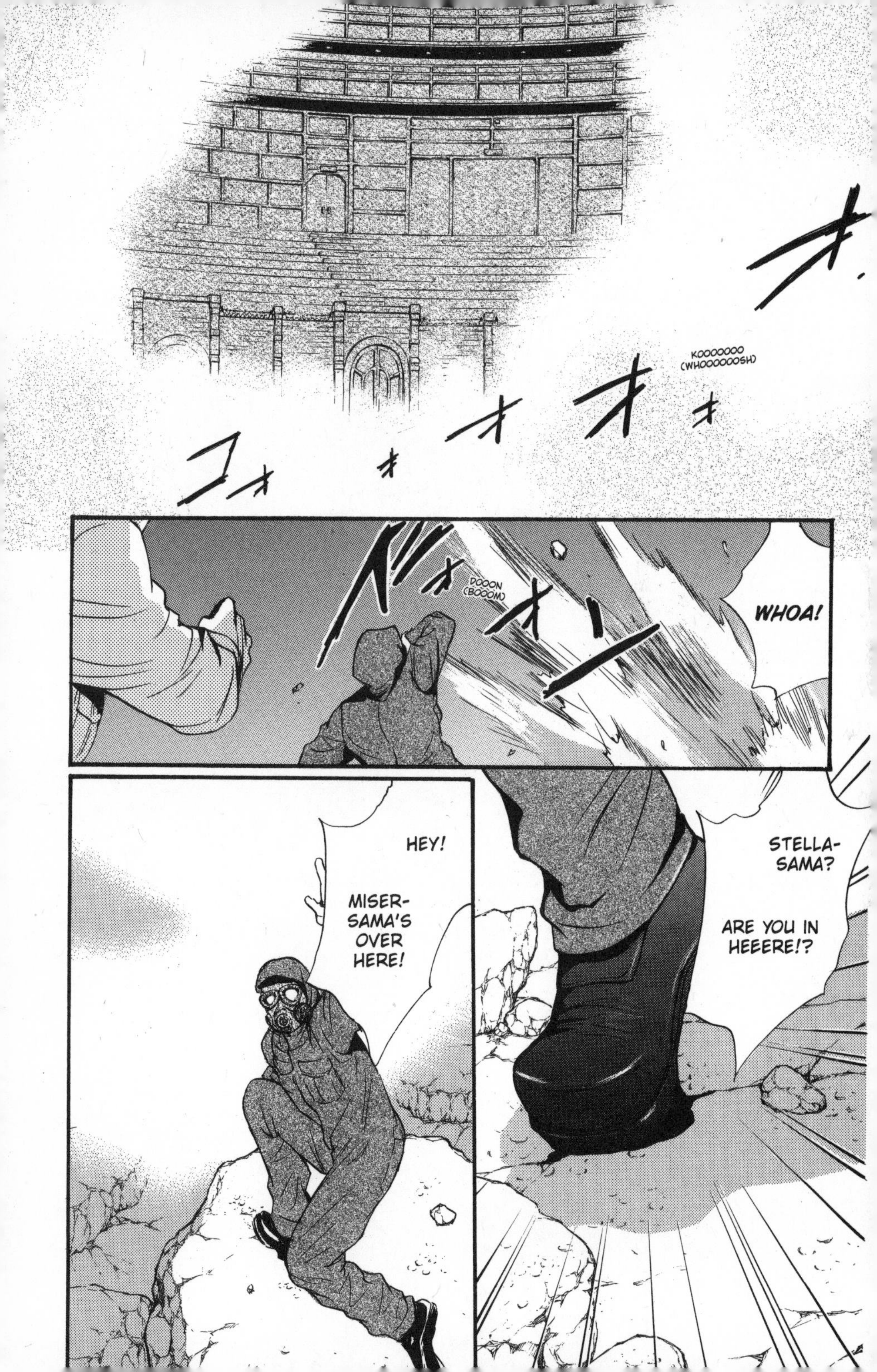
KOOOOOOO (WHOOOOOOSH)
DOOON (BOOOM)
WHOA!
STELLA-SAMA?
ARE YOU IN HEEERE!?
HEY!
MISER-SAMA'S OVER HERE!

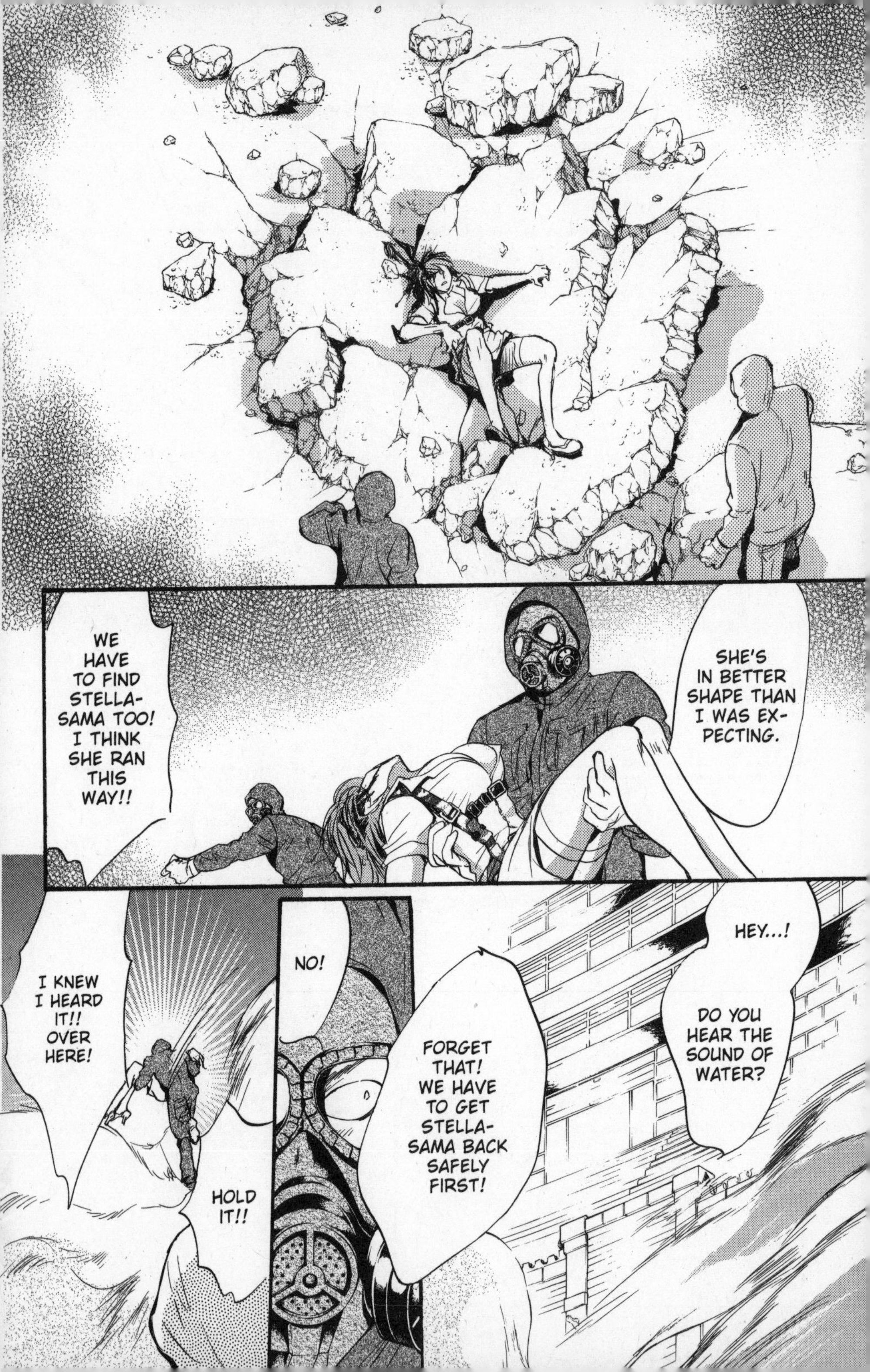
SHE'S IN BETTER SHAPE THAN I WAS EX-PECTING.
WE HAVE TO FIND STELLA-SAMA TOO! I THINK SHE RAN THIS WAY!!
HEY...!
DO YOU HEAR THE SOUND OF WATER?
FORGET THAT! WE HAVE TO GET STELLA-SAMA BACK SAFELY FIRST!
NO!
I KNEW I HEARD IT!! OVER HERE!
HOLD IT!!

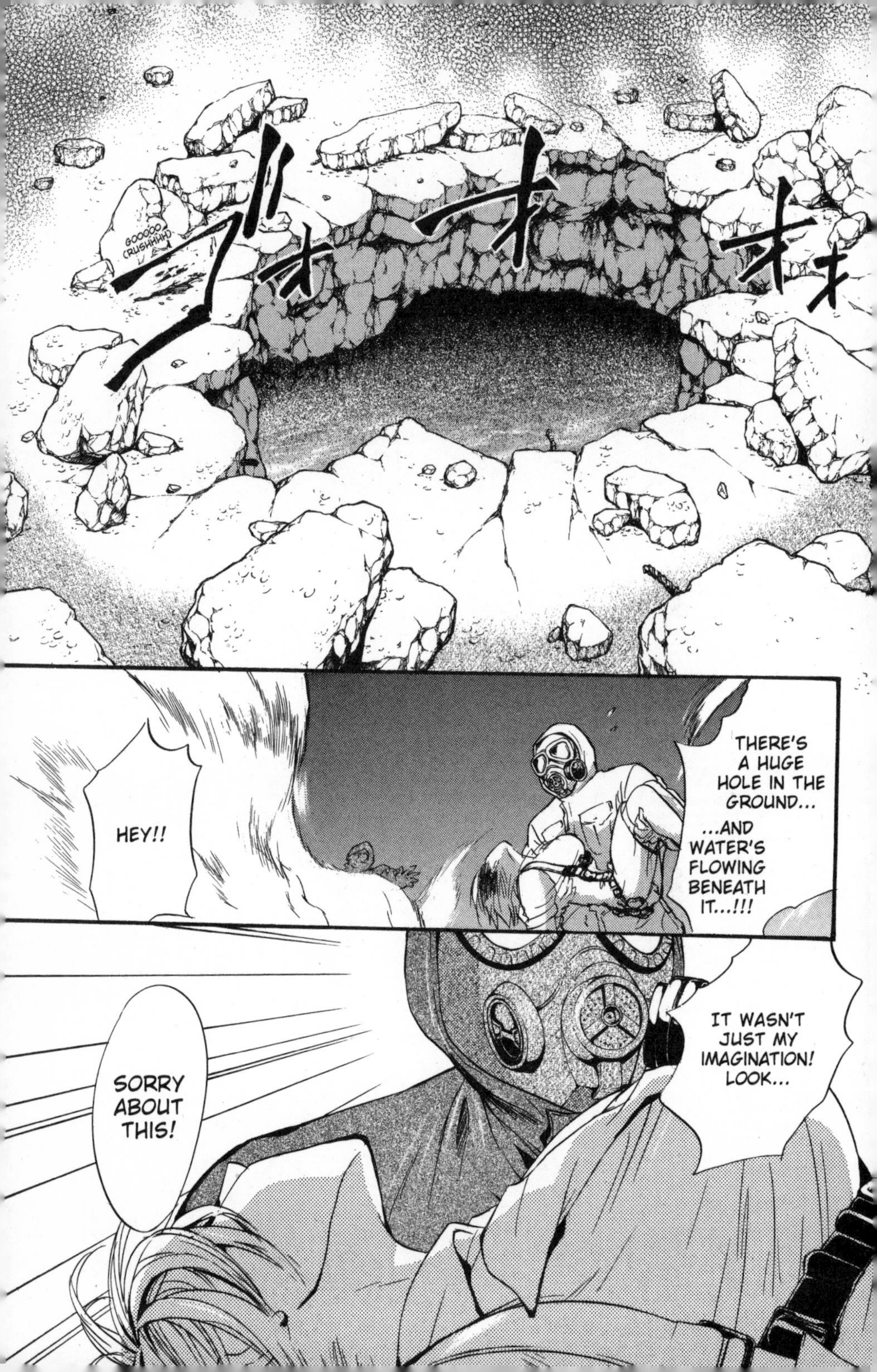
GOOOOOO (RUSHHHH)
THERE'S A HUGE HOLE IN THE GROUND...
...AND WATER'S FLOWING BENEATH IT...!!!
HEY!!
IT WASN'T JUST MY IMAGINATION! LOOK...
SORRY ABOUT THIS!

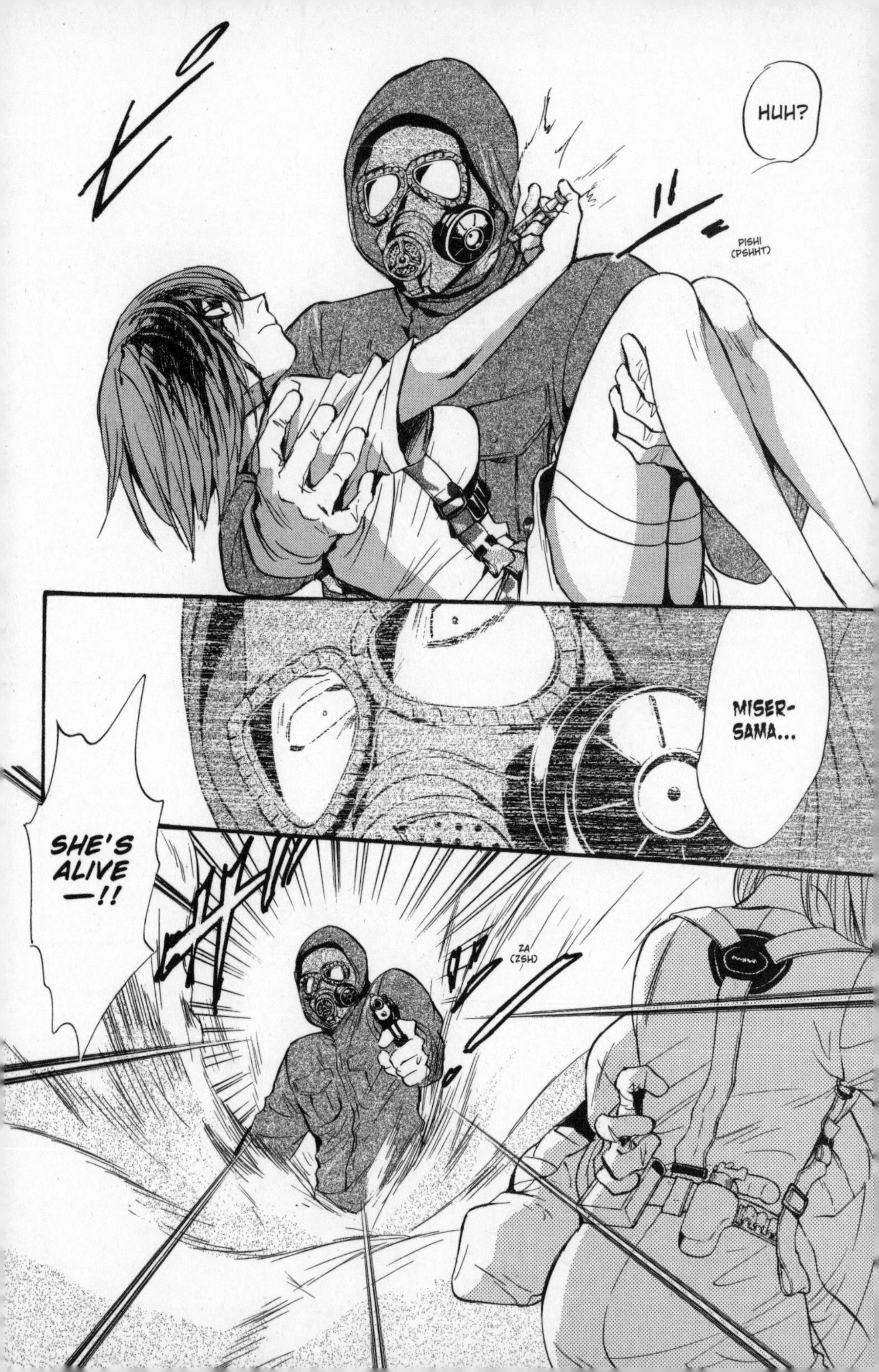
HUH?
PISHI (PSHHT)
MISER-SAMA...
ZA (ZSH)
SHE'S ALIVE—!!

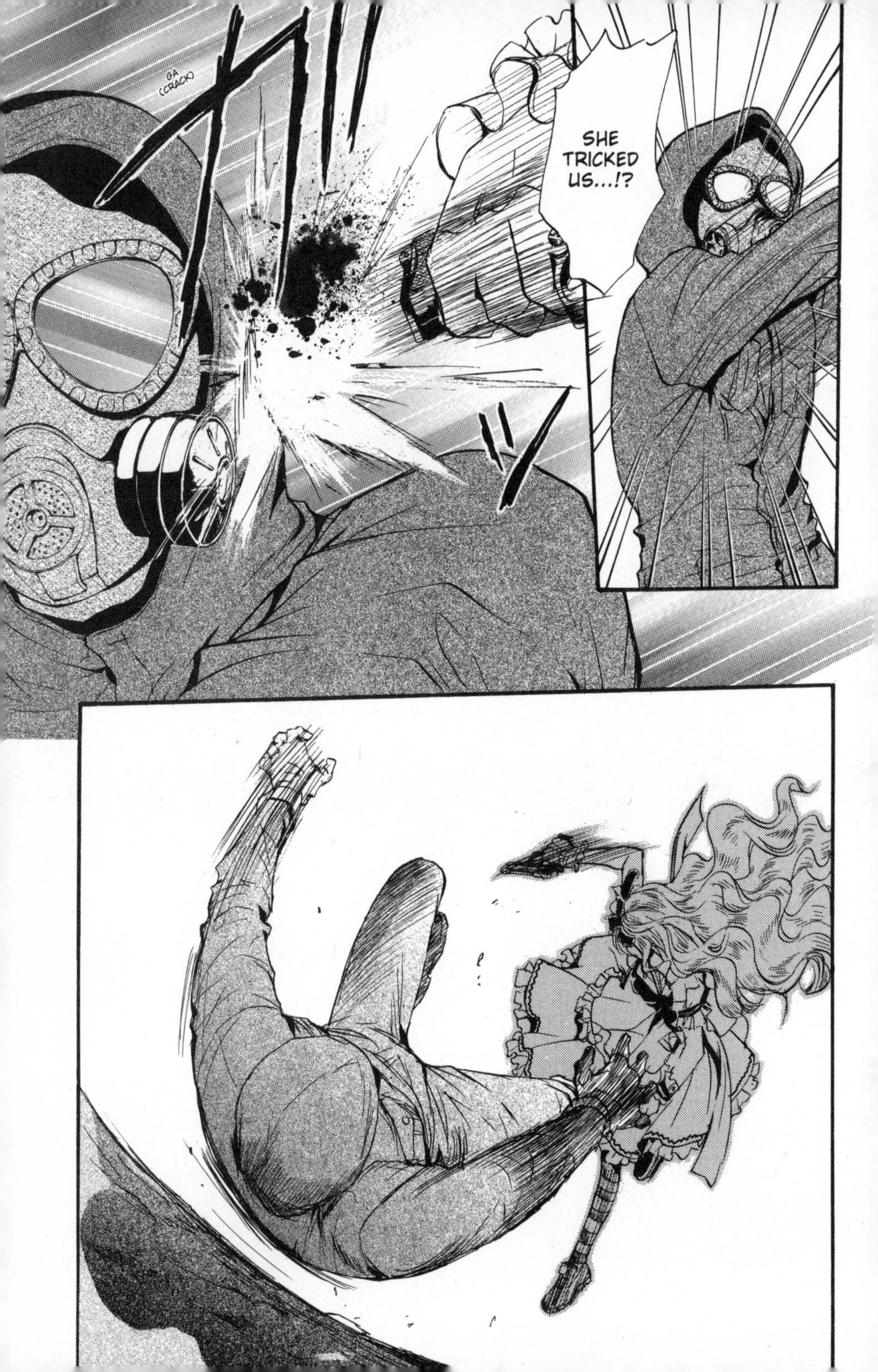
SHE TRICKED US...!?
GA (CRACK)

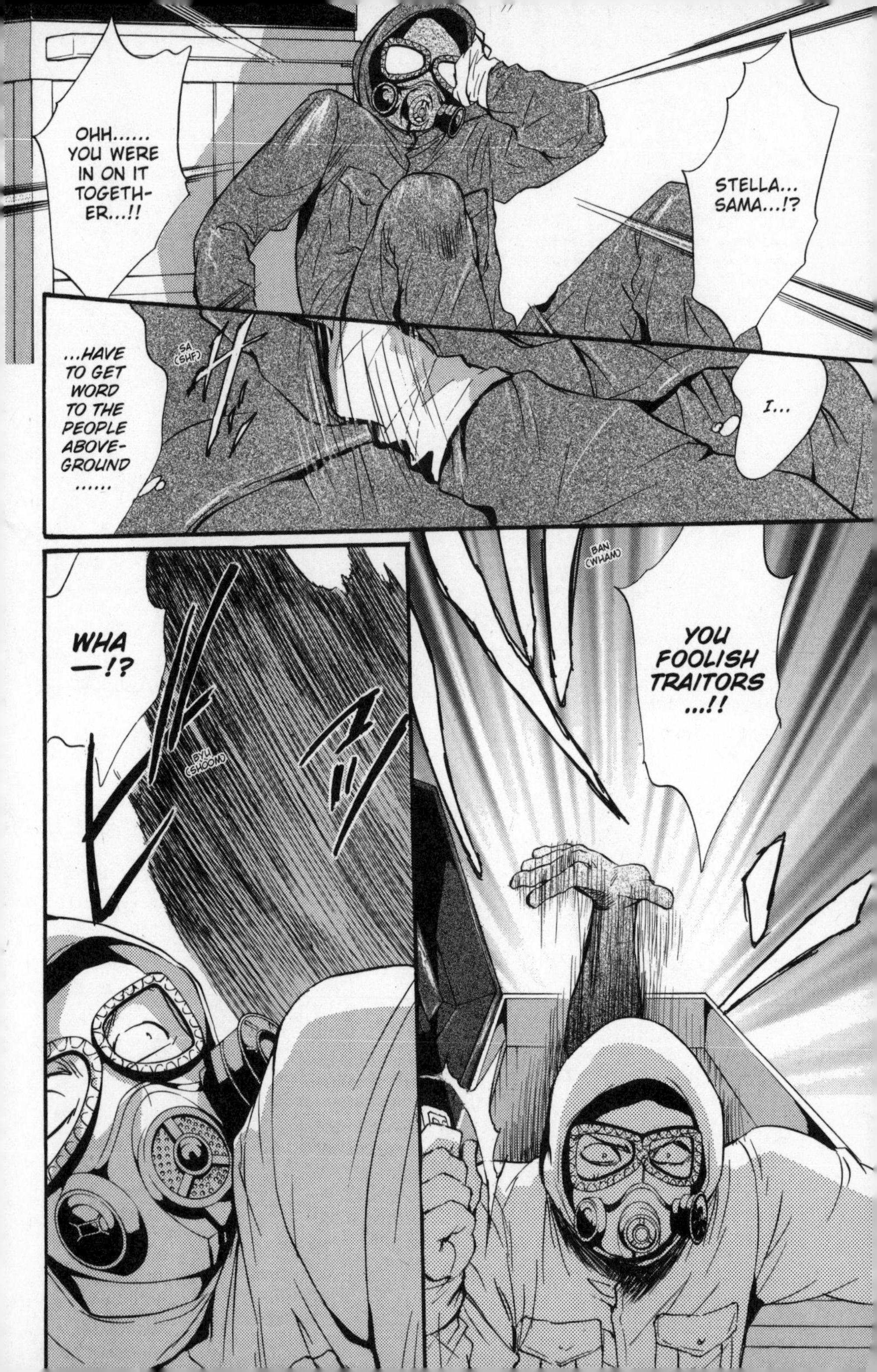
STELLA... SAMA...!?
OHH...... YOU WERE IN ON IT TOGETHER...!!
I...
SA (SHF)
...HAVE TO GET WORD TO THE PEOPLE ABOVEGROUND......
BAN (WHAM)
YOU FOOLISH TRAITORS ...!!
WHA—!?
BYU (SHOOM)

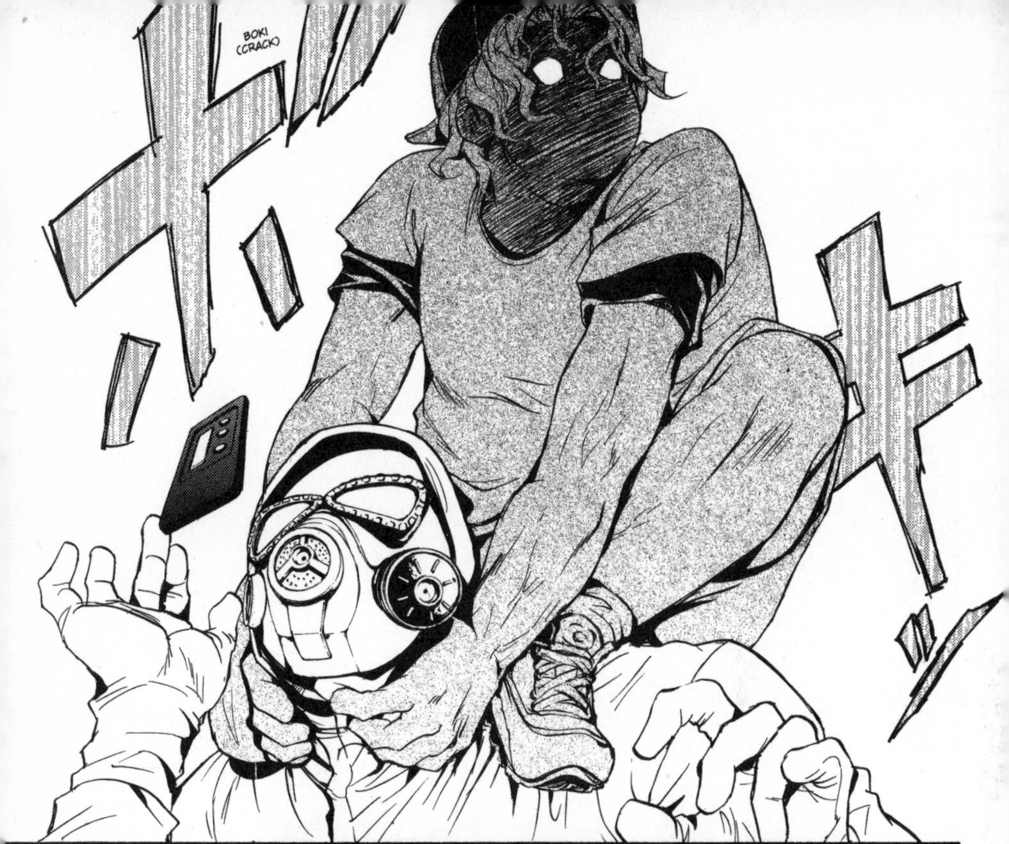
BOKI (CRACK)

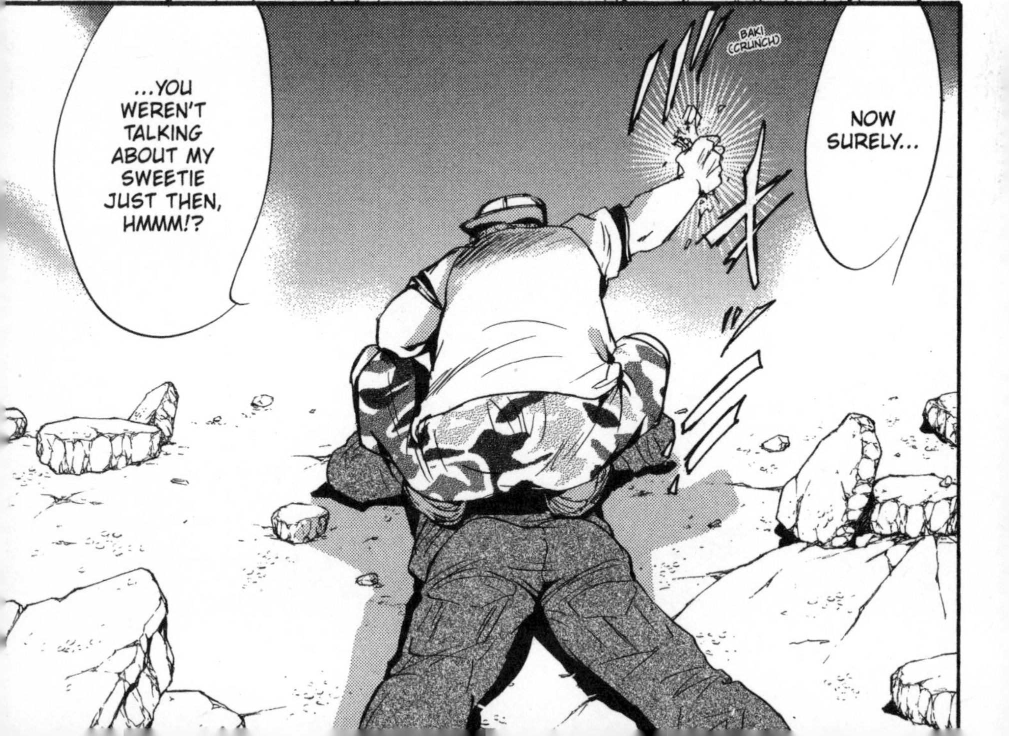
BAKI (CRUNCH)
NOW SURELY...
...YOU WEREN'T TALKING ABOUT MY SWEETIE JUST THEN, HMMM!?

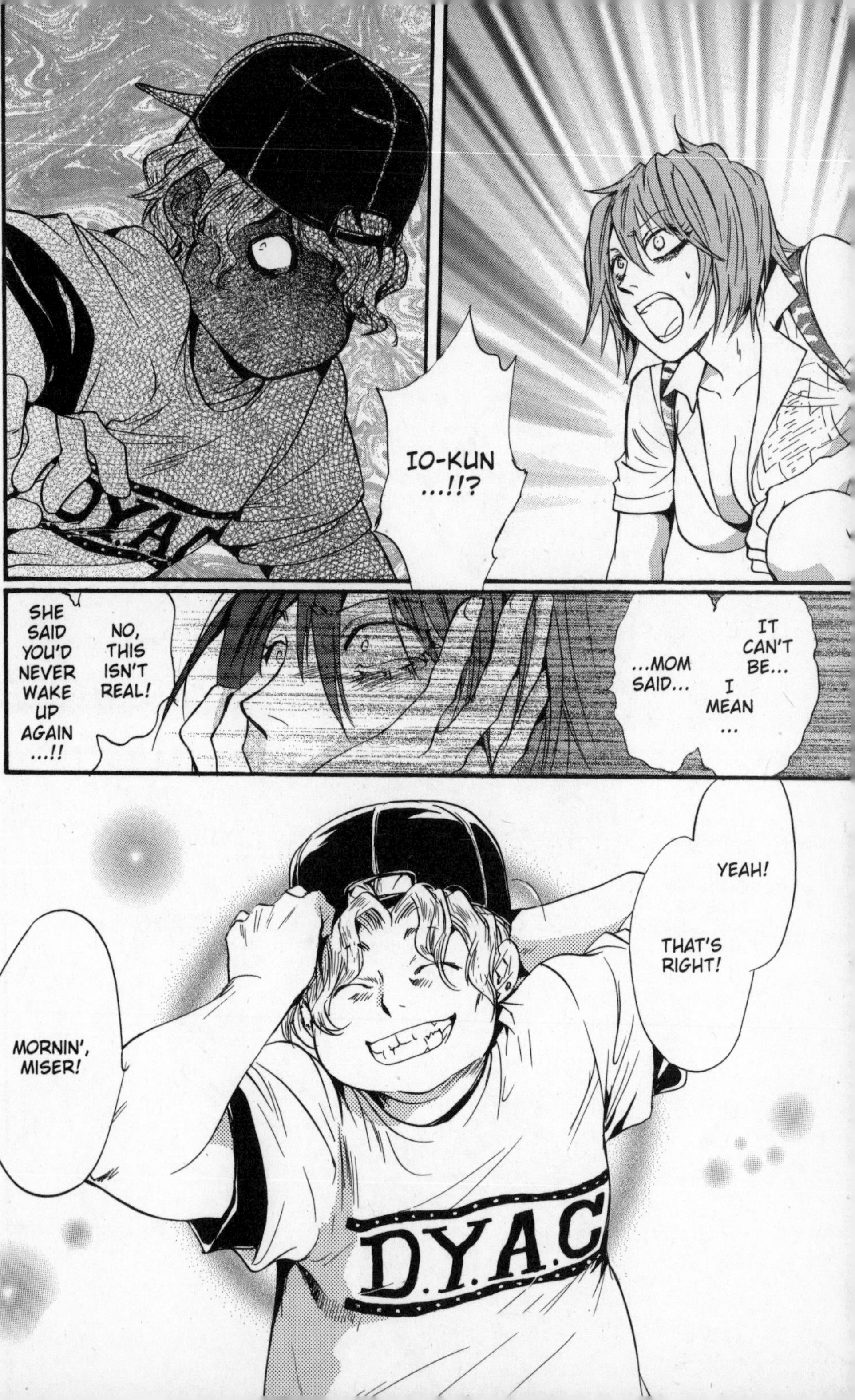
IO-KUN ...!!?
IT CAN'T BE... I MEAN ...
...MOM SAID...
NO, THIS ISN'T REAL!
SHE SAID YOU'D NEVER WAKE UP AGAIN ...!!
YEAH! THAT'S RIGHT!
MORNIN', MISER!

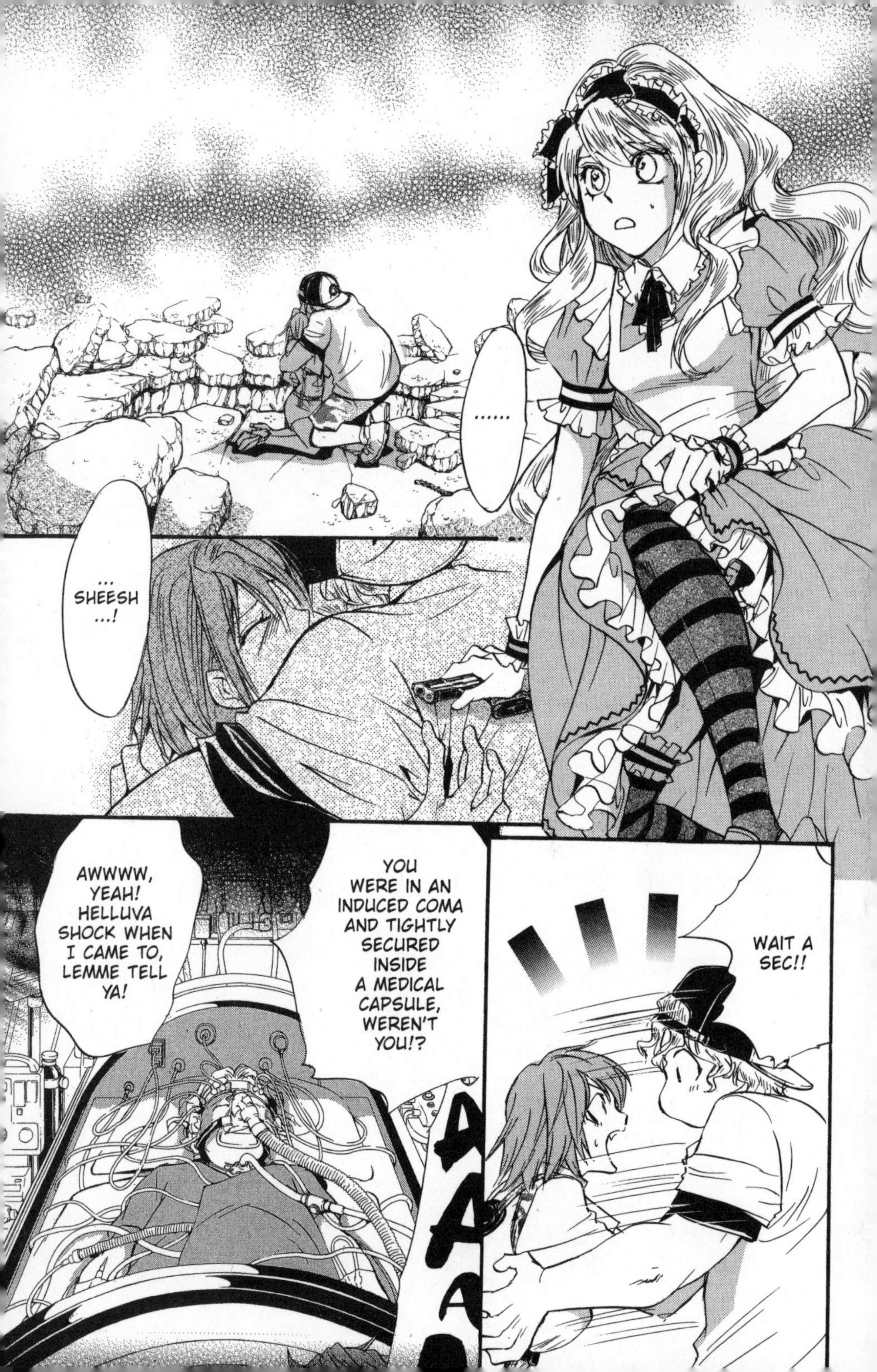
......
...SHEESH...!
WAIT A SEC!!
YOU WERE IN AN INDUCED COMA AND TIGHTLY SECURED INSIDE A MEDICAL CAPSULE, WEREN'T YOU!?
AWWWW, YEAH! HELLUVA SHOCK WHEN I CAME TO, LEMME TELL YA!
AAA

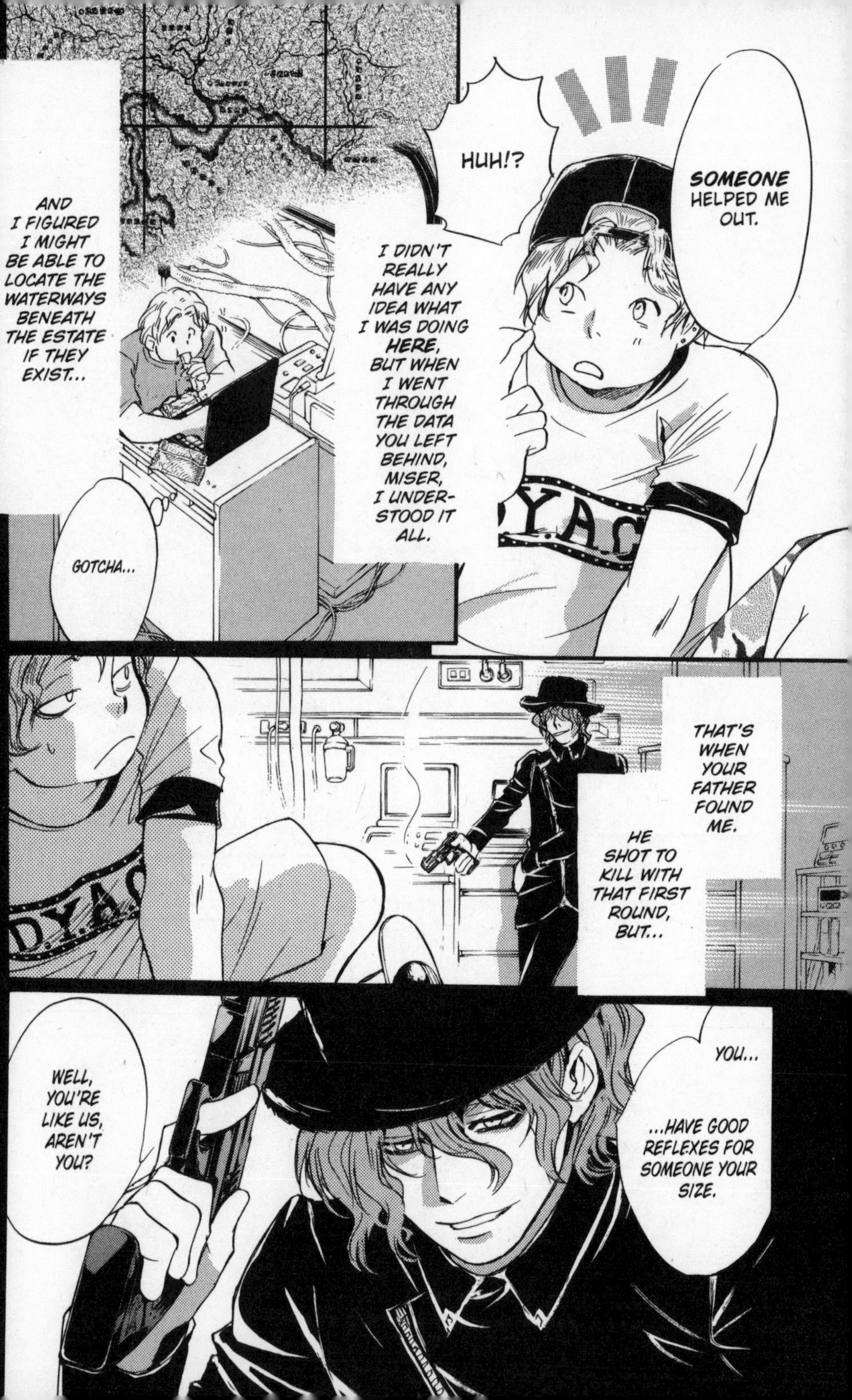
SOMEONE HELPED ME OUT.
HUH!?
I DIDN'T REALLY HAVE ANY IDEA WHAT I WAS DOING HERE, BUT WHEN I WENT THROUGH THE DATA YOU LEFT BEHIND, MISER, I UNDERSTOOD IT ALL.
AND I FIGURED I MIGHT BE ABLE TO LOCATE THE WATERWAYS BENEATH THE ESTATE IF THEY EXIST...
GOTCHA...
D.Y.A.C.
THAT'S WHEN YOUR FATHER FOUND ME.
HE SHOT TO KILL WITH THAT FIRST ROUND, BUT...
D.Y.A.
YOU...
...HAVE GOOD REFLEXES FOR SOMEONE YOUR SIZE.
WELL, YOU'RE LIKE US, AREN'T YOU?

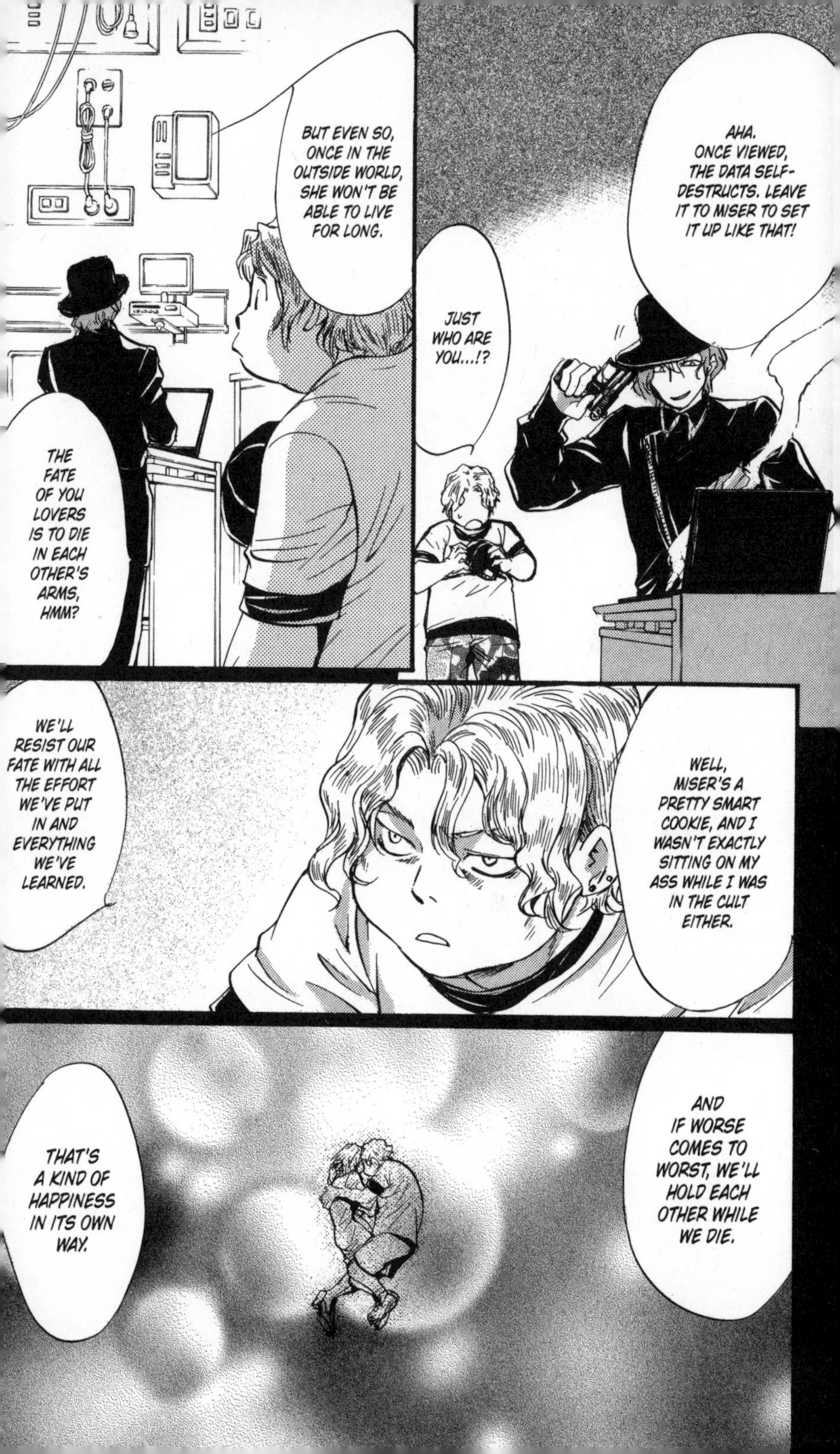
AHA. ONCE VIEWED, THE DATA SELF-DESTRUCTS. LEAVE IT TO MISER TO SET IT UP LIKE THAT!
JUST WHO ARE YOU...!?
BUT EVEN SO, ONCE IN THE OUTSIDE WORLD, SHE WON'T BE ABLE TO LIVE FOR LONG.
THE FATE OF YOU LOVERS IS TO DIE IN EACH OTHER'S ARMS, HMM?
WELL, MISER'S A PRETTY SMART COOKIE, AND I WASN'T EXACTLY SITTING ON MY ASS WHILE I WAS IN THE CULT EITHER.
WE'LL RESIST OUR FATE WITH ALL THE EFFORT WE'VE PUT IN AND EVERYTHING WE'VE LEARNED.
AND IF WORSE COMES TO WORST, WE'LL HOLD EACH OTHER WHILE WE DIE.
THAT'S A KIND OF HAPPINESS IN ITS OWN WAY.

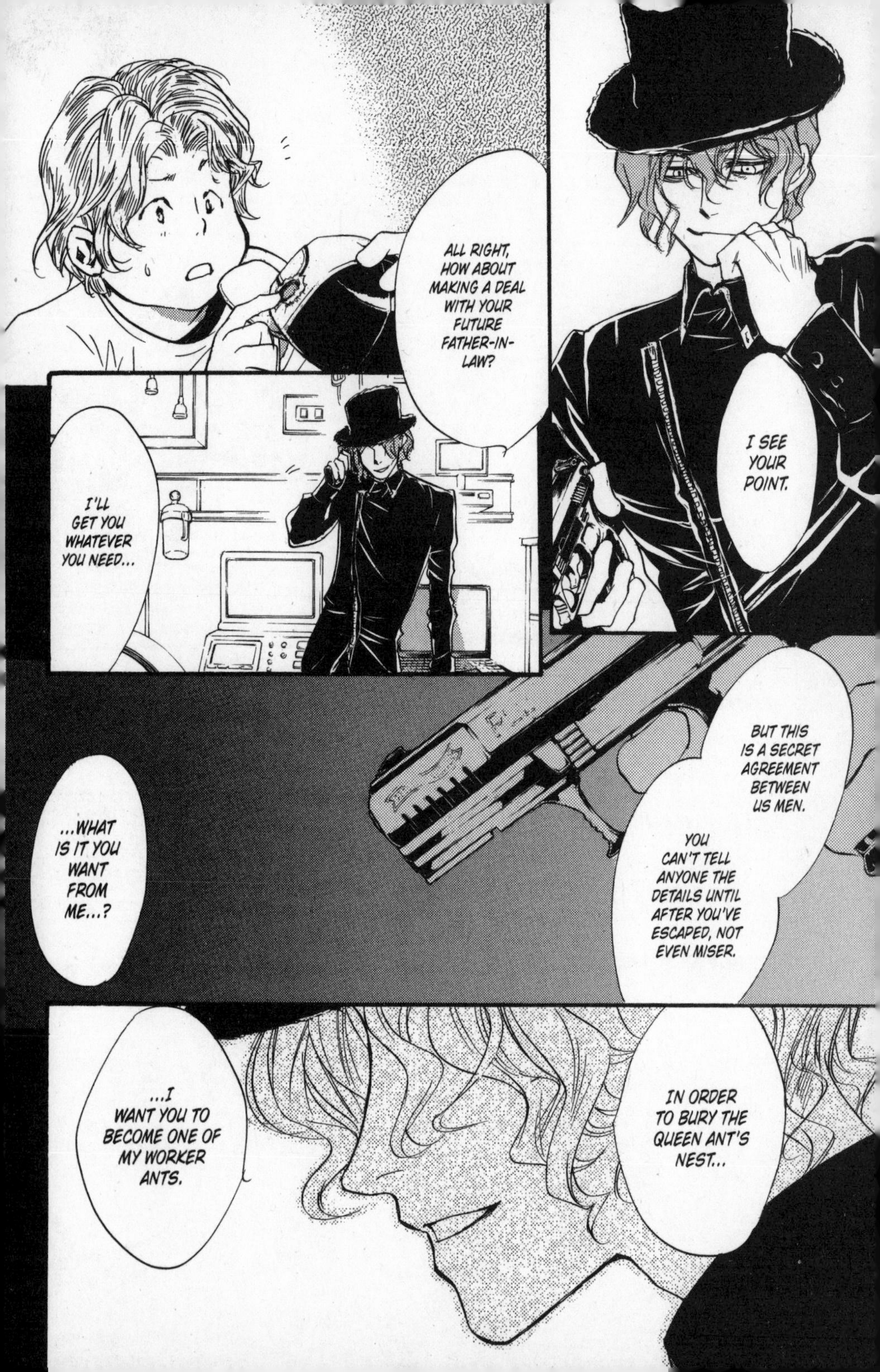
I SEE YOUR POINT.
ALL RIGHT, HOW ABOUT MAKING A DEAL WITH YOUR FUTURE FATHER-IN-LAW?
I'LL GET YOU WHATEVER YOU NEED...
BUT THIS IS A SECRET AGREEMENT BETWEEN US MEN.
YOU CAN'T TELL ANYONE THE DETAILS UNTIL AFTER YOU'VE ESCAPED, NOT EVEN MISER.
...WHAT IS IT YOU WANT FROM ME...?
IN ORDER TO BURY THE QUEEN ANT'S NEST...
...I WANT YOU TO BECOME ONE OF MY WORKER ANTS.

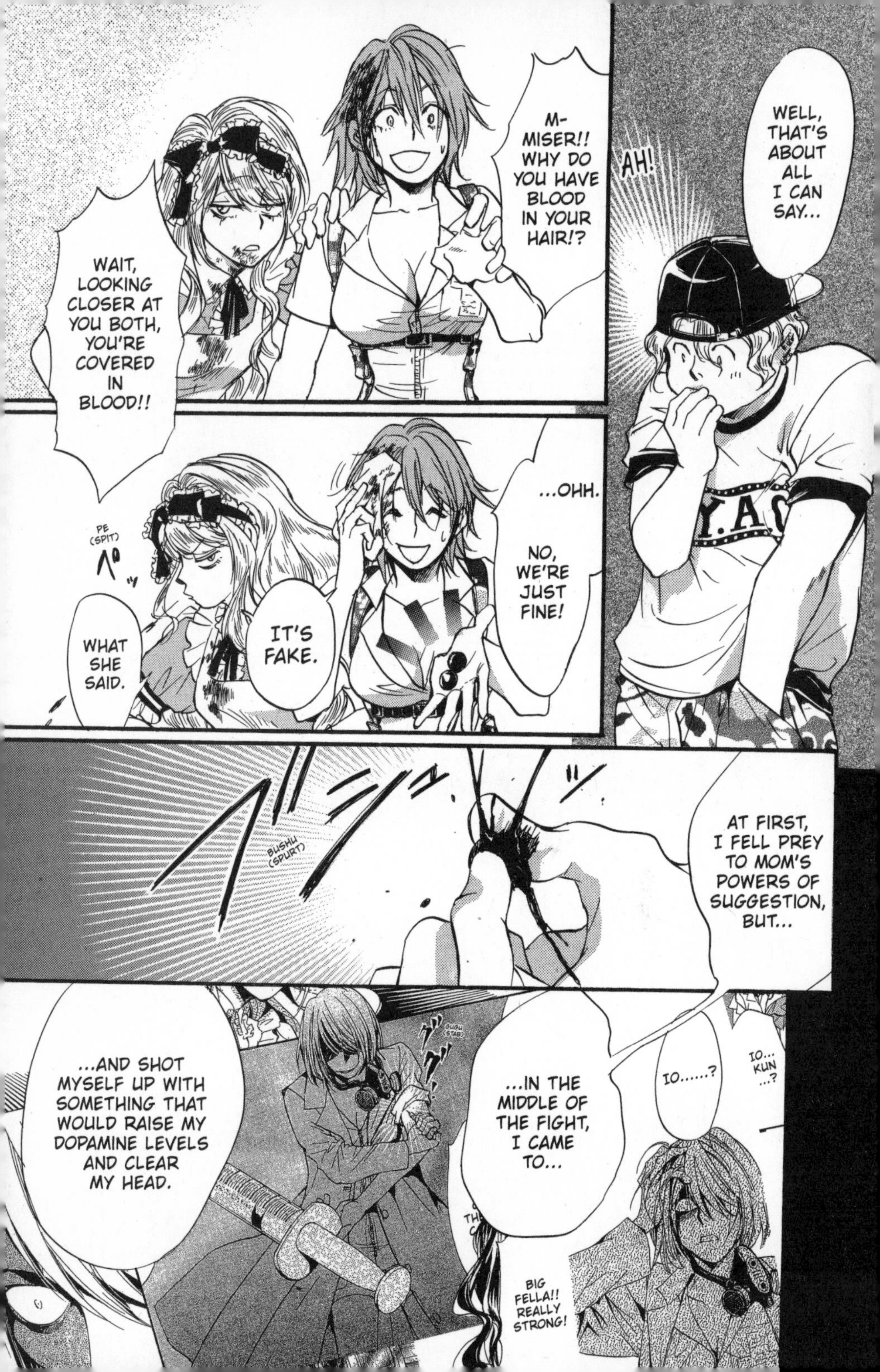
WELL, THAT'S ABOUT ALL I CAN SAY...
AH!
M-MISER!! WHY DO YOU HAVE BLOOD IN YOUR HAIR!?
WAIT, LOOKING CLOSER AT YOU BOTH, YOU'RE COVERED IN BLOOD!!
...OHH.
NO, WE'RE JUST FINE!
IT'S FAKE.
PE (SPIT)
WHAT SHE SAID.
AT FIRST, I FELL PREY TO MOM'S POWERS OF SUGGESTION, BUT...
BUSHU (SPURT)
IO... KUN ...?
IO......?
...IN THE MIDDLE OF THE FIGHT, I CAME TO...
GUGU (STAB)
...AND SHOT MYSELF UP WITH SOMETHING THAT WOULD RAISE MY DOPAMINE LEVELS AND CLEAR MY HEAD.
BIG FELLA!! REALLY STRONG!

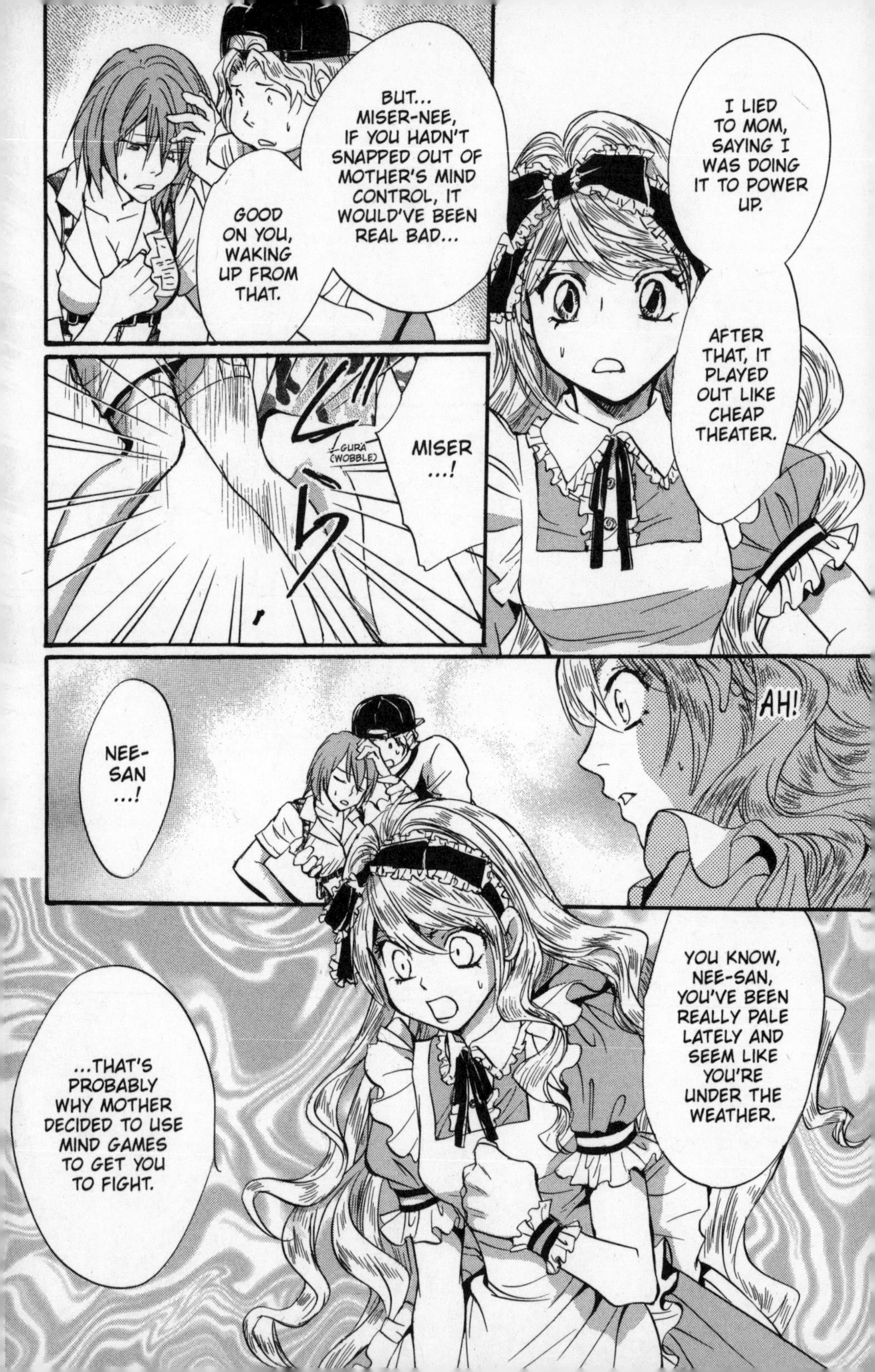
I LIED TO MOM, SAYING I WAS DOING IT TO POWER UP.
AFTER THAT, IT PLAYED OUT LIKE CHEAP THEATER.
BUT... MISER-NEE, IF YOU HADN'T SNAPPED OUT OF MOTHER'S MIND CONTROL, IT WOULD'VE BEEN REAL BAD...
GOOD ON YOU, WAKING UP FROM THAT.
MISER ...!
GURA (WOBBLE)
AH!
NEE-SAN ...!
YOU KNOW, NEE-SAN, YOU'VE BEEN REALLY PALE LATELY AND SEEM LIKE YOU'RE UNDER THE WEATHER.
...THAT'S PROBABLY WHY MOTHER DECIDED TO USE MIND GAMES TO GET YOU TO FIGHT.

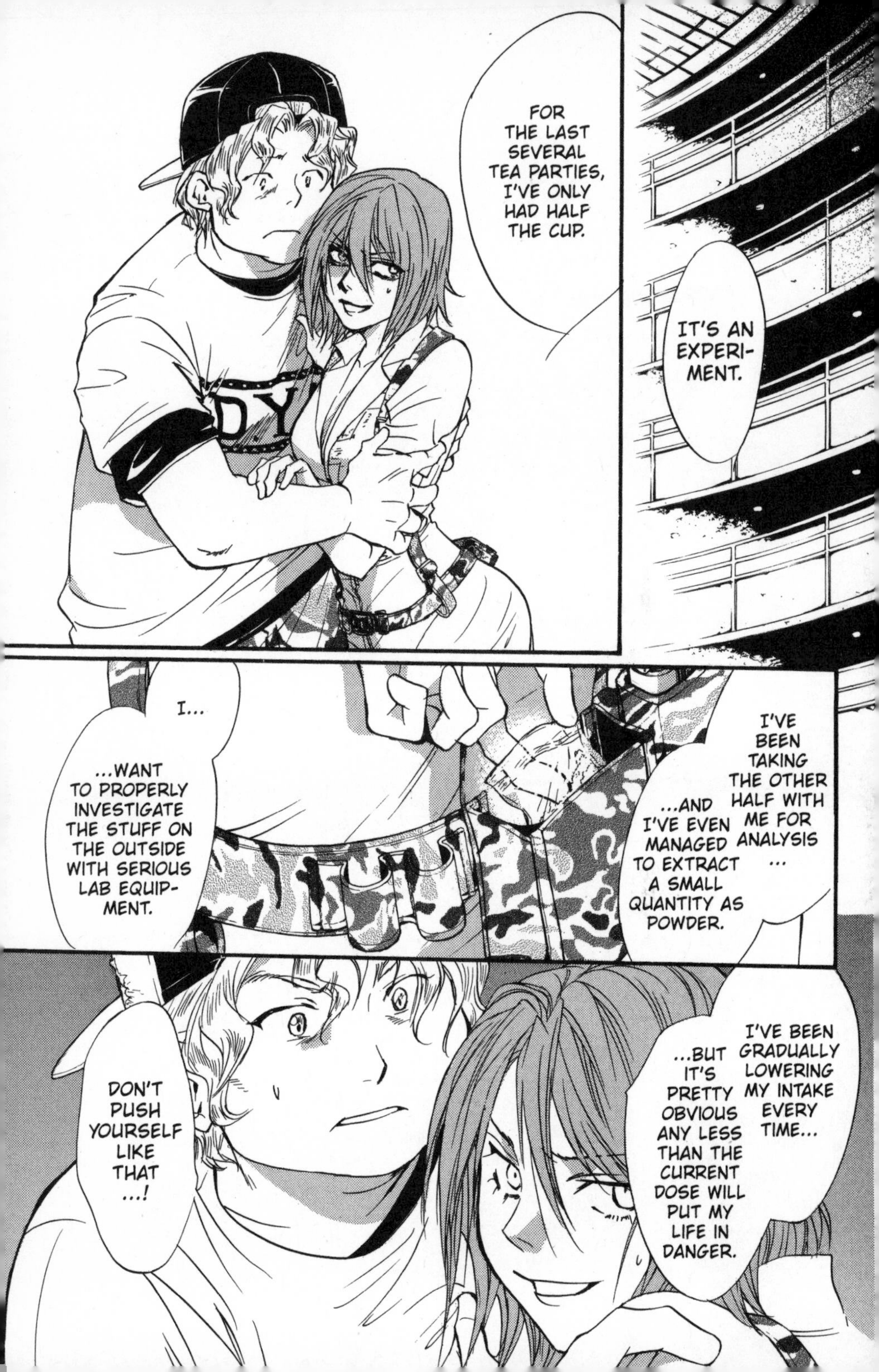
IT'S AN EXPERIMENT.
FOR THE LAST SEVERAL TEA PARTIES, I'VE ONLY HAD HALF THE CUP.
I'VE BEEN TAKING THE OTHER HALF WITH ME FOR ANALYSIS...
...AND I'VE EVEN MANAGED TO EXTRACT A SMALL QUANTITY AS POWDER.
I...
...WANT TO PROPERLY INVESTIGATE THE STUFF ON THE OUTSIDE WITH SERIOUS LAB EQUIPMENT.
I'VE BEEN GRADUALLY LOWERING MY INTAKE EVERY TIME...
...BUT IT'S PRETTY OBVIOUS ANY LESS THAN THE CURRENT DOSE WILL PUT MY LIFE IN DANGER.
DON'T PUSH YOURSELF LIKE THAT...!

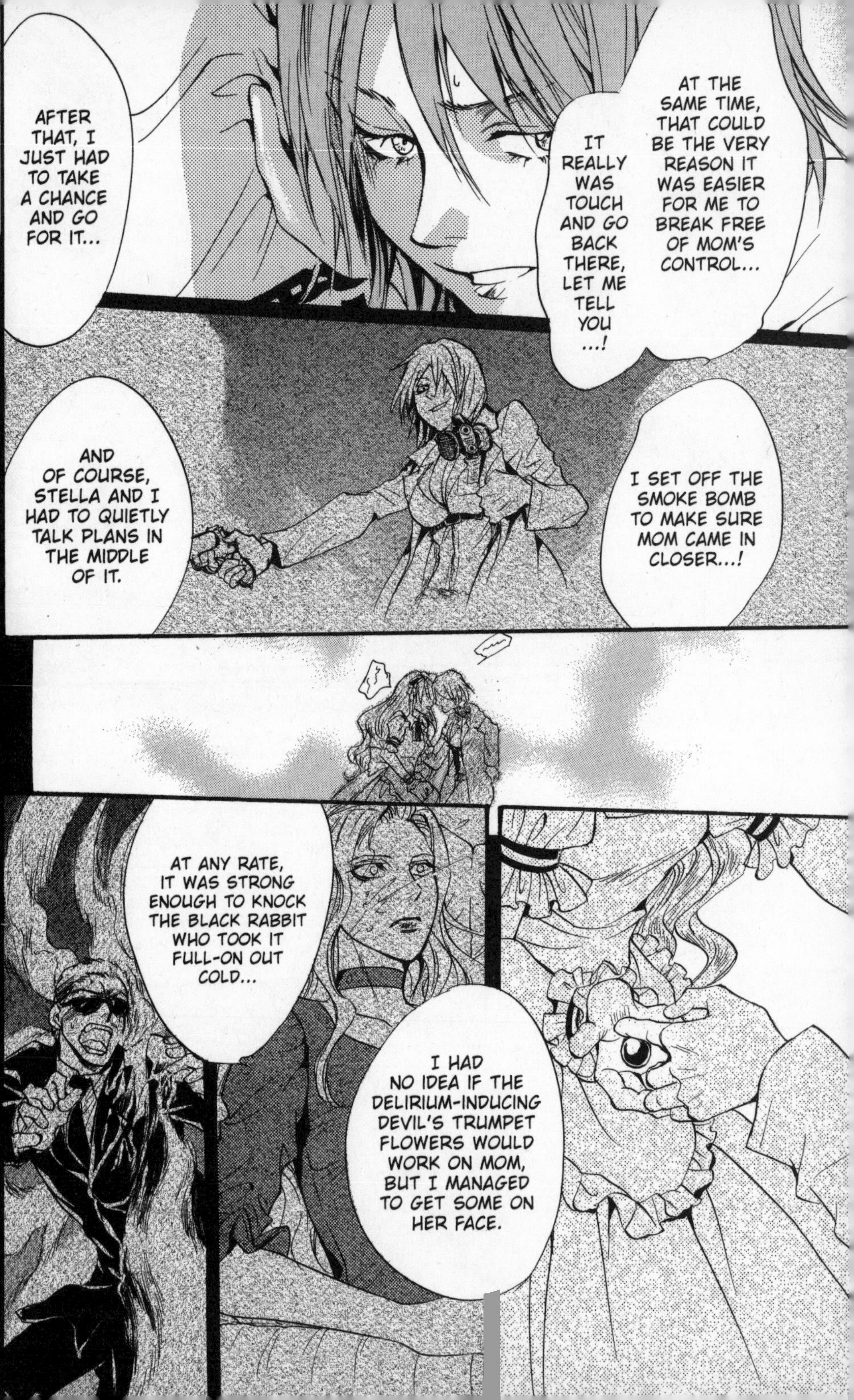
AT THE SAME TIME, THAT COULD BE THE VERY REASON IT WAS EASIER FOR ME TO BREAK FREE OF MOM'S CONTROL...
IT REALLY WAS TOUCH AND GO BACK THERE, LET ME TELL YOU ...!
AFTER THAT, I JUST HAD TO TAKE A CHANCE AND GO FOR IT...
I SET OFF THE SMOKE BOMB TO MAKE SURE MOM CAME IN CLOSER...!
AND OF COURSE, STELLA AND I HAD TO QUIETLY TALK PLANS IN THE MIDDLE OF IT.
I HAD NO IDEA IF THE DELIRIUM-INDUCING DEVIL'S TRUMPET FLOWERS WOULD WORK ON MOM, BUT I MANAGED TO GET SOME ON HER FACE.
AT ANY RATE, IT WAS STRONG ENOUGH TO KNOCK THE BLACK RABBIT WHO TOOK IT FULL-ON OUT COLD...

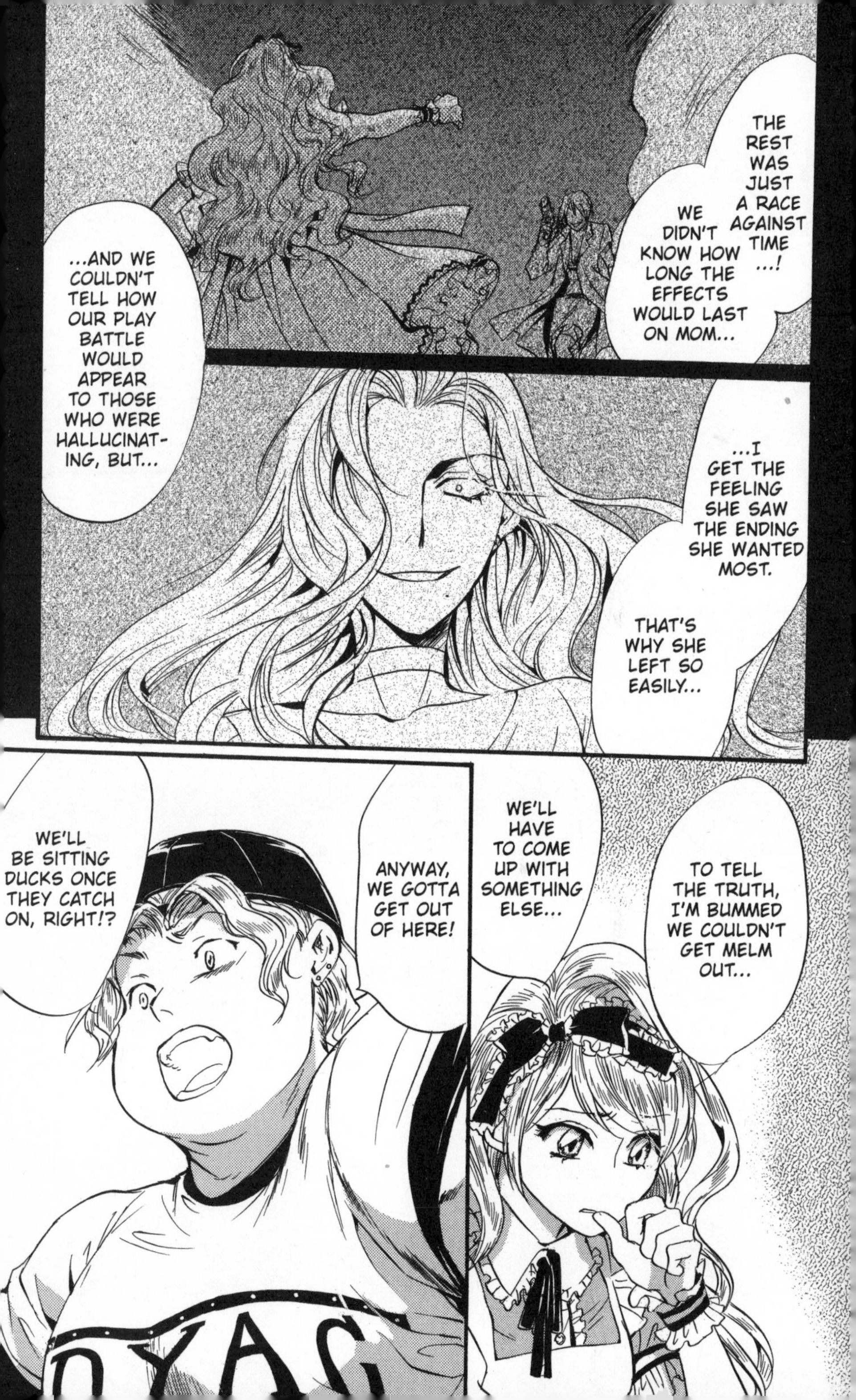
THE REST WAS JUST A RACE AGAINST TIME ...!
WE DIDN'T KNOW HOW LONG THE EFFECTS WOULD LAST ON MOM...
...AND WE COULDN'T TELL HOW OUR PLAY BATTLE WOULD APPEAR TO THOSE WHO WERE HALLUCINAT-ING, BUT...
...I GET THE FEELING SHE SAW THE ENDING SHE WANTED MOST.
THAT'S WHY SHE LEFT SO EASILY...
TO TELL THE TRUTH, I'M BUMMED WE COULDN'T GET MELM OUT...
WE'LL HAVE TO COME UP WITH SOMETHING ELSE...
ANYWAY, WE GOTTA GET OUT OF HERE!
WE'LL BE SITTING DUCKS ONCE THEY CATCH ON, RIGHT!?

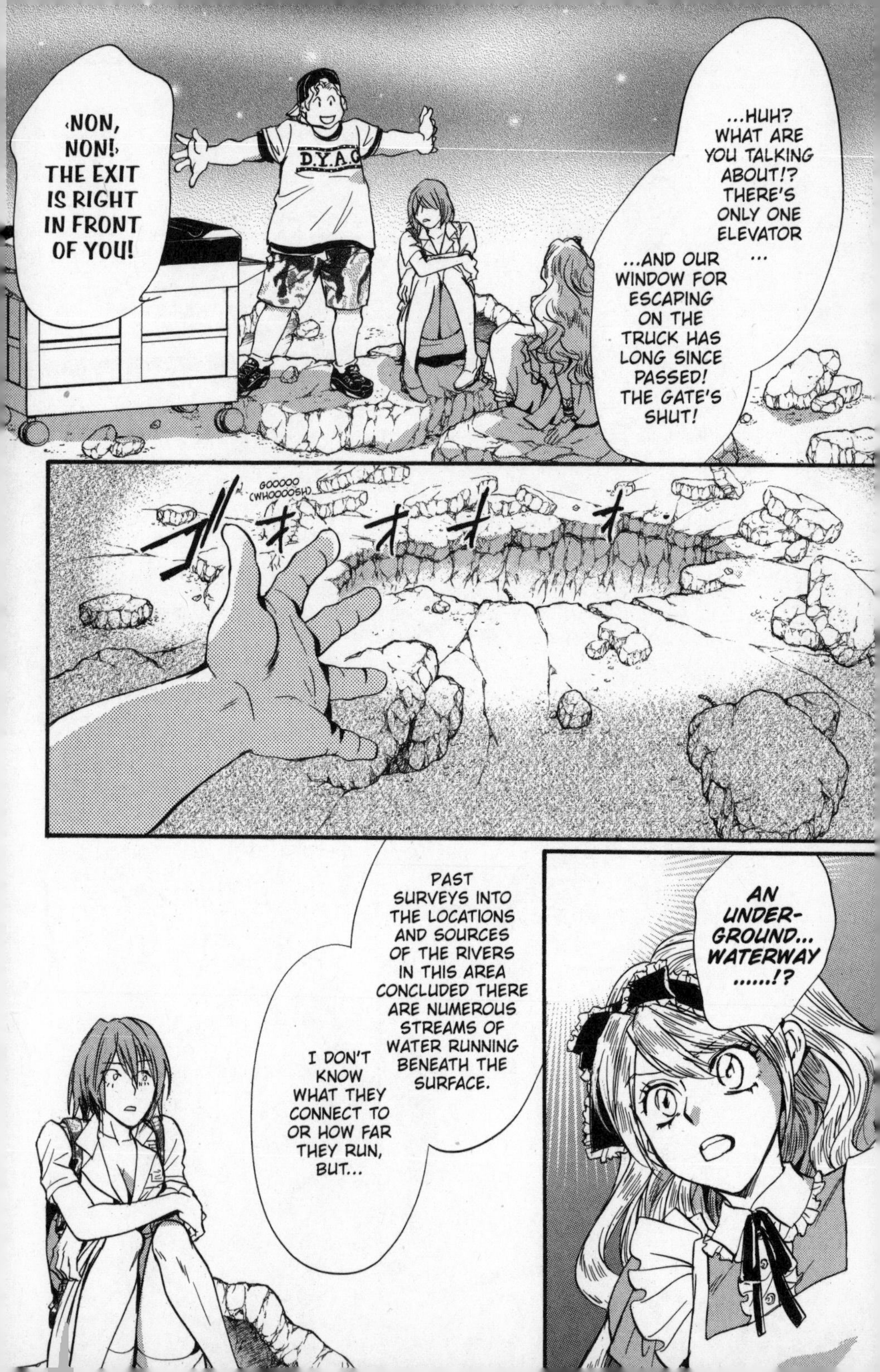
...HUH? WHAT ARE YOU TALKING ABOUT!? THERE'S ONLY ONE ELEVATOR ...
...AND OUR WINDOW FOR ESCAPING ON THE TRUCK HAS LONG SINCE PASSED! THE GATE'S SHUT!
‹NON, NON!› THE EXIT IS RIGHT IN FRONT OF YOU!
GOOOOO (WHOOOOSH)
AN UNDER-GROUND... WATERWAY ......!?
PAST SURVEYS INTO THE LOCATIONS AND SOURCES OF THE RIVERS IN THIS AREA CONCLUDED THERE ARE NUMEROUS STREAMS OF WATER RUNNING BENEATH THE SURFACE.
I DON'T KNOW WHAT THEY CONNECT TO OR HOW FAR THEY RUN, BUT...

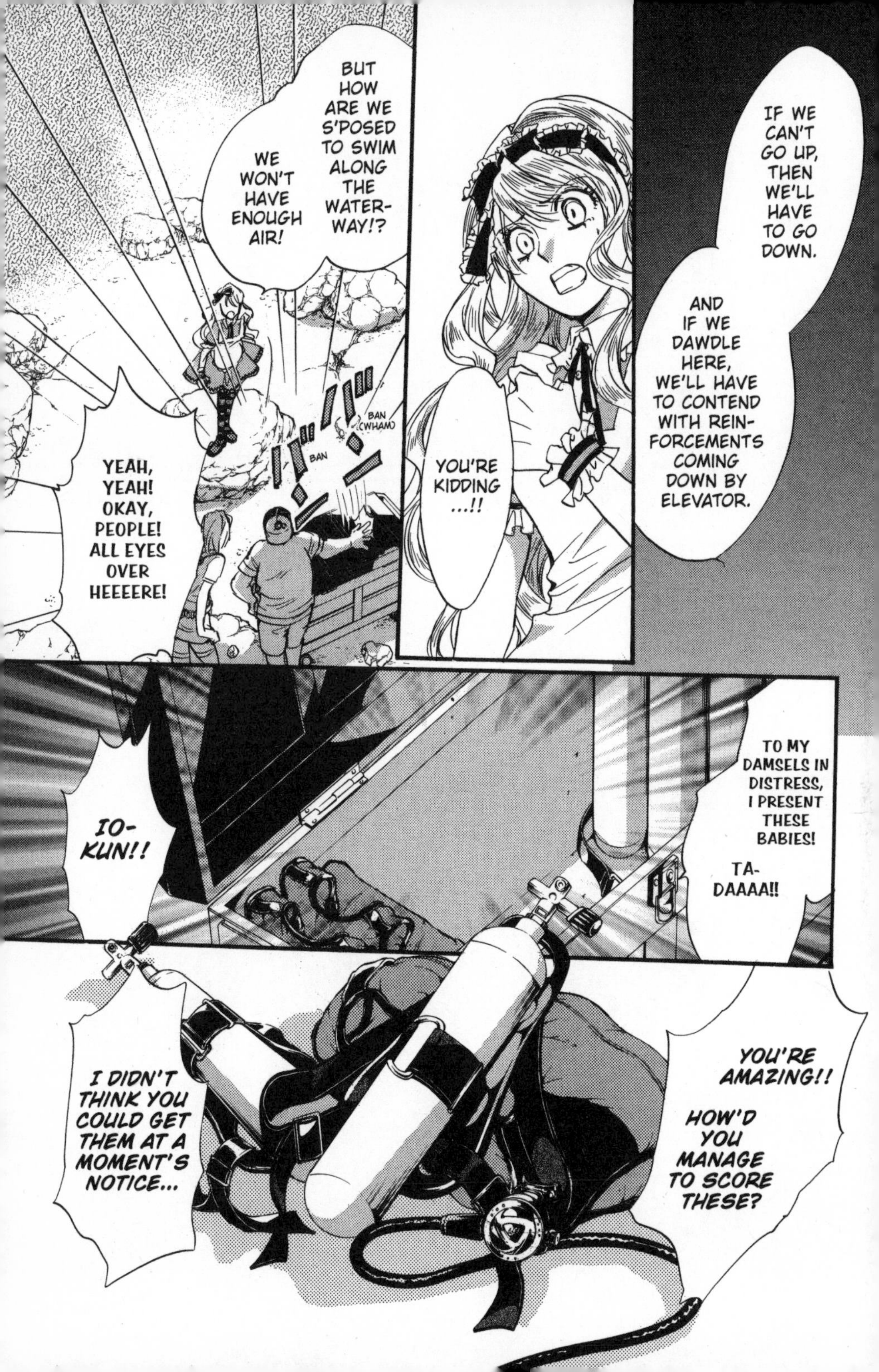
IF WE CAN'T GO UP, THEN WE'LL HAVE TO GO DOWN.
AND IF WE DAWDLE HERE, WE'LL HAVE TO CONTEND WITH REIN-FORCEMENTS COMING DOWN BY ELEVATOR.
YOU'RE KIDDING ...!!
BUT HOW ARE WE S'POSED TO SWIM ALONG THE WATER-WAY!?
WE WON'T HAVE ENOUGH AIR!
BAN (WHAM)
BAN
YEAH, YEAH! OKAY, PEOPLE! ALL EYES OVER HEEEERE!
TO MY DAMSELS IN DISTRESS, I PRESENT THESE BABIES!
TA-DAAAA!!
IO-KUN!!
YOU'RE AMAZING!!
HOW'D YOU MANAGE TO SCORE THESE?
I DIDN'T THINK YOU COULD GET THEM AT A MOMENT'S NOTICE...

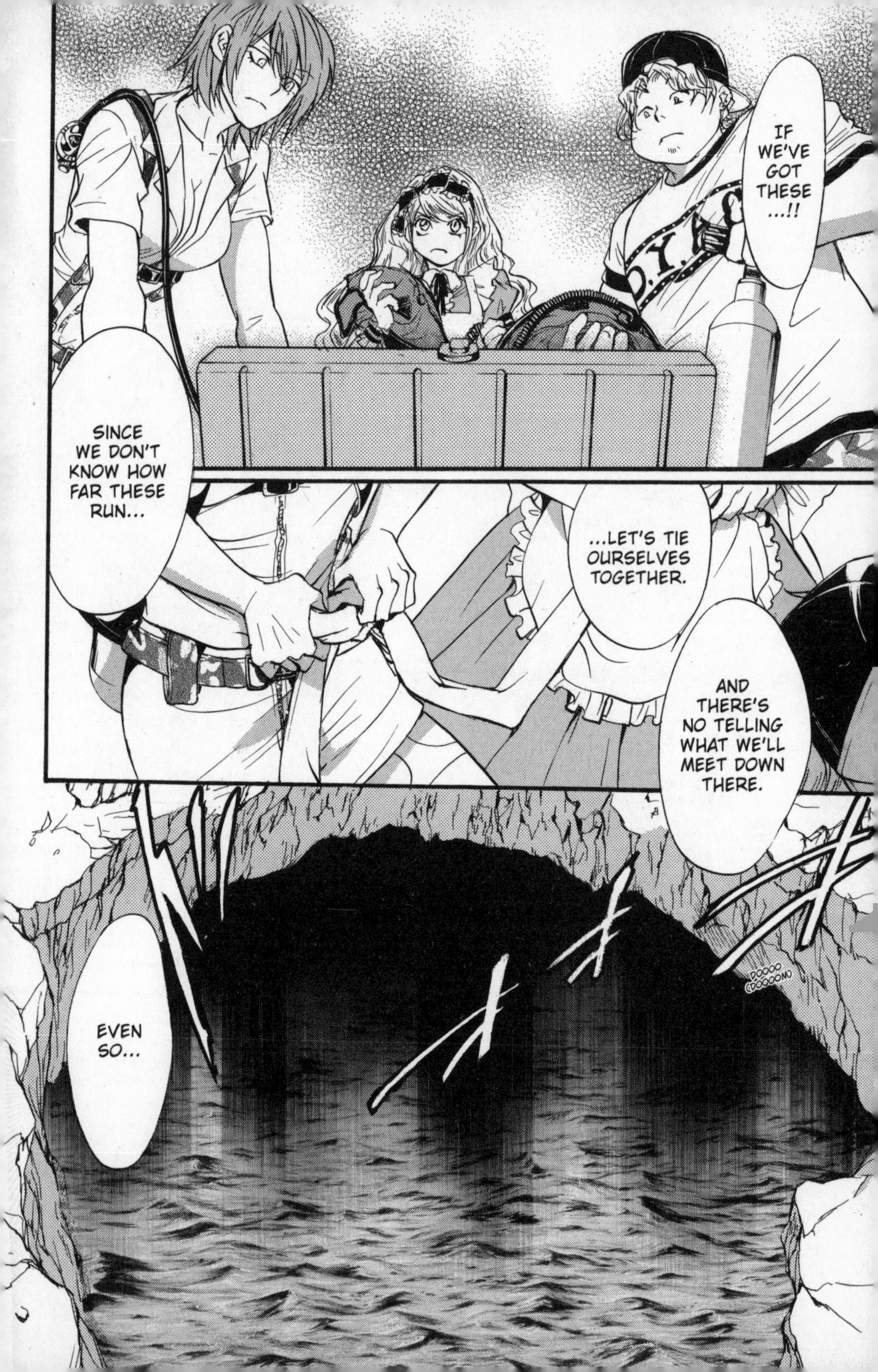
IF WE'VE GOT THESE ...!!
SINCE WE DON'T KNOW HOW FAR THESE RUN...
...LET'S TIE OURSELVES TOGETHER.
AND THERE'S NO TELLING WHAT WE'LL MEET DOWN THERE.
DOOOO (DOOOOM)
EVEN SO...

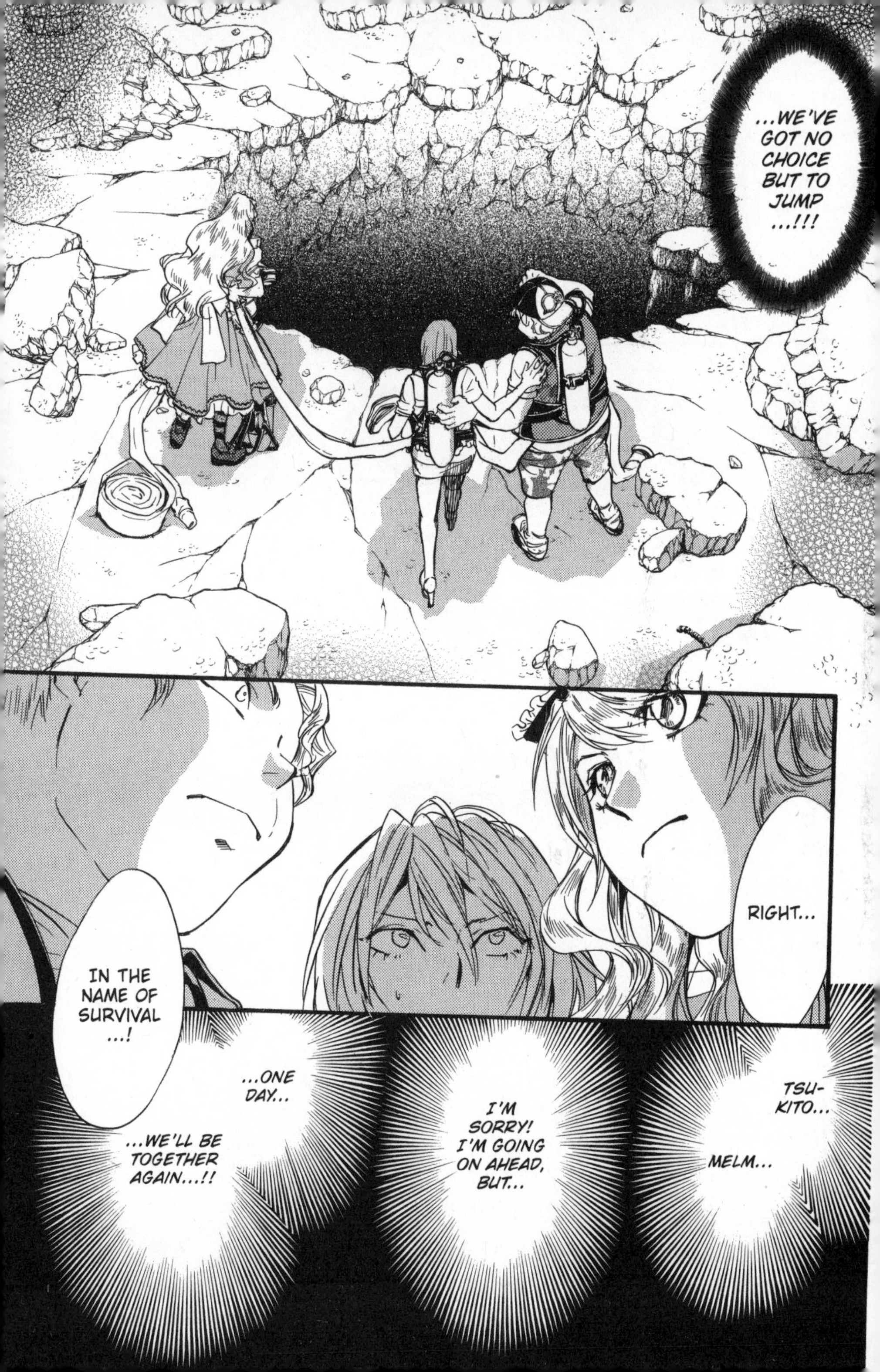
...WE'VE GOT NO CHOICE BUT TO JUMP ...!!!
RIGHT...
IN THE NAME OF SURVIVAL ...!
TSU-KITO...
MELM...
I'M SORRY! I'M GOING ON AHEAD, BUT...
...ONE DAY...
...WE'LL BE TOGETHER AGAIN...!!

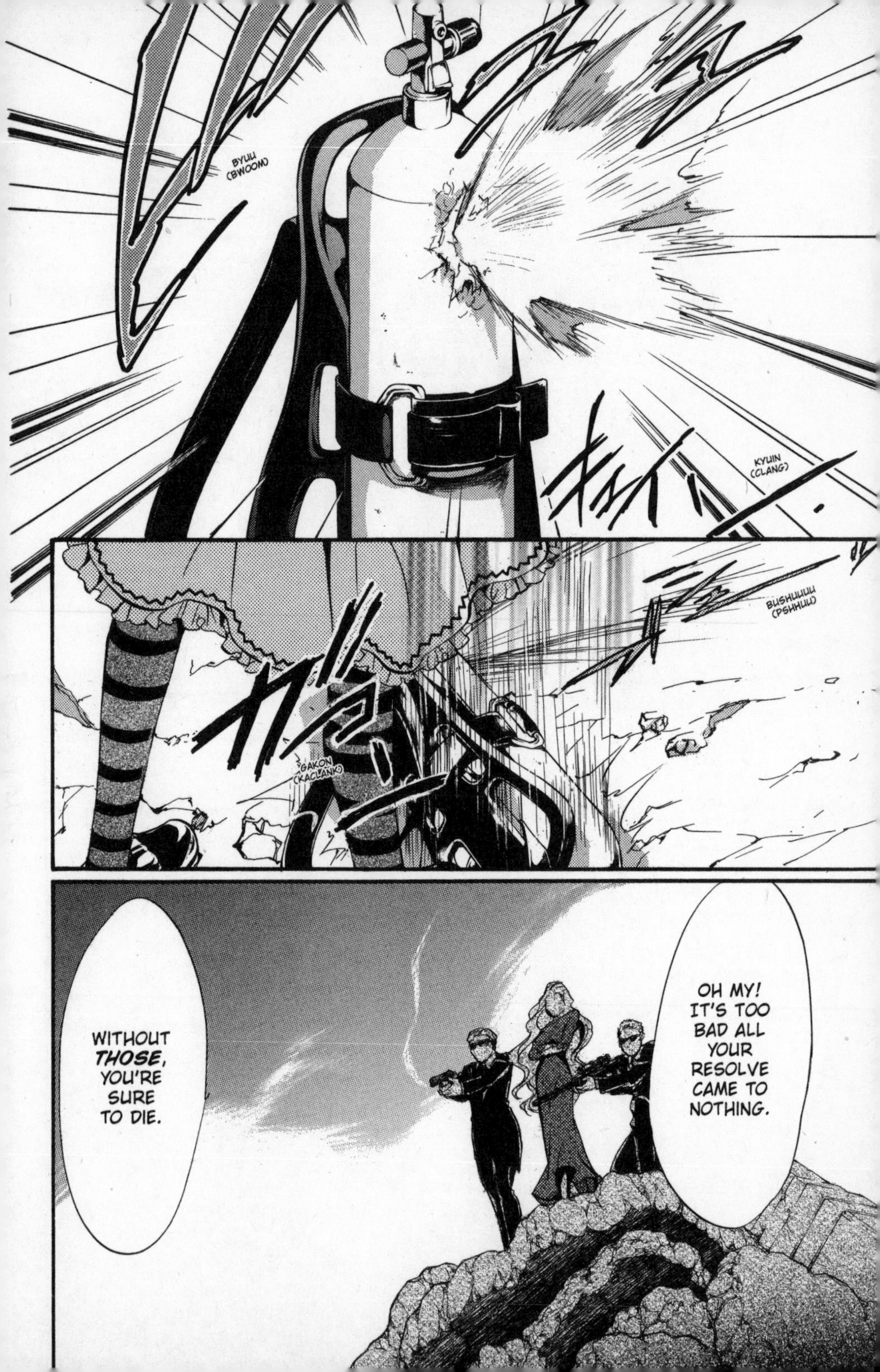

BYUU (BWOOM)
KYUIN (CLANG)
BUSHUUUU (PSHHUU)
GAKON (KACLANK)
OH MY! IT'S TOO BAD ALL YOUR RESOLVE CAME TO NOTHING.
WITHOUT *THOSE*, YOU'RE SURE TO DIE.

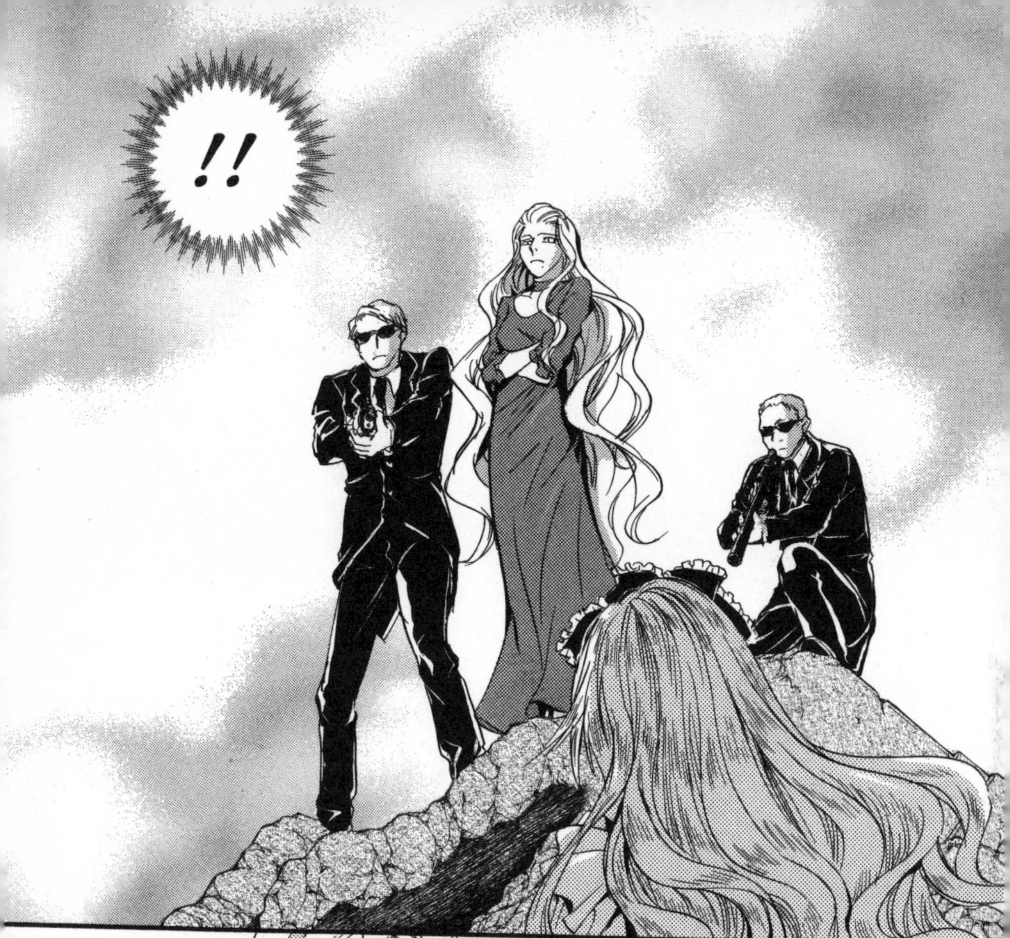
!!

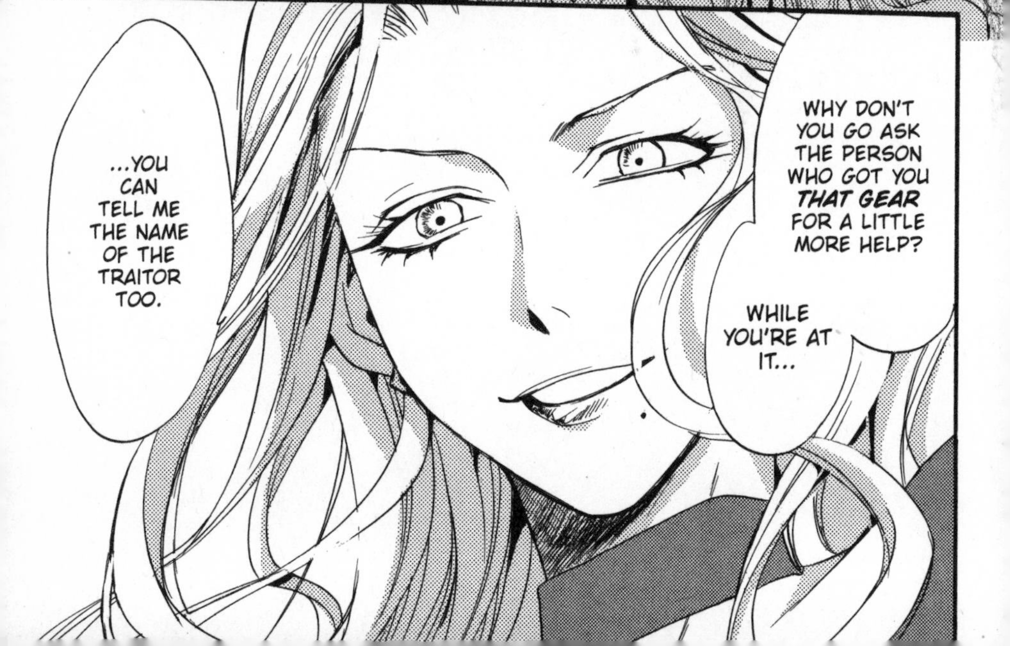
WHY DON'T YOU GO ASK THE PERSON WHO GOT YOU **THAT GEAR** FOR A LITTLE MORE HELP?
WHILE YOU'RE AT IT...
...YOU CAN TELL ME THE NAME OF THE TRAITOR TOO.

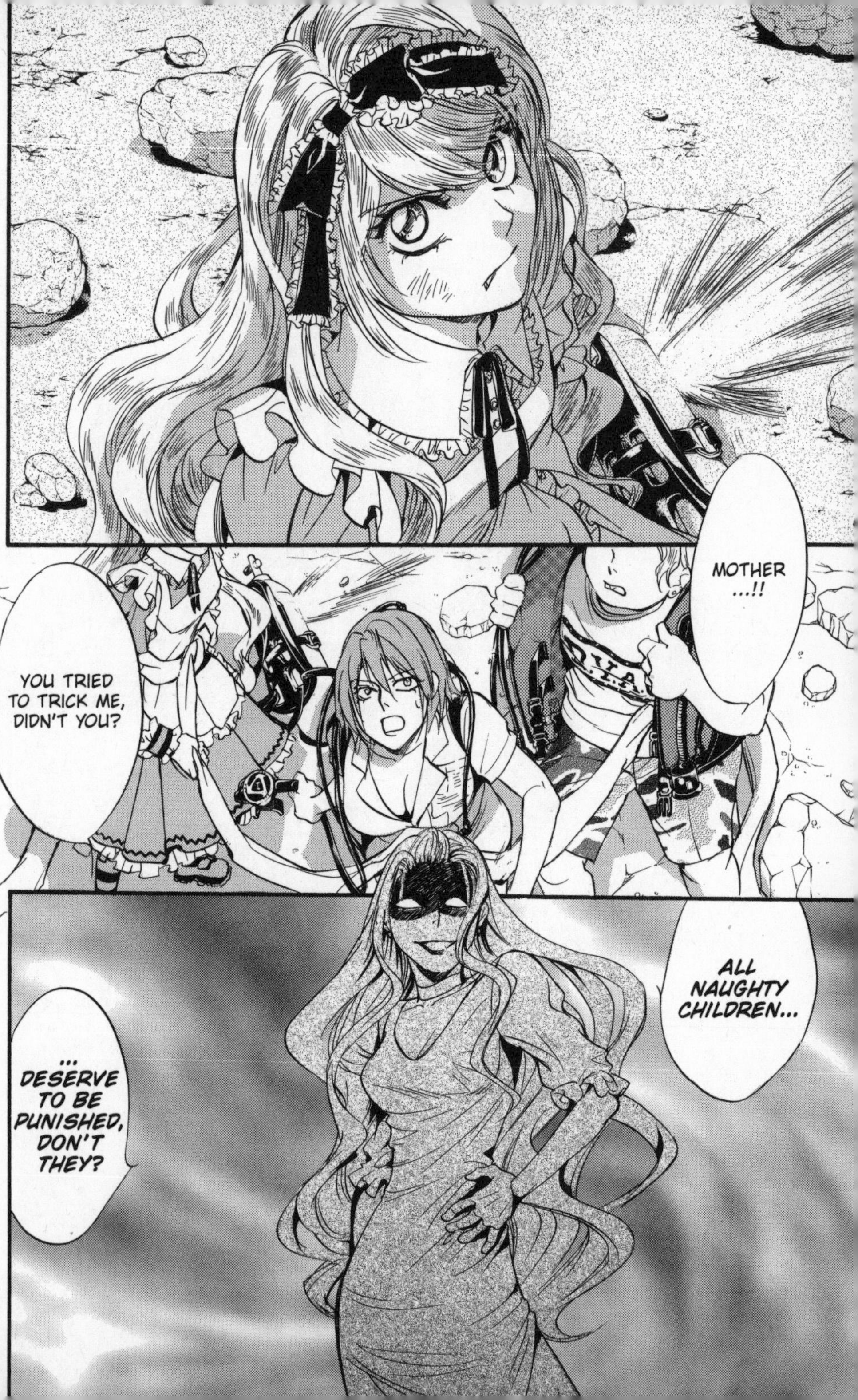
MOTHER ...!!
YOU TRIED TO TRICK ME, DIDN'T YOU?
ALL NAUGHTY CHILDREN...
... DESERVE TO BE PUNISHED, DON'T THEY?

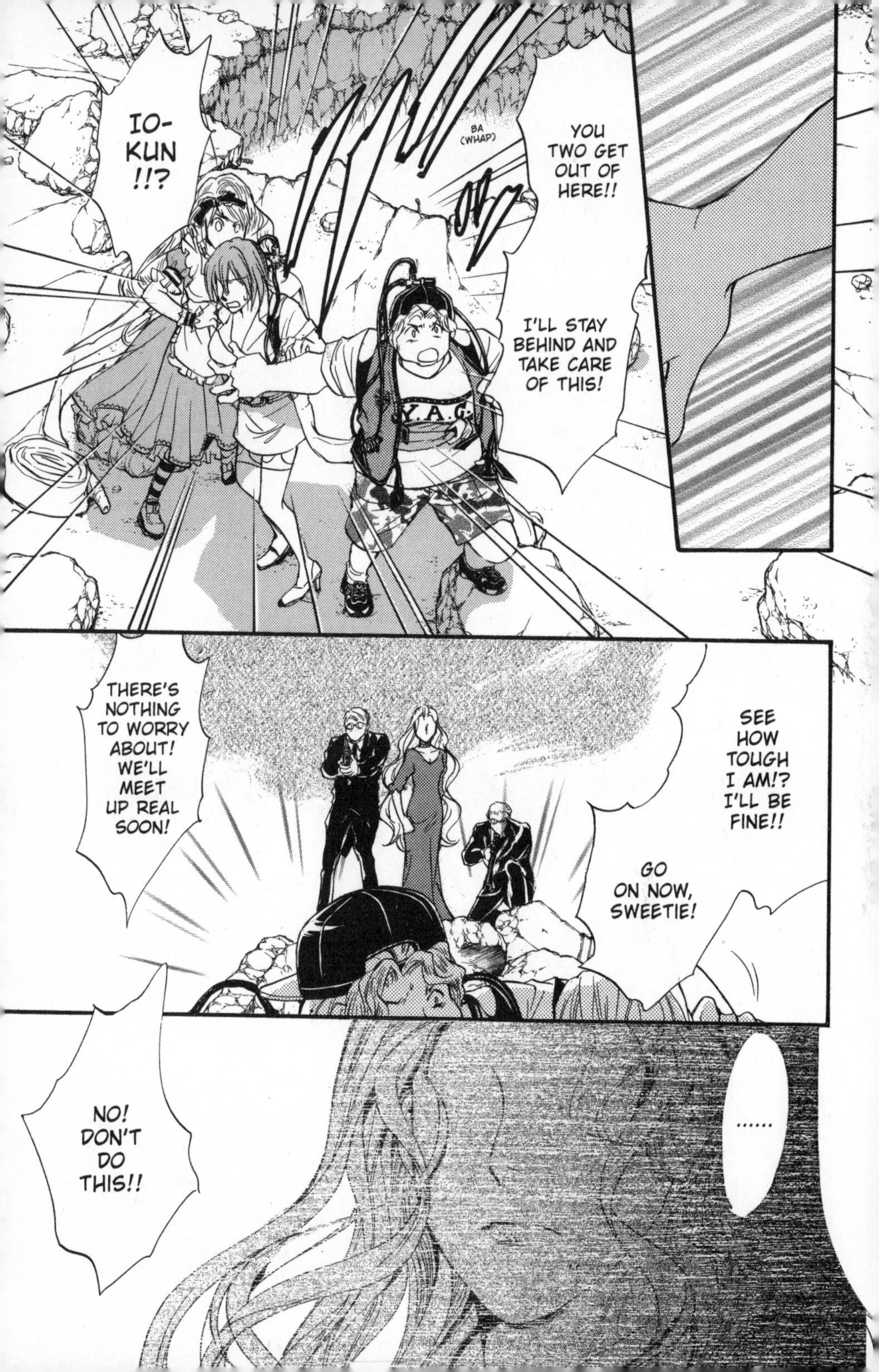
BA (WHAP)
YOU TWO GET OUT OF HERE!!
I'LL STAY BEHIND AND TAKE CARE OF THIS!
IO-KUN!!?
SEE HOW TOUGH I AM!? I'LL BE FINE!!
GO ON NOW, SWEETIE!
THERE'S NOTHING TO WORRY ABOUT! WE'LL MEET UP REAL SOON!
......
NO! DON'T DO THIS!!

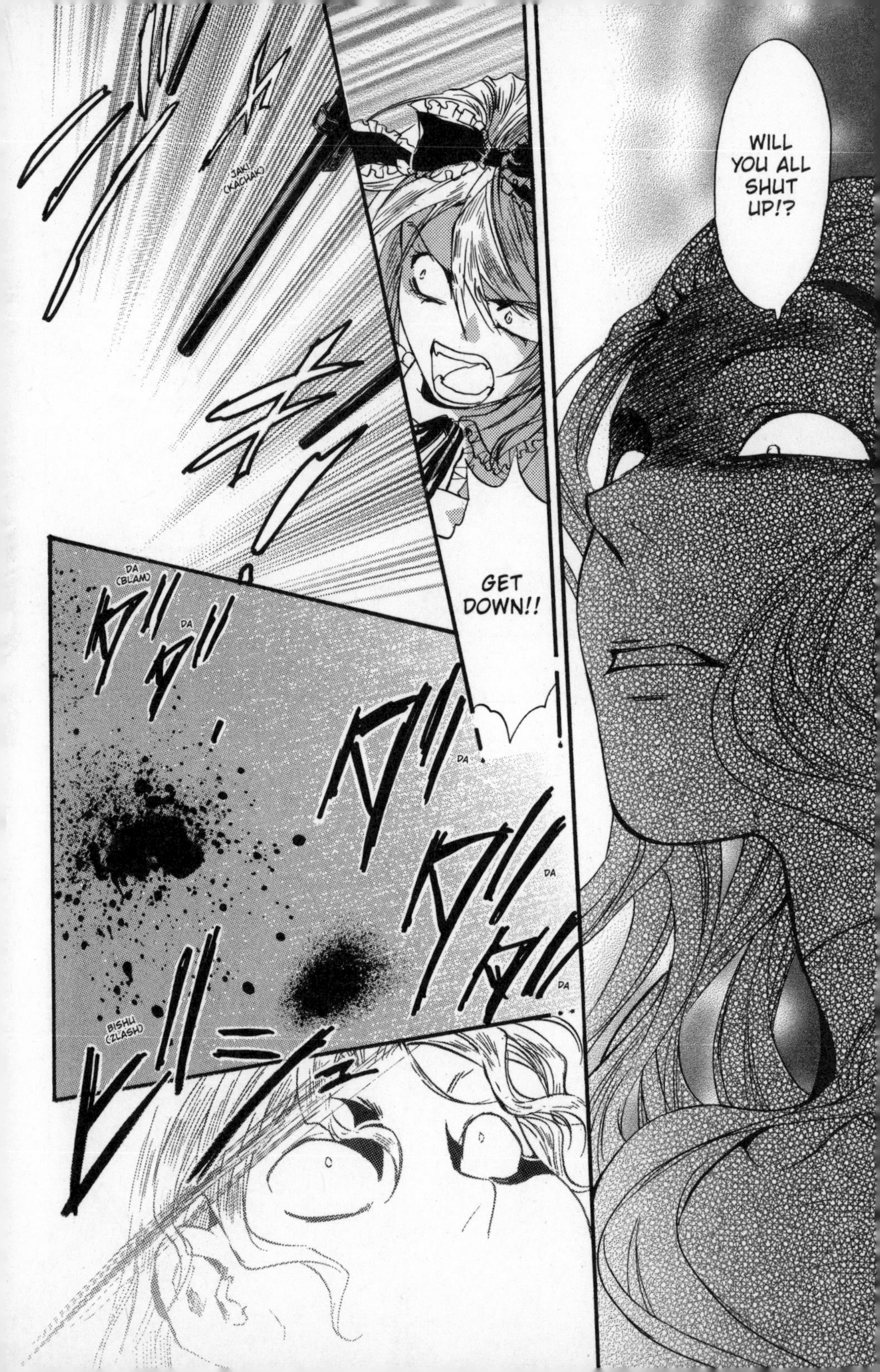
WILL YOU ALL SHUT UP!?
JAKI (KACHAK)
GET DOWN!!
DA (BLAM)
DA
DA
DA
DA
BISHU (ZLASH)

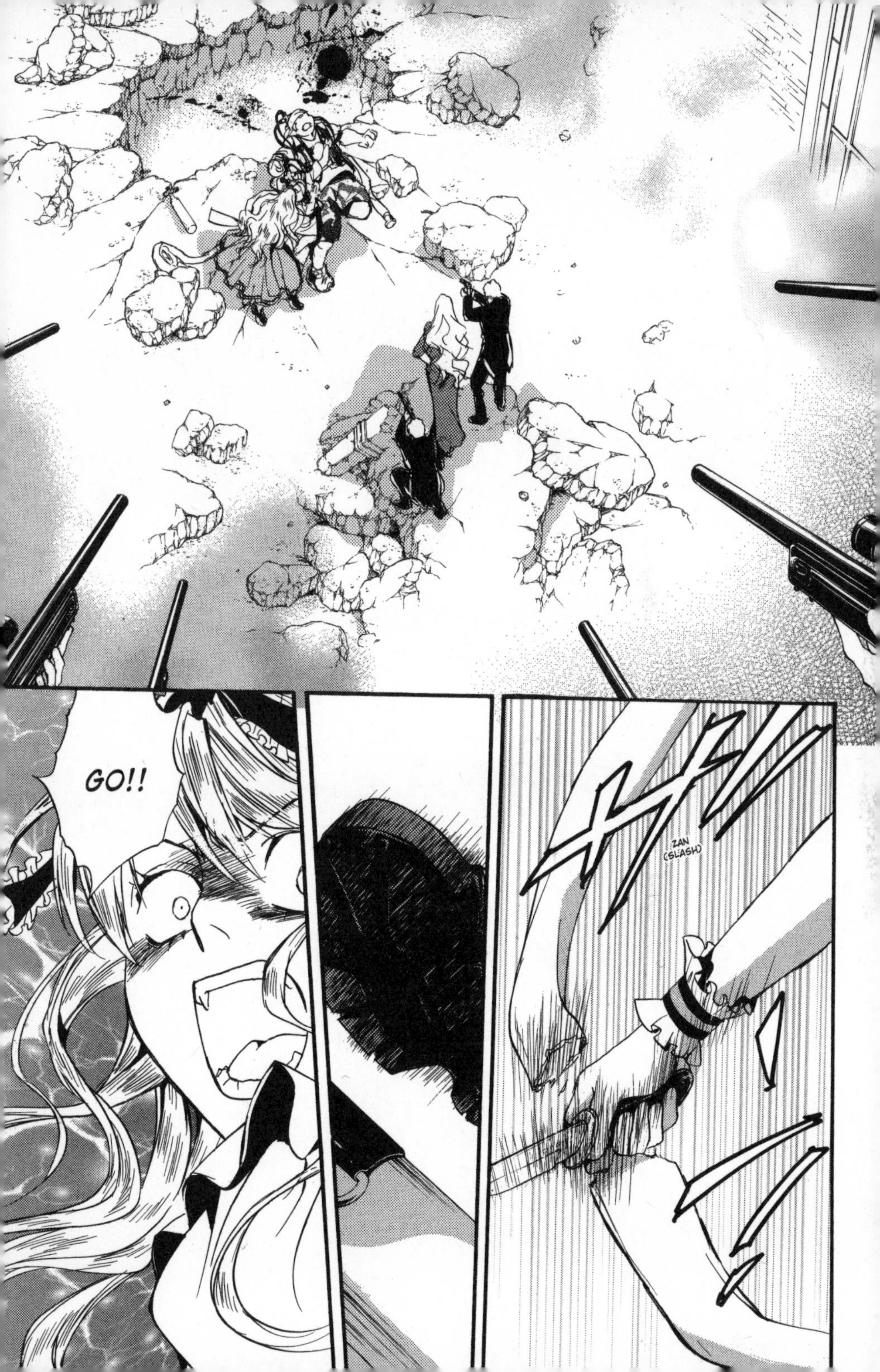
ZAN
(SLASH)
GO!!

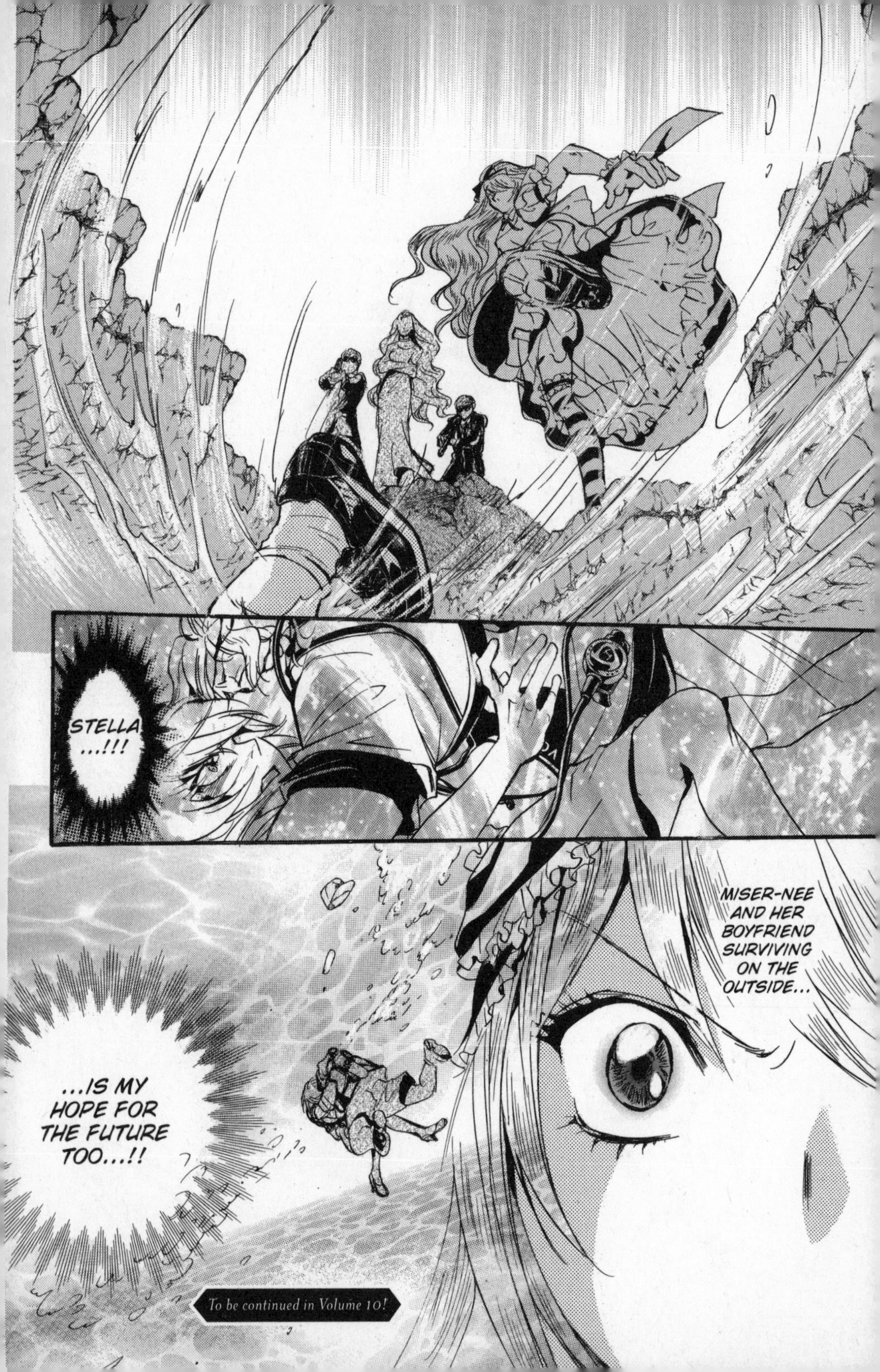
STELLA ...!!!
MISER-NEE AND HER BOYFRIEND SURVIVING ON THE OUTSIDE...
...IS MY HOPE FOR THE FUTURE TOO...!!
To be continued in Volume 10!

Alice in Murderland

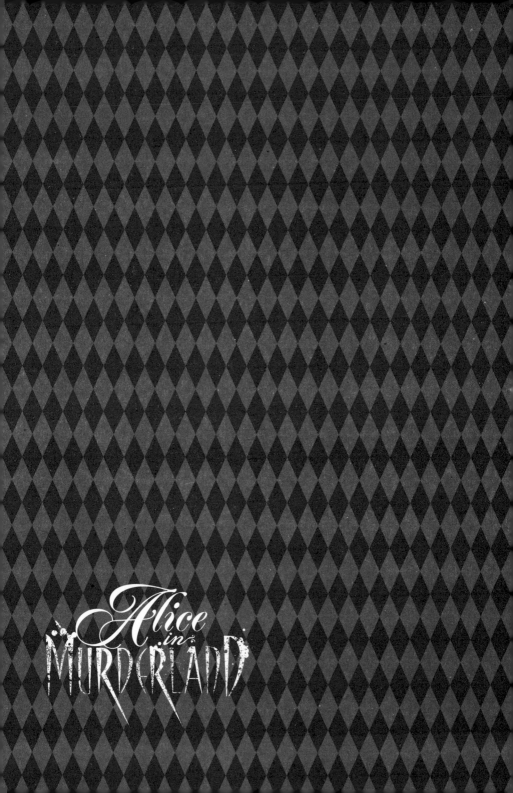

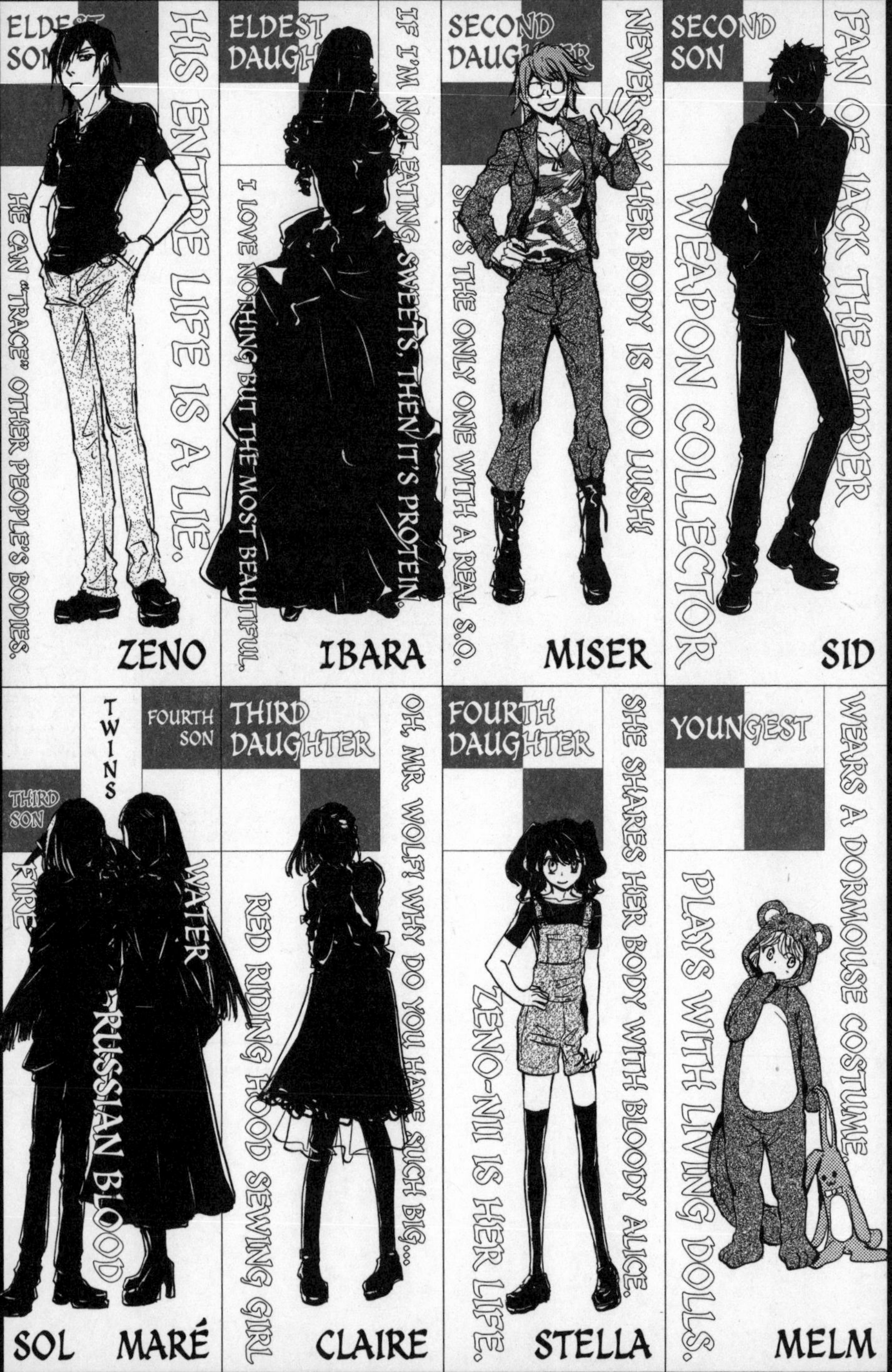
SECOND SON
FAN OF JACK THE RIPPER
WEAPON COLLECTOR
SID
SECOND DAUGHTER
NEVER SAY HER BODY IS TOO LUSH!
SHE'S THE ONLY ONE WITH A REAL S.O.
MISER
ELDEST DAUGHTER
IF I'M NOT EATING SWEETS, THEN IT'S PROTEIN.
I LOVE NOTHING BUT THE MOST BEAUTIFUL.
IBARA
ELDEST SON
HIS ENTIRE LIFE IS A LIE.
HE CAN "TRACE" OTHER PEOPLE'S BODIES.
ZENO
YOUNGEST
WEARS A DORMOUSE COSTUME.
PLAYS WITH LIVING DOLLS.
MELM
FOURTH DAUGHTER
SHE SHARES HER BODY WITH BLOODY ALICE.
ZENO-NII IS HER LIFE.
STELLA
THIRD DAUGHTER
OH, MR. WOLF! WHY DO YOU HAVE SUCH BIG...
RED RIDING HOOD SEWING GIRL
CLAIRE
TWINS
FOURTH SON
THIRD SON
WATER
FIRE
RUSSIAN BLOOD
MARÉ
SOL

Humpty ✦ Dumpty

The more the number of volumes,
the fewer the number of siblings...
We're getting close to the end of the series,
but since there are still a lot of threads to tie up,
it'd make me very happy if you'd stay for the rest of the ride.
I apologize for not providing any hints about how it will end,
but I've been worrying over whether I should make it a
happy ending like usual or go for something different.........
In the scene where Miser was killed, you might notice
that the borders of the page and space between panels
are black, so please think of that scene as being
seen through their mother's delirious gaze.
When I was talking to my assistants about Io,
I realized they didn't know who that was,
so instead, I call him "Chubby-chan,"
and they get it.

Twitter (Japanese): @angelaid
Kaori Yuki

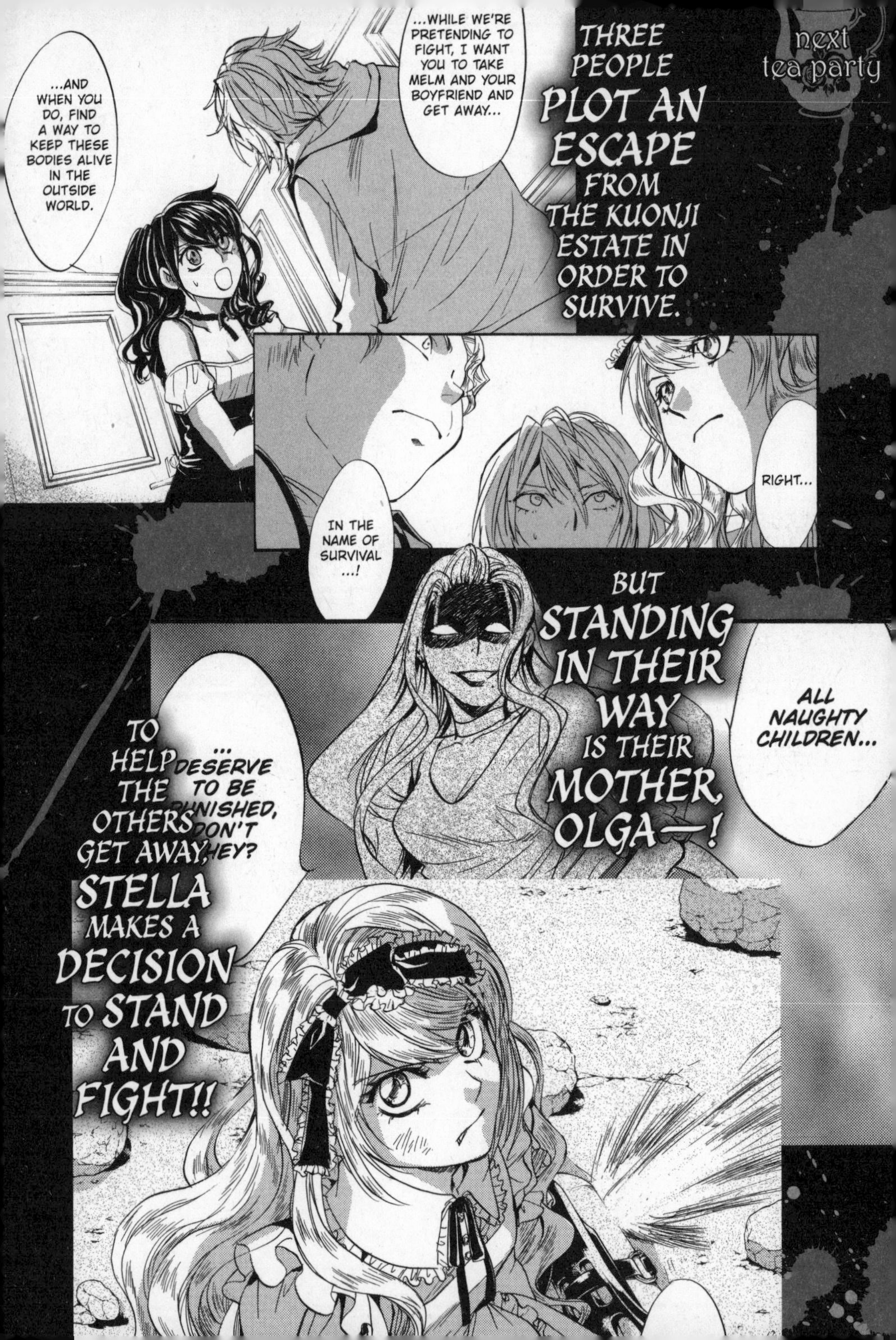
next tea party
THREE PEOPLE PLOT AN ESCAPE FROM THE KUONJI ESTATE IN ORDER TO SURVIVE.
...WHILE WE'RE PRETENDING TO FIGHT, I WANT YOU TO TAKE MELM AND YOUR BOYFRIEND AND GET AWAY...
...AND WHEN YOU DO, FIND A WAY TO KEEP THESE BODIES ALIVE IN THE OUTSIDE WORLD.
RIGHT...
IN THE NAME OF SURVIVAL ...!
BUT STANDING IN THEIR WAY IS THEIR MOTHER, OLGA—!
ALL NAUGHTY CHILDREN...
...DESERVE TO BE PUNISHED, DON'T THEY?
TO HELP THE OTHERS GET AWAY, STELLA MAKES A DECISION TO STAND AND FIGHT!!

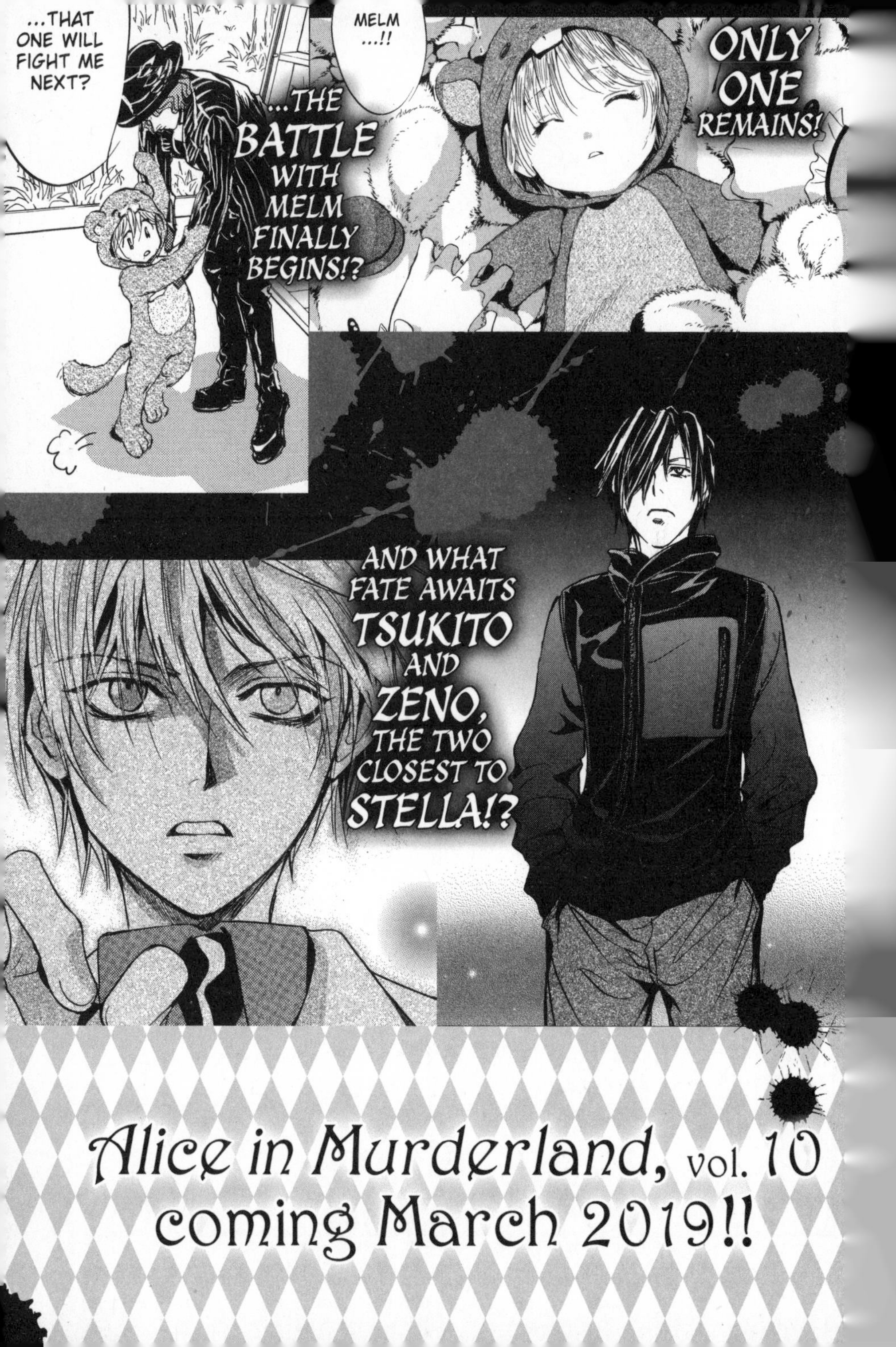
ONLY ONE REMAINS!
MELM ...!!
...THE BATTLE WITH MELM FINALLY BEGINS!?
...THAT ONE WILL FIGHT ME NEXT?
AND WHAT FATE AWAITS TSUKITO AND ZENO, THE TWO CLOSEST TO STELLA!?

Alice in Murderland, vol. 10 coming March 2019!!

Alice in Murderland 9

Kaori Yuki

Translation: William Flanagan Lettering: Lys Blakeslee

KAKEI NO ALICE
© 2017 Kaori Yuki. All rights reserved.
First published in Japan in 2017 by Kodansha Ltd., Tokyo. Publication rights for this English language edition arranged through Kodansha Ltd., Tokyo.

English translation © 2018 by Yen Press, LLC

Yen Press
1290 Avenue of the Americas
New York, NY 10104

Visit us at yenpress.com
facebook.com/yenpress
twitter.com/yenpress
yenpress.tumblr.com
instagram.com/yenpress

First Yen Press Edition: November 2018

Yen Press is an imprint of Yen Press, LLC.
The Yen Press name and logo are trademarks of Yen Press, LLC.

The publisher is not responsible for websites (or their content) that are not owned by the publisher.

Library of Congress Control Number: 2014504636

ISBN: 978-1-9753-2797-2

10 9 8 7 6 5 4 3 2 1

WOR

Printed in the United States of America